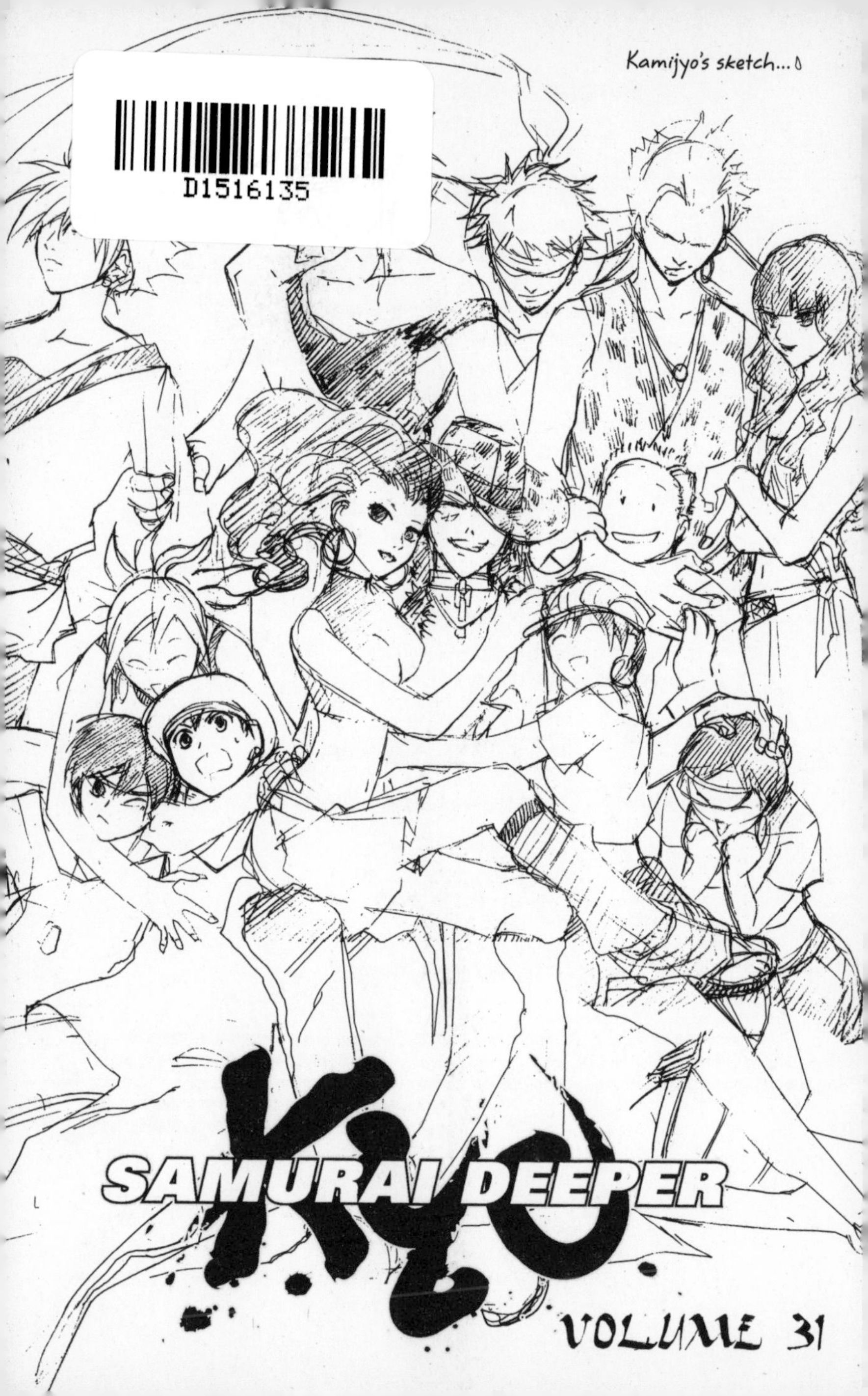
Kamijyo's sketch...♪
SAMURAI DEEPER KYO
VOLUME 31

Samurai Deeper Kyo Volume 31
Created by Akimine Kamijyo

Translation - Stephen Paul
English Adaptation - Matt Varosky
Retouch and Lettering - Star Print Brokers
Production Artist - Vicente Rivera, Jr.
Graphic Designer - Erika Terriquez

Editor - Hyun Joo Kim
Pre-Production Supervisor - Vicente Rivera, Jr.
Print-Production Specialist - Lucas Rivera
Managing Editor - Vy Nguyen
Senior Designer - Louis Csontos
Senior Designer - James Lee
Senior Editor - Bryce P. Coleman
Senior Editor - Jenna Winterberg
Associate Publisher - Marco F. Pavia
President and C.O.O. - John Parker
C.E.O. and Chief Creative Officer - Stu Levy

A **TOKYOPOP** Manga

TOKYOPOP and ⊙ are trademarks or registered trademarks of TOKYOPOP Inc.

TOKYOPOP Inc.
5900 Wilshire Blvd. Suite 2000
Los Angeles, CA 90036

E-mail: info@TOKYOPOP.com
Come visit us online at www.TOKYOPOP.com

ISBN: 978-1-59816-191-5

First TOKYOPOP printing: November 2008
10 9 8 7 6 5 4 3 2 1
Printed in the USA

SAMURAI DEEPER KYO

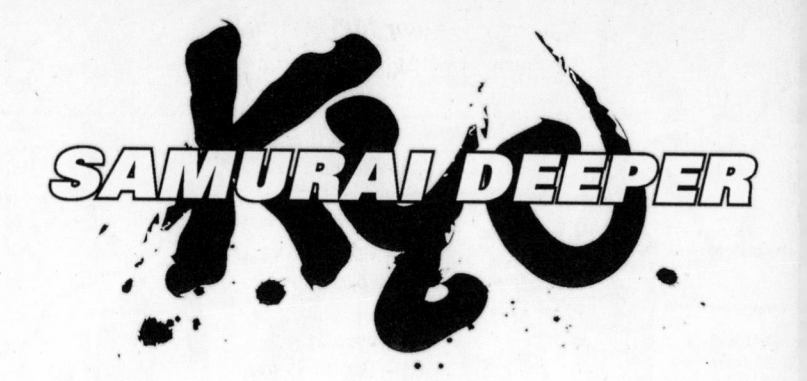

Vol. 31

by Akimine Kamijyo

TOKYOPOP®

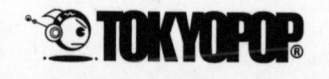

HAMBURG // LONDON // LOS ANGELES // TOKYO

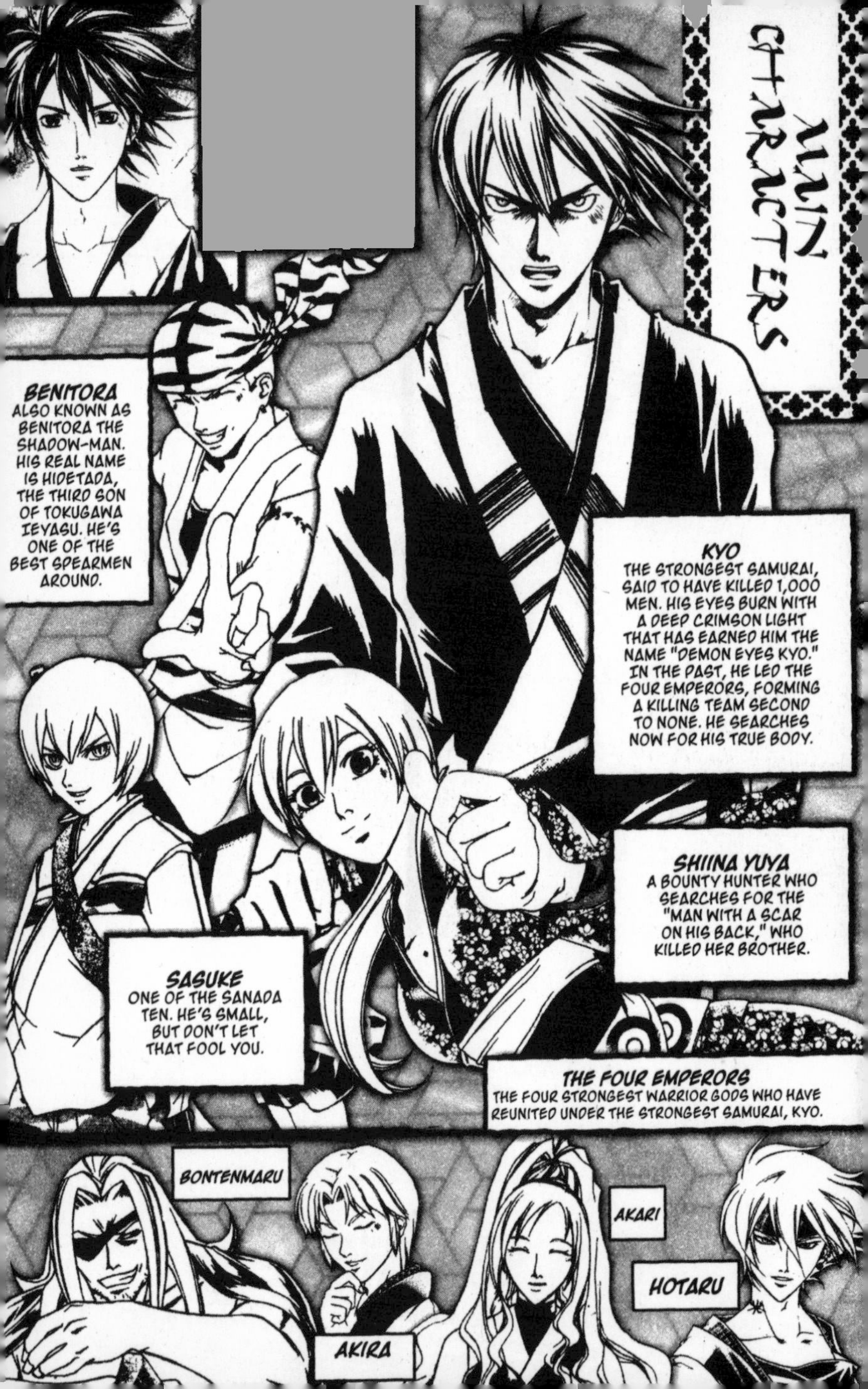
MAIN CHARACTERS
KYO
THE STRONGEST SAMURAI, SAID TO HAVE KILLED 1,000 MEN. HIS EYES BURN WITH A DEEP CRIMSON LIGHT THAT HAS EARNED HIM THE NAME "DEMON EYES KYO." IN THE PAST, HE LED THE FOUR EMPERORS, FORMING A KILLING TEAM SECOND TO NONE. HE SEARCHES NOW FOR HIS TRUE BODY.
BENITORA
ALSO KNOWN AS BENITORA THE SHADOW-MAN. HIS REAL NAME IS HIDETADA, THE THIRD SON OF TOKUGAWA IEYASU. HE'S ONE OF THE BEST SPEARMEN AROUND.
SHIINA YUYA
A BOUNTY HUNTER WHO SEARCHES FOR THE "MAN WITH A SCAR ON HIS BACK," WHO KILLED HER BROTHER.
SASUKE
ONE OF THE SANADA TEN. HE'S SMALL, BUT DON'T LET THAT FOOL YOU.
THE FOUR EMPERORS
THE FOUR STRONGEST WARRIOR GODS WHO HAVE REUNITED UNDER THE STRONGEST SAMURAI, KYO.
HOTARU
AKARI
AKIRA
BONTENMARU

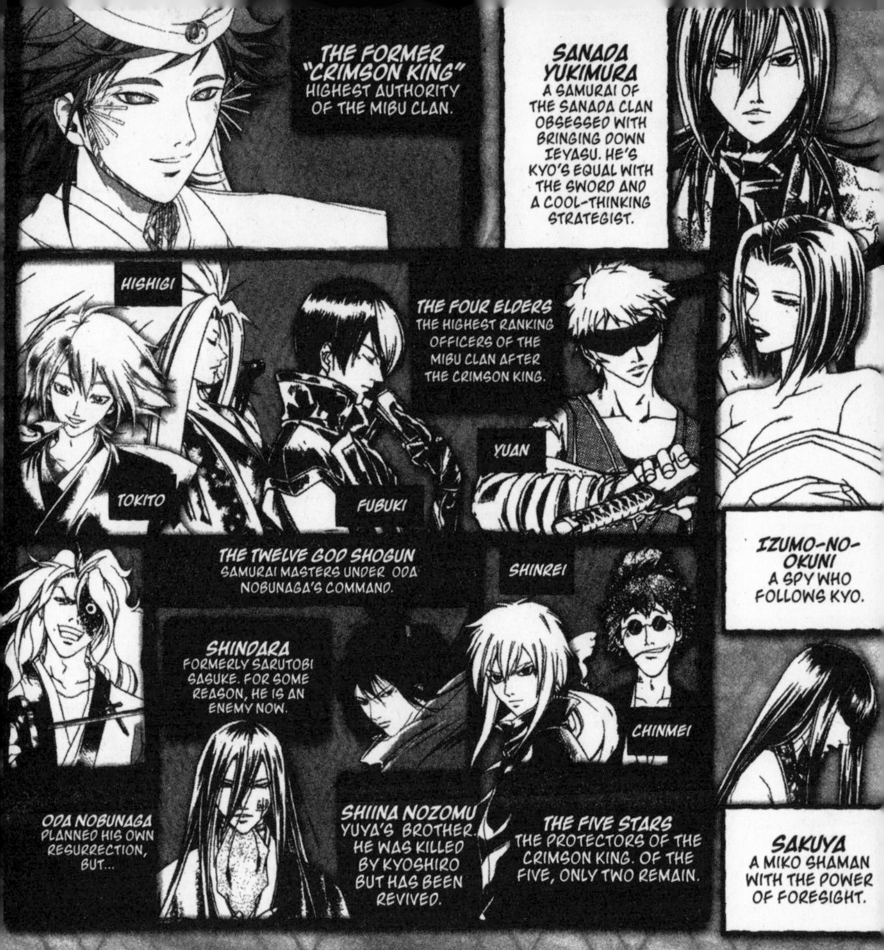
SANADA YUKIMURA
A SAMURAI OF THE SANADA CLAN OBSESSED WITH BRINGING DOWN IEYASU. HE'S KYO'S EQUAL WITH THE SWORD AND A COOL-THINKING STRATEGIST.
THE FORMER "CRIMSON KING"
HIGHEST AUTHORITY OF THE MIBU CLAN.
THE FOUR ELDERS
THE HIGHEST RANKING OFFICERS OF THE MIBU CLAN AFTER THE CRIMSON KING.
HISHIGI
YUAN
FUBUKI
TOKITO
IZUMO-NO-OKUNI
A SPY WHO FOLLOWS KYO.
SHINREI
THE TWELVE GOD SHOGUN
SAMURAI MASTERS UNDER ODA NOBUNAGA'S COMMAND.
SHINDARA
FORMERLY SARUTOBI SASUKE. FOR SOME REASON, HE IS AN ENEMY NOW.
CHINMEI
SAKUYA
A MIKO SHAMAN WITH THE POWER OF FORESIGHT.
THE FIVE STARS
THE PROTECTORS OF THE CRIMSON KING. OF THE FIVE, ONLY TWO REMAIN.
SHIINA NOZOMU
YUYA'S BROTHER. HE WAS KILLED BY KYOSHIRO BUT HAS BEEN REVIVED.
ODA NOBUNAGA
PLANNED HIS OWN RESURRECTION, BUT...

STORY SO FAR

YUYA'S BROTHER, NOZOMU, LONG THOUGHT DEAD, HAS BEEN REVEALED TO BE ALIVE, ALBEIT TAKEN OVER BY THE SPIRIT OF THE SIXTH DEMON KING, THE WICKED ODA NOBUNAGA! NOBUNAGA, SUMMONING THE DEAD TWELVE GOD SHOGUN BACK TO THE WORLD OF THE LIVING, SETS THEM LOOSE ON KYO. WITH KYO SEEMINGLY FALTERING UNDER THEIR ATTACK, YUYA JUMPS IN TO SAVE HIM, ONLY TO BE CUT DOWN BY HER BROTHER, NOZOMU, WHO TRAGICALLY FAILS TO RECOGNIZE HER WHILE UNDER THE INFLUENCE OF NOBUNAGA.

SOON AFTER, KYO IS REUNITED WITH HIS OWN BODY, AND RETURNING TO HIS TRUE FORM, EASILY CRUSHES THE EVIL NOBUNAGA. AKARI IS ABLE TO RESTORE YUYA ENOUGH THAT SHE MAY SPEAK, BUT IT SEEMS HER END IS NEAR. KYOSHIRO THEN FORCES KYO OUT OF HIS LONG LOST BODY AND CLAIMS IT FOR HIMSELF, LEAVING DEMON EYES TO RETURN TO THE BODY OF MIBU KYOSHIRO!

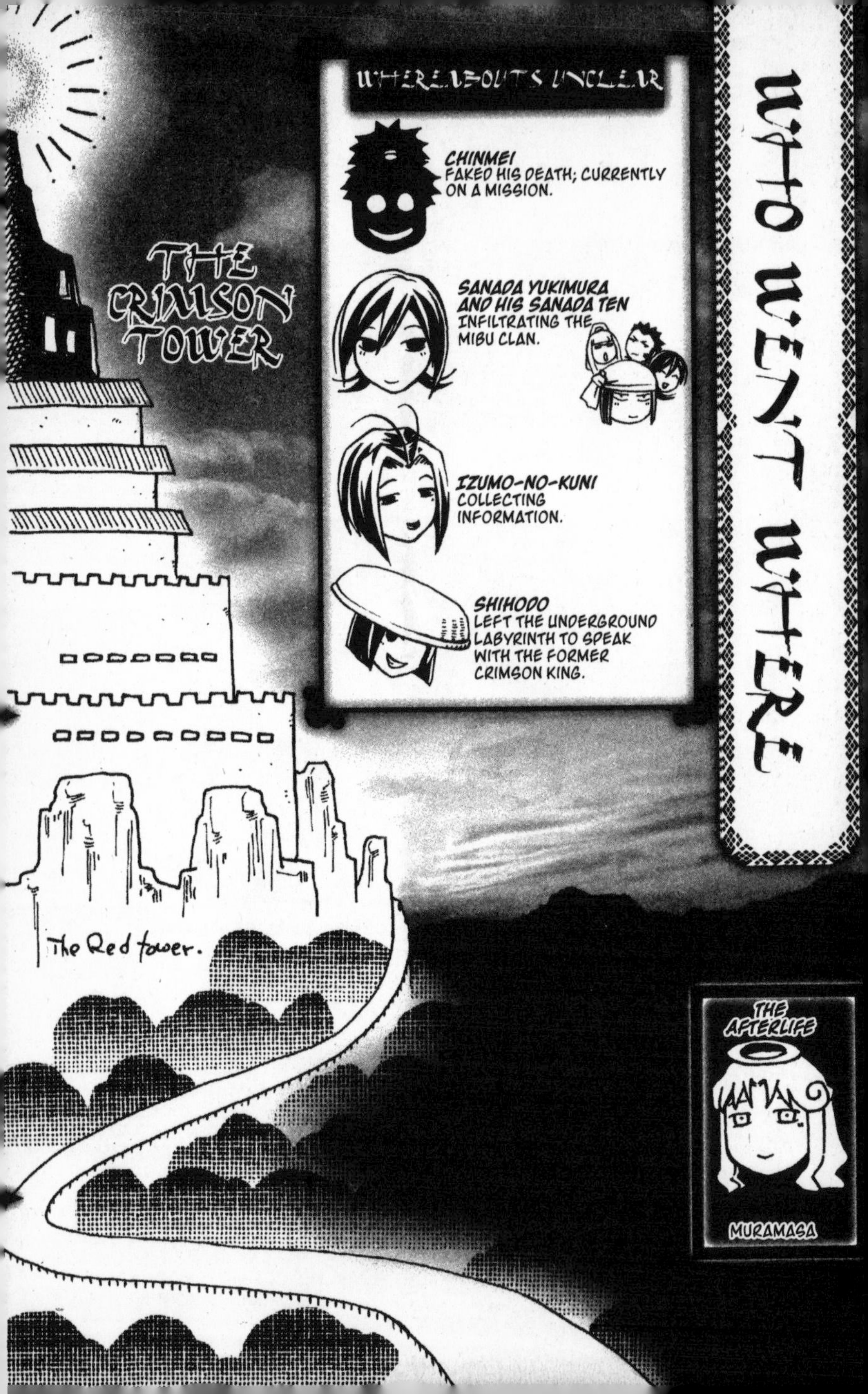
WHO WENT WHERE
WHEREABOUTS UNCLEAR
CHINMEI
FAKED HIS DEATH; CURRENTLY ON A MISSION.
SANADA YUKIMURA AND HIS SANADA TEN
INFILTRATING THE MIBU CLAN.
IZUMO-NO-KUNI
COLLECTING INFORMATION.
SHIHODO
LEFT THE UNDERGROUND LABYRINTH TO SPEAK WITH THE FORMER CRIMSON KING.
THE CRIMSON TOWER
The Red tower.
THE AFTERLIFE
MURAMASA

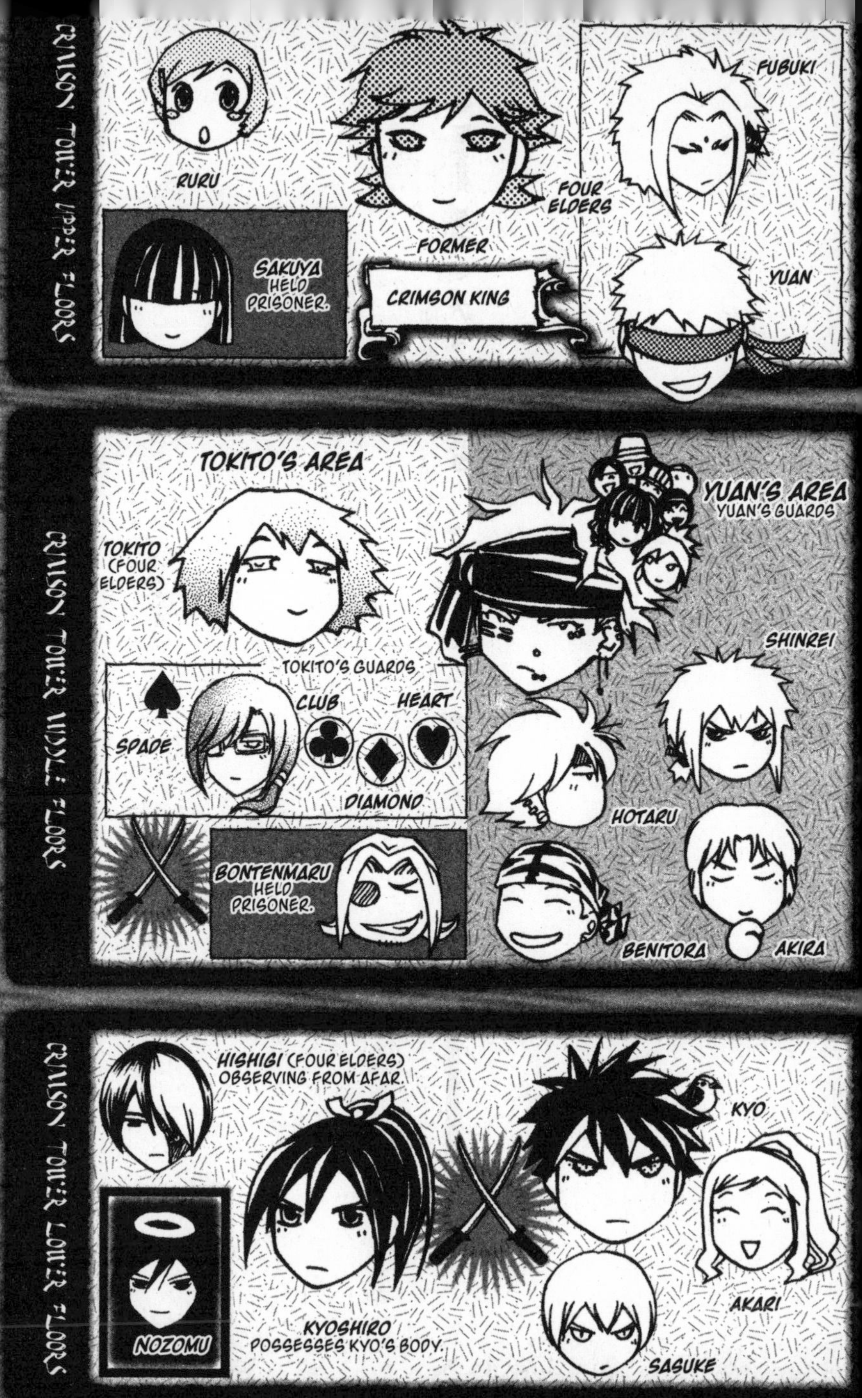
CRIMSON TOWER UPPER FLOORS
FUBUKI
YUAN
FOUR ELDERS
FORMER
CRIMSON KING
RURU
SAKUYA HELD PRISONER.
CRIMSON TOWER MIDDLE FLOORS
YUAN'S AREA
YUAN'S GUARDS
SHINREI
HOTARU
AKIRA
BENITORA
TOKITO'S AREA
TOKITO (FOUR ELDERS)
TOKITO'S GUARDS
HEART
CLUB
DIAMOND
SPADE
BONTENMARU HELD PRISONER.
CRIMSON TOWER LOWER FLOORS
KYO
AKARI
SASUKE
HISHIGI (FOUR ELDERS) OBSERVING FROM AFAR.
KYOSHIRO POSSESSES KYO'S BODY.
NOZOMU

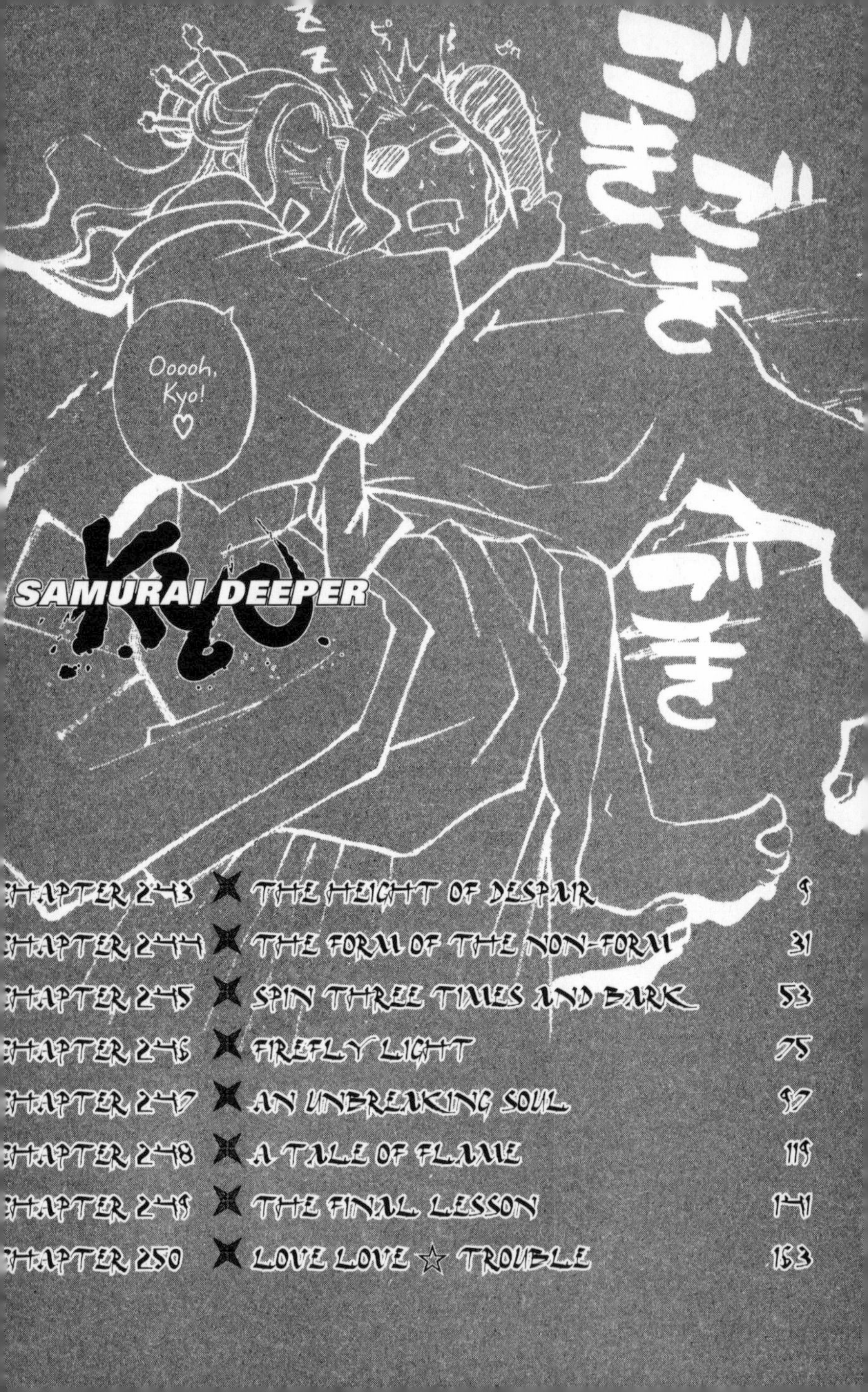
Ooooh, Kyo! ♡
SAMURAI DEEPER KYO

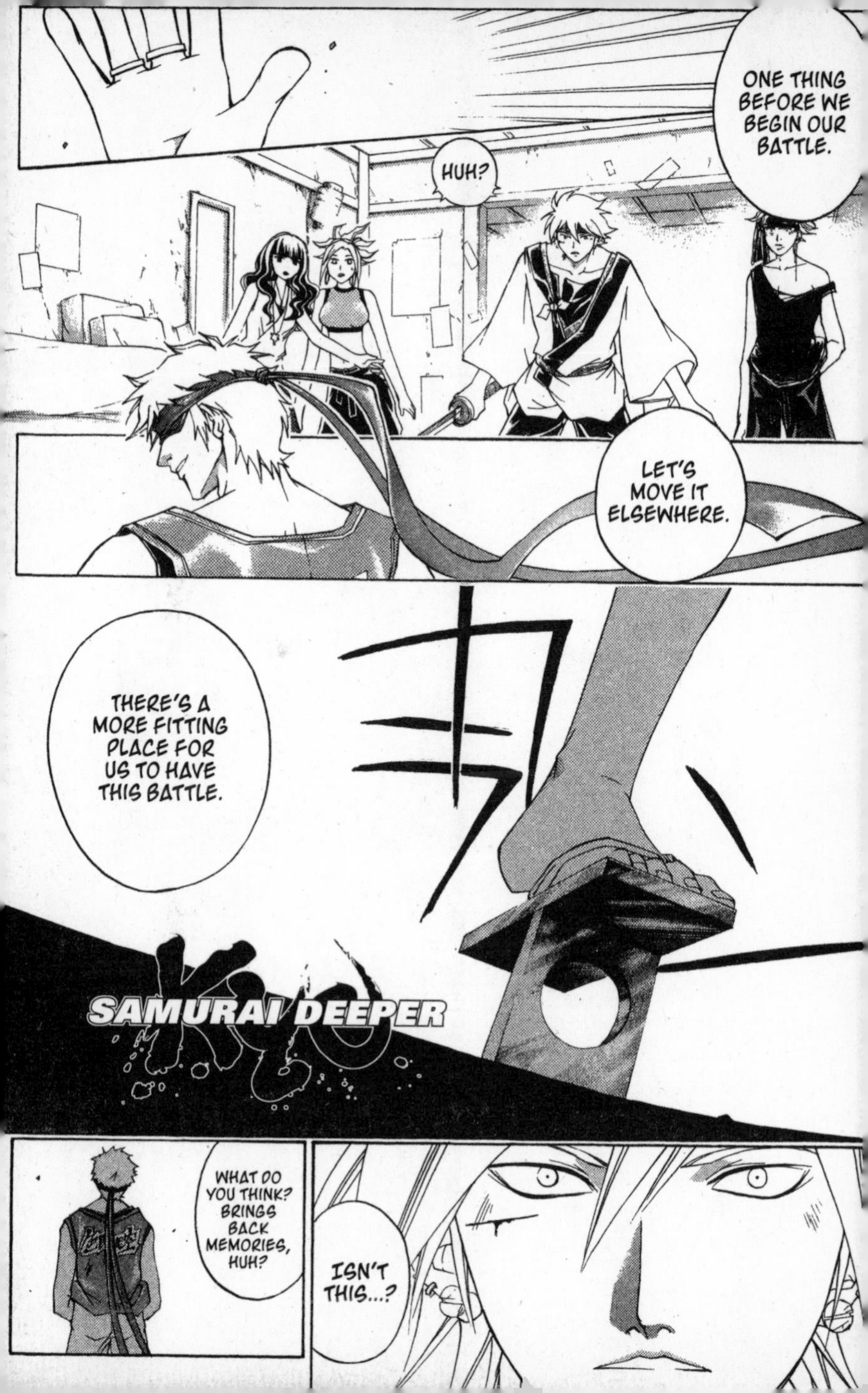
ONE THING BEFORE WE BEGIN OUR BATTLE.
HUH?
LET'S MOVE IT ELSEWHERE.
THERE'S A MORE FITTING PLACE FOR US TO HAVE THIS BATTLE.
SAMURAI DEEPER KYO
ISN'T THIS...?
WHAT DO YOU THINK? BRINGS BACK MEMORIES, HUH?

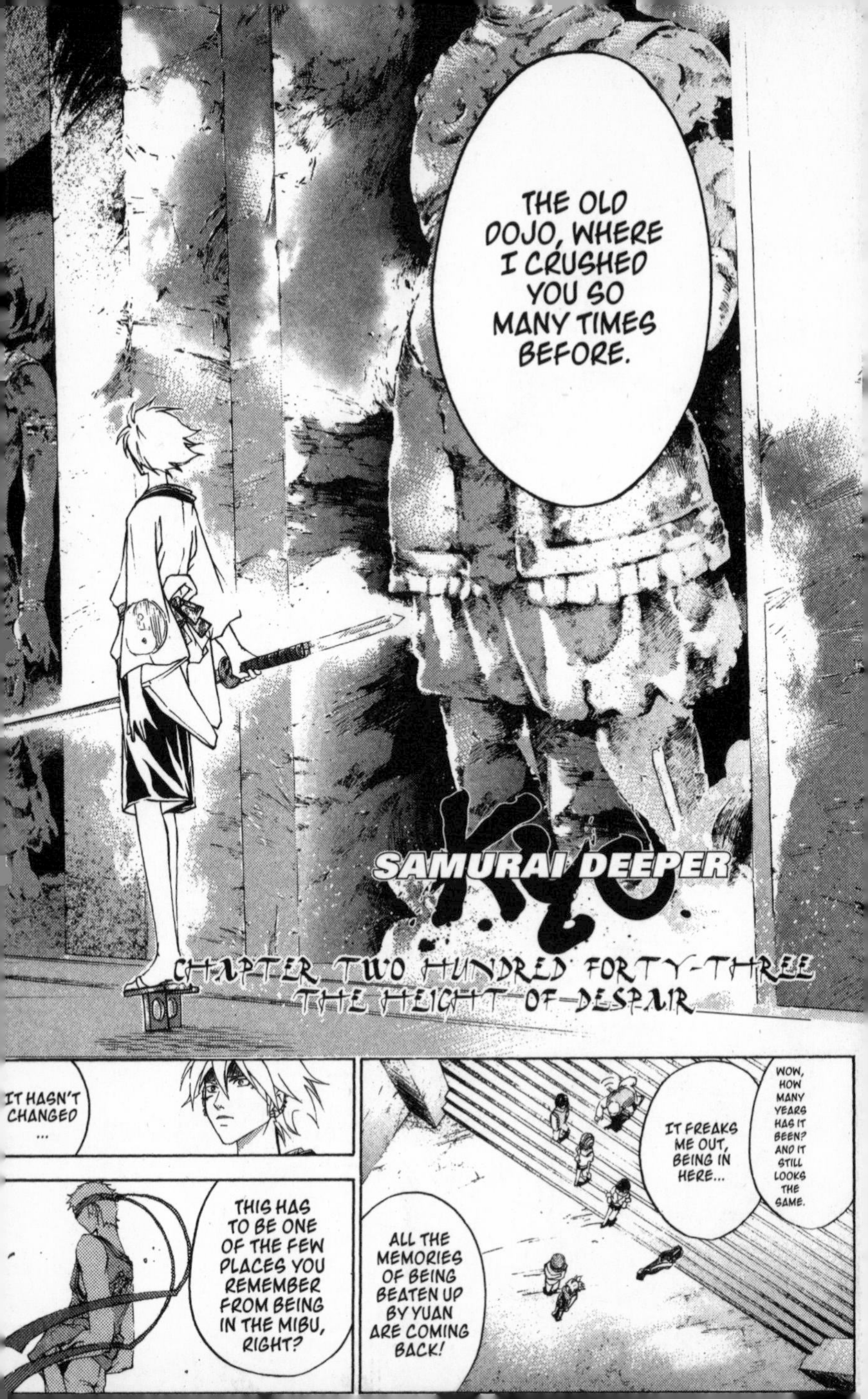
THE OLD DOJO, WHERE I CRUSHED YOU SO MANY TIMES BEFORE.
SAMURAI DEEPER KYO
CHAPTER TWO HUNDRED FORTY-THREE
THE HEIGHT OF DESPAIR
WOW, HOW MANY YEARS HAS IT BEEN? AND IT STILL LOOKS THE SAME.
IT FREAKS ME OUT, BEING IN HERE...
ALL THE MEMORIES OF BEING BEATEN UP BY YUAN ARE COMING BACK!
IT HASN'T CHANGED...
THIS HAS TO BE ONE OF THE FEW PLACES YOU REMEMBER FROM BEING IN THE MIBU, RIGHT?

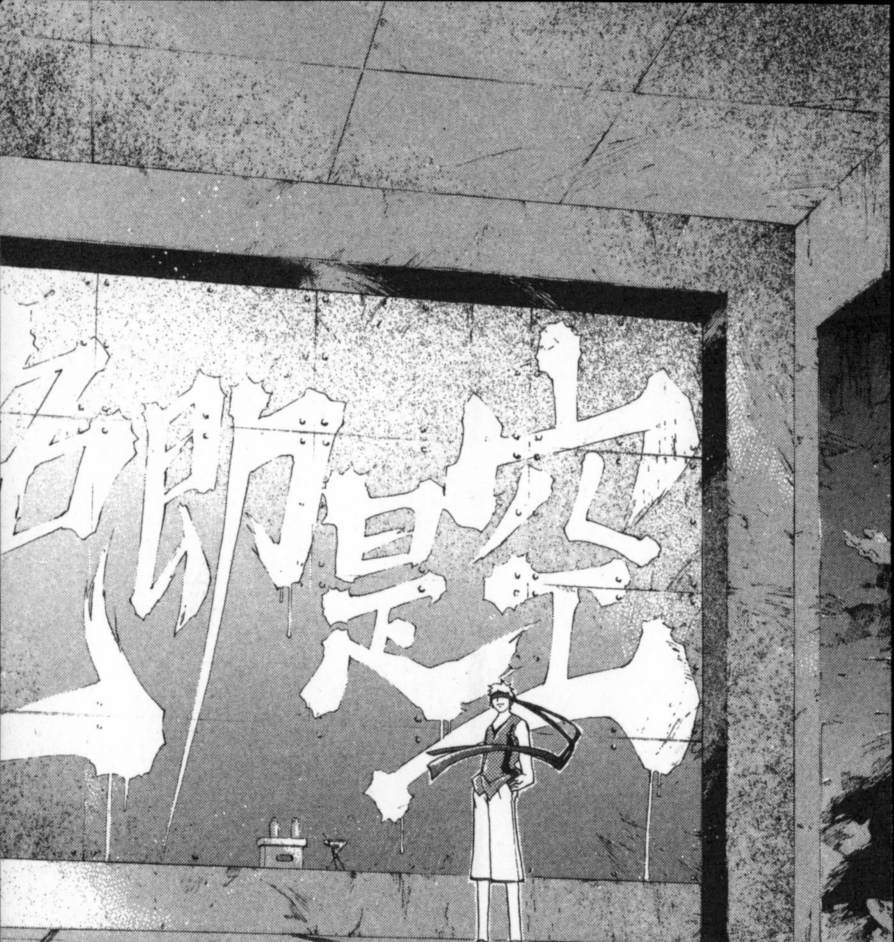

Note: Mural reads, "Matter is void--all is vanity."

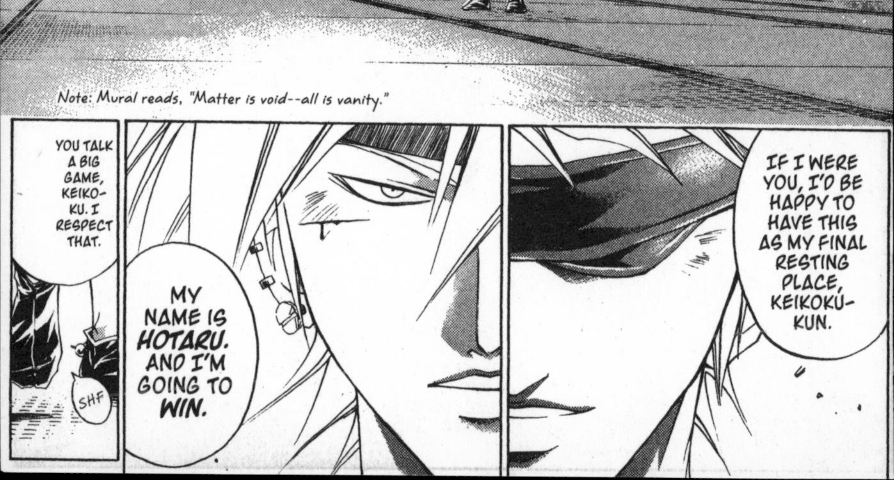
IF I WERE YOU, I'D BE HAPPY TO HAVE THIS AS MY FINAL RESTING PLACE, KEIKOKU-KUN.
MY NAME IS **HOTARU.** AND I'M GOING TO **WIN.**
YOU TALK A BIG GAME, KEIKO-KU. I RESPECT THAT.
SHF

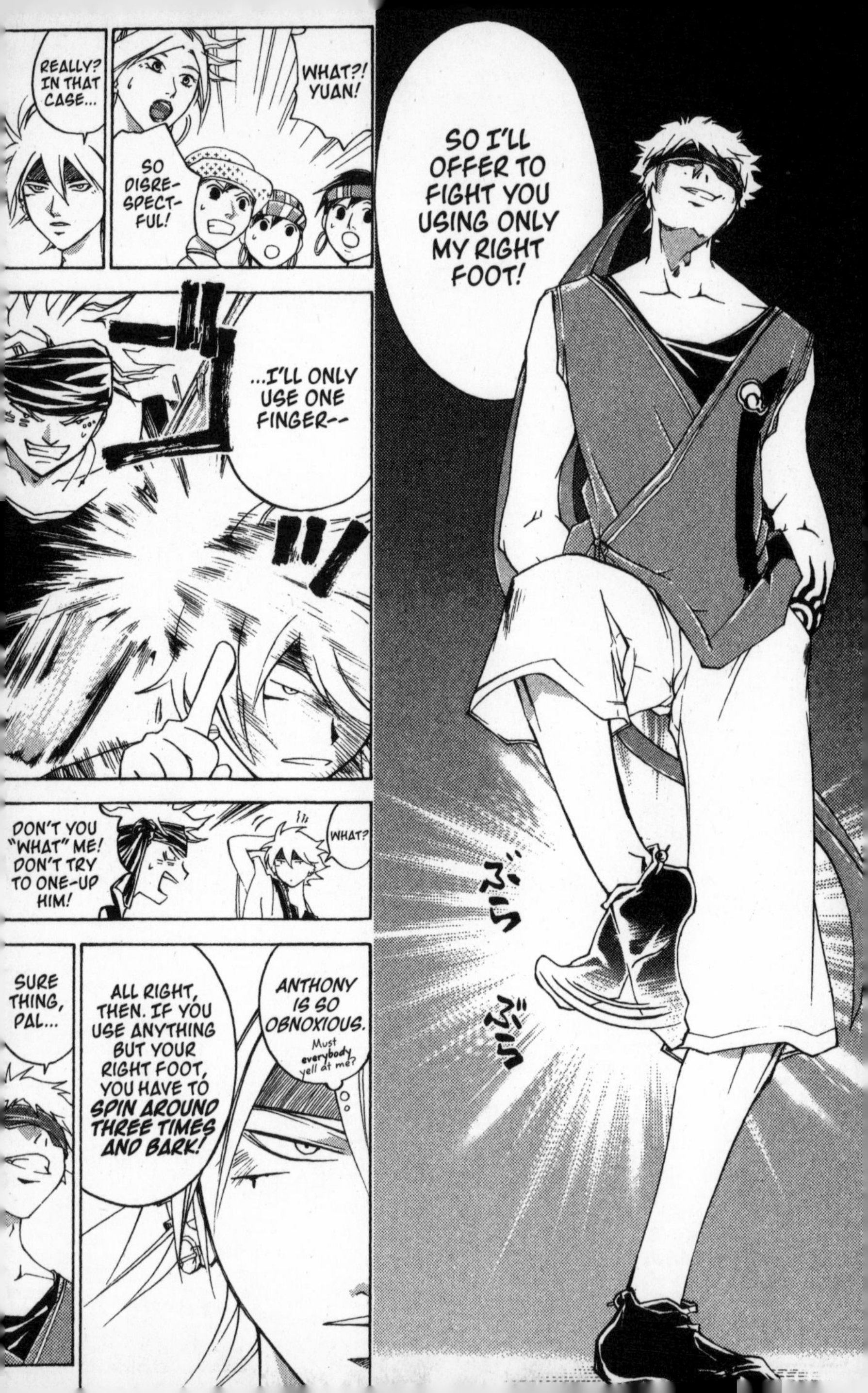
SO I'LL OFFER TO FIGHT YOU USING ONLY MY RIGHT FOOT!
WHAT?! YUAN!
SO DISRESPECTFUL!
REALLY? IN THAT CASE...
...I'LL ONLY USE ONE FINGER--
WHAT?
DON'T YOU "WHAT" ME! DON'T TRY TO ONE-UP HIM!
ANTHONY IS SO OBNOXIOUS.
Must everybody yell at me?
ALL RIGHT, THEN. IF YOU USE ANYTHING BUT YOUR RIGHT FOOT, YOU HAVE TO SPIN AROUND THREE TIMES AND BARK!
SURE THING, PAL...

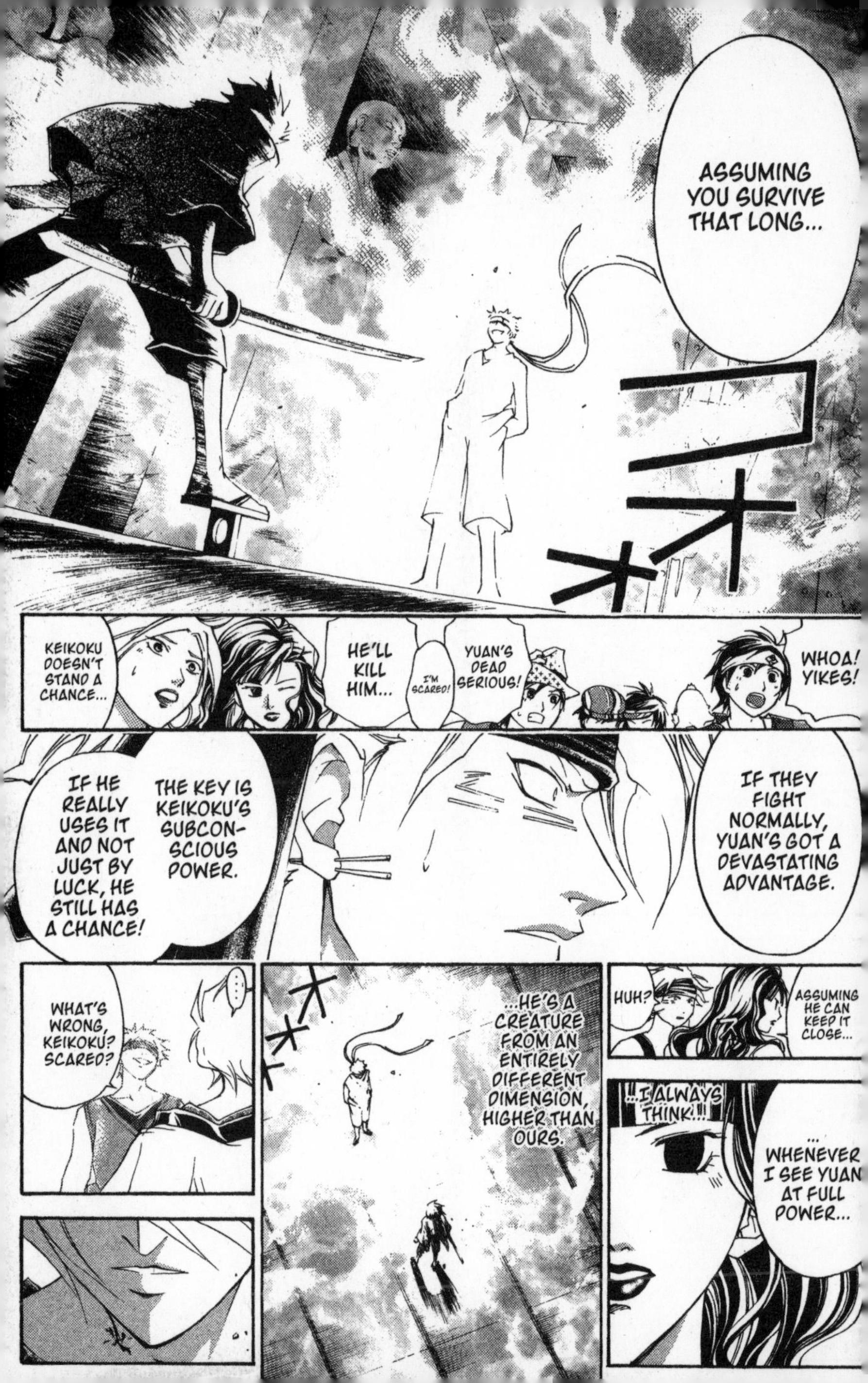
ASSUMING YOU SURVIVE THAT LONG...
WHOA! YIKES!
YUAN'S DEAD SERIOUS!
I'M SCARED!
HE'LL KILL HIM...
KEIKOKU DOESN'T STAND A CHANCE...
IF THEY FIGHT NORMALLY, YUAN'S GOT A DEVASTATING ADVANTAGE.
THE KEY IS KEIKOKU'S SUBCON-SCIOUS POWER.
IF HE REALLY USES IT AND NOT JUST BY LUCK, HE STILL HAS A CHANCE!
ASSUMING HE CAN KEEP IT CLOSE...
HUH?
...WHENEVER I SEE YUAN AT FULL POWER...
...I ALWAYS THINK!!!
...HE'S A CREATURE FROM AN ENTIRELY DIFFERENT DIMENSION, HIGHER THAN OURS.
...
WHAT'S WRONG, KEIKOKU? SCARED?

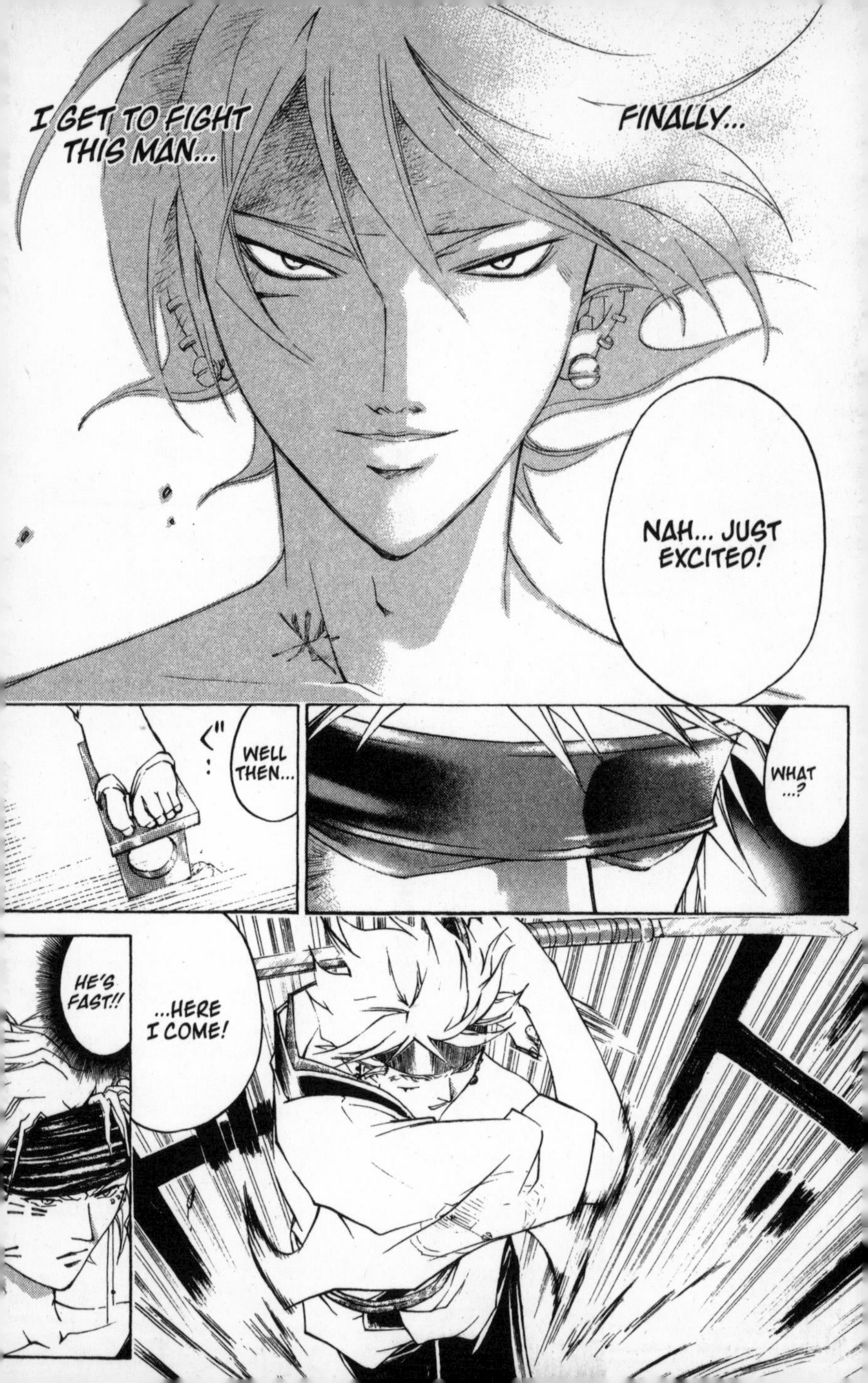
FINALLY...
I GET TO FIGHT THIS MAN...
NAH... JUST EXCITED!
WHAT ...?
WELL THEN...
...HERE I COME!
HE'S FAST!!

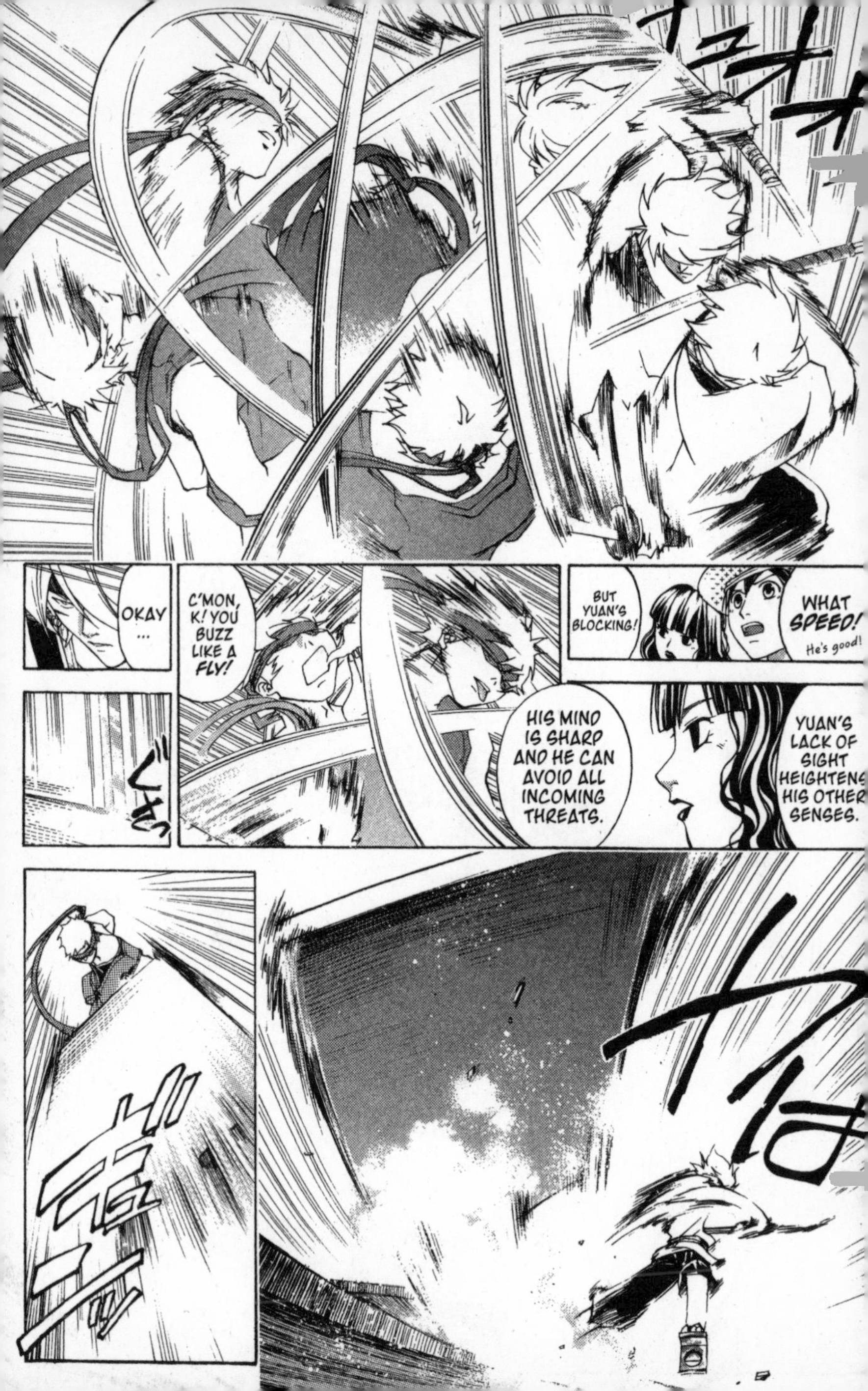
WHAT SPEED!
He's good!
BUT YUAN'S BLOCKING!
YUAN'S LACK OF SIGHT HEIGHTENS HIS OTHER SENSES.
HIS MIND IS SHARP AND HE CAN AVOID ALL INCOMING THREATS.
C'MON, K! YOU BUZZ LIKE A FLY!
OKAY ...

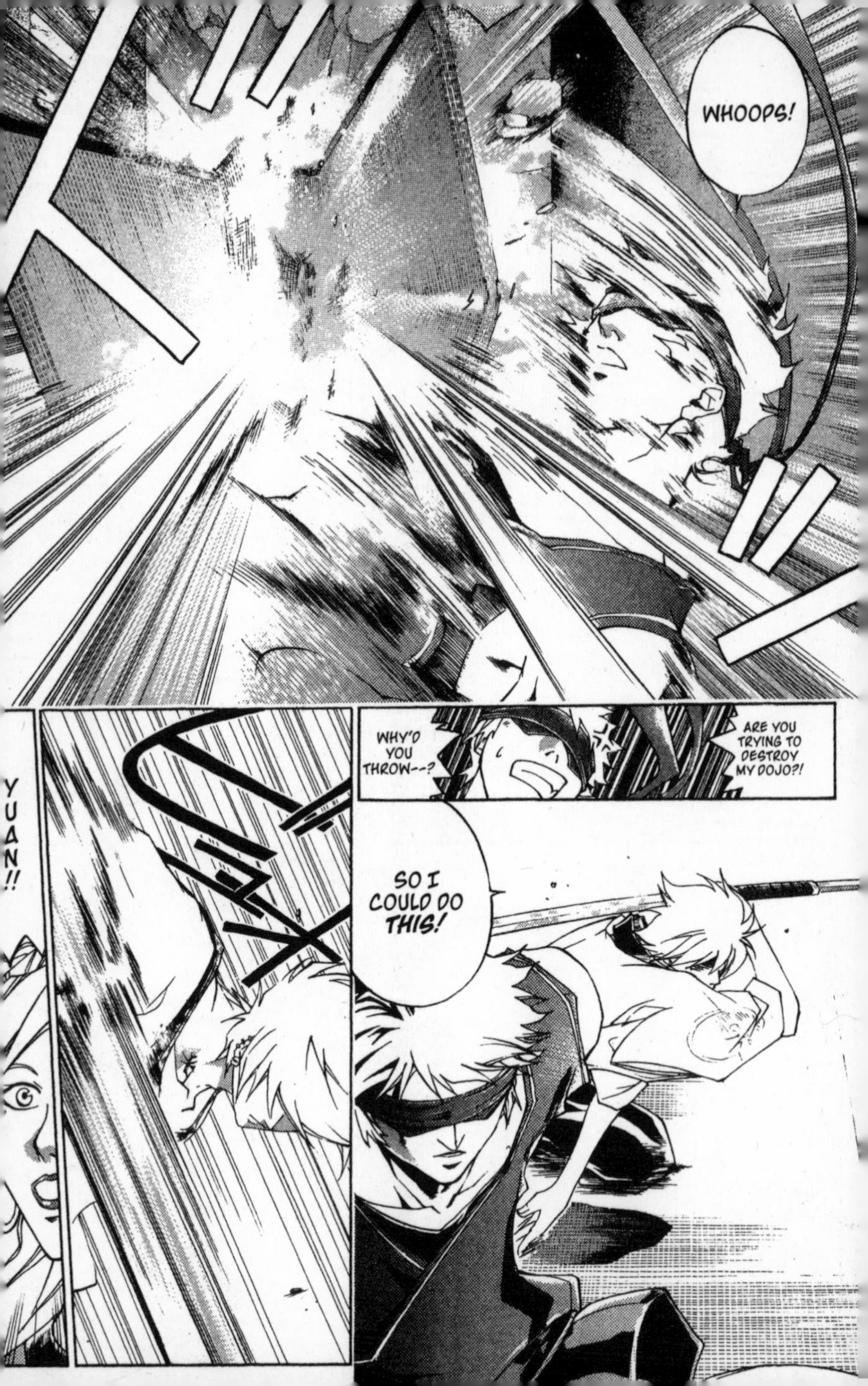
WHOOPS!
ARE YOU TRYING TO DESTROY MY DOJO?!
WHY'D YOU THROW--?
SO I COULD DO THIS!
YUAN!!

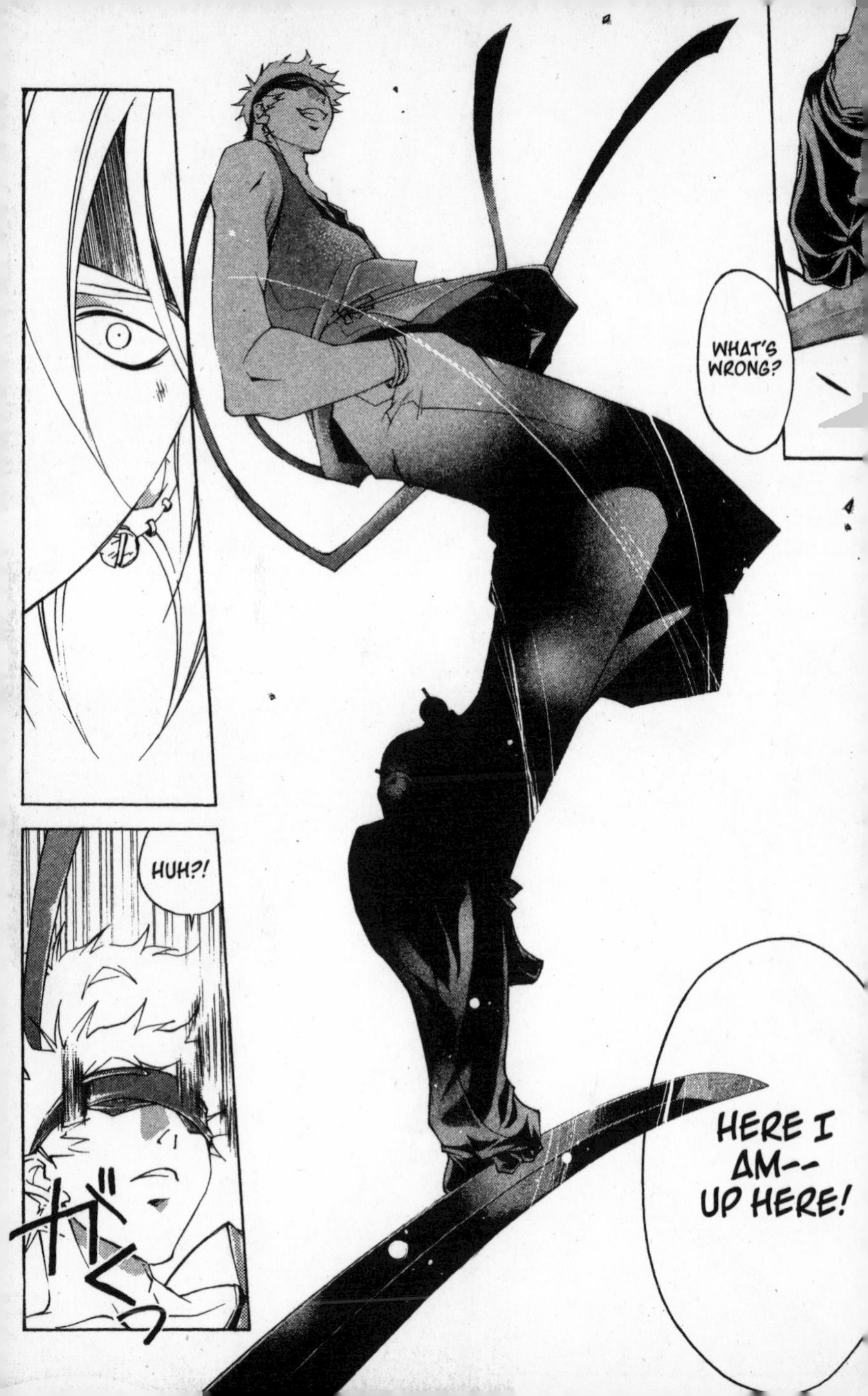
WHAT'S WRONG?
HERE I AM-- UP HERE!
HUH?!
ガくっ

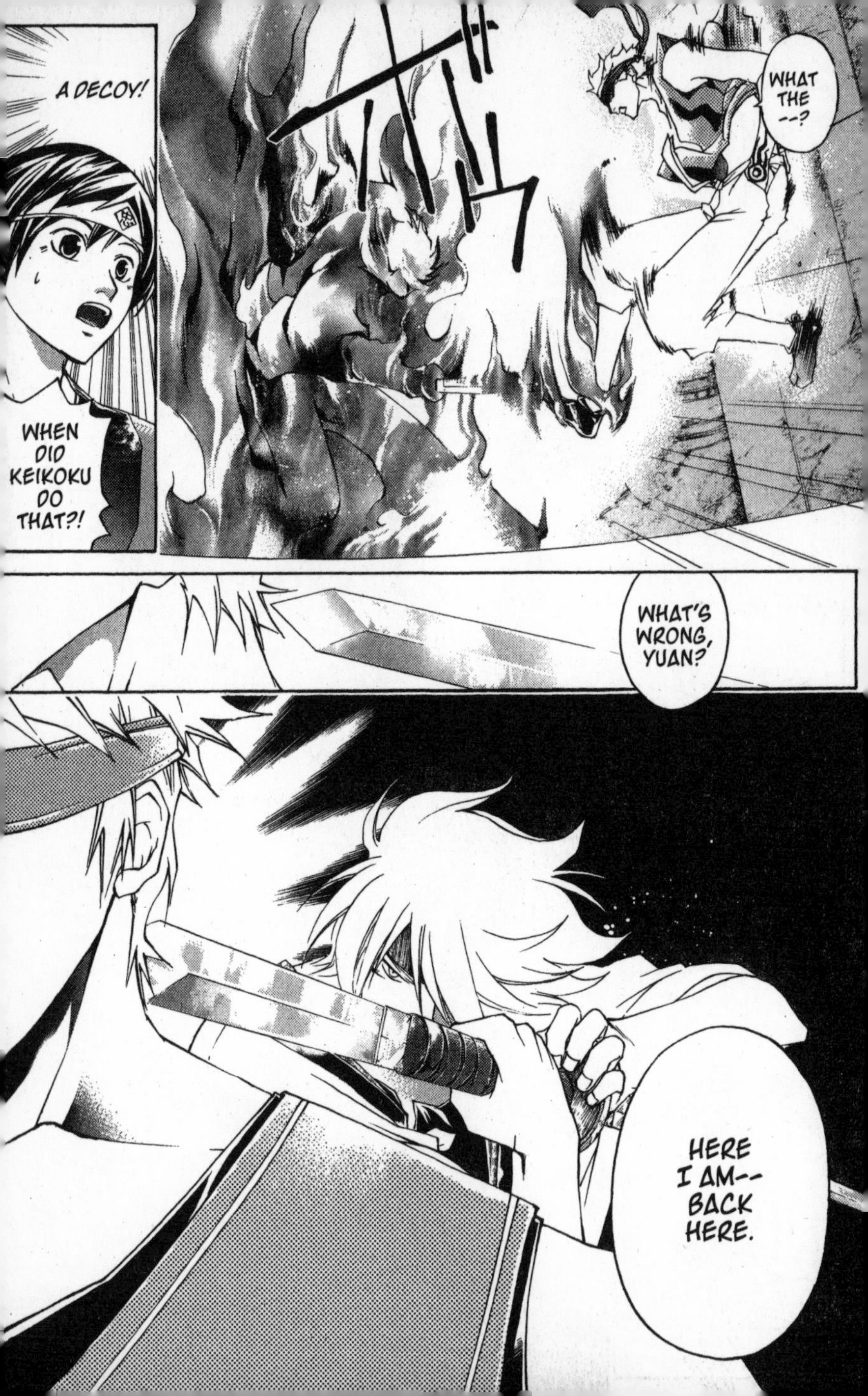
WHAT THE --?
A DECOY!
WHEN DID KEIKOKU DO THAT?!
WHAT'S WRONG, YUAN?
HERE I AM-- BACK HERE.

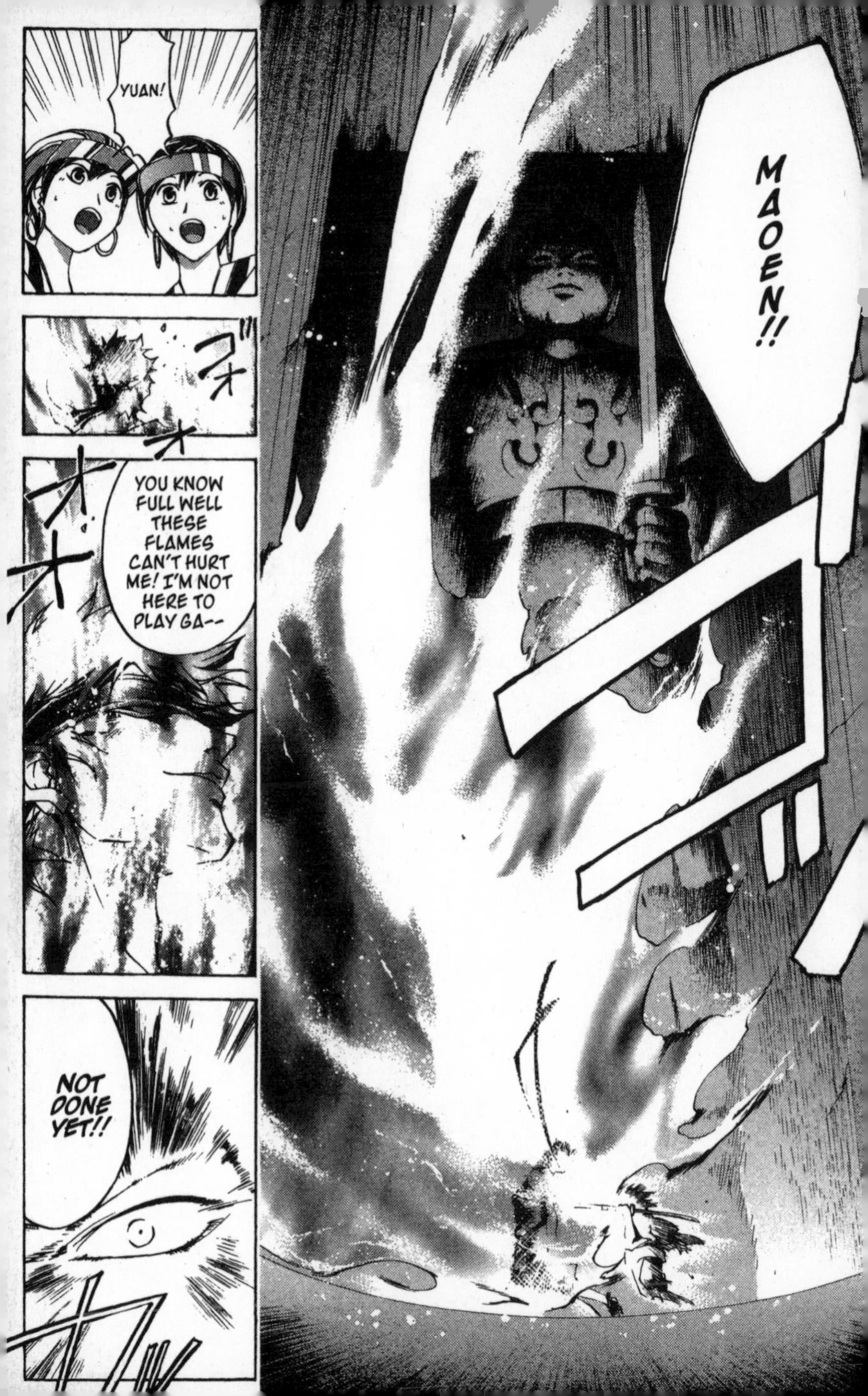
MAOEN!!
YUAN!
YOU KNOW FULL WELL THESE FLAMES CAN'T HURT ME! I'M NOT HERE TO PLAY GA--
NOT DONE YET!!

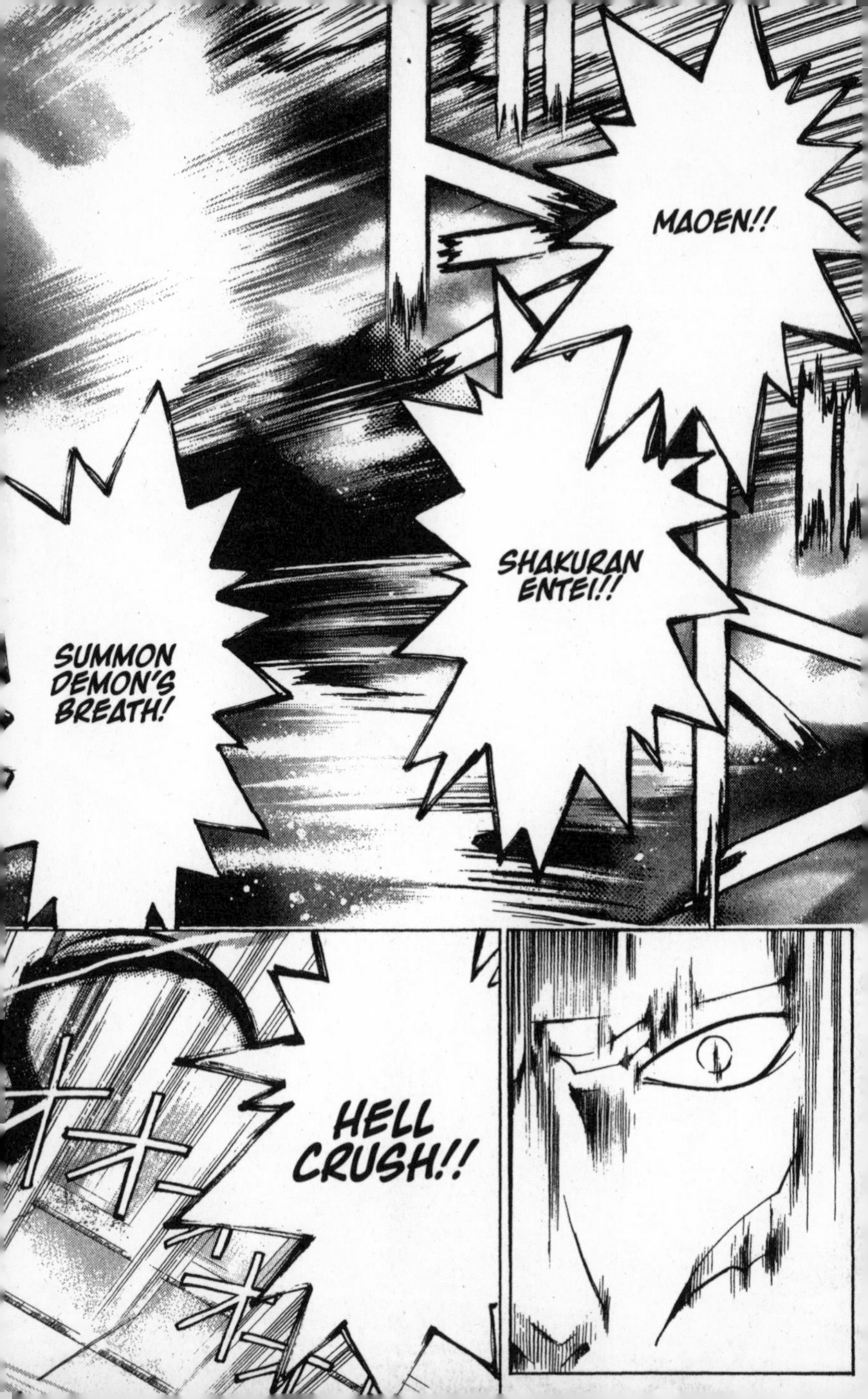
MAOEN!!
SHAKURAN ENTEI!!
SUMMON DEMON'S BREATH!
HELL CRUSH!!

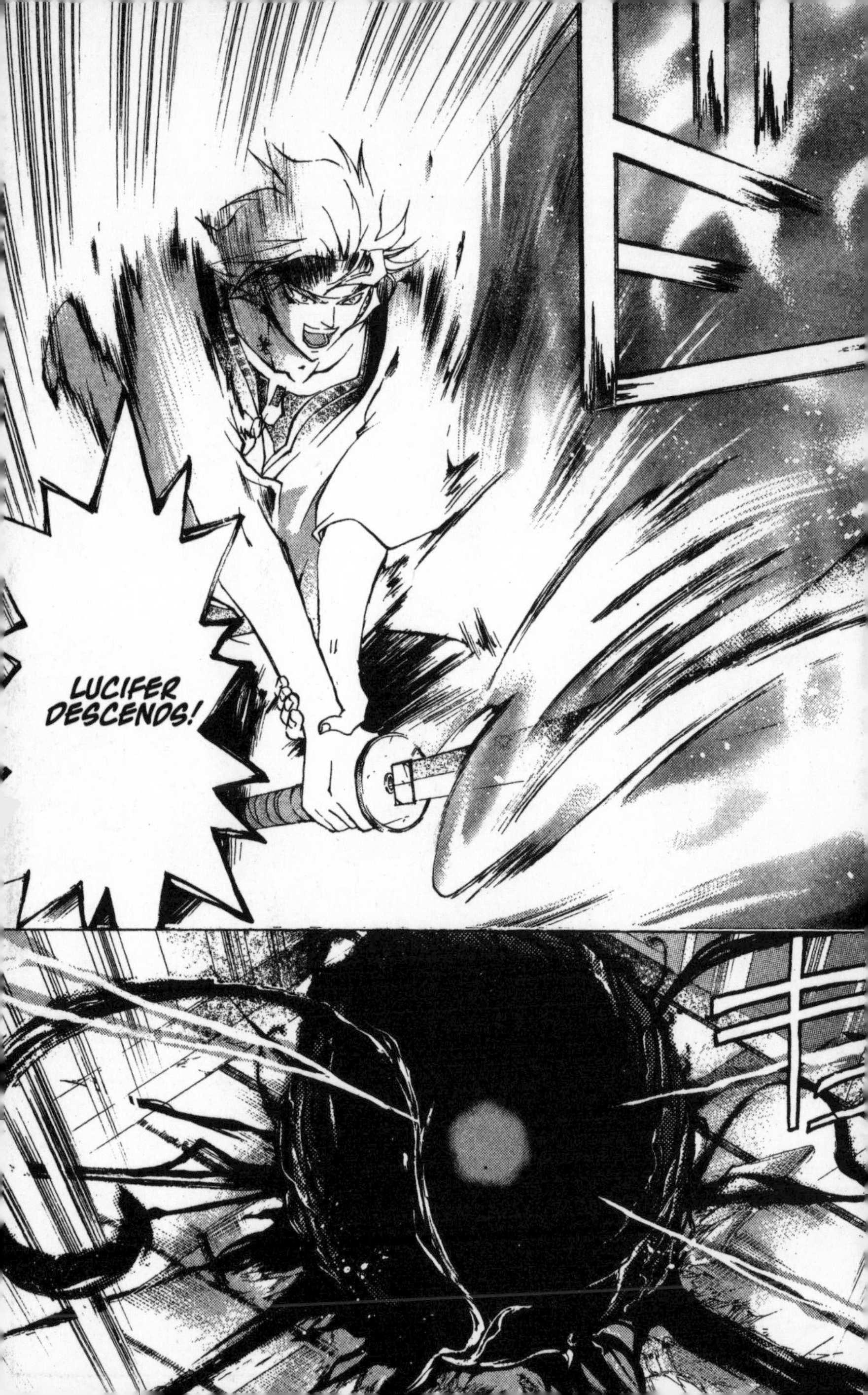
LUCIFER DESCENDS!

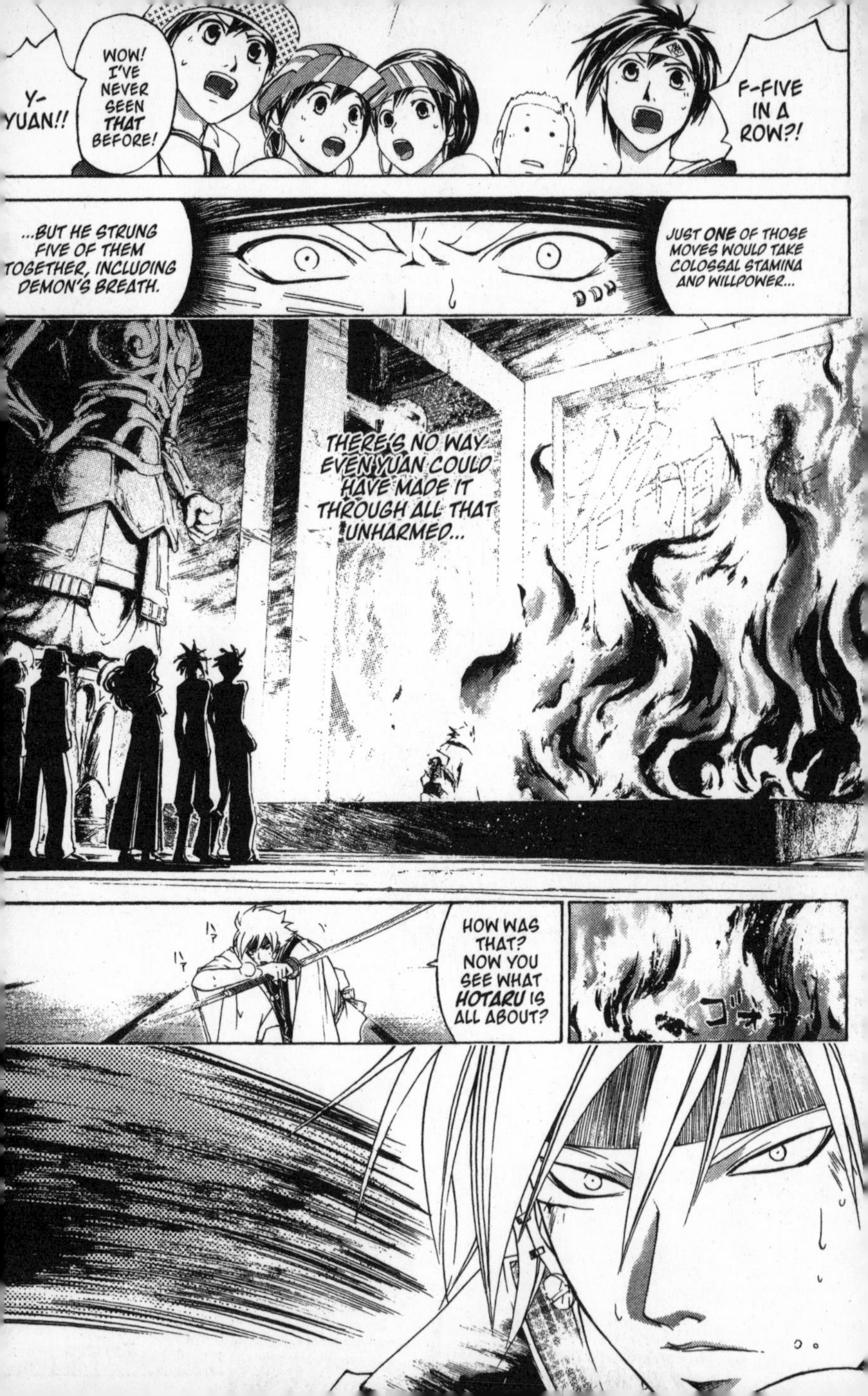
F-FIVE IN A ROW?!
WOW! I'VE NEVER SEEN THAT BEFORE!
Y-YUAN!!
JUST ONE OF THOSE MOVES WOULD TAKE COLOSSAL STAMINA AND WILLPOWER...
...BUT HE STRUNG FIVE OF THEM TOGETHER, INCLUDING DEMON'S BREATH.
THERE'S NO WAY EVEN YUAN COULD HAVE MADE IT THROUGH ALL THAT UNHARMED...
HOW WAS THAT? NOW YOU SEE WHAT HOTARU IS ALL ABOUT?

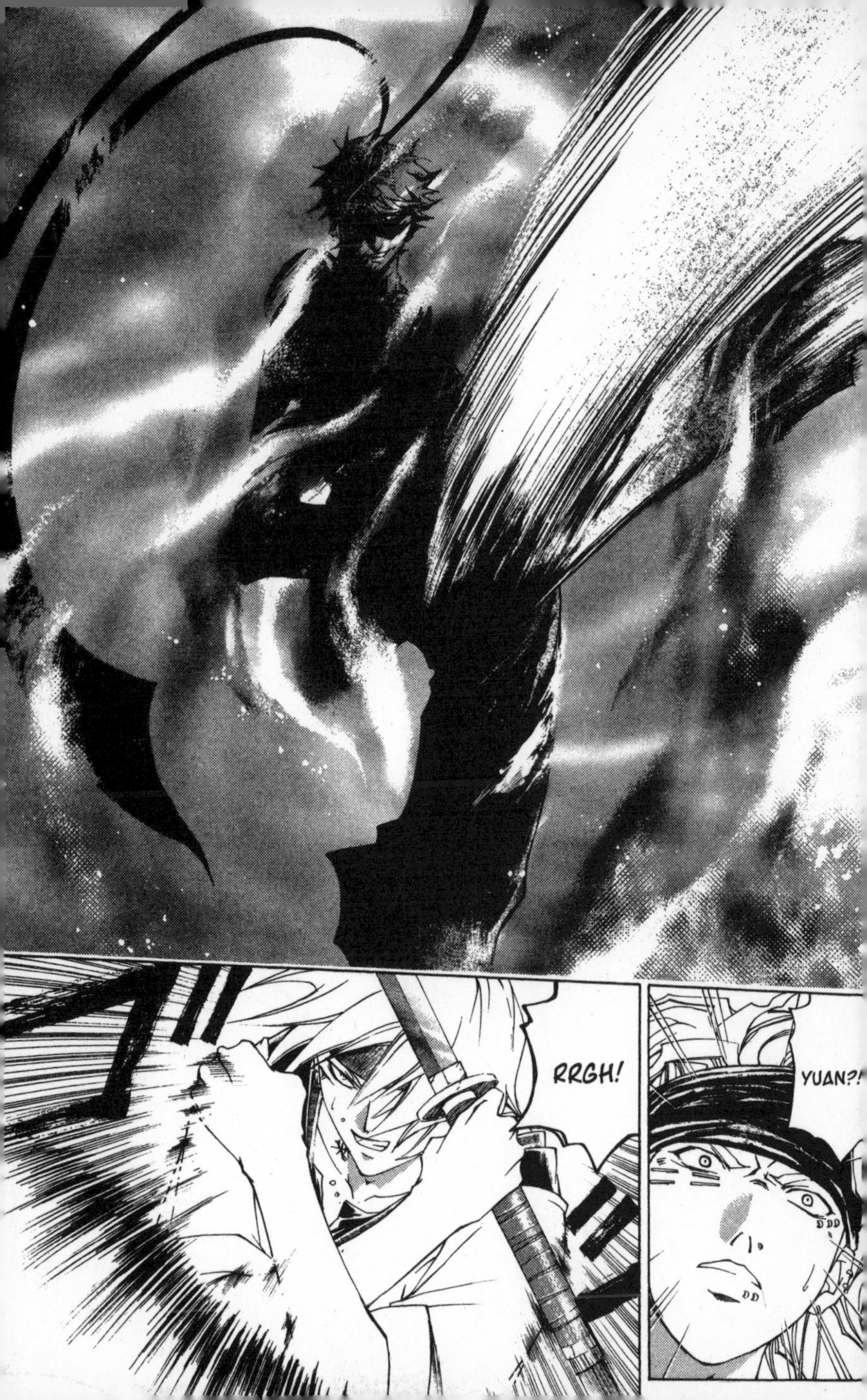
YUAN?!
RRGH!

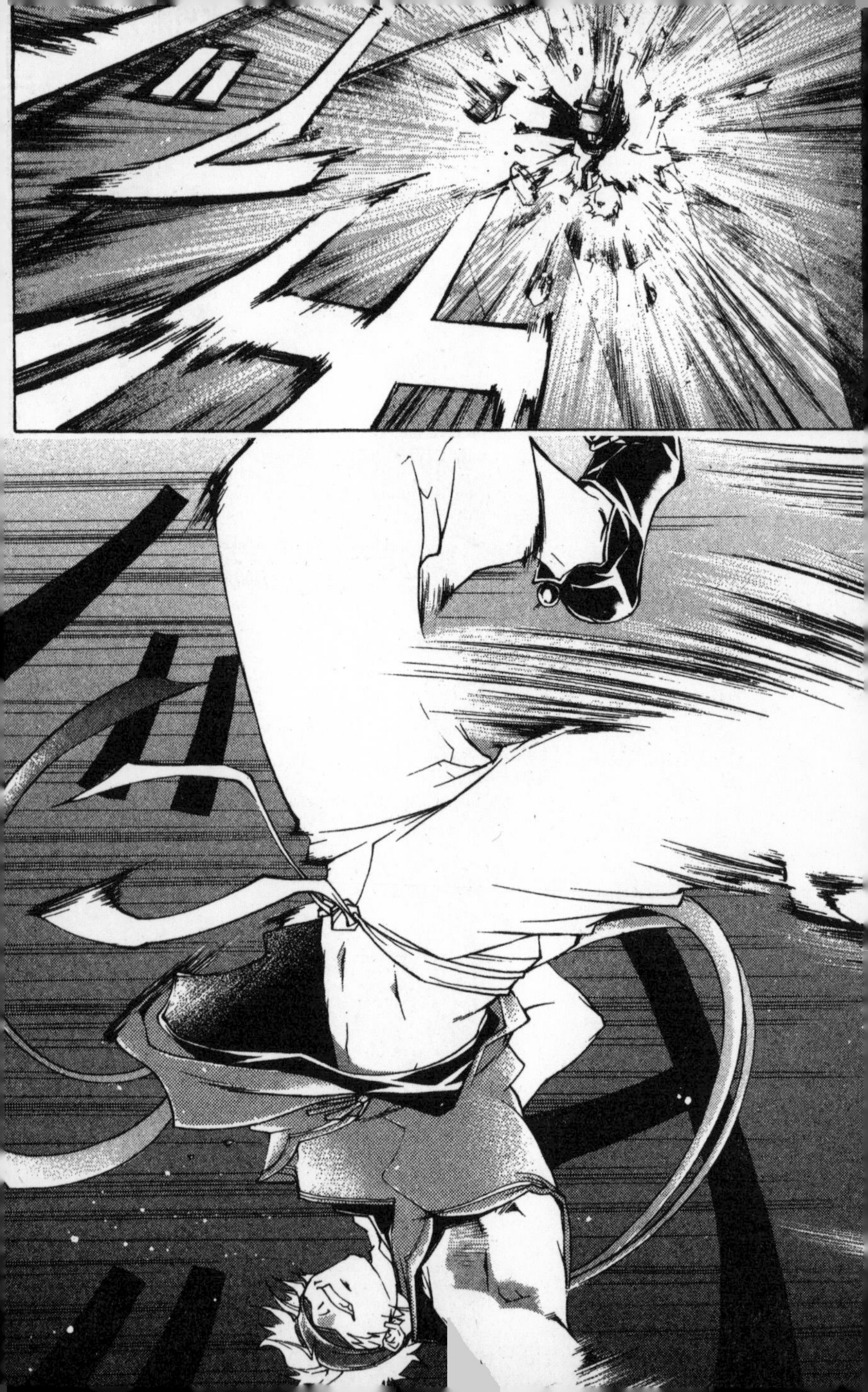

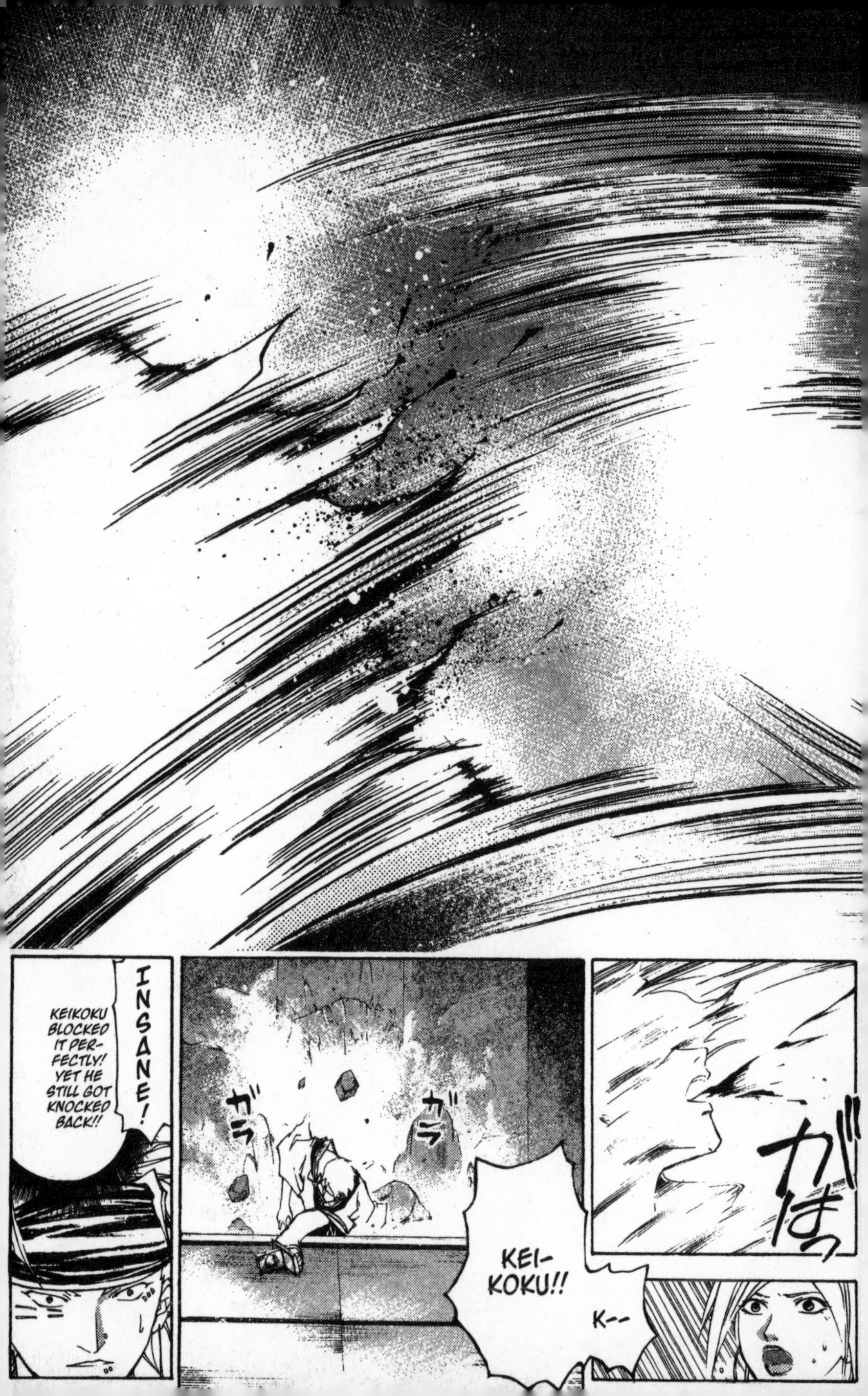
がはっ
ガラ
ガラ
KEI-KOKU!!
K--
INSANE!
KEIKOKU BLOCKED IT PERFECTLY! YET HE STILL GOT KNOCKED BACK!!

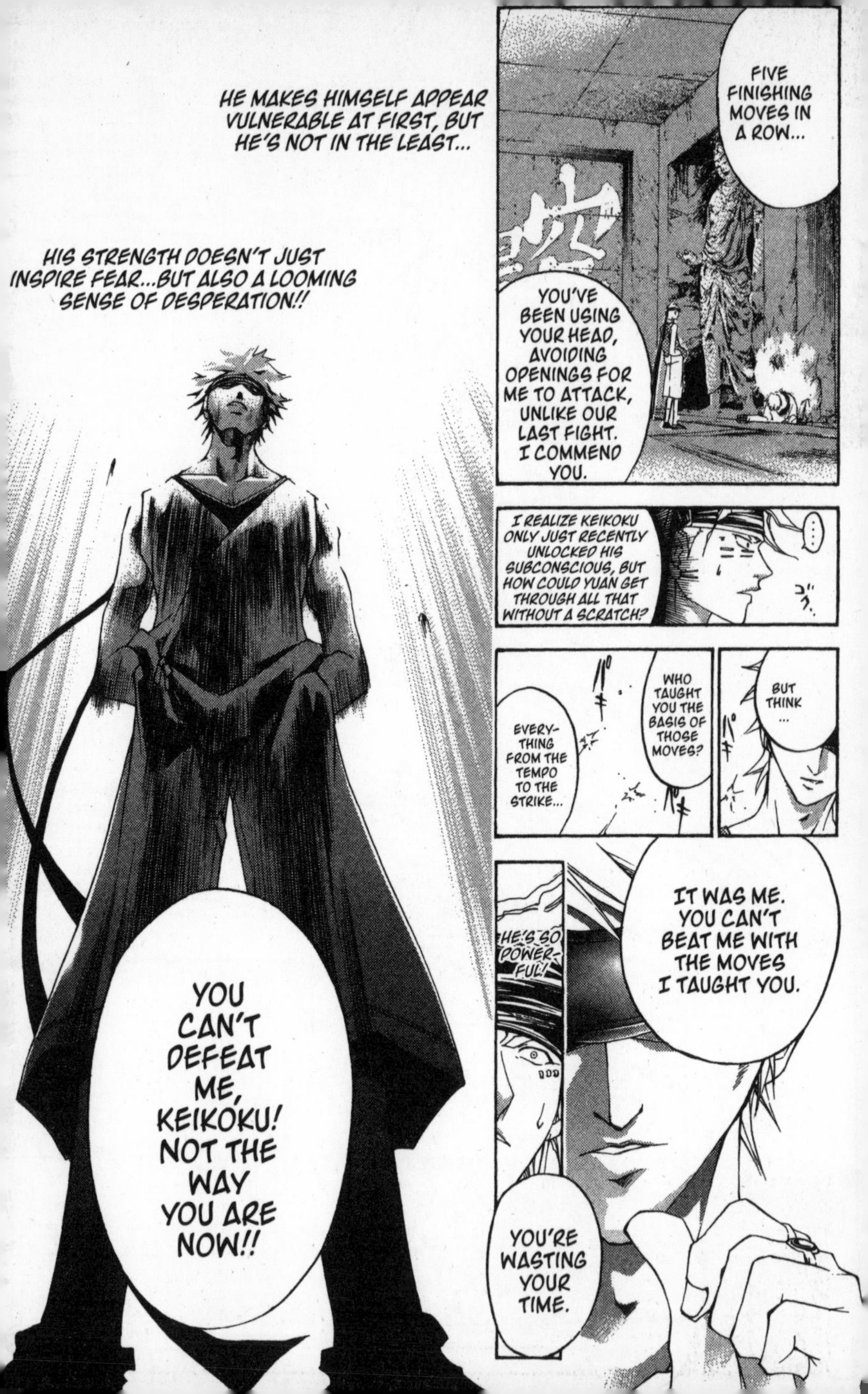
FIVE FINISHING MOVES IN A ROW...
YOU'VE BEEN USING YOUR HEAD, AVOIDING OPENINGS FOR ME TO ATTACK, UNLIKE OUR LAST FIGHT. I COMMEND YOU.
I REALIZE KEIKOKU ONLY JUST RECENTLY UNLOCKED HIS SUBCONSCIOUS, BUT HOW COULD YUAN GET THROUGH ALL THAT WITHOUT A SCRATCH?
...
BUT THINK ...
WHO TAUGHT YOU THE BASIS OF THOSE MOVES?
EVERYTHING FROM THE TEMPO TO THE STRIKE...
IT WAS ME. YOU CAN'T BEAT ME WITH THE MOVES I TAUGHT YOU.
HE'S SO POWERFUL!
YOU'RE WASTING YOUR TIME.
HE MAKES HIMSELF APPEAR VULNERABLE AT FIRST, BUT HE'S NOT IN THE LEAST...
HIS STRENGTH DOESN'T JUST INSPIRE FEAR...BUT ALSO A LOOMING SENSE OF DESPERATION!!
YOU CAN'T DEFEAT ME, KEIKOKU! NOT THE WAY YOU ARE NOW!!

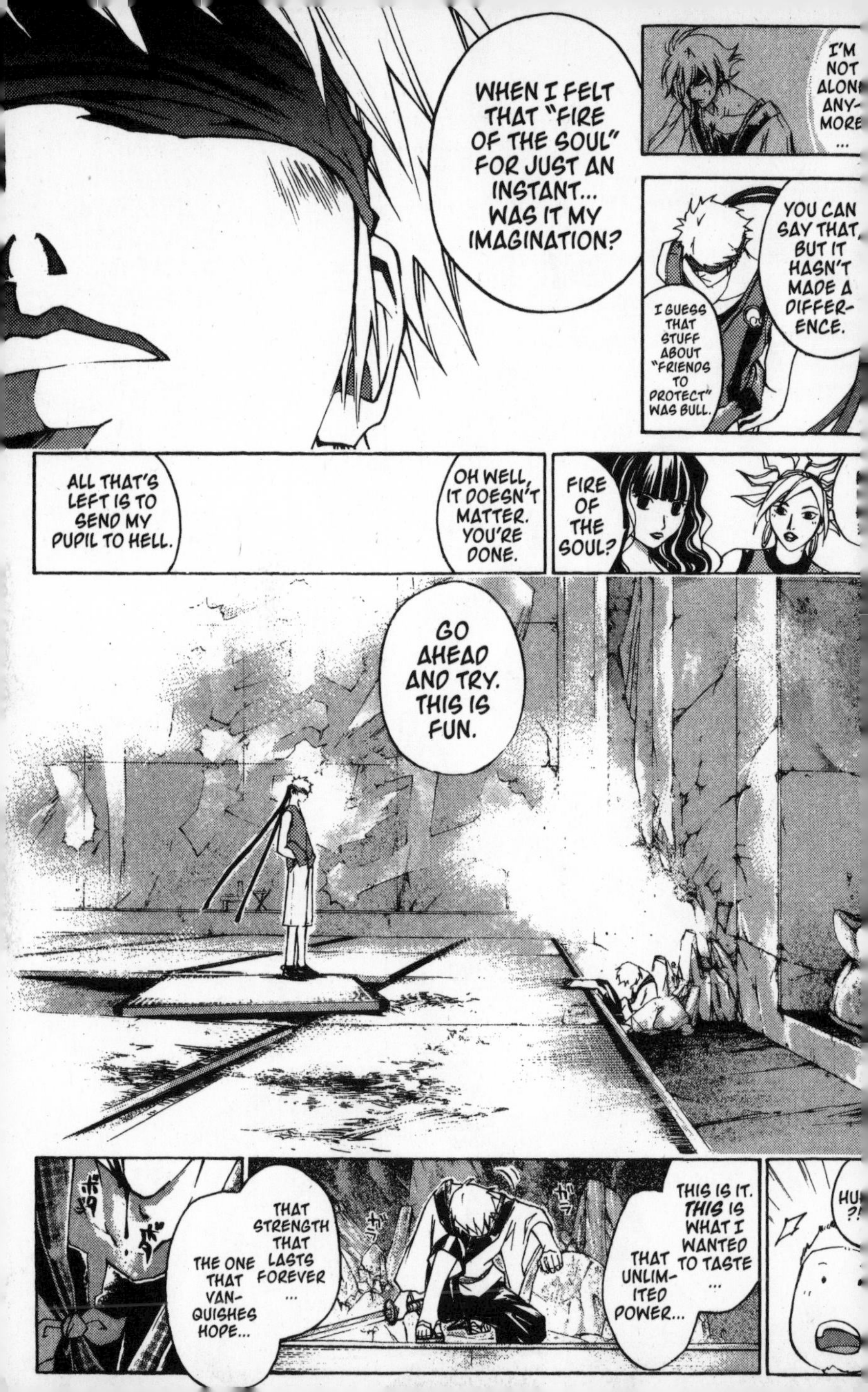
I'M NOT ALON[E] ANY-MORE ...
YOU CAN SAY THAT, BUT IT HASN'T MADE A DIFFER-ENCE.
I GUESS THAT STUFF ABOUT "FRIENDS TO PROTECT" WAS BULL.
WHEN I FELT THAT "FIRE OF THE SOUL" FOR JUST AN INSTANT... WAS IT MY IMAGINATION?
FIRE OF THE SOUL?
OH WELL, IT DOESN'T MATTER. YOU'RE DONE.
ALL THAT'S LEFT IS TO SEND MY PUPIL TO HELL.
GO AHEAD AND TRY. THIS IS FUN.
HU ?!
THIS IS IT. THIS IS WHAT I WANTED TO TASTE ...
THAT UNLIM-ITED POWER...
THAT STRENGTH THAT LASTS FOREVER ...
THE ONE THAT VAN-QUISHES HOPE...

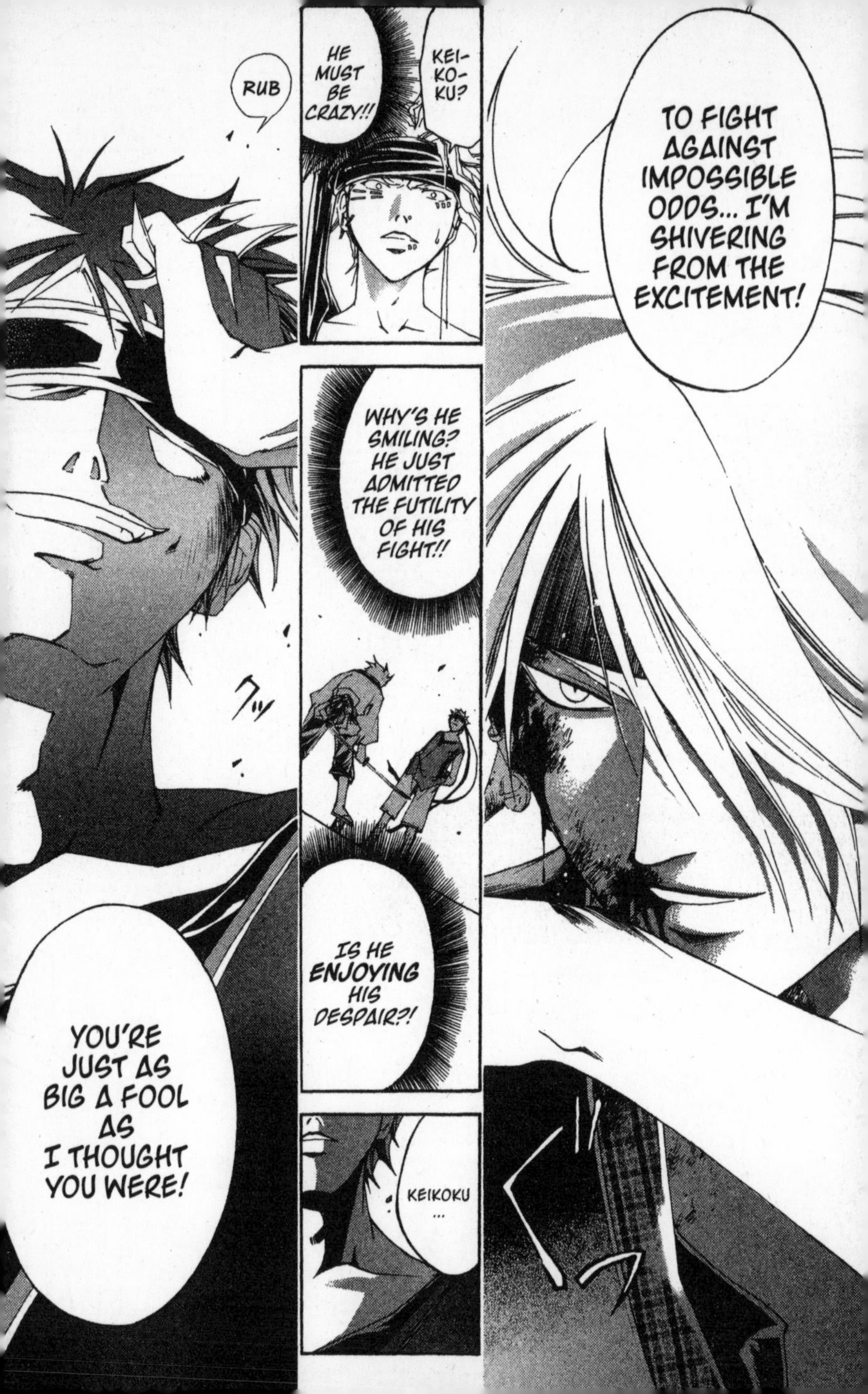
TO FIGHT AGAINST IMPOSSIBLE ODDS... I'M SHIVERING FROM THE EXCITEMENT!
KEI-KO-KU?
HE MUST BE CRAZY!!
WHY'S HE SMILING? HE JUST ADMITTED THE FUTILITY OF HIS FIGHT!!
IS HE ENJOYING HIS DESPAIR?!
KEIKOKU ...
RUB
YOU'RE JUST AS BIG A FOOL AS I THOUGHT YOU WERE!

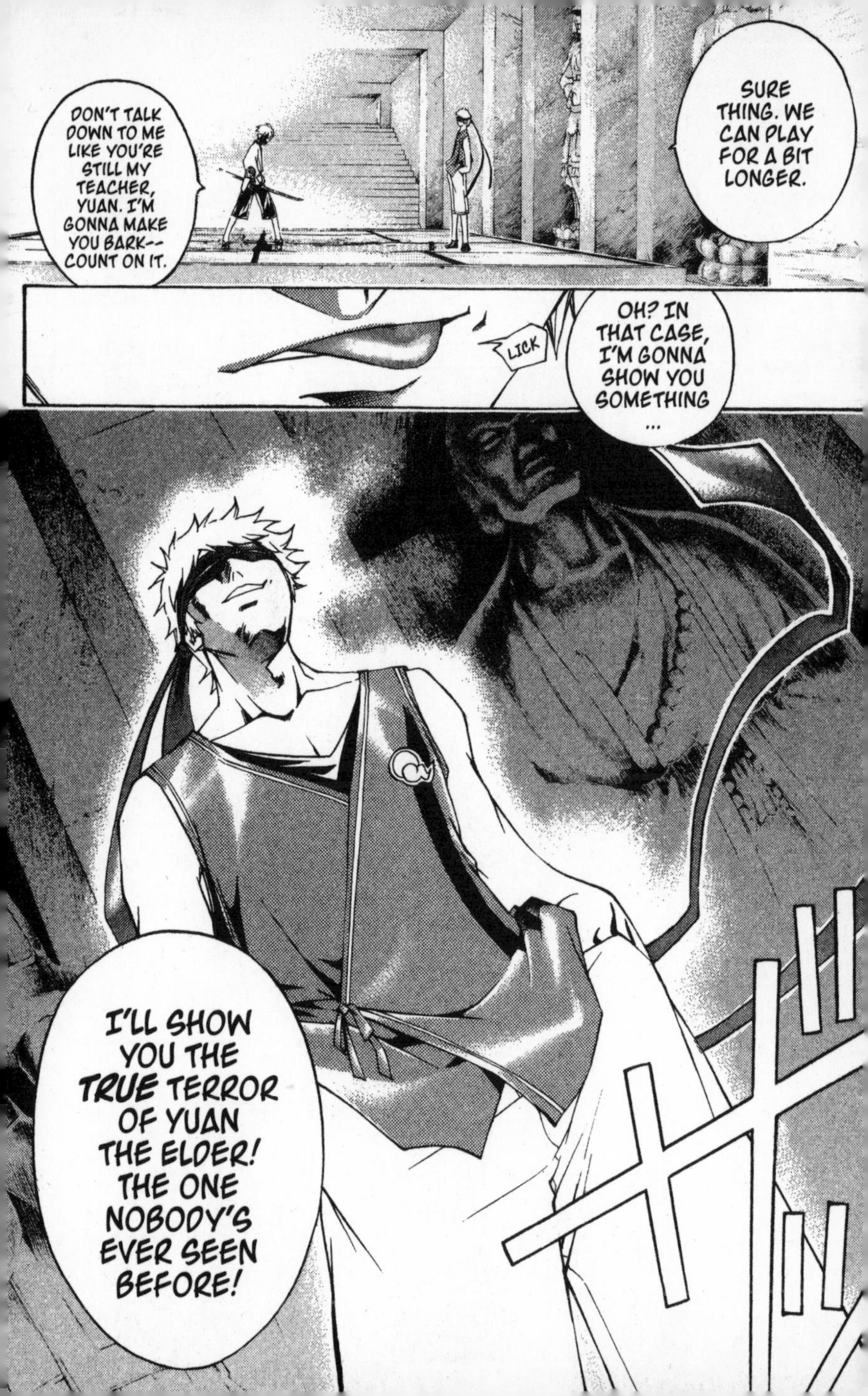
SURE THING. WE CAN PLAY FOR A BIT LONGER.
DON'T TALK DOWN TO ME LIKE YOU'RE STILL MY TEACHER, YUAN. I'M GONNA MAKE YOU BARK-- COUNT ON IT.
OH? IN THAT CASE, I'M GONNA SHOW YOU SOMETHING ...
LICK
I'LL SHOW YOU THE TRUE TERROR OF YUAN THE ELDER! THE ONE NOBODY'S EVER SEEN BEFORE!

Mad Skillz!

DRAW LIKE KAMIJYO!

[Toyama/Kuro] ⬇

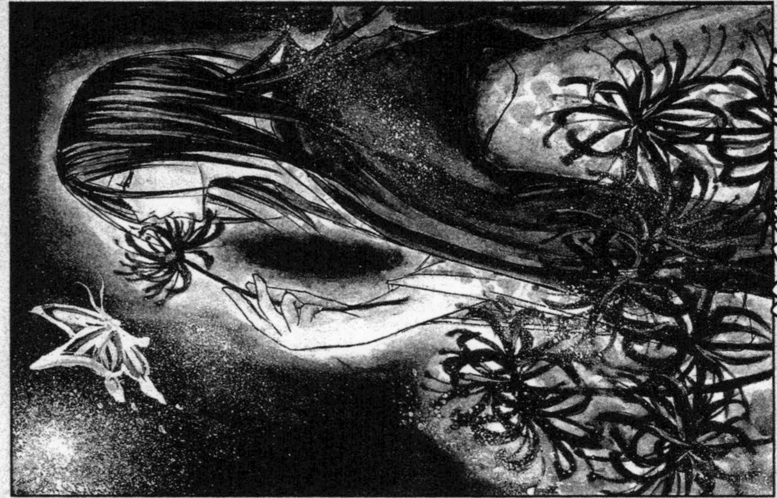

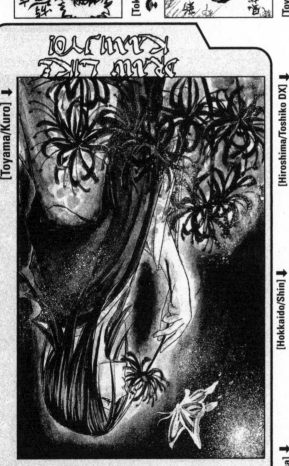

What beauty! The amaryllis and butterfly motif is gorgeous. This entire picture just screams Yukimura!

[Shizuoka/Kabuto] ⬇

Tough guys!

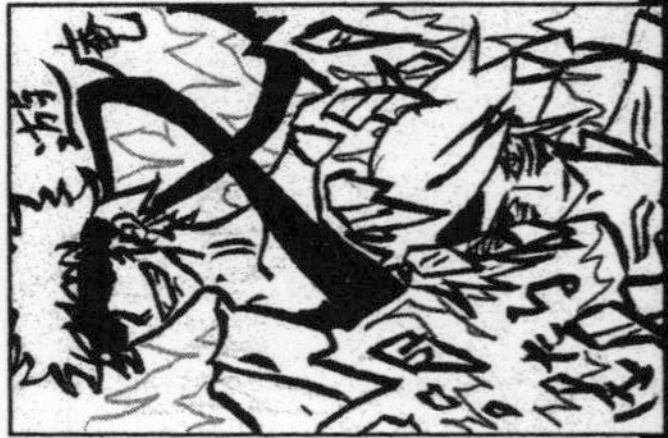

[Tokyo/Hina] ⬇

What a peaceful smile.

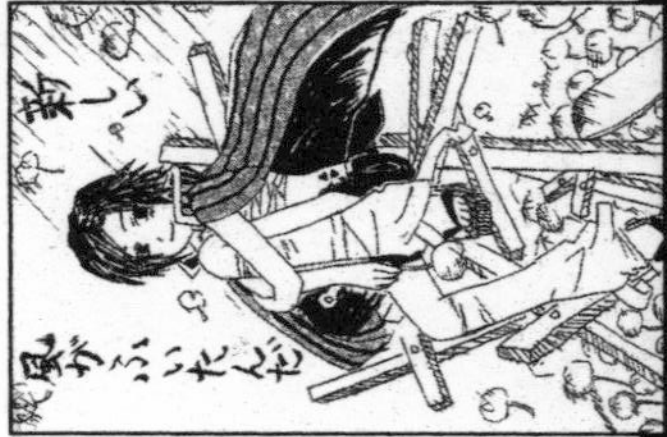

[Miyazaki/Misa] ⬇

What's wrong, Bon-chan?

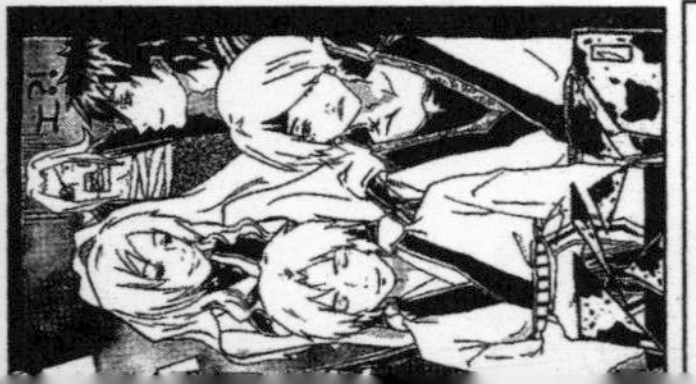

[Hokkaido/Shin] ⬇

Where ya goin', Sasuke?

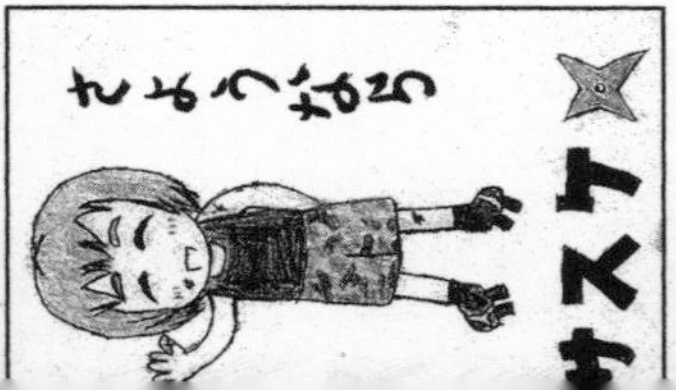
さようなら
サスケ

[Hiroshima/Toshiko DX] ⬇

Nice and friendly!

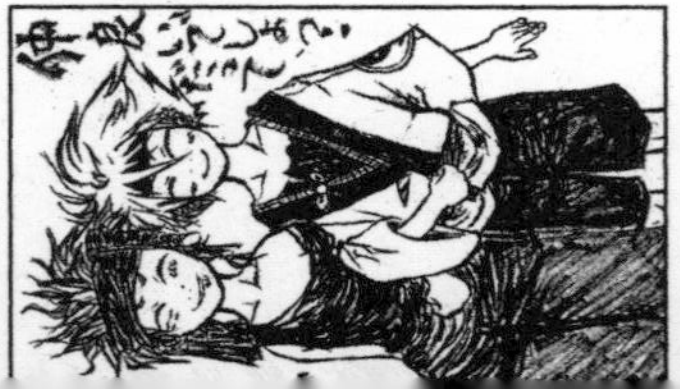

[Toyama/Eriko Odera] ⬇

Does Hotaru write poems, too?

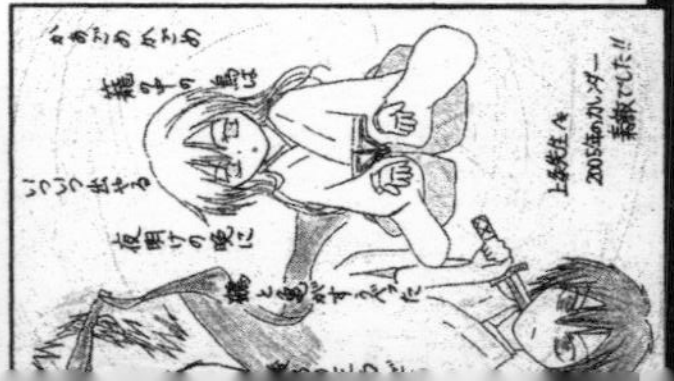

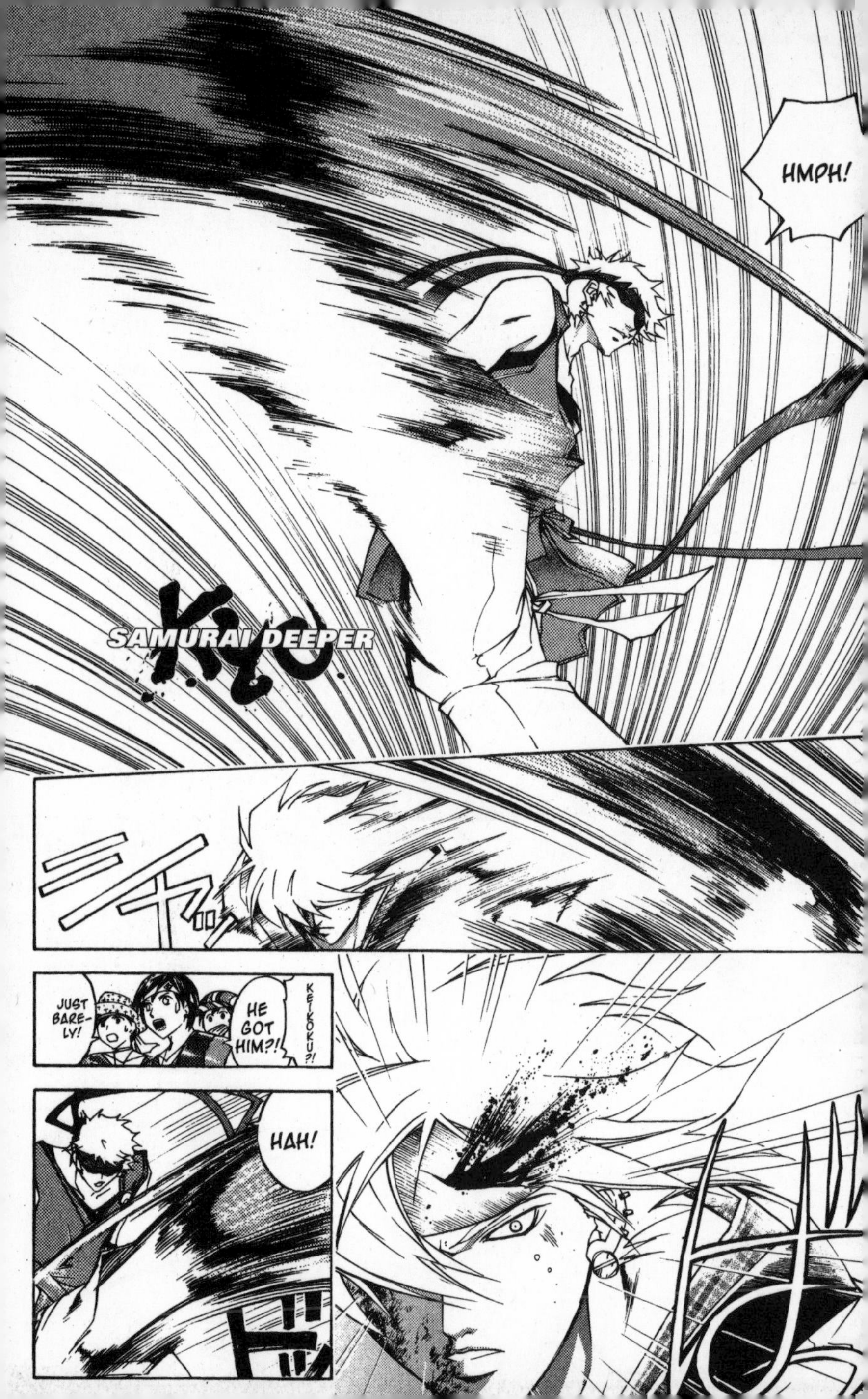
HMPH!
SAMURAI DEEPER KYO
KEIKOKU?!
HE GOT HIM?!
JUST BARE-LY!
HAH!

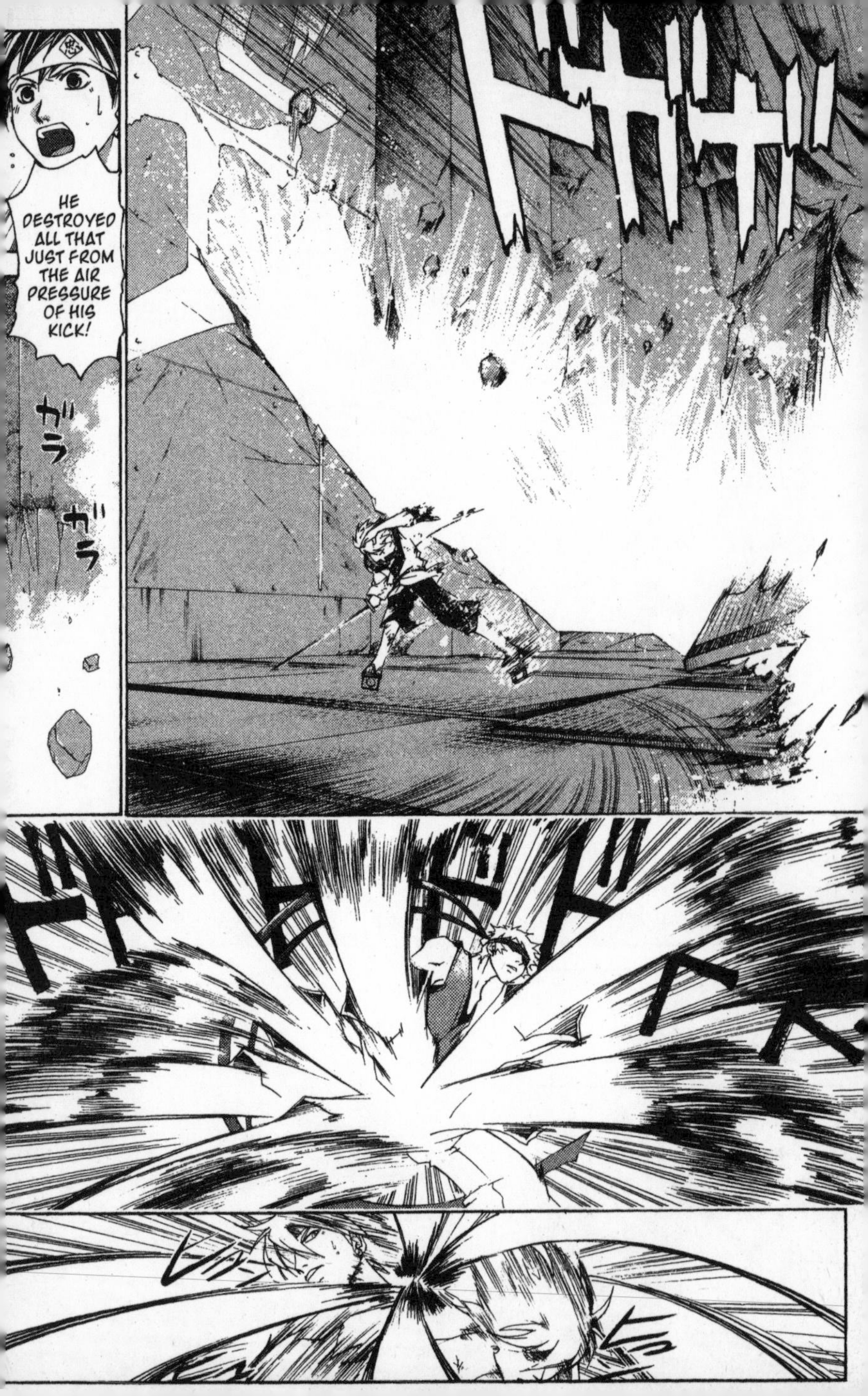
HE DESTROYED ALL THAT JUST FROM THE AIR PRESSURE OF HIS KICK!
ガラ
ガラ

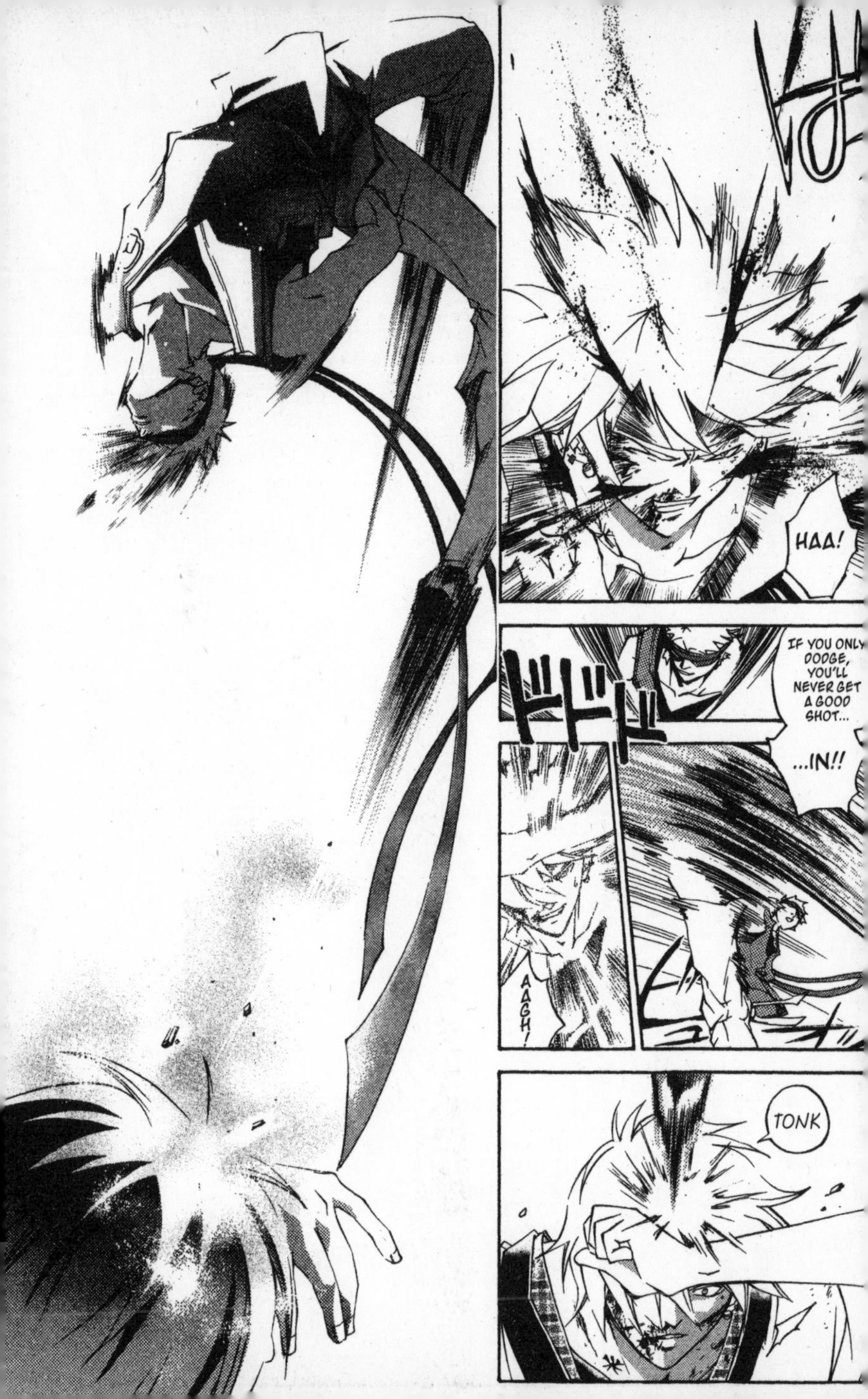
HAA!
IF YOU ONLY DODGE, YOU'LL NEVER GET A GOOD SHOT...
...IN!!
AAGH!
TONK

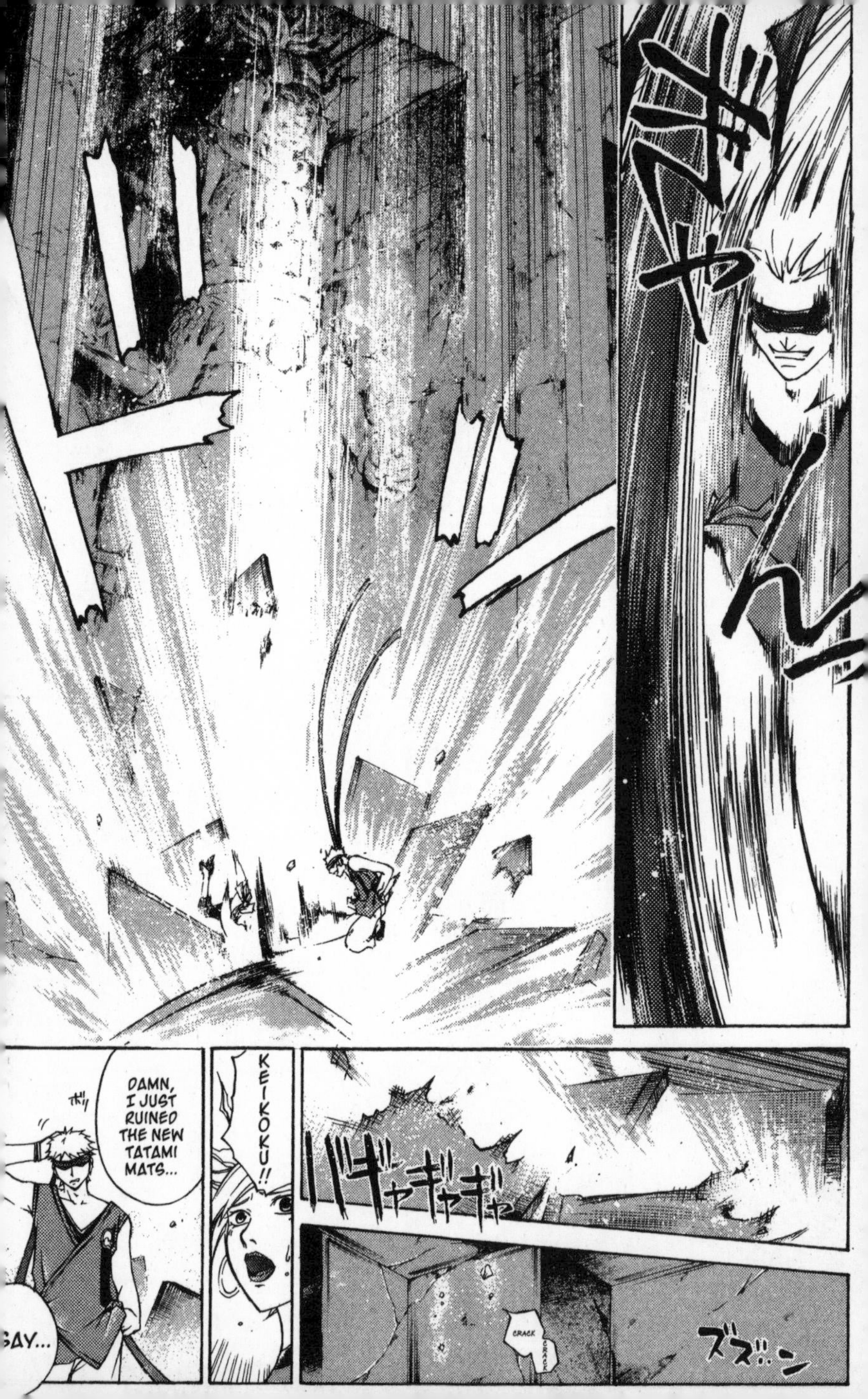
ぎゃん
バギャギャギャ
CRACK
CRACK
ズズ!!ン
KEIKOKU!!
ボリ
DAMN, I JUST RUINED THE NEW TATAMI MATS...
SAY...

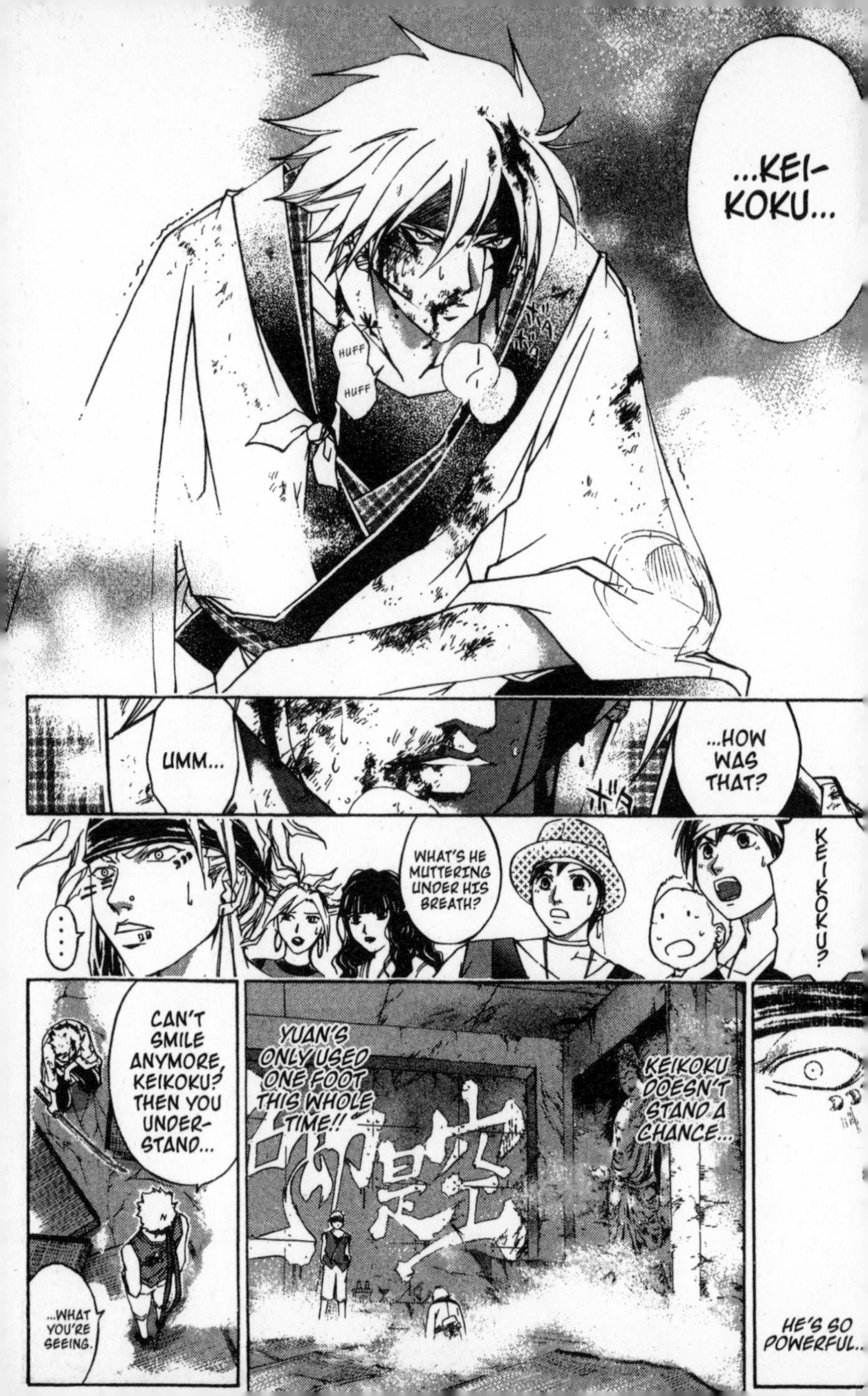
...KEI-KOKU...
HUFF
HUFF
...HOW WAS THAT?
UMM...
KEIKOKU?
WHAT'S HE MUTTERING UNDER HIS BREATH?
....
HE'S SO POWERFUL...
KEIKOKU DOESN'T STAND A CHANCE...
YUAN'S ONLY USED ONE FOOT THIS WHOLE TIME!!
CAN'T SMILE ANYMORE, KEIKOKU? THEN YOU UNDER-STAND...
...WHAT YOU'RE SEEING.

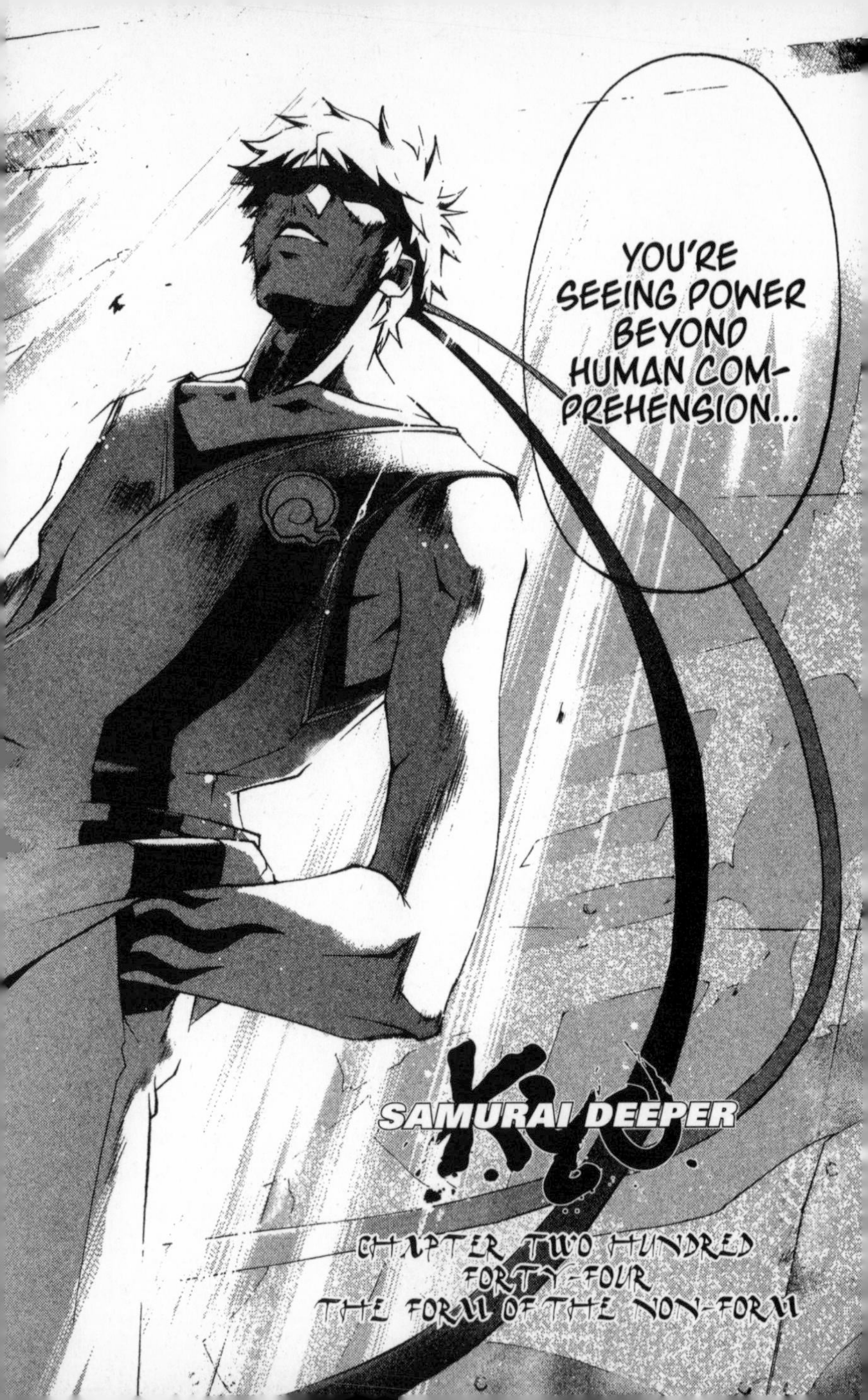
YOU'RE SEEING POWER BEYOND HUMAN COM-PREHENSION...
SAMURAI DEEPER KYO
CHAPTER TWO HUNDRED FORTY-FOUR
THE FORM OF THE NON-FORM

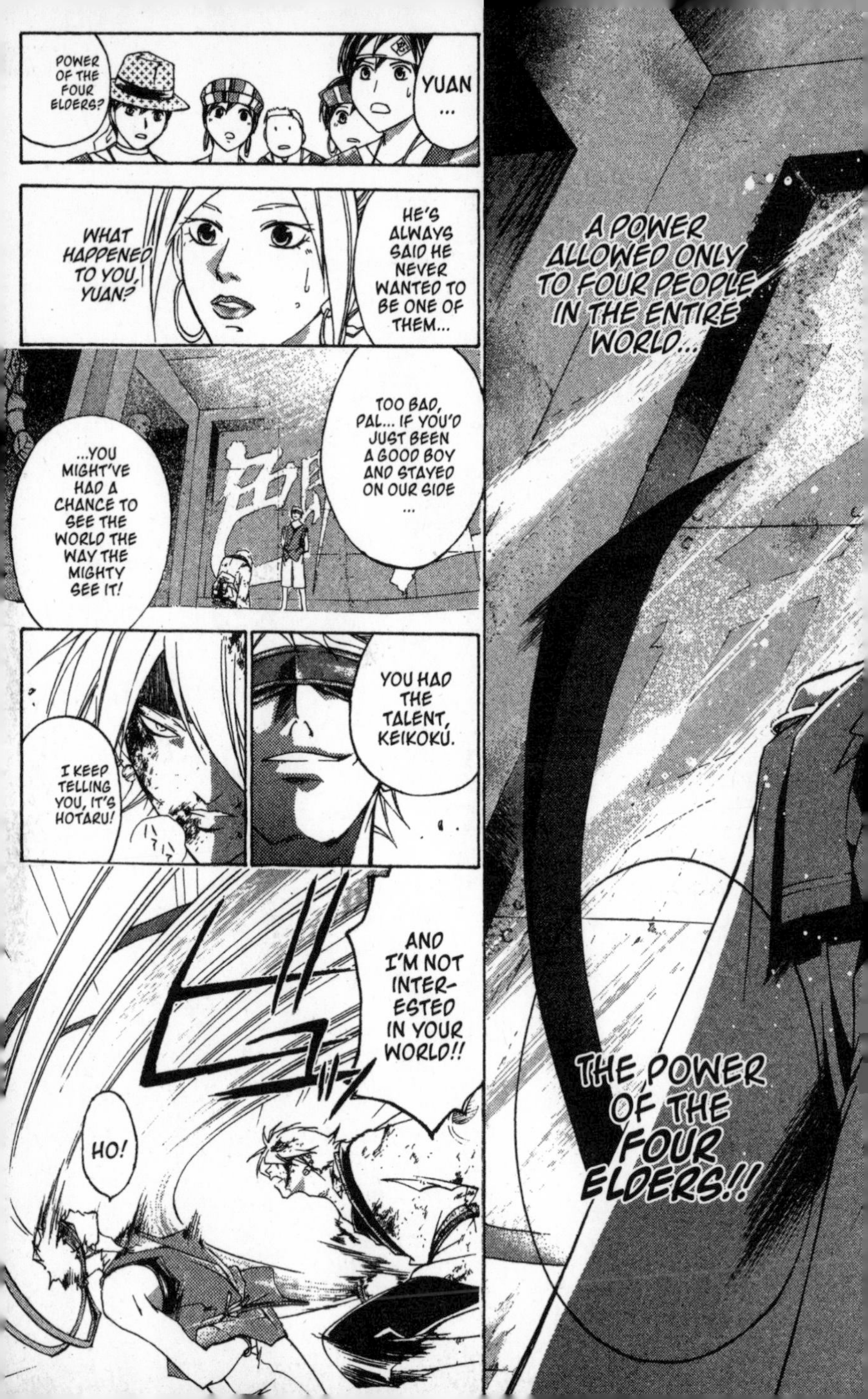
A POWER ALLOWED ONLY TO FOUR PEOPLE IN THE ENTIRE WORLD...
THE POWER OF THE FOUR ELDERS!!
YUAN ...
POWER OF THE FOUR ELDERS?
HE'S ALWAYS SAID HE NEVER WANTED TO BE ONE OF THEM...
WHAT HAPPENED TO YOU, YUAN?
TOO BAD, PAL... IF YOU'D JUST BEEN A GOOD BOY AND STAYED ON OUR SIDE ...
...YOU MIGHT'VE HAD A CHANCE TO SEE THE WORLD THE WAY THE MIGHTY SEE IT!
YOU HAD THE TALENT, KEIKOKU.
I KEEP TELLING YOU, IT'S HOTARU!
AND I'M NOT INTER-ESTED IN YOUR WORLD!!
HO!

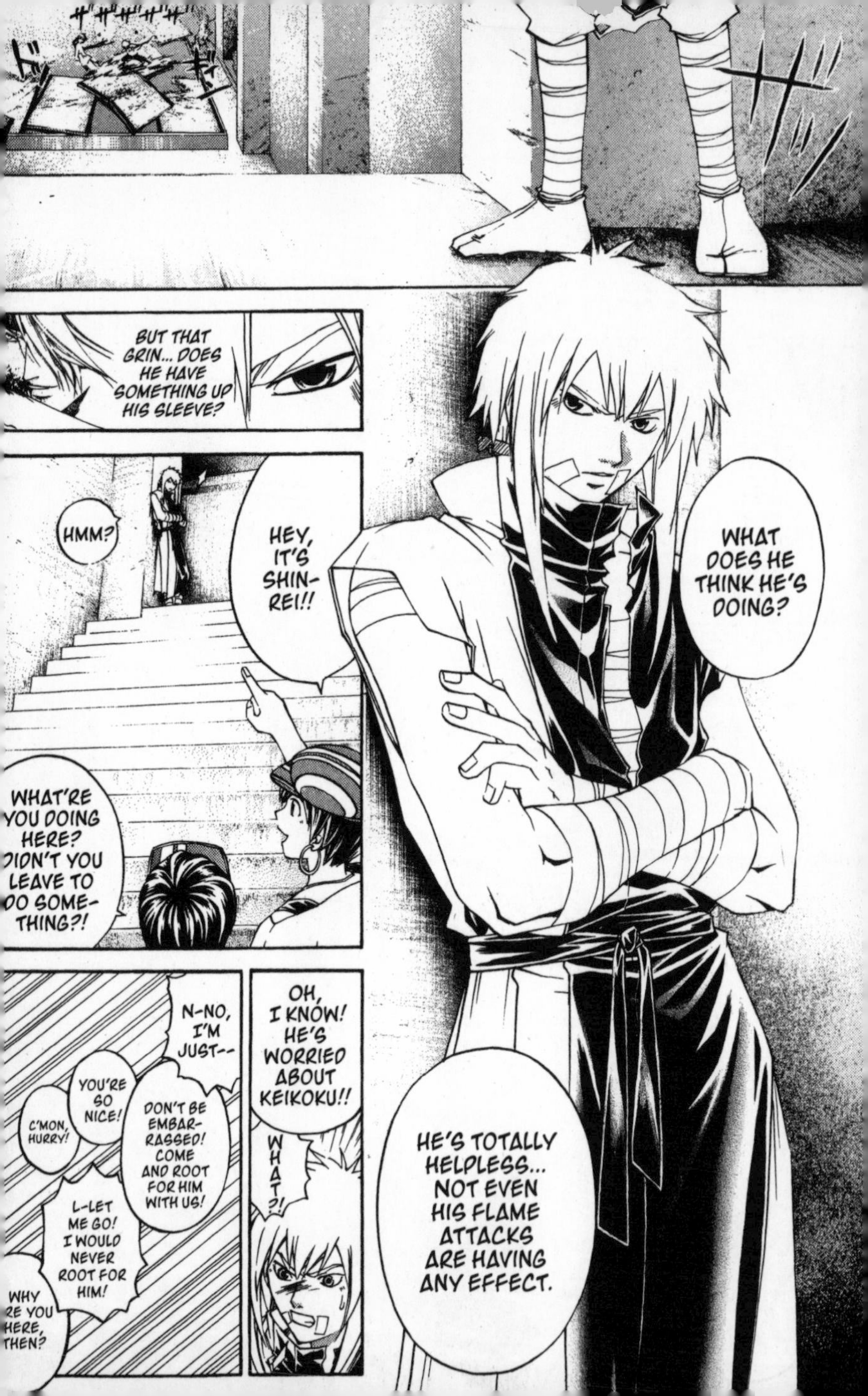
WHAT DOES HE THINK HE'S DOING?
HE'S TOTALLY HELPLESS... NOT EVEN HIS FLAME ATTACKS ARE HAVING ANY EFFECT.
BUT THAT GRIN... DOES HE HAVE SOMETHING UP HIS SLEEVE?
HEY, IT'S SHIN-REI!!
HMM?
WHAT'RE YOU DOING HERE? DIDN'T YOU LEAVE TO DO SOME-THING?!
OH, I KNOW! HE'S WORRIED ABOUT KEIKOKU!!
WHAT?!
N-NO, I'M JUST--
YOU'RE SO NICE!
DON'T BE EMBAR-RASSED! COME AND ROOT FOR HIM WITH US!
C'MON, HURRY!
L-LET ME GO! I WOULD NEVER ROOT FOR HIM!
WHY RE YOU HERE, THEN?

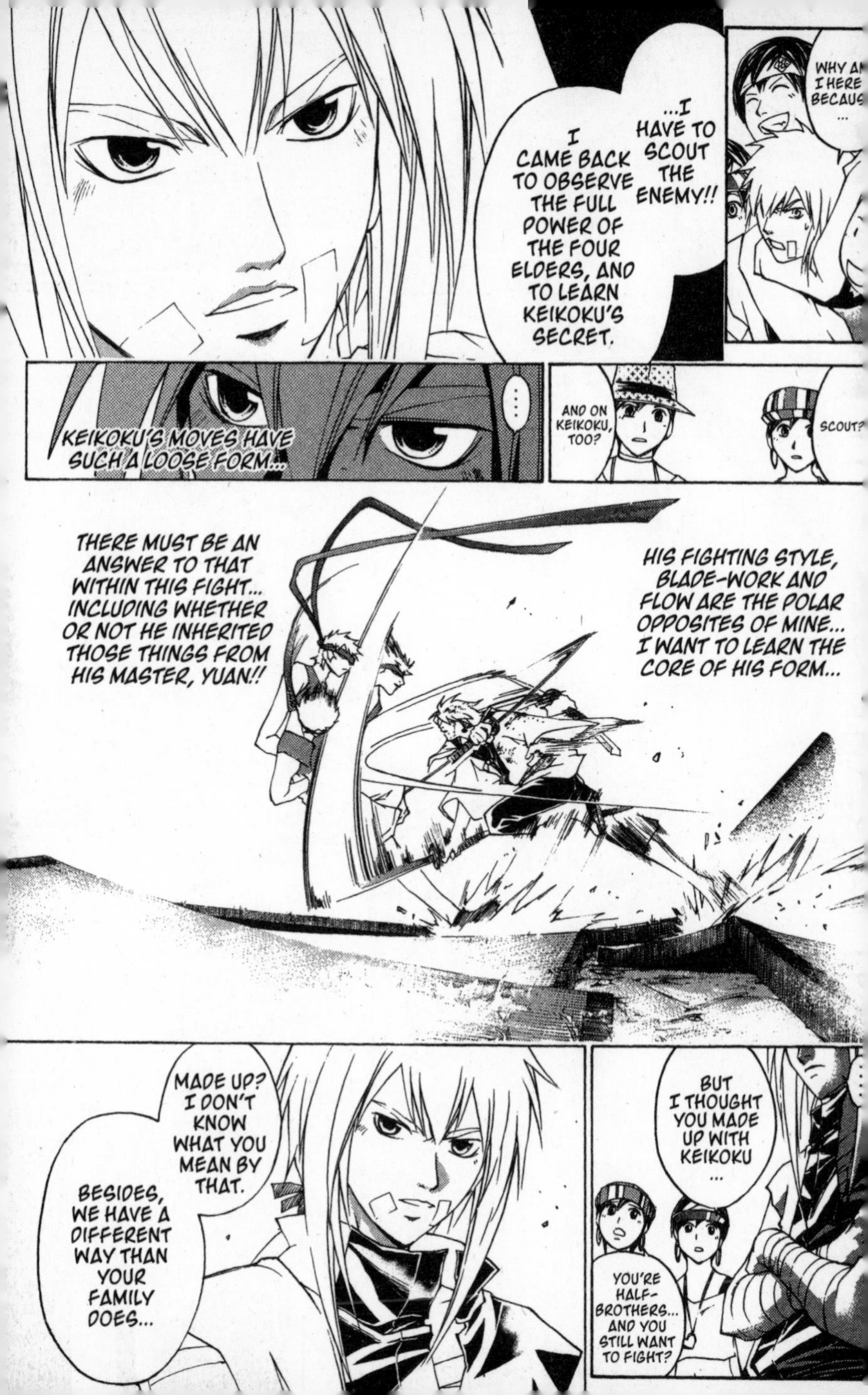
WHY A I HERE BECAUS ...
...I HAVE TO SCOUT THE ENEMY!!
I CAME BACK TO OBSERVE THE FULL POWER OF THE FOUR ELDERS, AND TO LEARN KEIKOKU'S SECRET.
SCOUT?
AND ON KEIKOKU, TOO?
....
KEIKOKU'S MOVES HAVE SUCH A LOOSE FORM...
HIS FIGHTING STYLE, BLADE-WORK AND FLOW ARE THE POLAR OPPOSITES OF MINE... I WANT TO LEARN THE CORE OF HIS FORM...
THERE MUST BE AN ANSWER TO THAT WITHIN THIS FIGHT... INCLUDING WHETHER OR NOT HE INHERITED THOSE THINGS FROM HIS MASTER, YUAN!!
BUT I THOUGHT YOU MADE UP WITH KEIKOKU ...
YOU'RE HALF-BROTHERS... AND YOU STILL WANT TO FIGHT?
MADE UP? I DON'T KNOW WHAT YOU MEAN BY THAT.
BESIDES, WE HAVE A DIFFERENT WAY THAN YOUR FAMILY DOES...

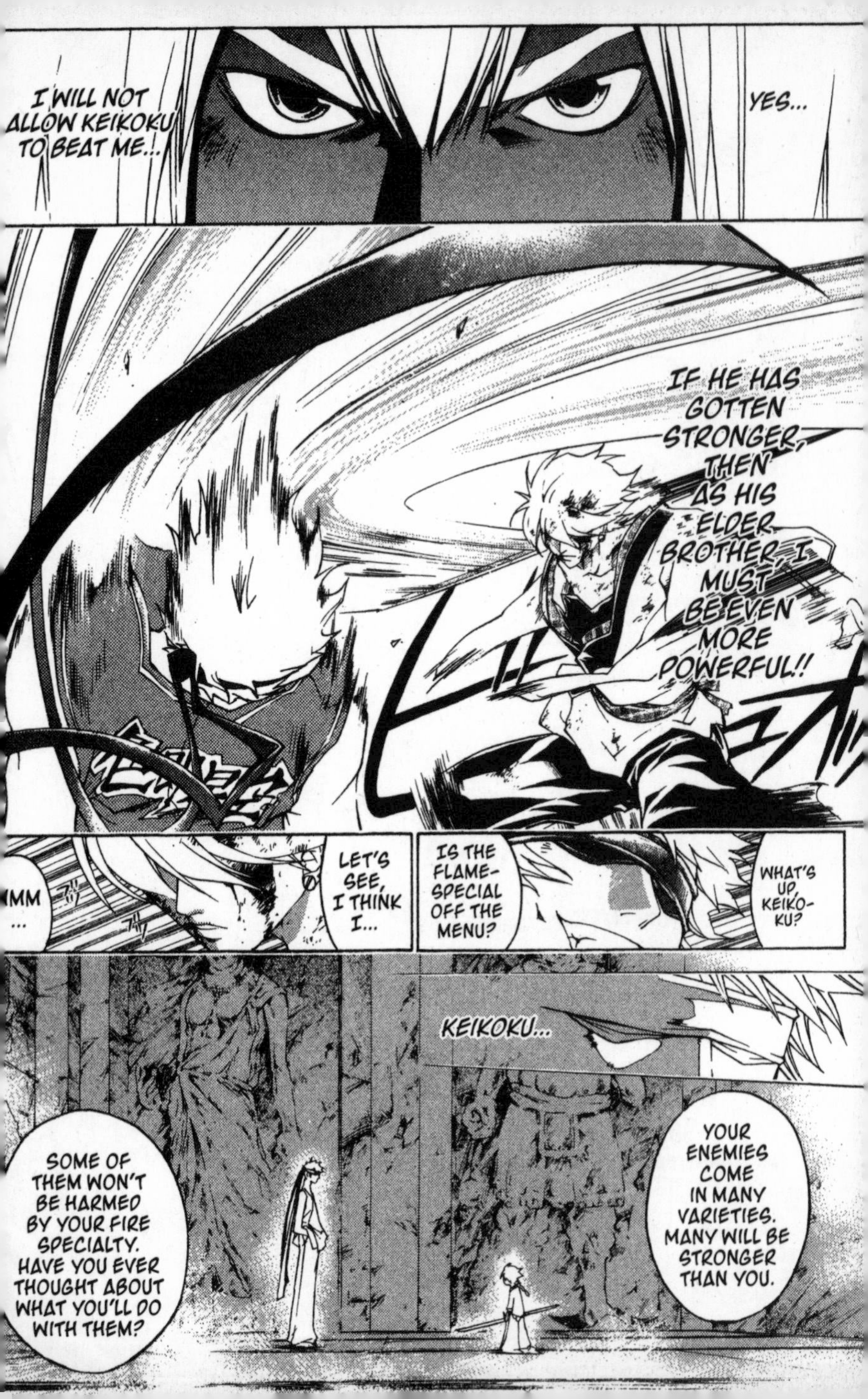
YES...
I WILL NOT ALLOW KEIKOKU TO BEAT ME...
IF HE HAS GOTTEN STRONGER, THEN AS HIS ELDER BROTHER, I MUST BE EVEN MORE POWERFUL!!
WHAT'S UP, KEIKOKU?
IS THE FLAME-SPECIAL OFF THE MENU?
LET'S SEE, I THINK I...
IMM ...
KEIKOKU...
YOUR ENEMIES COME IN MANY VARIETIES. MANY WILL BE STRONGER THAN YOU.
SOME OF THEM WON'T BE HARMED BY YOUR FIRE SPECIALTY. HAVE YOU EVER THOUGHT ABOUT WHAT YOU'LL DO WITH THEM?

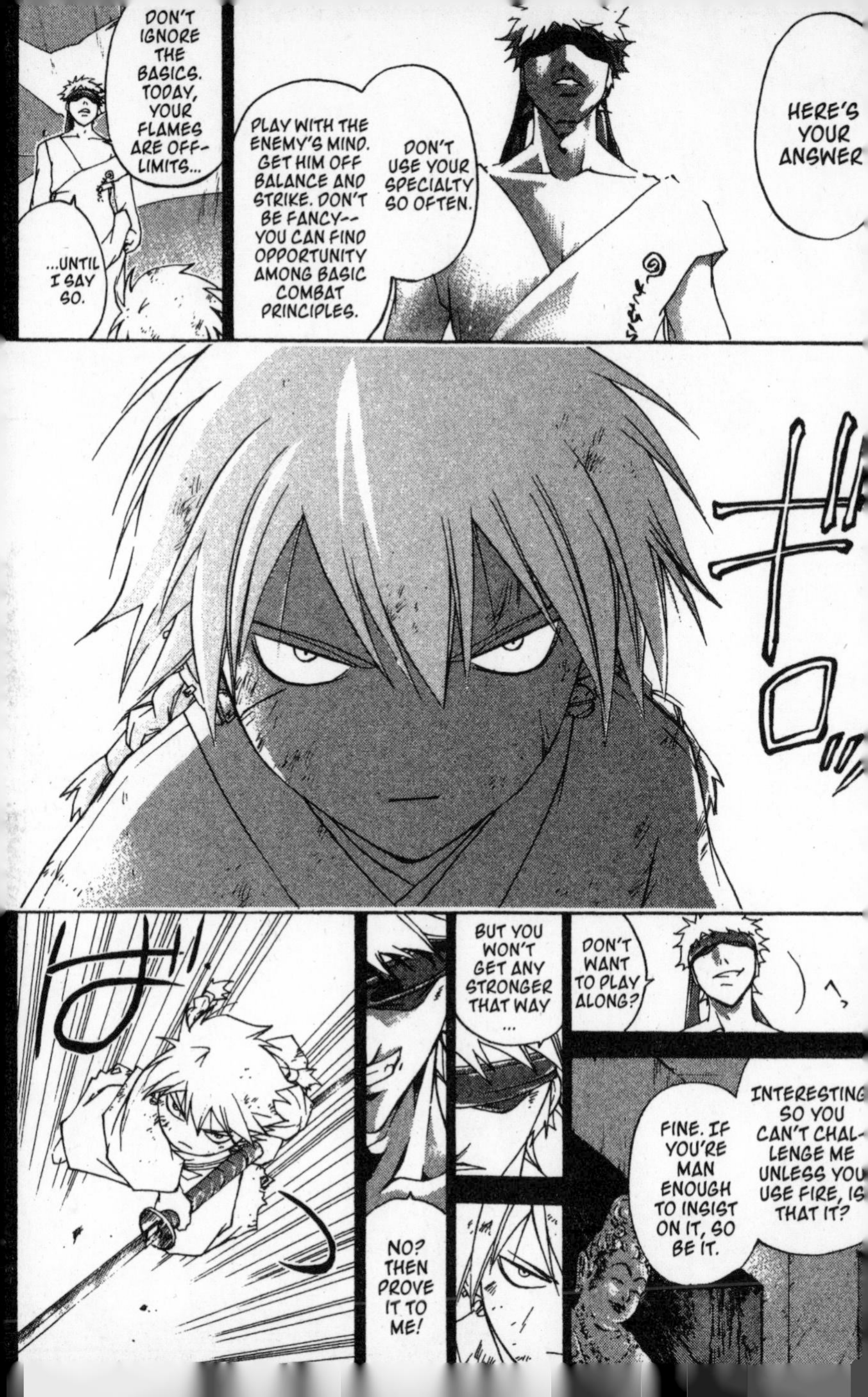
HERE'S YOUR ANSWER
DON'T USE YOUR SPECIALTY SO OFTEN.
PLAY WITH THE ENEMY'S MIND. GET HIM OFF BALANCE AND STRIKE. DON'T BE FANCY-- YOU CAN FIND OPPORTUNITY AMONG BASIC COMBAT PRINCIPLES.
DON'T IGNORE THE BASICS. TODAY, YOUR FLAMES ARE OFF-LIMITS...
...UNTIL I SAY SO.
DON'T WANT TO PLAY ALONG?
BUT YOU WON'T GET ANY STRONGER THAT WAY ...
INTERESTING SO YOU CAN'T CHAL-LENGE ME UNLESS YOU USE FIRE, IS THAT IT?
FINE. IF YOU'RE MAN ENOUGH TO INSIST ON IT, SO BE IT.
NO? THEN PROVE IT TO ME!

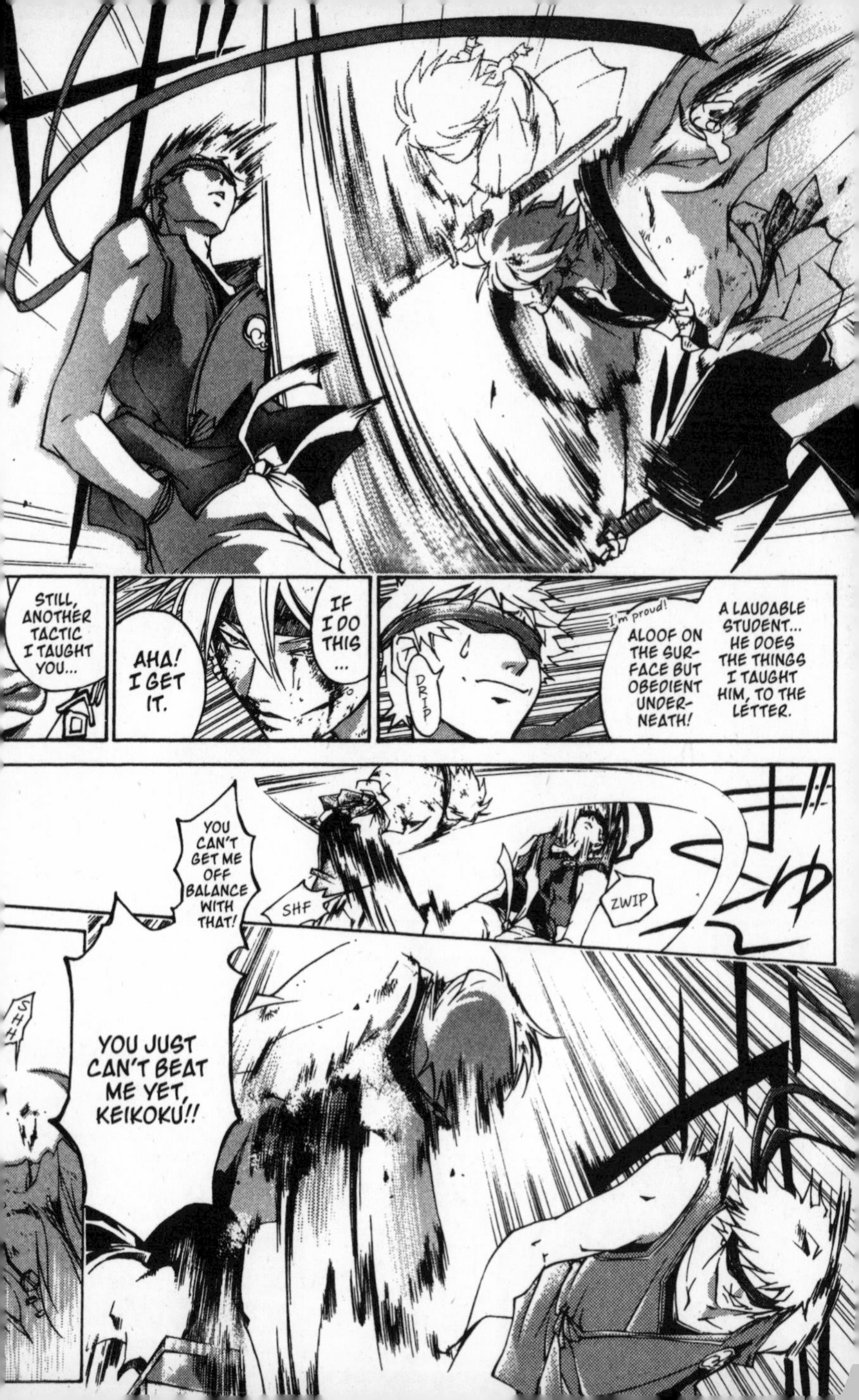
A LAUDABLE STUDENT... HE DOES THE THINGS I TAUGHT HIM, TO THE LETTER.
I'm proud!
ALOOF ON THE SURFACE BUT OBEDIENT UNDERNEATH!
DRIP
IF I DO THIS ...
AHA! I GET IT.
STILL, ANOTHER TACTIC I TAUGHT YOU...
ZWIP
SHF
YOU CAN'T GET ME OFF BALANCE WITH THAT!
SHH
YOU JUST CAN'T BEAT ME YET, KEIKOKU!!

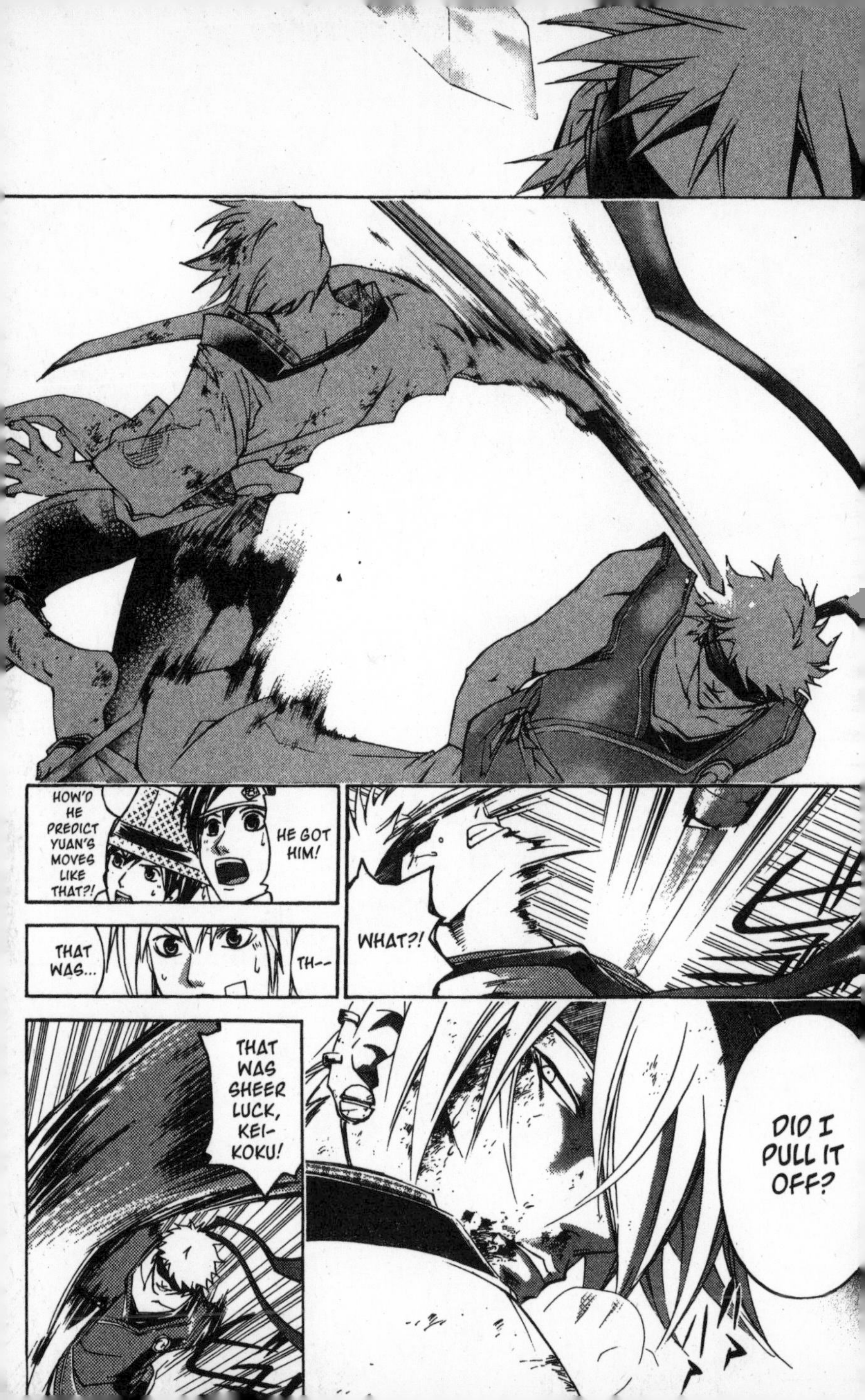
WHAT?!
HE GOT HIM!
HOW'D HE PREDICT YUAN'S MOVES LIKE THAT?!
TH--
THAT WAS...
DID I PULL IT OFF?
THAT WAS SHEER LUCK, KEI-KOKU!

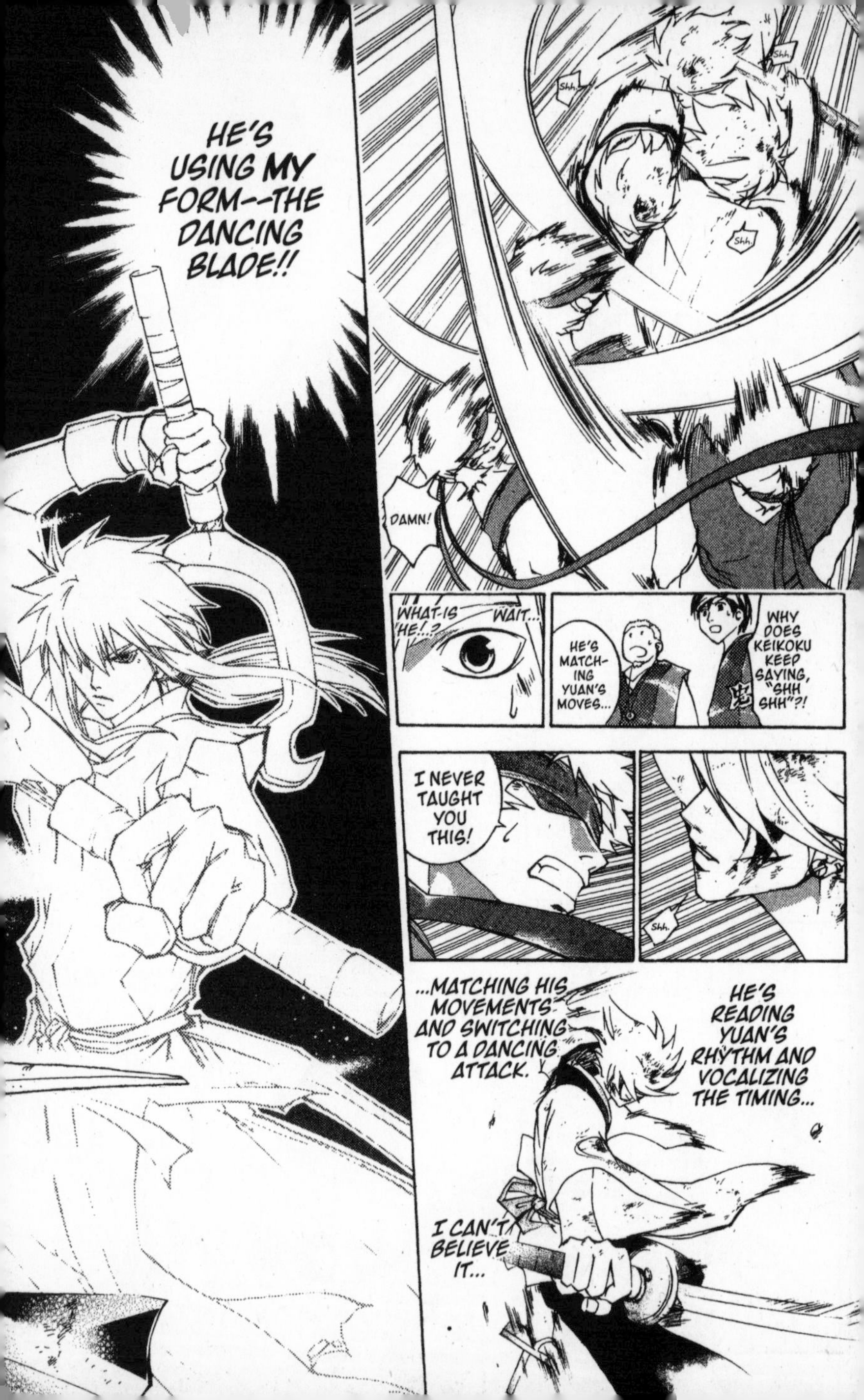
Shh.
Shh.
Shh.
DAMN!
WHY DOES KEIKOKU KEEP SAYING, "SHH SHH"?!
HE'S MATCHING YUAN'S MOVES...
WAIT...
WHAT-IS HE!..?
Shh.
I NEVER TAUGHT YOU THIS!
HE'S READING YUAN'S RHYTHM AND VOCALIZING THE TIMING...
...MATCHING HIS MOVEMENTS AND SWITCHING TO A DANCING ATTACK.
I CAN'T BELIEVE IT...
HE'S USING MY FORM--THE DANCING BLADE!!

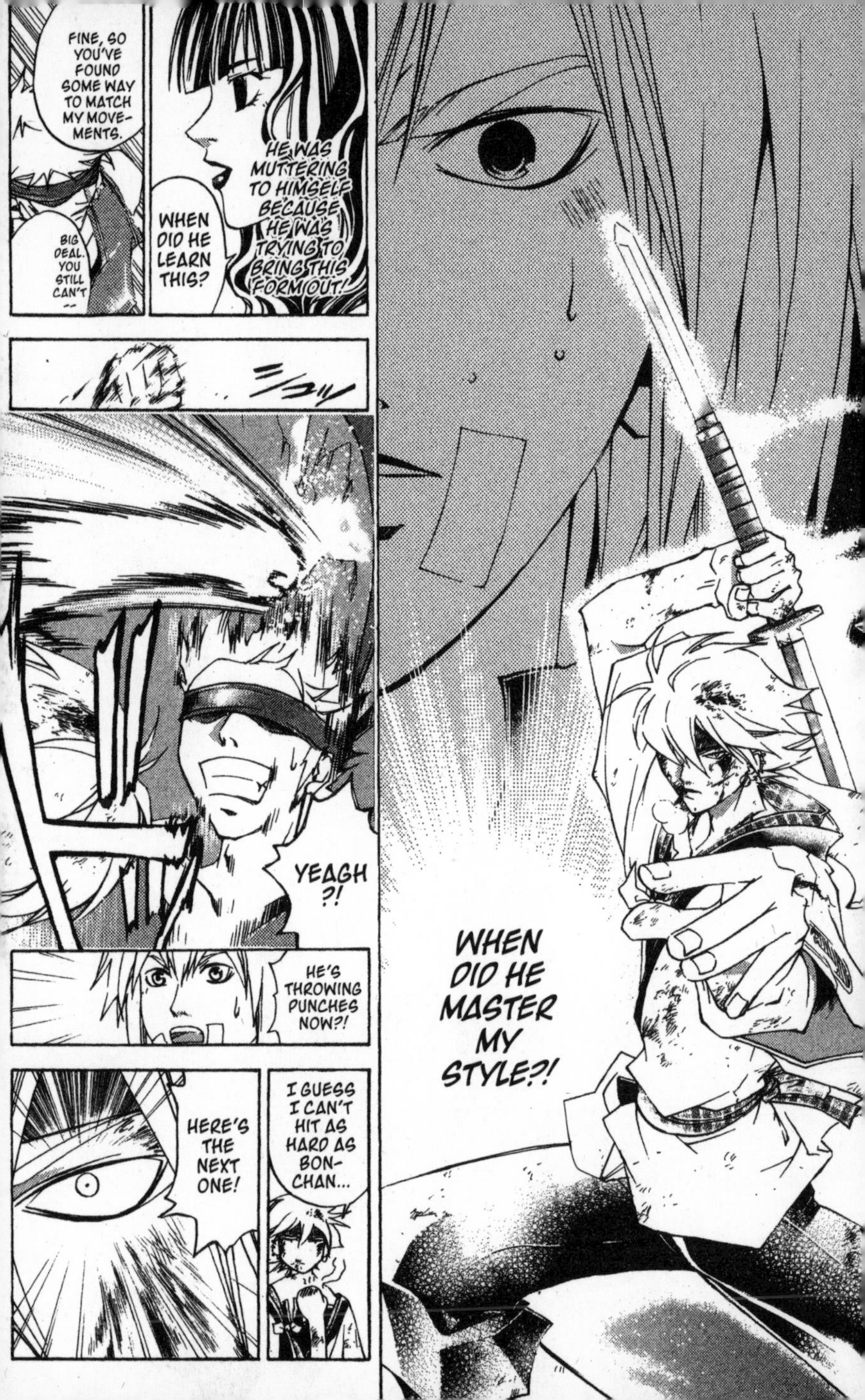
WHEN DID HE MASTER MY STYLE?!
FINE, SO YOU'VE FOUND SOME WAY TO MATCH MY MOVEMENTS.
BIG DEAL. YOU STILL CAN'T --
HE WAS MUTTERING TO HIMSELF BECAUSE HE WAS TRYING TO BRING THIS FORM OUT!
WHEN DID HE LEARN THIS?
YEAGH ?!
HE'S THROWING PUNCHES NOW?!
I GUESS I CAN'T HIT AS HARD AS BON-CHAN...
HERE'S THE NEXT ONE!

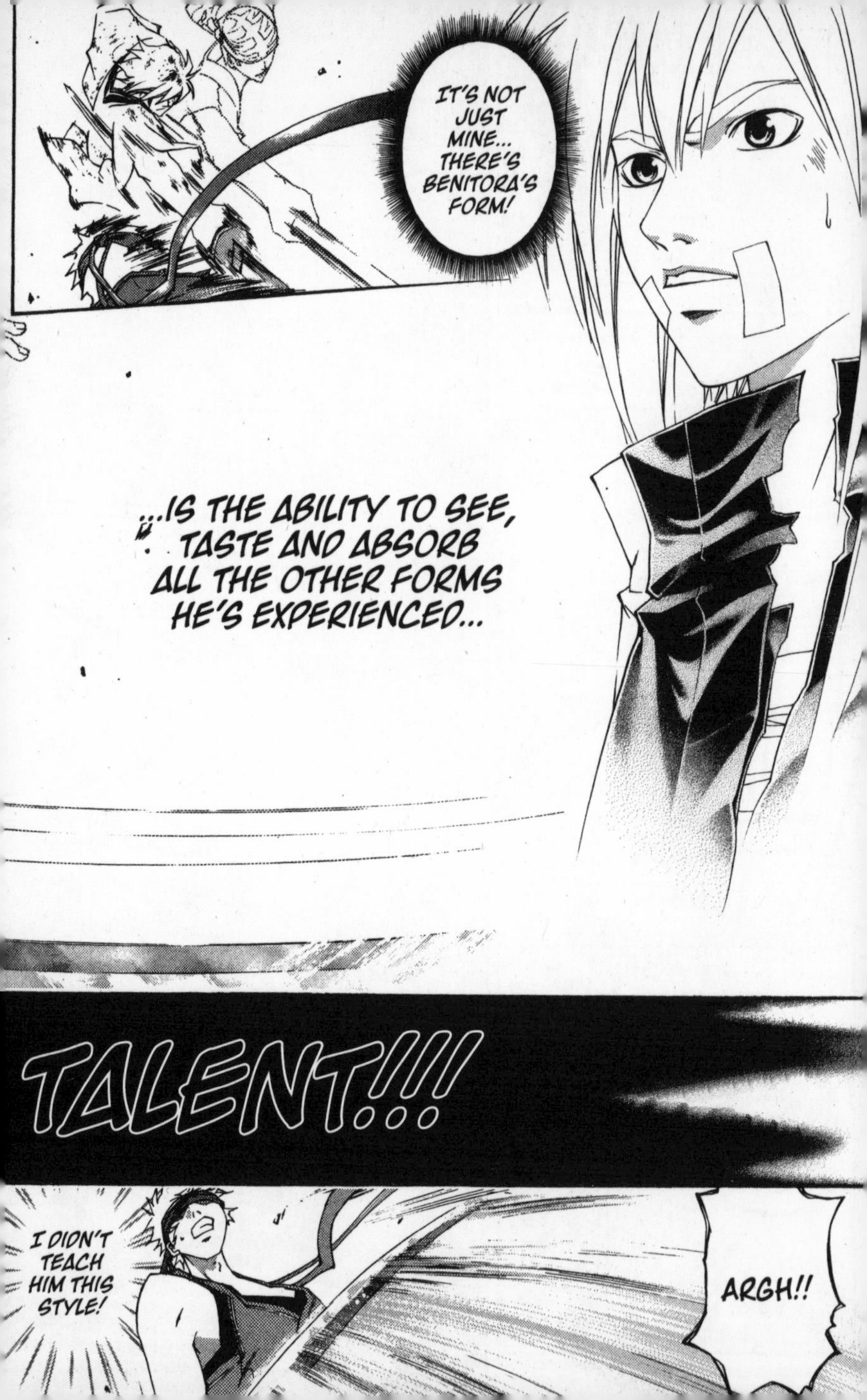
IT'S NOT JUST MINE... THERE'S BENITORA'S FORM!
...IS THE ABILITY TO SEE, TASTE AND ABSORB ALL THE OTHER FORMS HE'S EXPERIENCED...
TALENT!!!
ARGH!!
I DIDN'T TEACH HIM THIS STYLE!

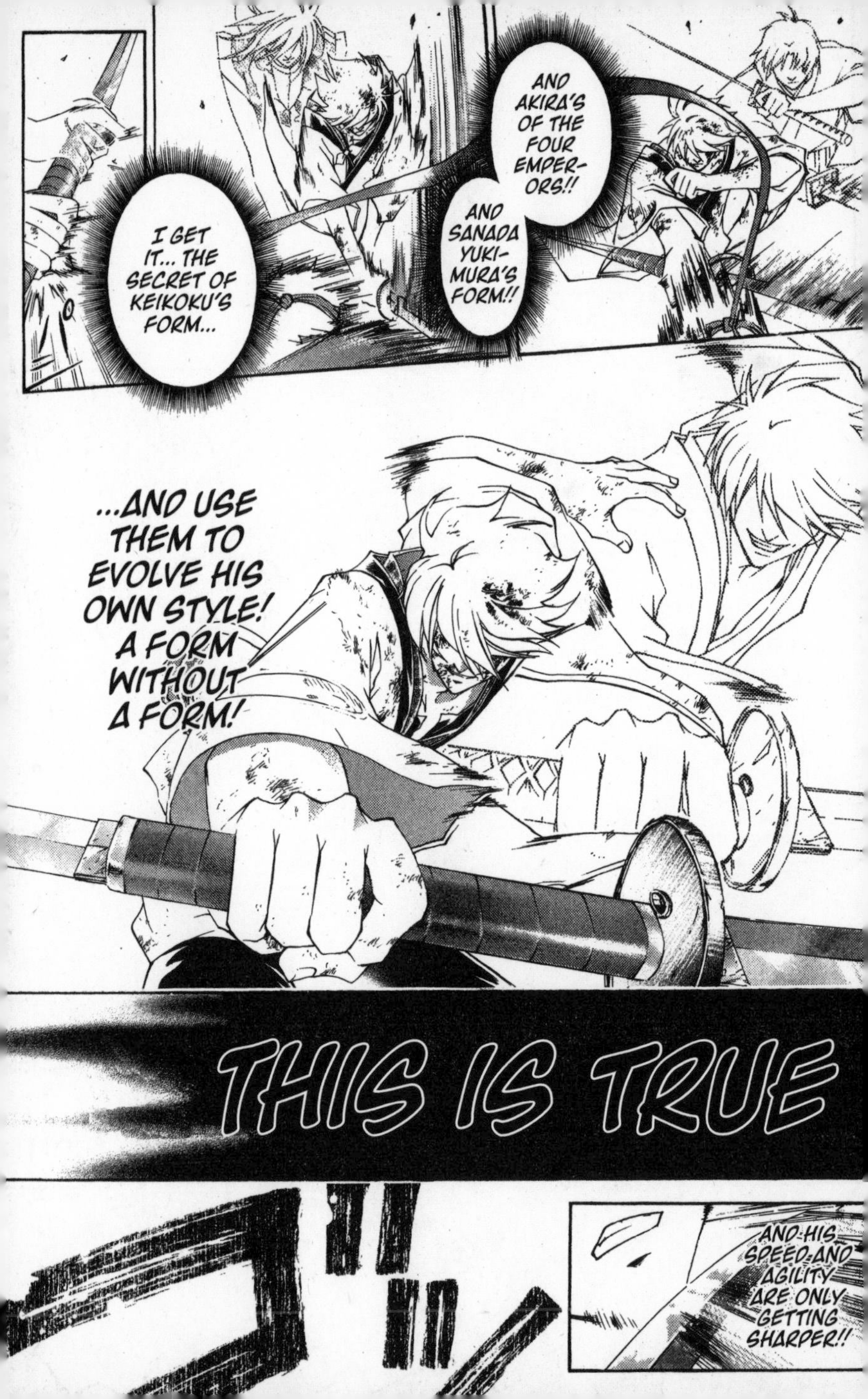
AND AKIRA'S OF THE FOUR EMPEROR-ORS!!
AND SANADA YUKI-MURA'S FORM!!
I GET IT... THE SECRET OF KEIKOKU'S FORM...
...AND USE THEM TO EVOLVE HIS OWN STYLE! A FORM WITHOUT A FORM!
THIS IS TRUE
AND HIS SPEED AND AGILITY ARE ONLY GETTING SHARPER!!

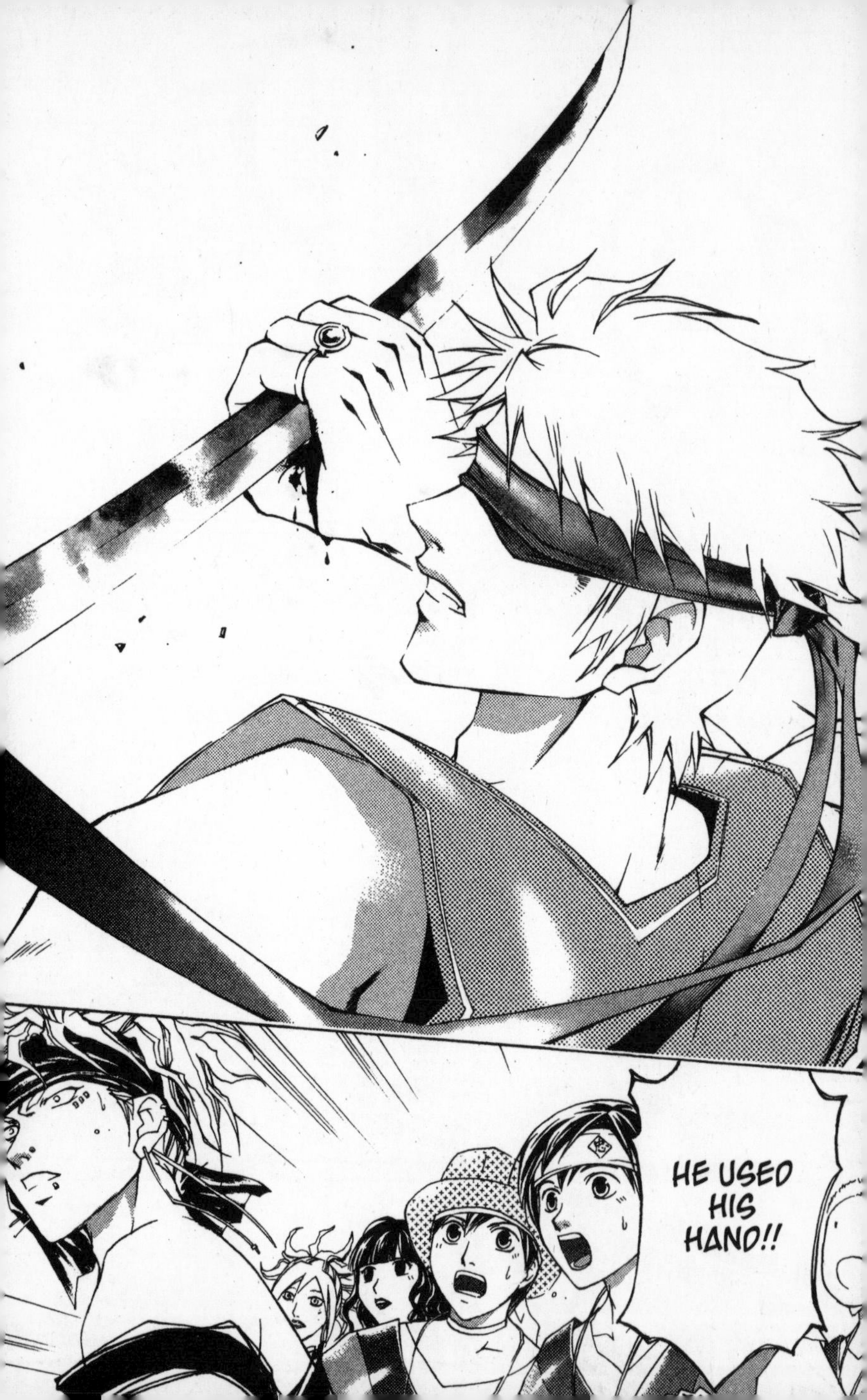
HE USED HIS HAND!!

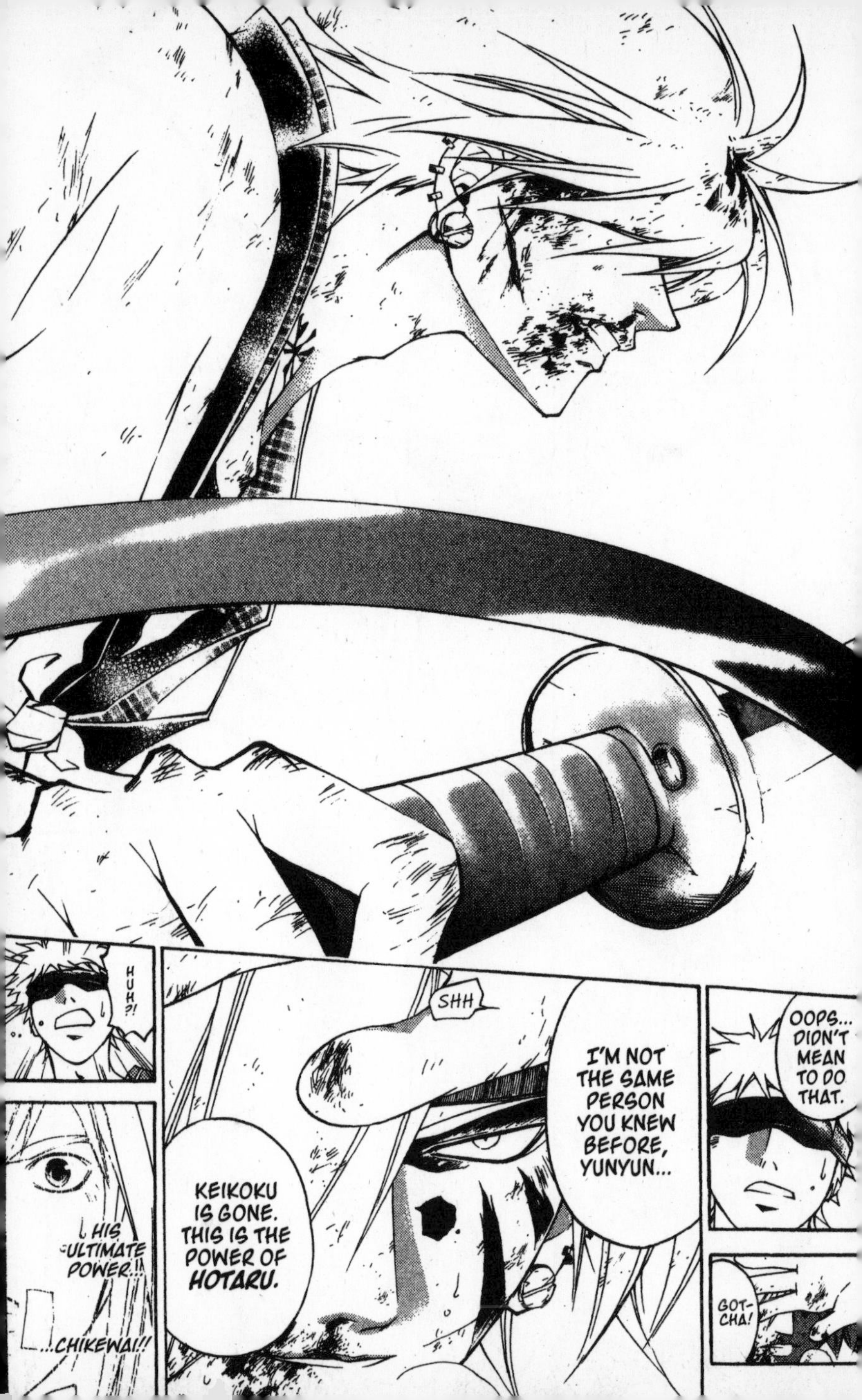
OOPS... DIDN'T MEAN TO DO THAT.
GOT-CHA!
SHH
I'M NOT THE SAME PERSON YOU KNEW BEFORE, YUNYUN...
KEIKOKU IS GONE. THIS IS THE POWER OF HOTARU.
HUH?!
HIS ULTIMATE POWER...!!
...CHIKEWAI!!

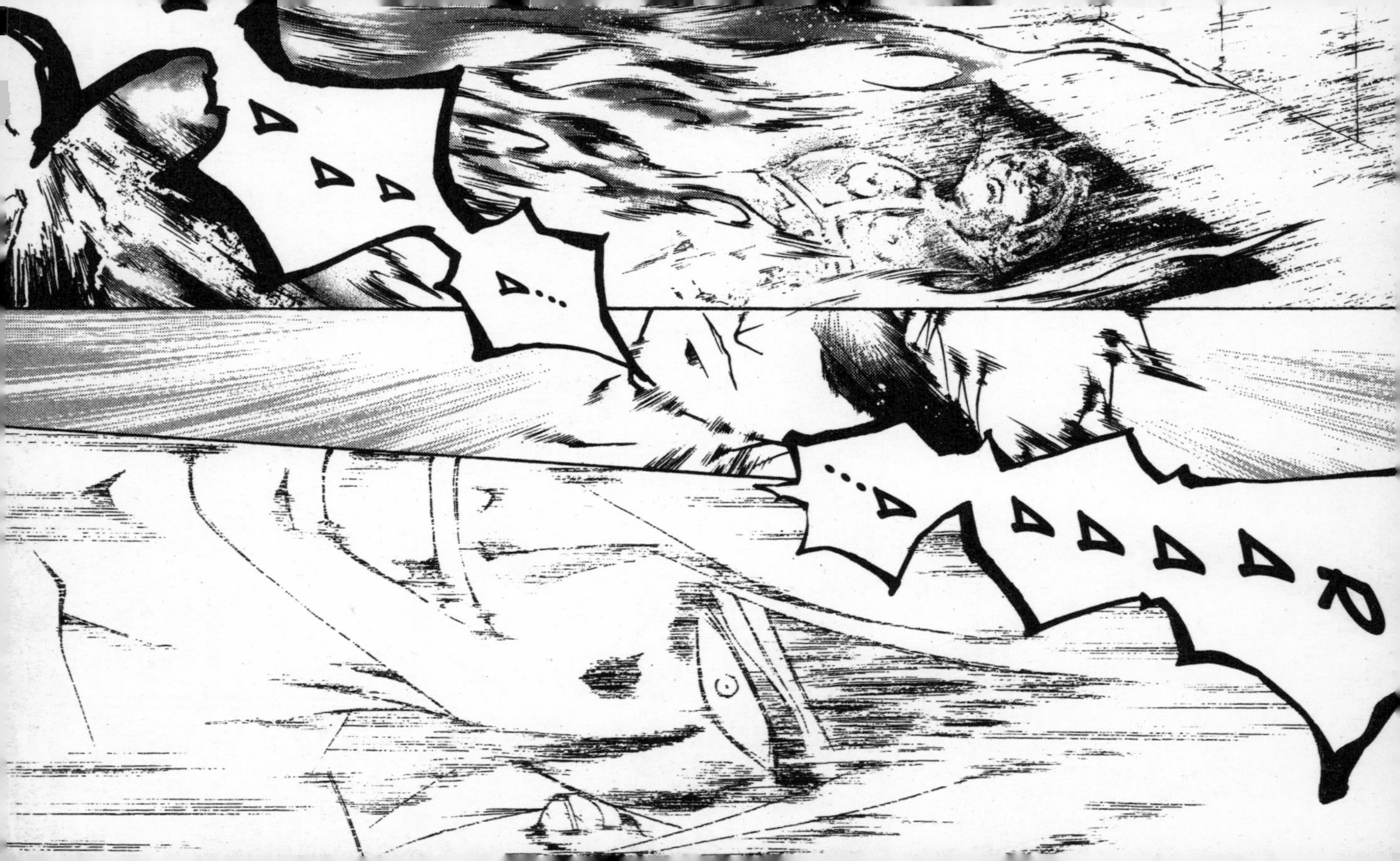
AAA
A...
...AAAAAR

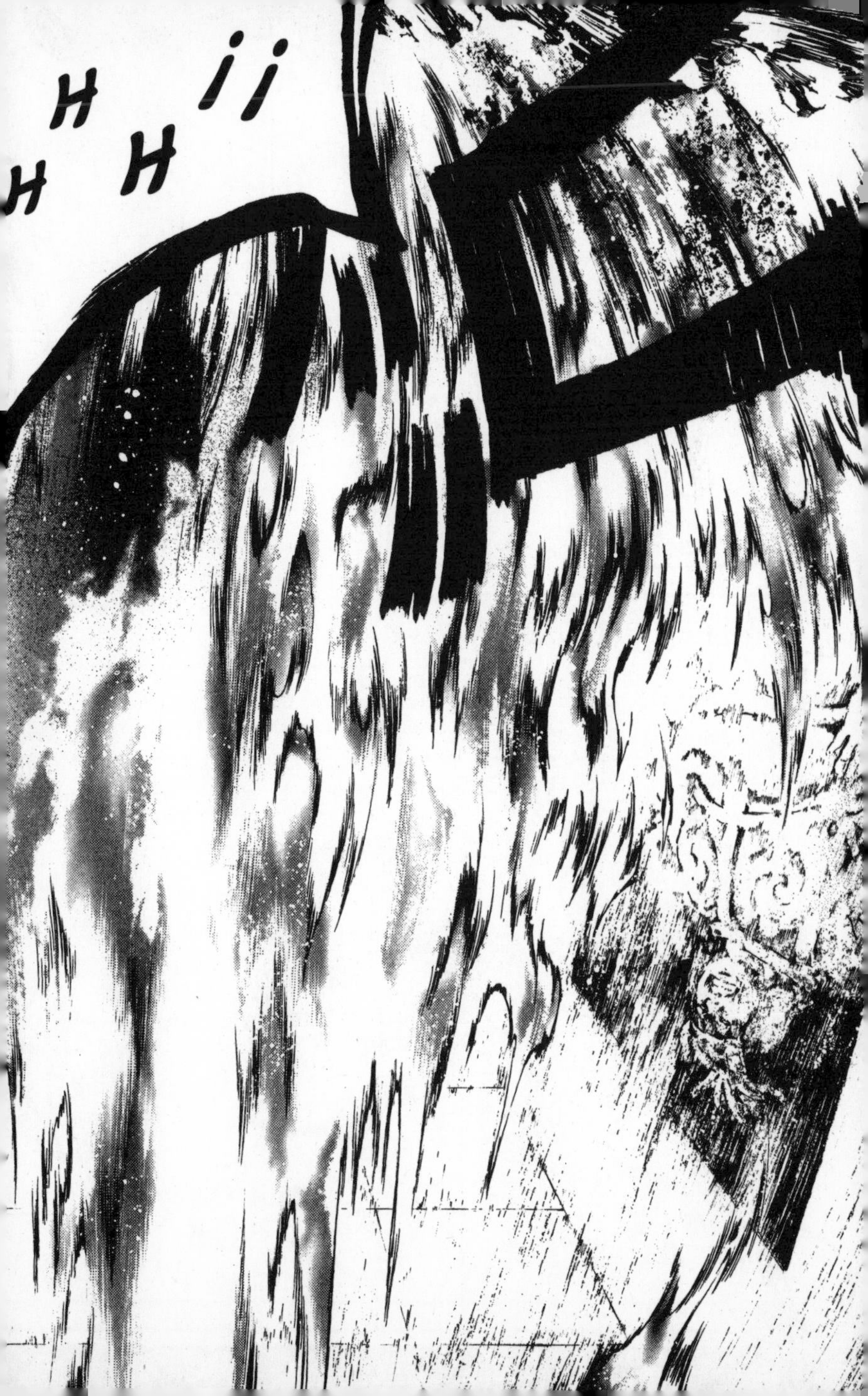
HHH¡¡

Pretty Good!

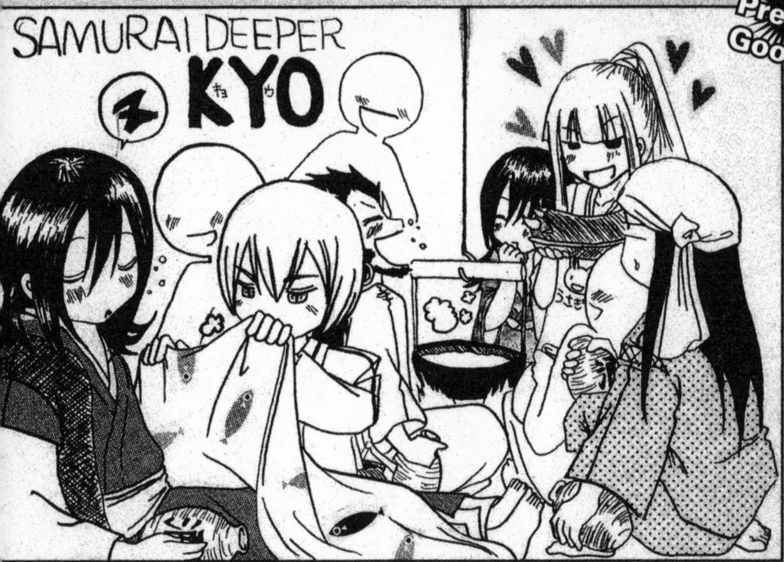
SAMURAI DEEPER
KYO

[Shizuoka/Aoi]⬆

Is Sasuke the most grown-up person in this shot? You can really tell each personality by the expressions!

Draw Like Kamijyo!

[Hokkaido/Okame Natto]⬇

Akira's a hard worker!

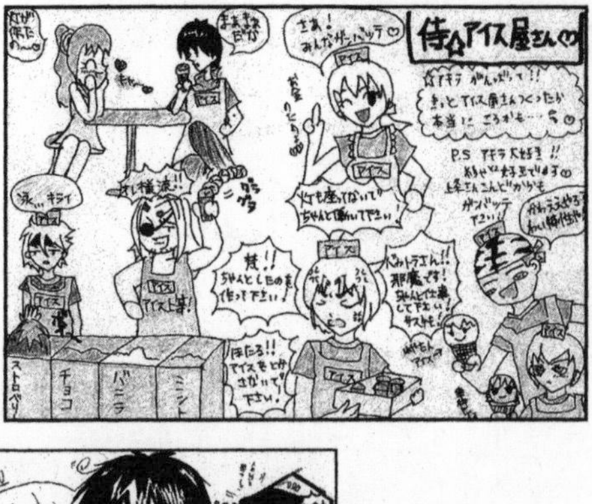

[Kagoshima/Kyutaro]⬇

They're all over the place!

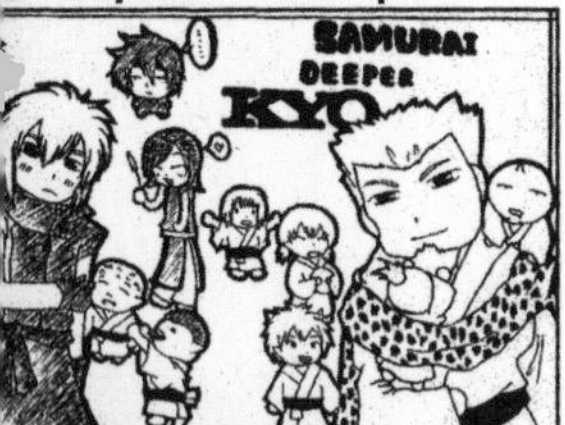
SAMURAI
DEEPER
KYO

[Kumamoto/Ryo]⬇

The contrast draws the eye.

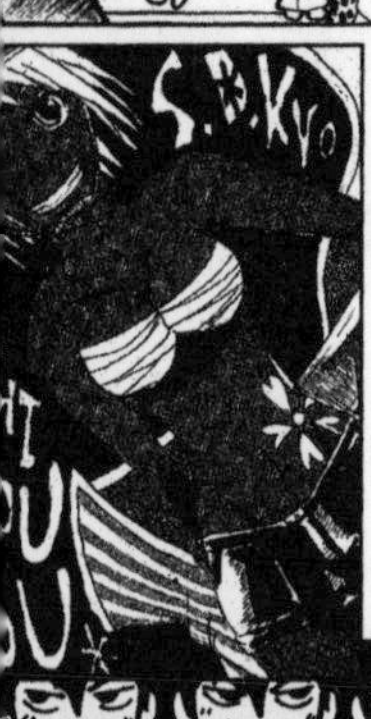

⬅ [Osaka/Keely]

Sometimes you just gotta complain.

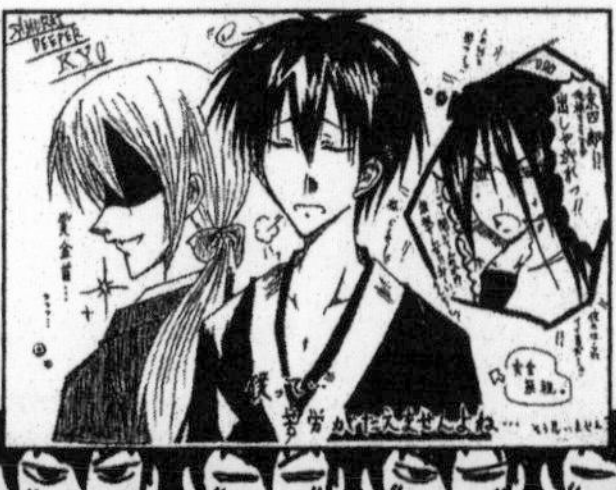
SAMURAI DEEPER KYO

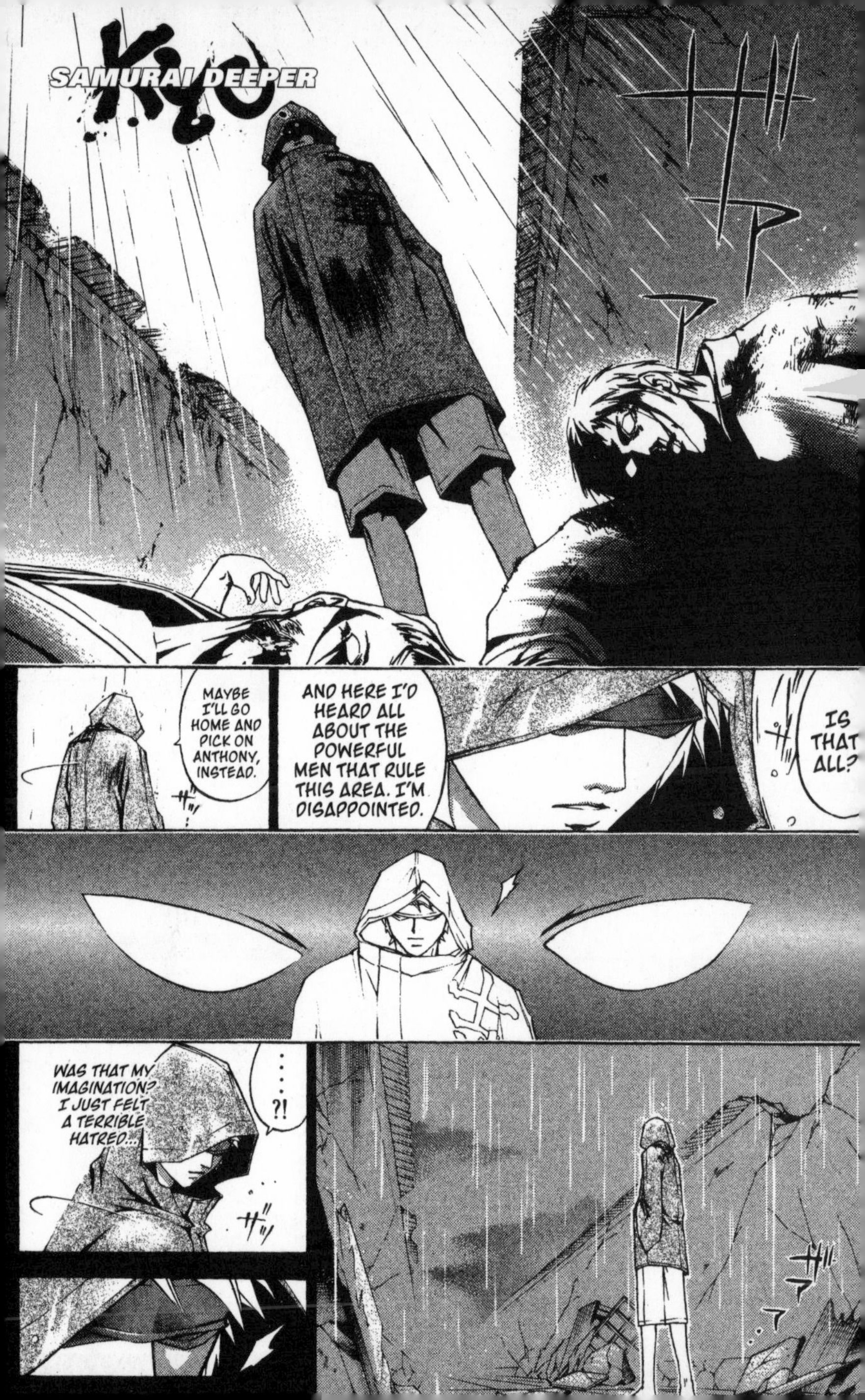
SAMURAI DEEPER KYO
IS THAT ALL?
AND HERE I'D HEARD ALL ABOUT THE POWERFUL MEN THAT RULE THIS AREA. I'M DISAPPOINTED.
MAYBE I'LL GO HOME AND PICK ON ANTHONY, INSTEAD.
....?!
WAS THAT MY IMAGINATION? I JUST FELT A TERRIBLE HATRED...

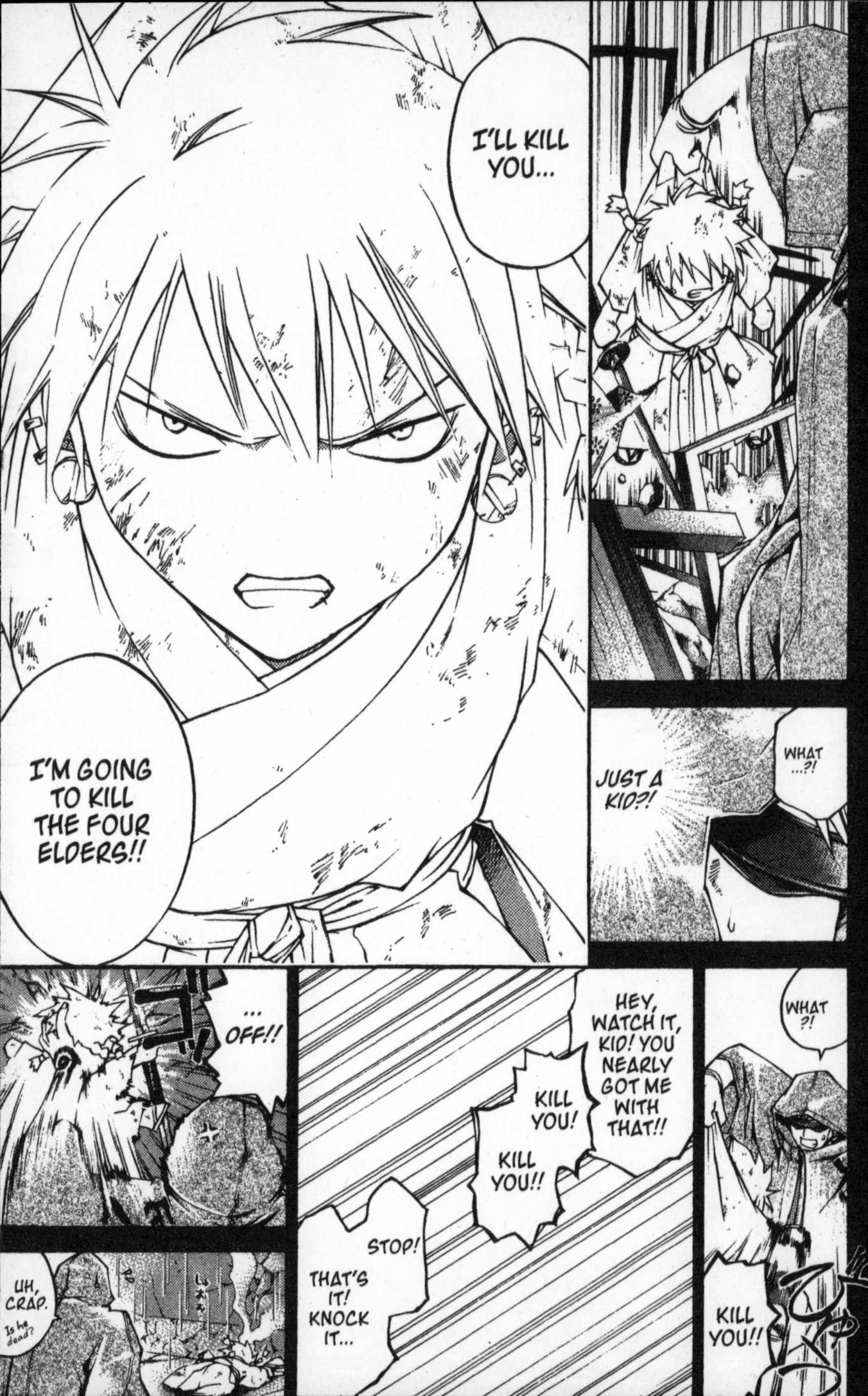
WHAT ...?!
JUST A KID?!
I'LL KILL YOU...
I'M GOING TO KILL THE FOUR ELDERS!!
WHAT ?!
KILL YOU!!
HEY, WATCH IT, KID! YOU NEARLY GOT ME WITH THAT!!
KILL YOU!
KILL YOU!!
STOP!
THAT'S IT! KNOCK IT...
... OFF!!
UH, CRAP.
Is he dead?

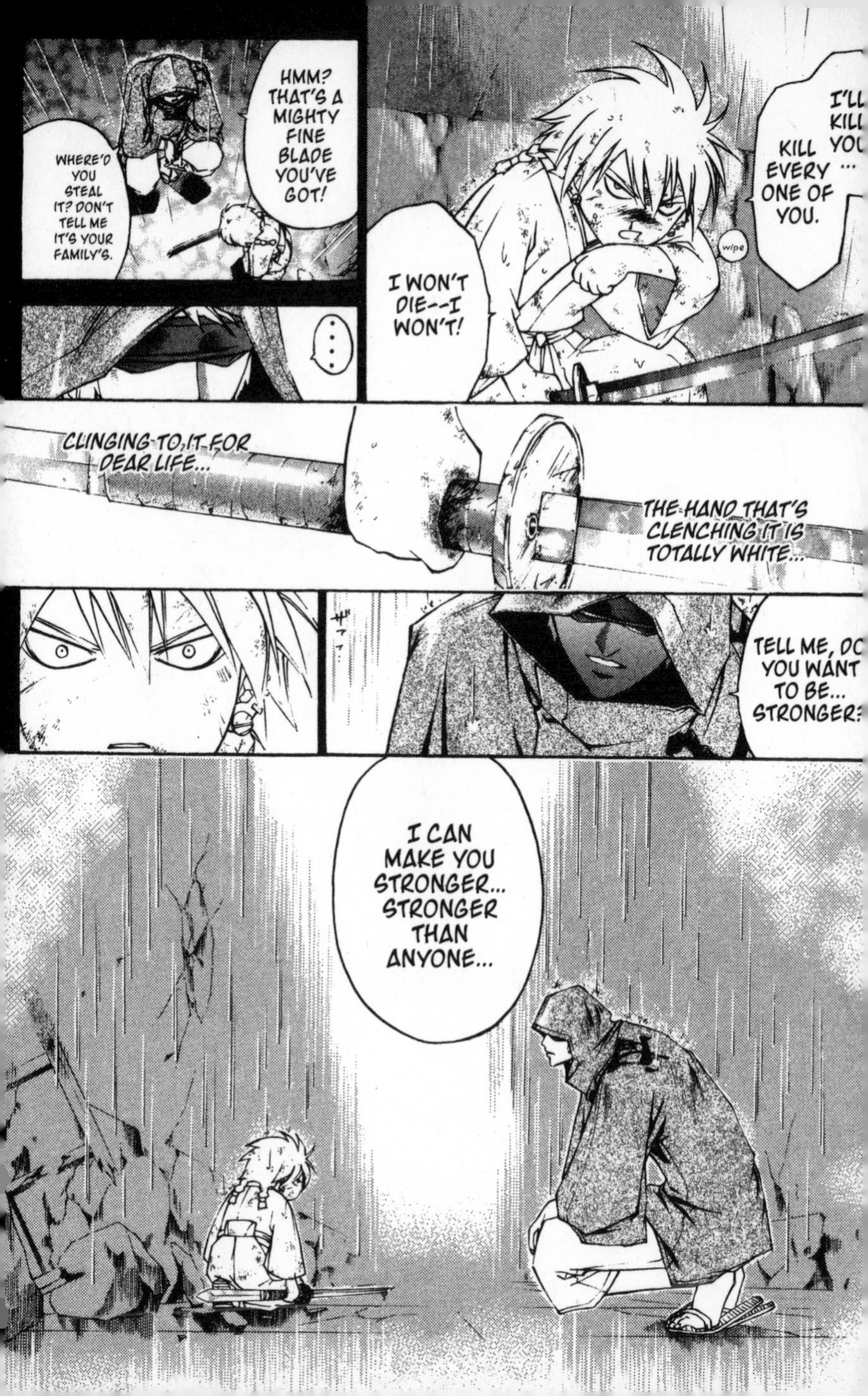
I'LL KILL YOU ... KILL EVERY ONE OF YOU.
wipe
I WON'T DIE--I WON'T!
HMM? THAT'S A MIGHTY FINE BLADE YOU'VE GOT!
WHERE'D YOU STEAL IT? DON'T TELL ME IT'S YOUR FAMILY'S.
...
THE HAND THAT'S CLENCHING IT IS TOTALLY WHITE...
CLINGING TO IT FOR DEAR LIFE...
TELL ME, DO YOU WANT TO BE... STRONGER?
I CAN MAKE YOU STRONGER... STRONGER THAN ANYONE...

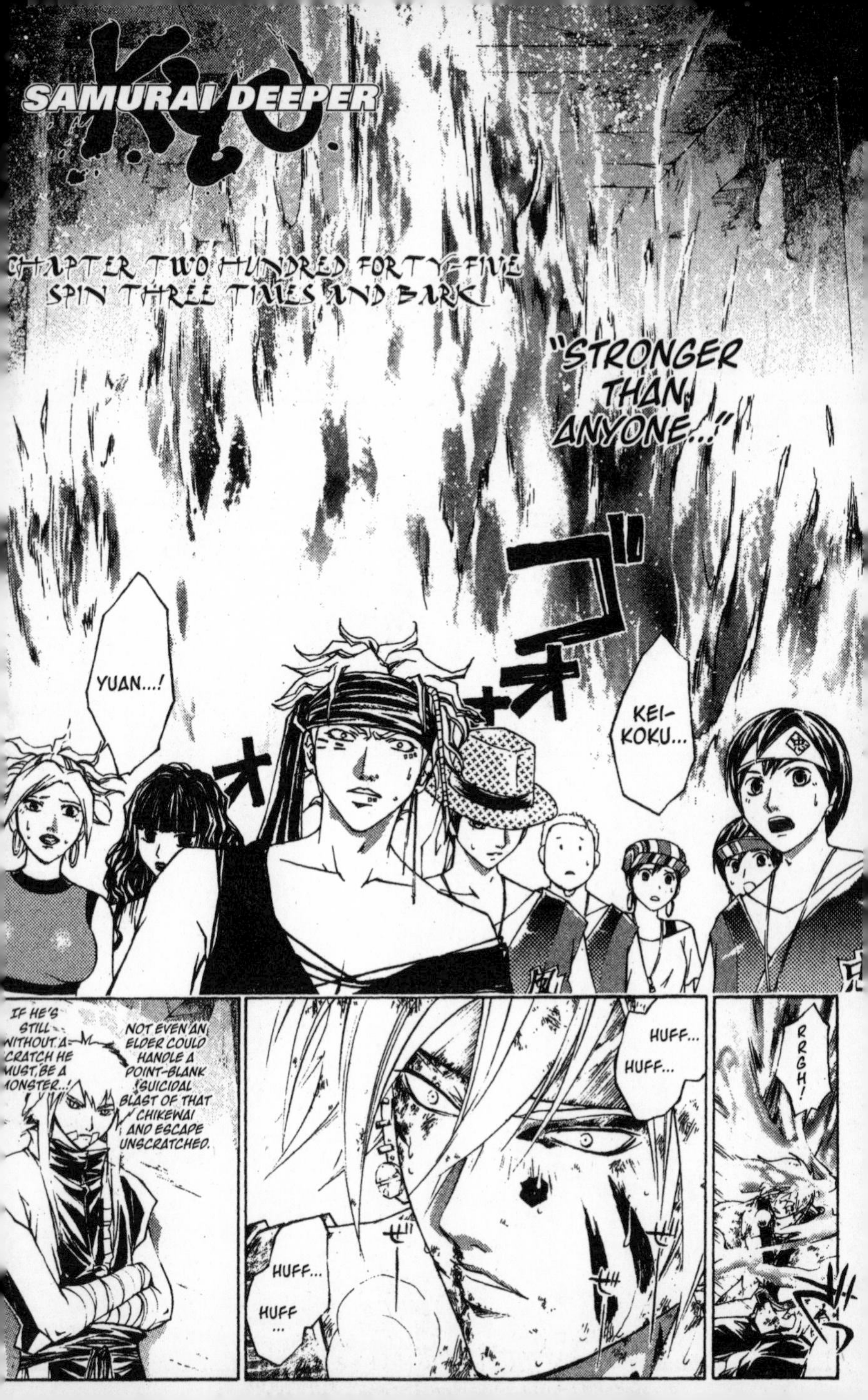
SAMURAI DEEPER KYO
CHAPTER TWO HUNDRED FORTY-FIVE
SPIN THREE TIMES AND BARK
"STRONGER THAN ANYONE...!"
KEI-KOKU...
YUAN...!
RRGH!
HUFF... HUFF...
HUFF... HUFF...
IF HE'S STILL WITHOUT A SCRATCH HE MUST BE A MONSTER...!
NOT EVEN AN ELDER COULD HANDLE A POINT-BLANK SUICIDAL BLAST OF THAT CHIKEWAI AND ESCAPE UNSCRATCHED.

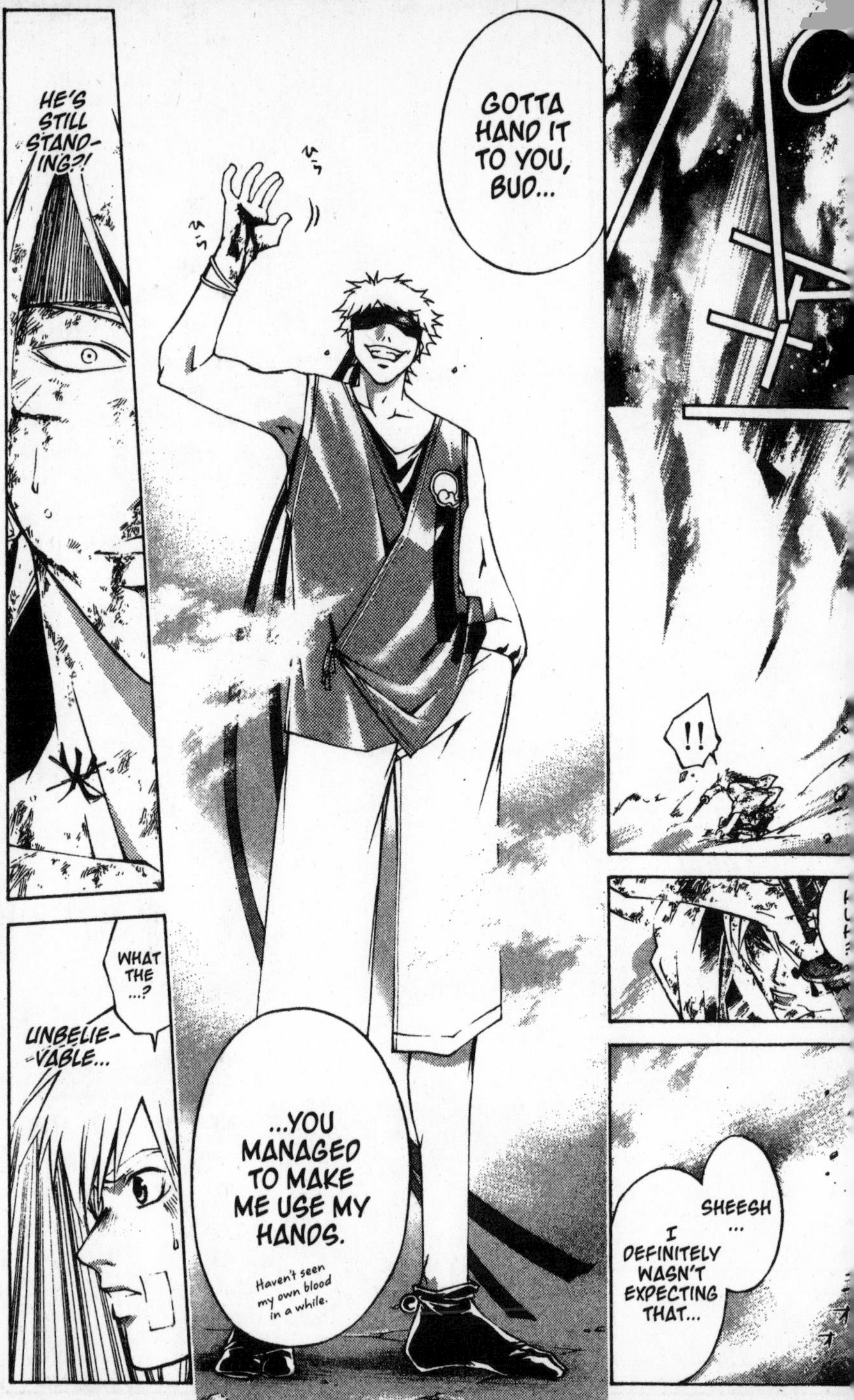
!!
SHEESH ... I DEFINITELY WASN'T EXPECTING THAT...
GOTTA HAND IT TO YOU, BUD...
...YOU MANAGED TO MAKE ME USE MY HANDS.
Haven't seen my own blood in a while.
HE'S STILL STAND-ING?!
WHAT THE ...?
UNBELIE-VABLE...

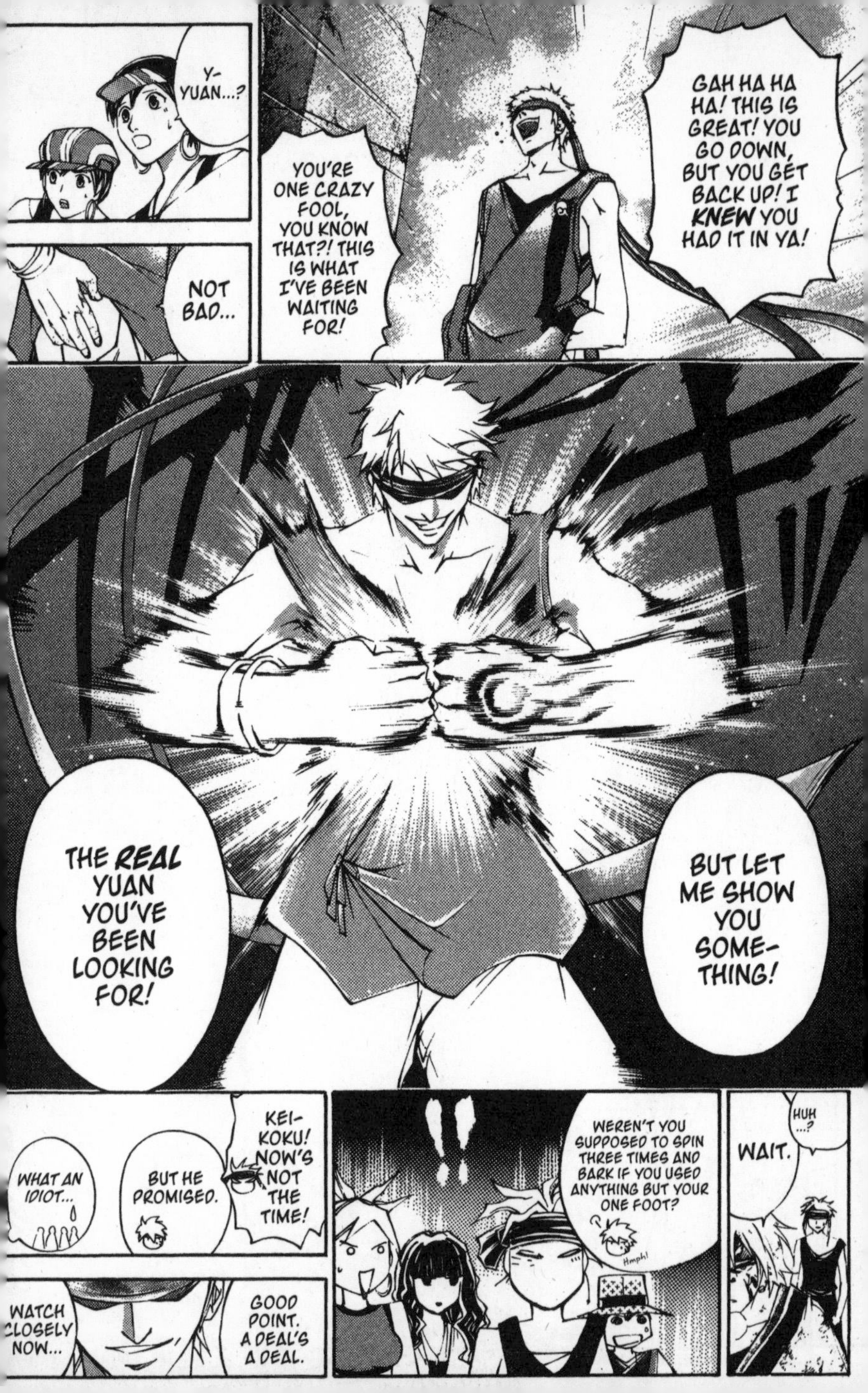
GAH HA HA HA! THIS IS GREAT! YOU GO DOWN, BUT YOU GET BACK UP! I KNEW YOU HAD IT IN YA!
YOU'RE ONE CRAZY FOOL, YOU KNOW THAT?! THIS IS WHAT I'VE BEEN WAITING FOR!
Y-YUAN...?
NOT BAD...
BUT LET ME SHOW YOU SOME-THING!
THE REAL YUAN YOU'VE BEEN LOOKING FOR!
WAIT.
HUH ...?
WEREN'T YOU SUPPOSED TO SPIN THREE TIMES AND BARK IF YOU USED ANYTHING BUT YOUR ONE FOOT?
Hmph!
!!
KEI-KOKU! NOW'S NOT THE TIME!
BUT HE PROMISED.
WHAT AN IDIOT...
GOOD POINT. A DEAL'S A DEAL.
WATCH CLOSELY NOW...

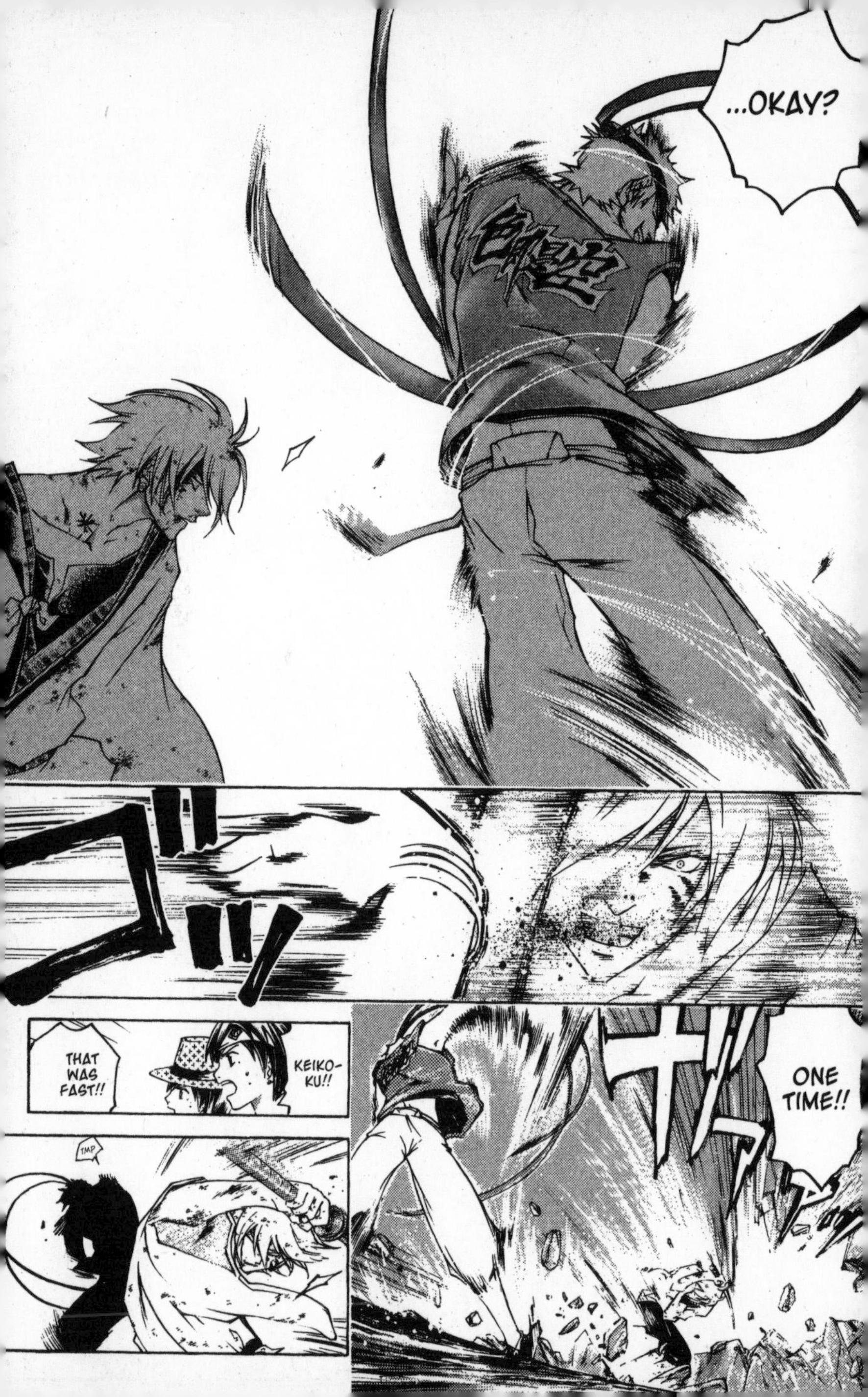
...OKAY?
ONE TIME!!
KEIKO-KU!!
THAT WAS FAST!!
TMP

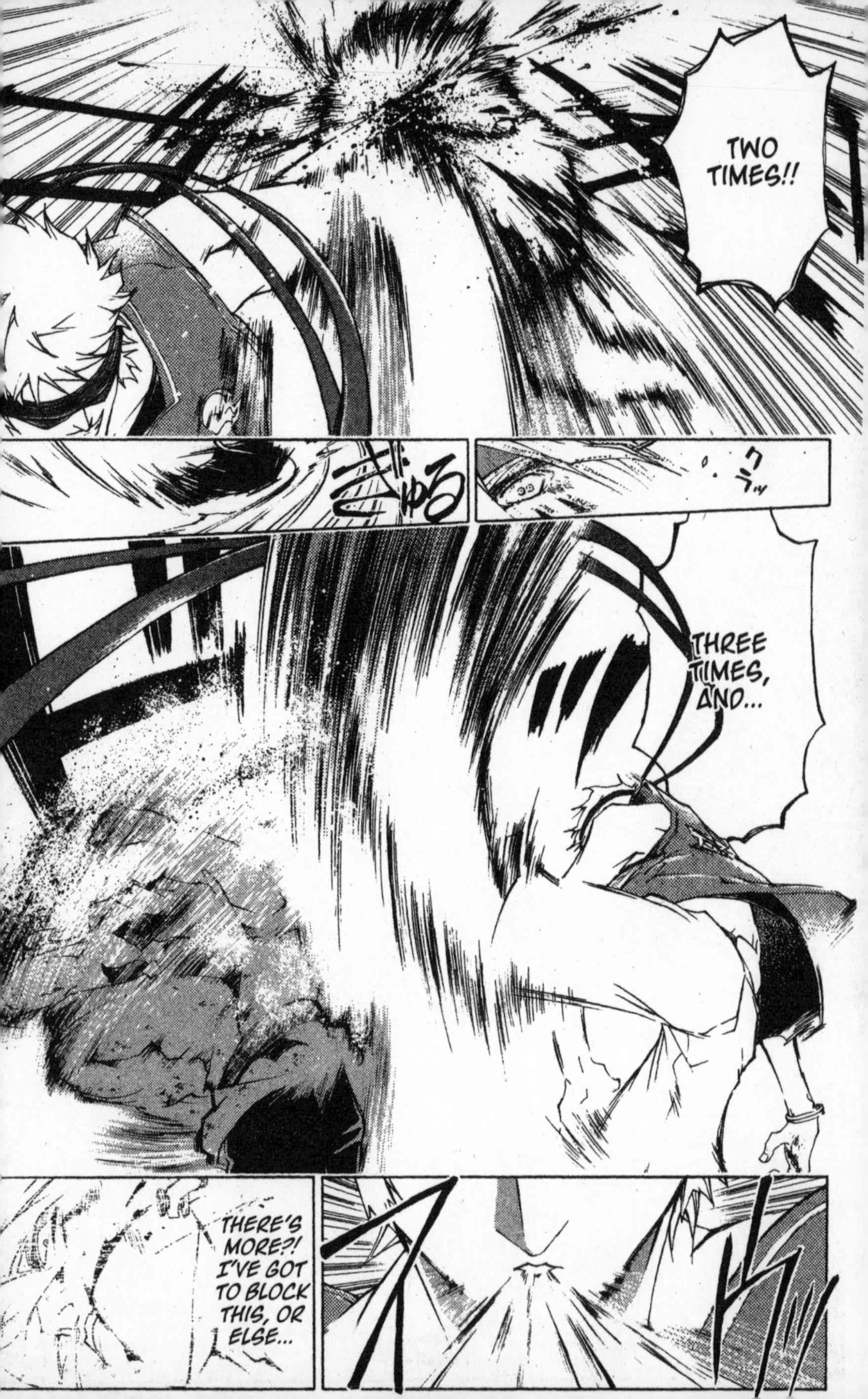
TWO TIMES!!
クラッ
ぎゅる
THREE TIMES, AND...
THERE'S MORE?! I'VE GOT TO BLOCK THIS, OR ELSE...

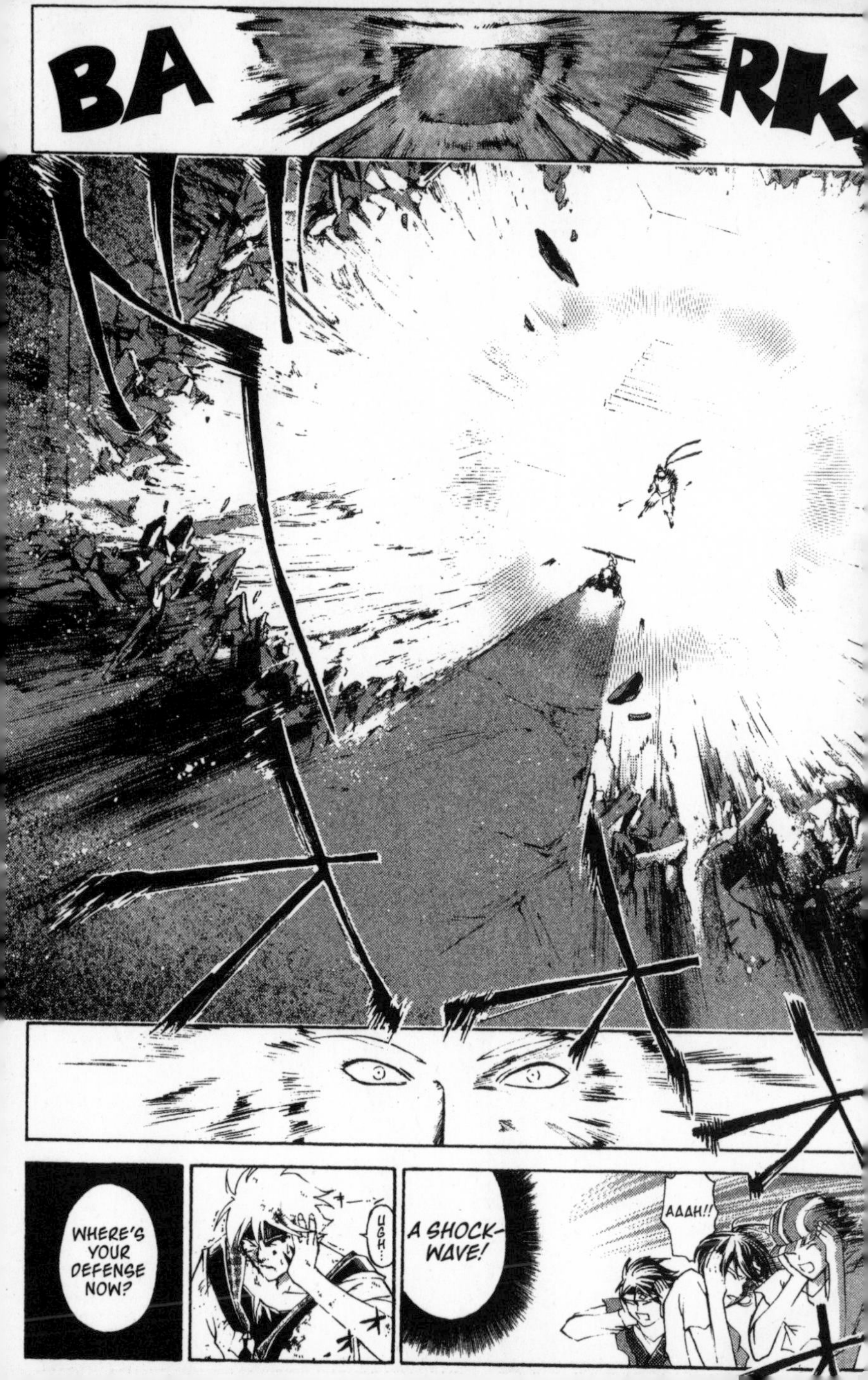
BARK
AAAH!!
A SHOCK-WAVE!
UGH...
WHERE'S YOUR DEFENSE NOW?

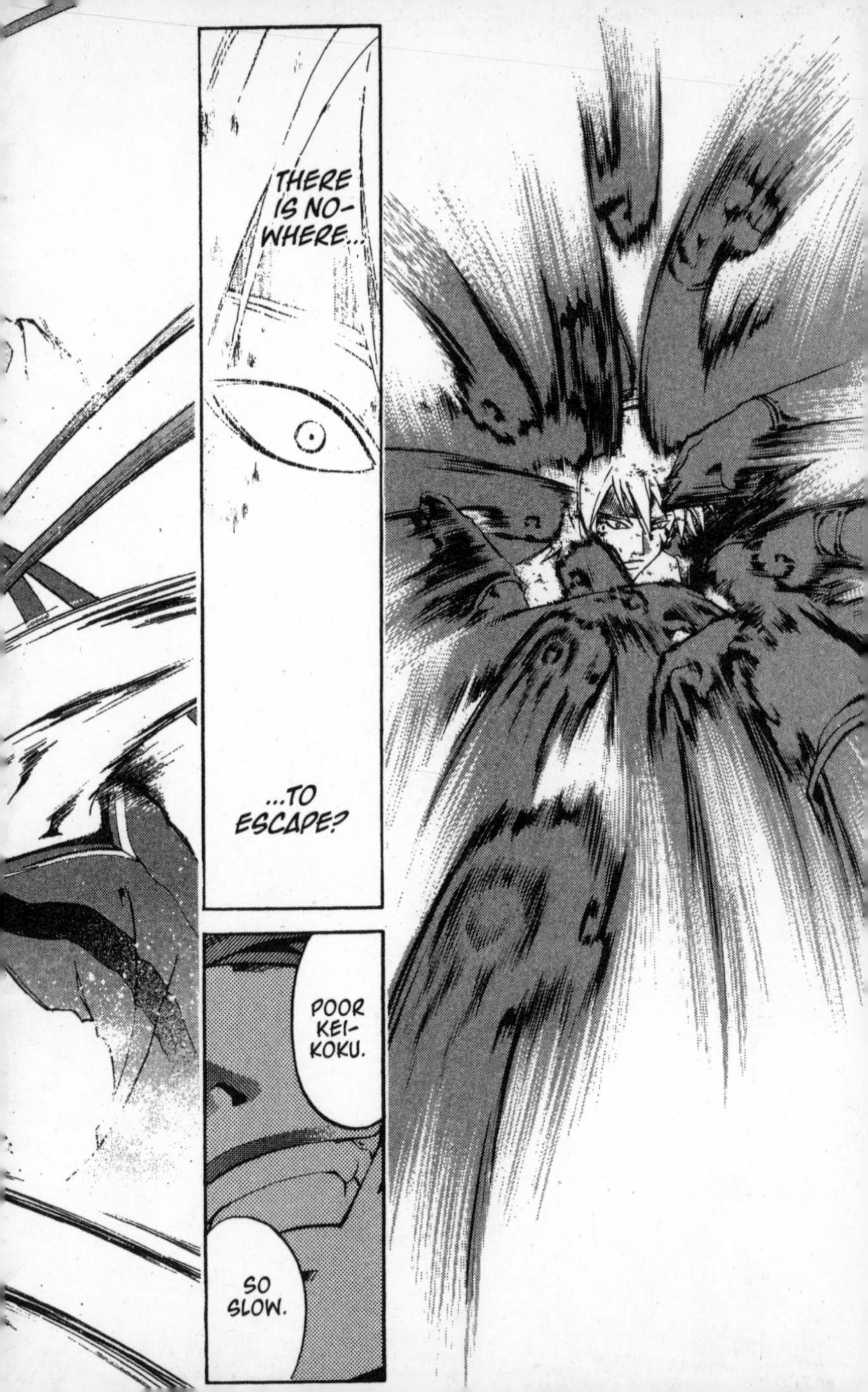
THERE IS NO-WHERE...
...TO ESCAPE?
POOR KEI-KOKU.
SO SLOW.

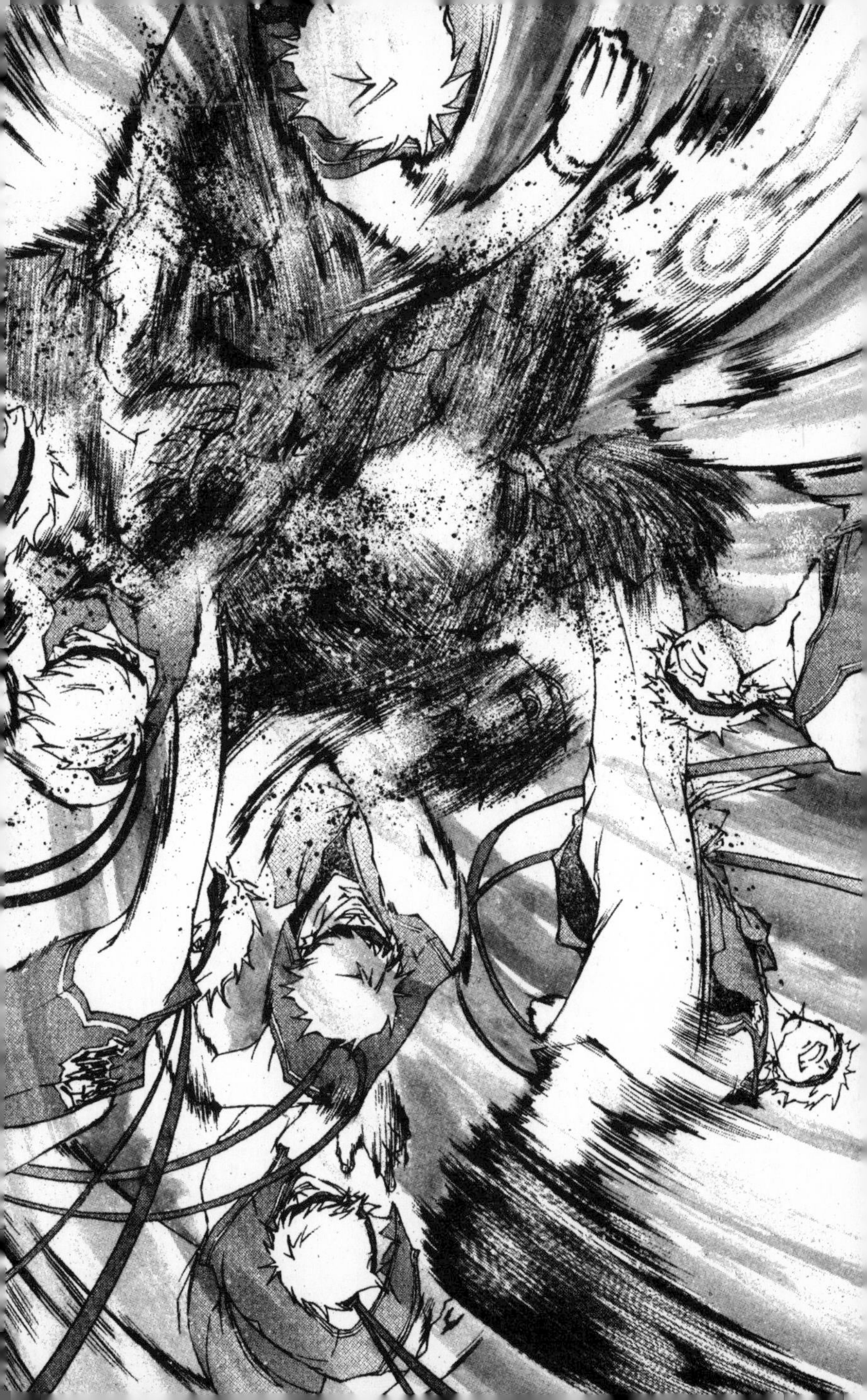

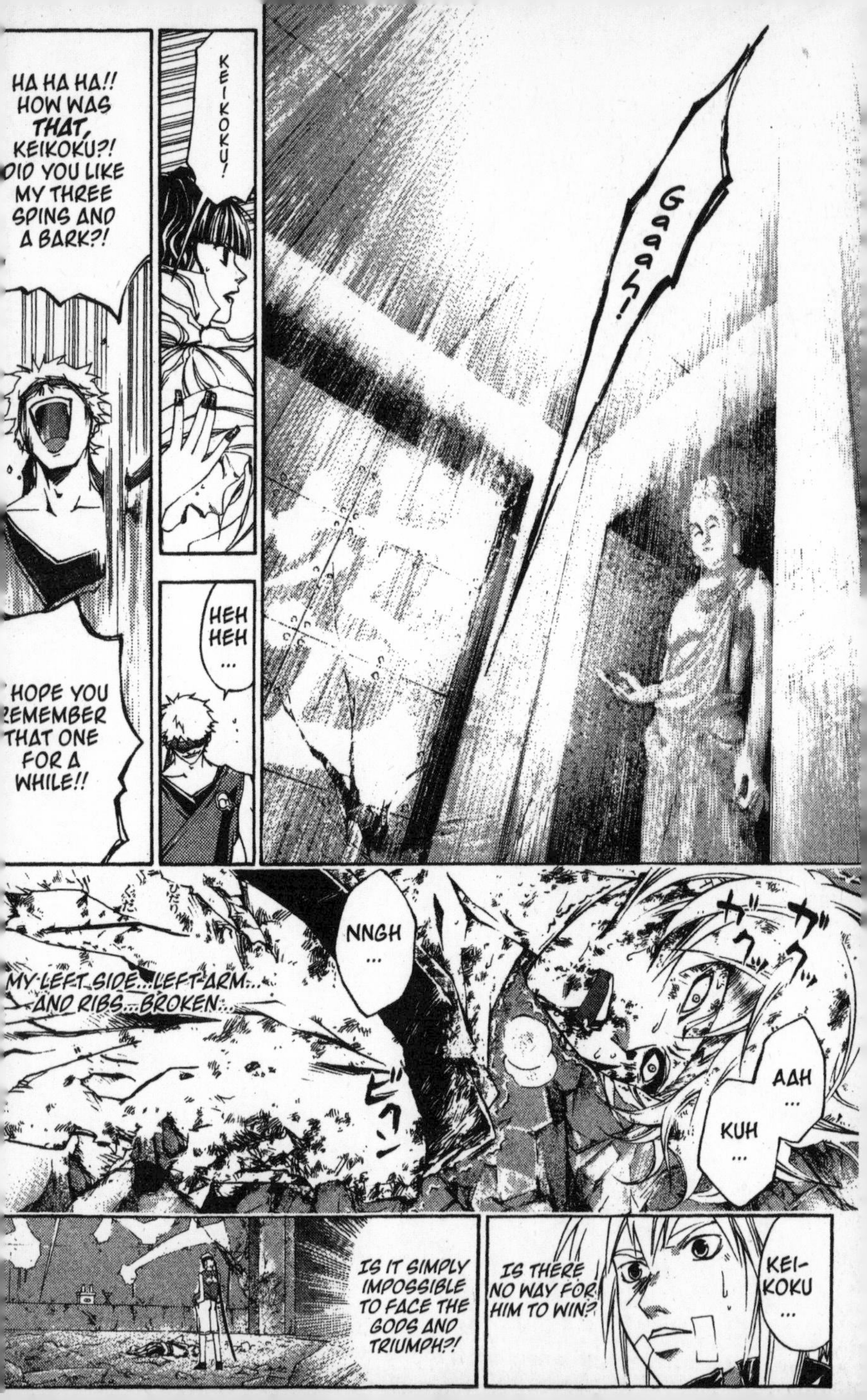
Gaaah!
KEIKOKU!
HEH HEH ...
HA HA HA!! HOW WAS THAT, KEIKOKU?! DID YOU LIKE MY THREE SPINS AND A BARK?!
I HOPE YOU REMEMBER THAT ONE FOR A WHILE!!
AAH ... KUH ...
NNGH ...
MY LEFT SIDE... LEFT ARM... AND RIBS... BROKEN...
KEI-KOKU ...
IS THERE NO WAY FOR HIM TO WIN?
IS IT SIMPLY IMPOSSIBLE TO FACE THE GODS AND TRIUMPH?!

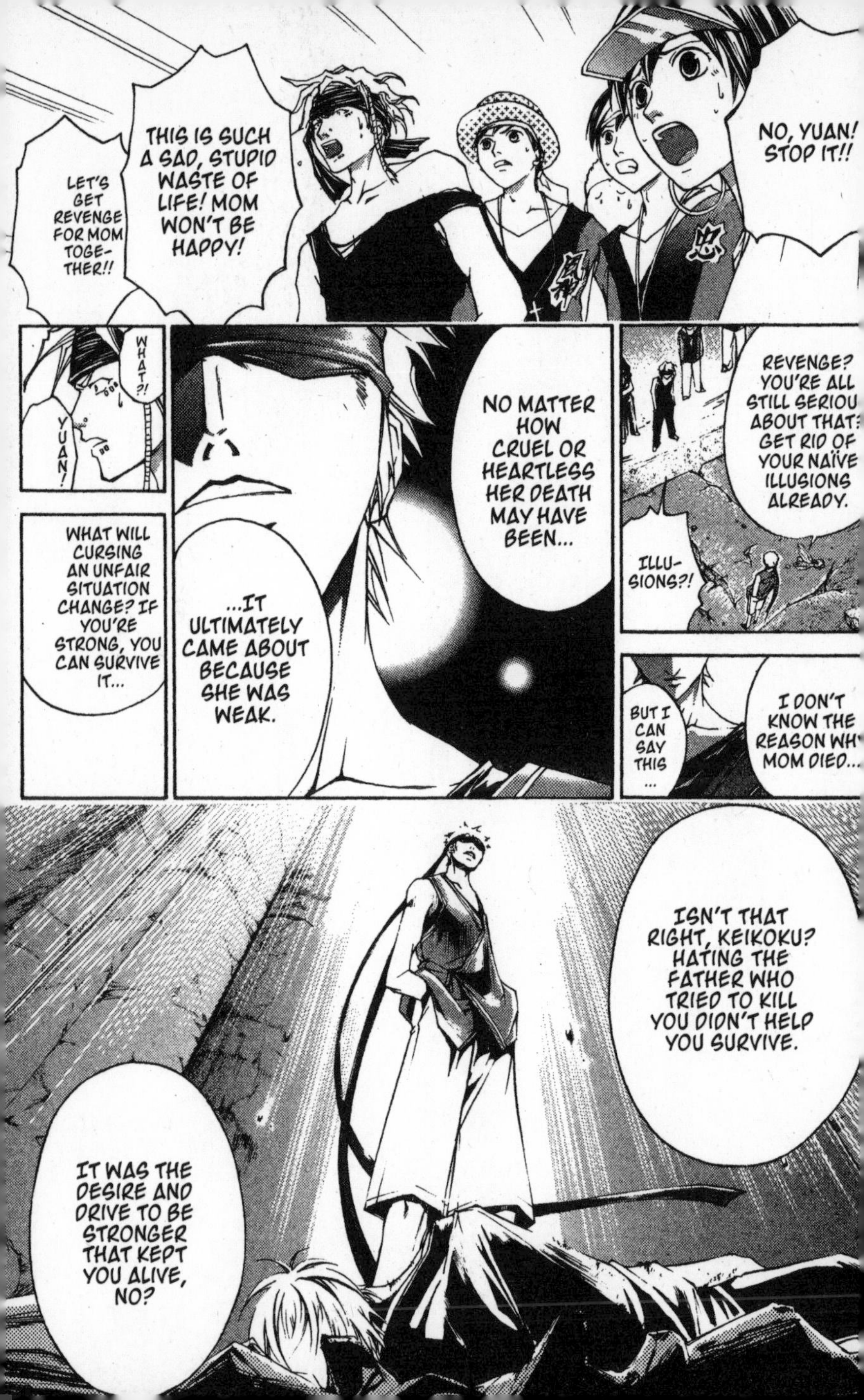
NO, YUAN! STOP IT!!
THIS IS SUCH A SAD, STUPID WASTE OF LIFE! MOM WON'T BE HAPPY!
LET'S GET REVENGE FOR MOM TOGE- THER!!
REVENGE? YOU'RE ALL STILL SERIOU ABOUT THAT GET RID OF YOUR NAÏVE ILLUSIONS ALREADY.
ILLU- SIONS?!
I DON'T KNOW THE REASON WH MOM DIED...
BUT I CAN SAY THIS ...
NO MATTER HOW CRUEL OR HEARTLESS HER DEATH MAY HAVE BEEN...
...IT ULTIMATELY CAME ABOUT BECAUSE SHE WAS WEAK.
WHAT?!
YUAN!
WHAT WILL CURSING AN UNFAIR SITUATION CHANGE? IF YOU'RE STRONG, YOU CAN SURVIVE IT...
ISN'T THAT RIGHT, KEIKOKU? HATING THE FATHER WHO TRIED TO KILL YOU DIDN'T HELP YOU SURVIVE.
IT WAS THE DESIRE AND DRIVE TO BE STRONGER THAT KEPT YOU ALIVE, NO?

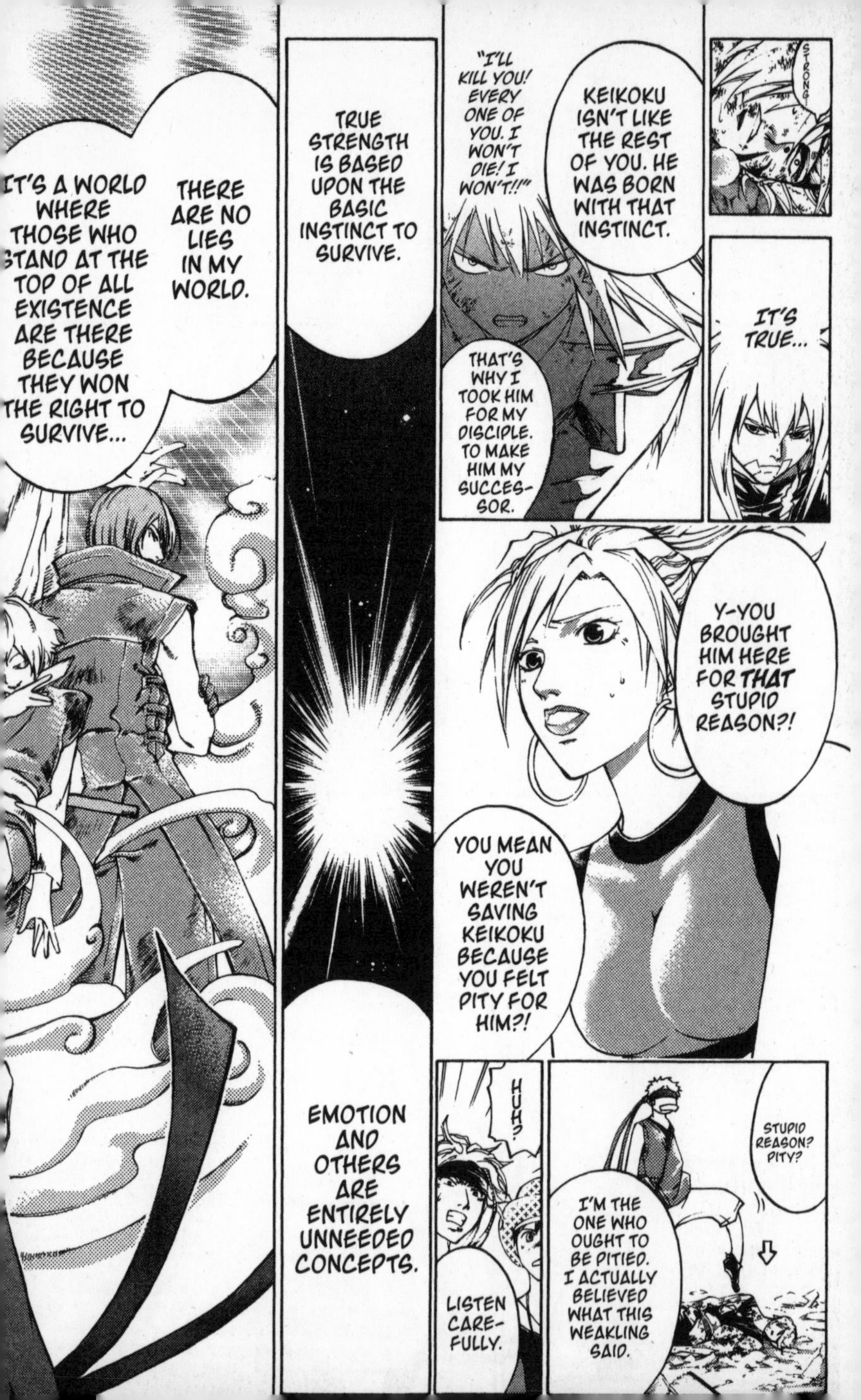
STRONG!
IT'S TRUE...
KEIKOKU ISN'T LIKE THE REST OF YOU. HE WAS BORN WITH THAT INSTINCT.
"I'LL KILL YOU! EVERY ONE OF YOU. I WON'T DIE! I WON'T!!"
THAT'S WHY I TOOK HIM FOR MY DISCIPLE. TO MAKE HIM MY SUCCES-SOR.
Y-YOU BROUGHT HIM HERE FOR **THAT** STUPID REASON?!
YOU MEAN YOU WEREN'T SAVING KEIKOKU BECAUSE YOU FELT PITY FOR HIM?!
STUPID REASON? PITY?
I'M THE ONE WHO OUGHT TO BE PITIED. I ACTUALLY BELIEVED WHAT THIS WEAKLING SAID.
HUH?
LISTEN CARE-FULLY.
TRUE STRENGTH IS BASED UPON THE BASIC INSTINCT TO SURVIVE.
EMOTION AND OTHERS ARE ENTIRELY UNNEEDED CONCEPTS.
THERE ARE NO LIES IN MY WORLD.
IT'S A WORLD WHERE THOSE WHO STAND AT THE TOP OF ALL EXISTENCE ARE THERE BECAUSE THEY WON THE RIGHT TO SURVIVE...

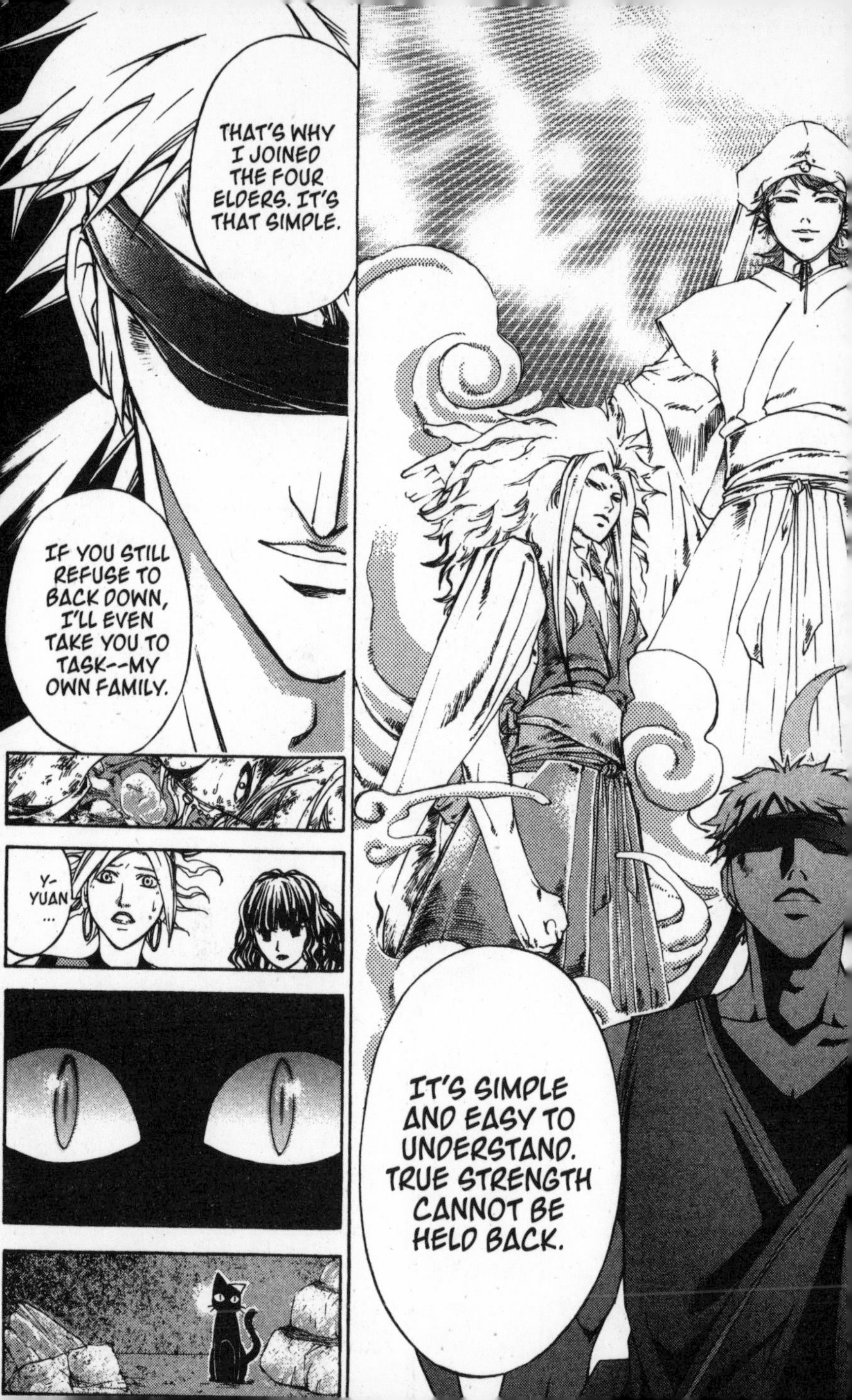
IT'S SIMPLE AND EASY TO UNDERSTAND. TRUE STRENGTH CANNOT BE HELD BACK.
THAT'S WHY I JOINED THE FOUR ELDERS. IT'S THAT SIMPLE.
IF YOU STILL REFUSE TO BACK DOWN, I'LL EVEN TAKE YOU TO TASK--MY OWN FAMILY.
Y-YUAN ...

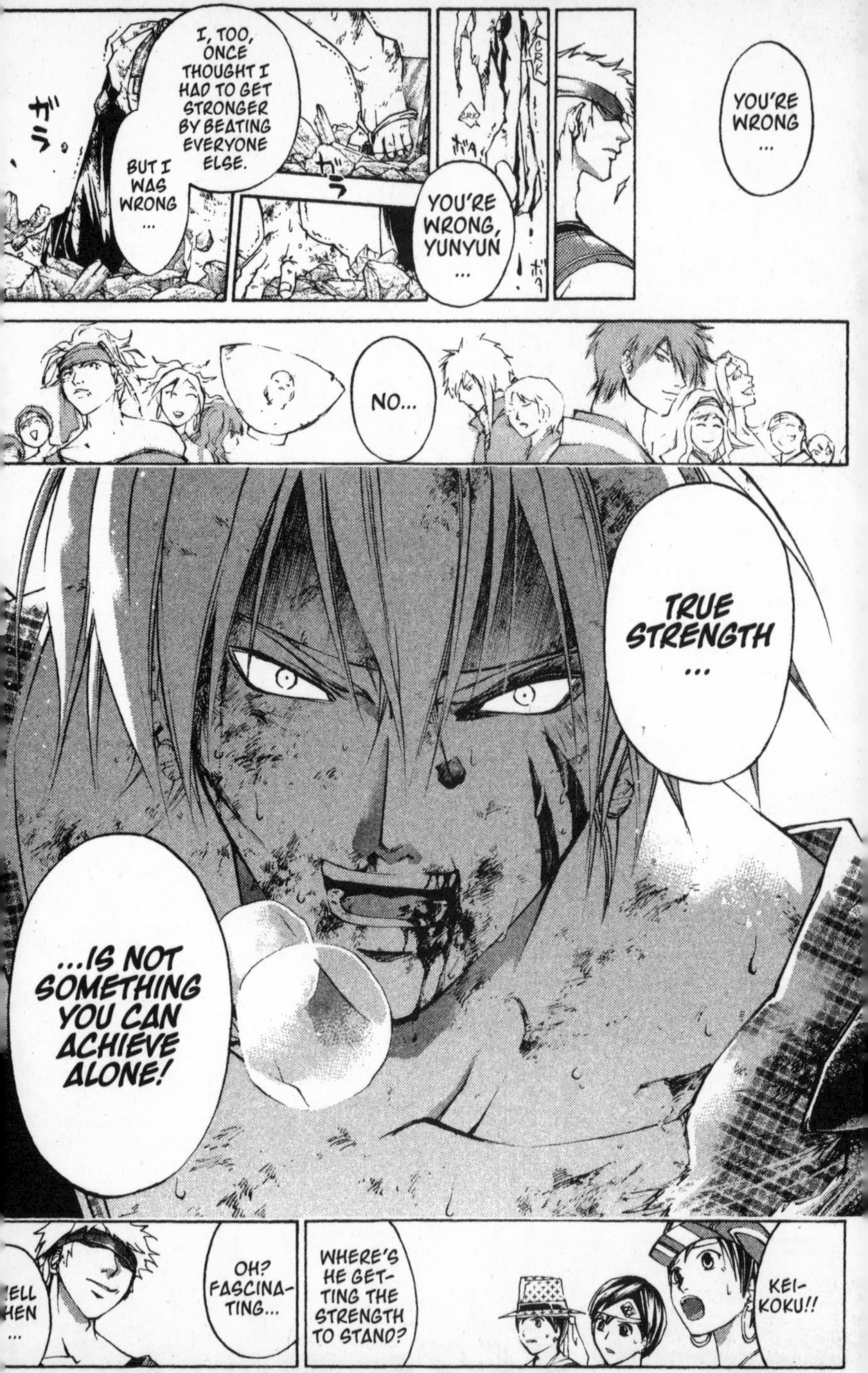
YOU'RE WRONG ...
YOU'RE WRONG, YUNYUN ...
CRK
I, TOO, ONCE THOUGHT I HAD TO GET STRONGER BY BEATING EVERYONE ELSE.
BUT I WAS WRONG ...
NO...
TRUE STRENGTH ...
...IS NOT SOMETHING YOU CAN ACHIEVE ALONE!
KEI-KOKU!!
WHERE'S HE GET-TING THE STRENGTH TO STAND?
OH? FASCINA-TING...
ELL HEN ...

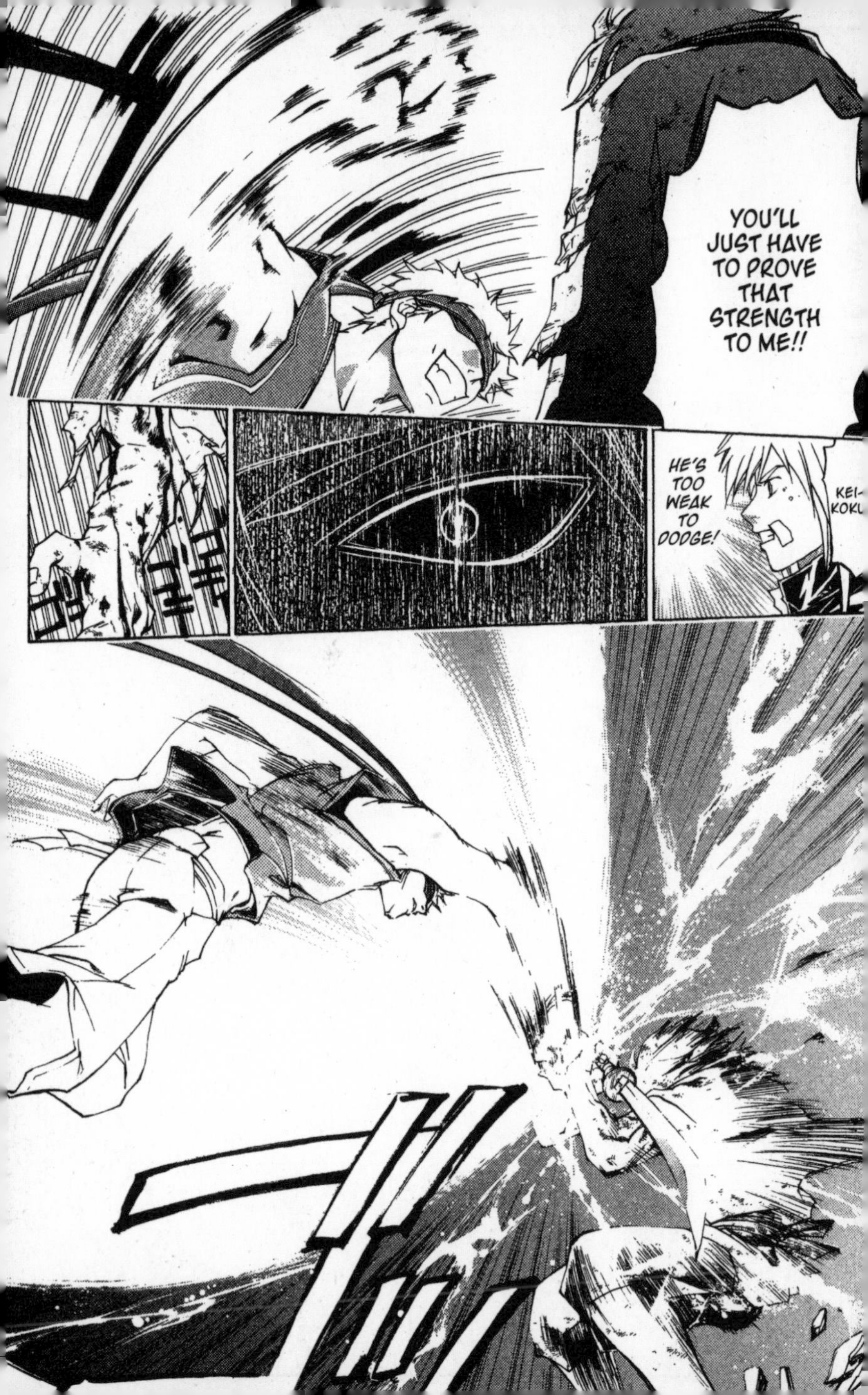
YOU'LL JUST HAVE TO PROVE THAT STRENGTH TO ME!!
KEI-KOKU
HE'S TOO WEAK TO DODGE!

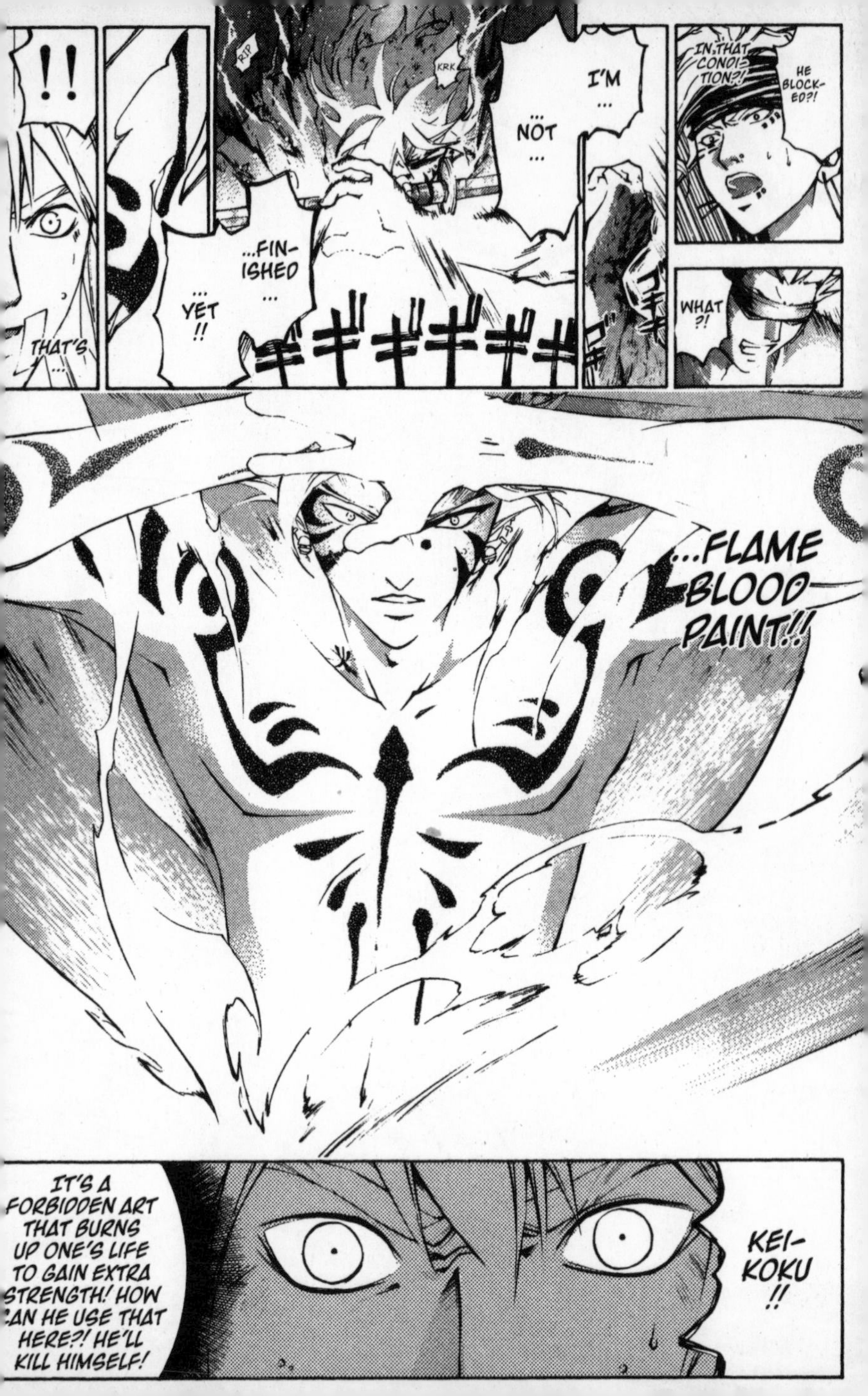
IN THAT CONDITION?!
HE BLOCKED?!
WHAT ?!
RIP
KRK
I'M ... NOT ...
...FINISHED ...
... YET !!
!!
THAT'S ...
...FLAME BLOOD-PAINT!!
KEI-KOKU !!
IT'S A FORBIDDEN ART THAT BURNS UP ONE'S LIFE TO GAIN EXTRA STRENGTH! HOW CAN HE USE THAT HERE?! HE'LL KILL HIMSELF!

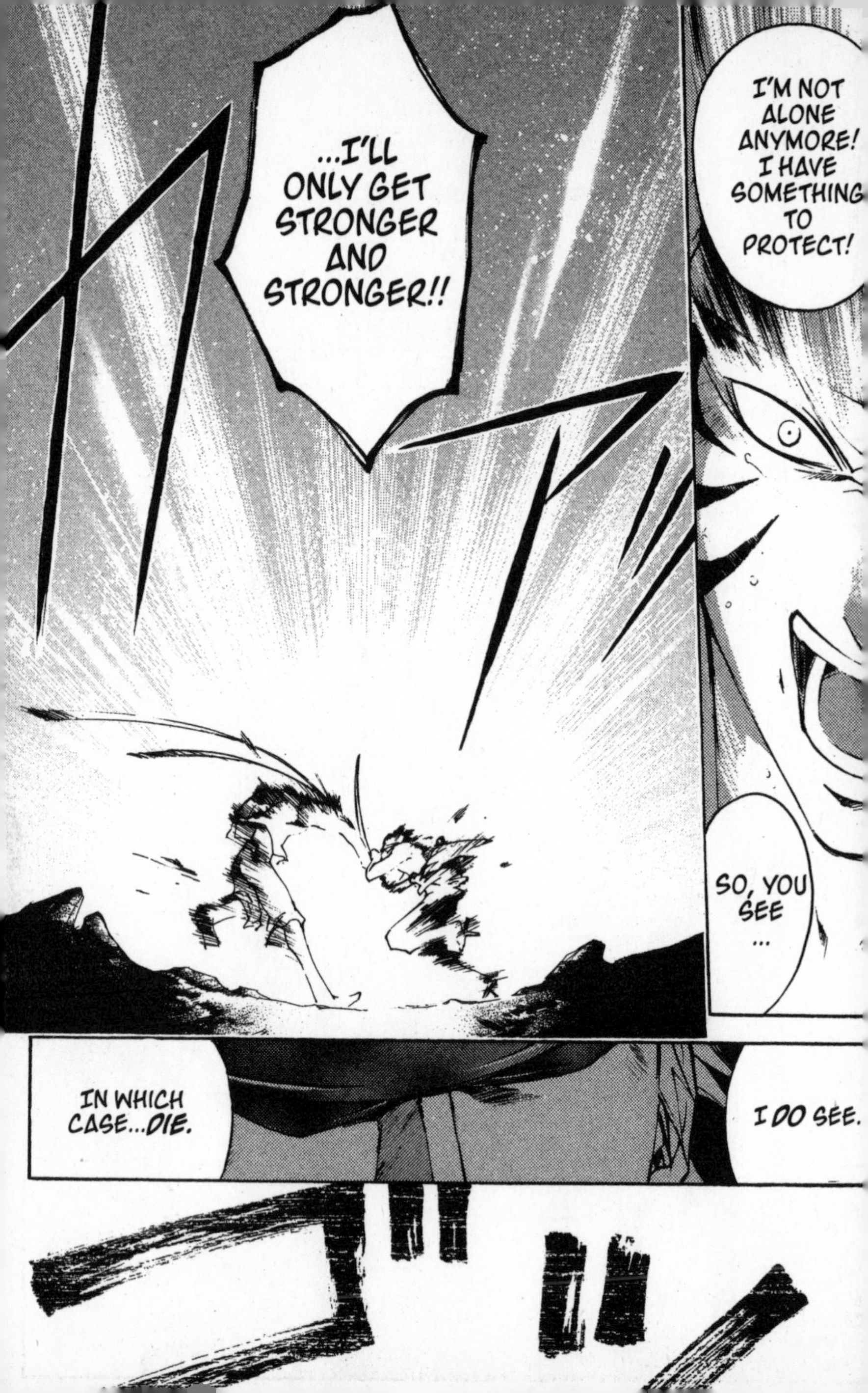
I'M NOT ALONE ANYMORE! I HAVE SOMETHING TO PROTECT!
SO, YOU SEE ...
...I'LL ONLY GET STRONGER AND STRONGER!!
I DO SEE.
IN WHICH CASE...DIE.

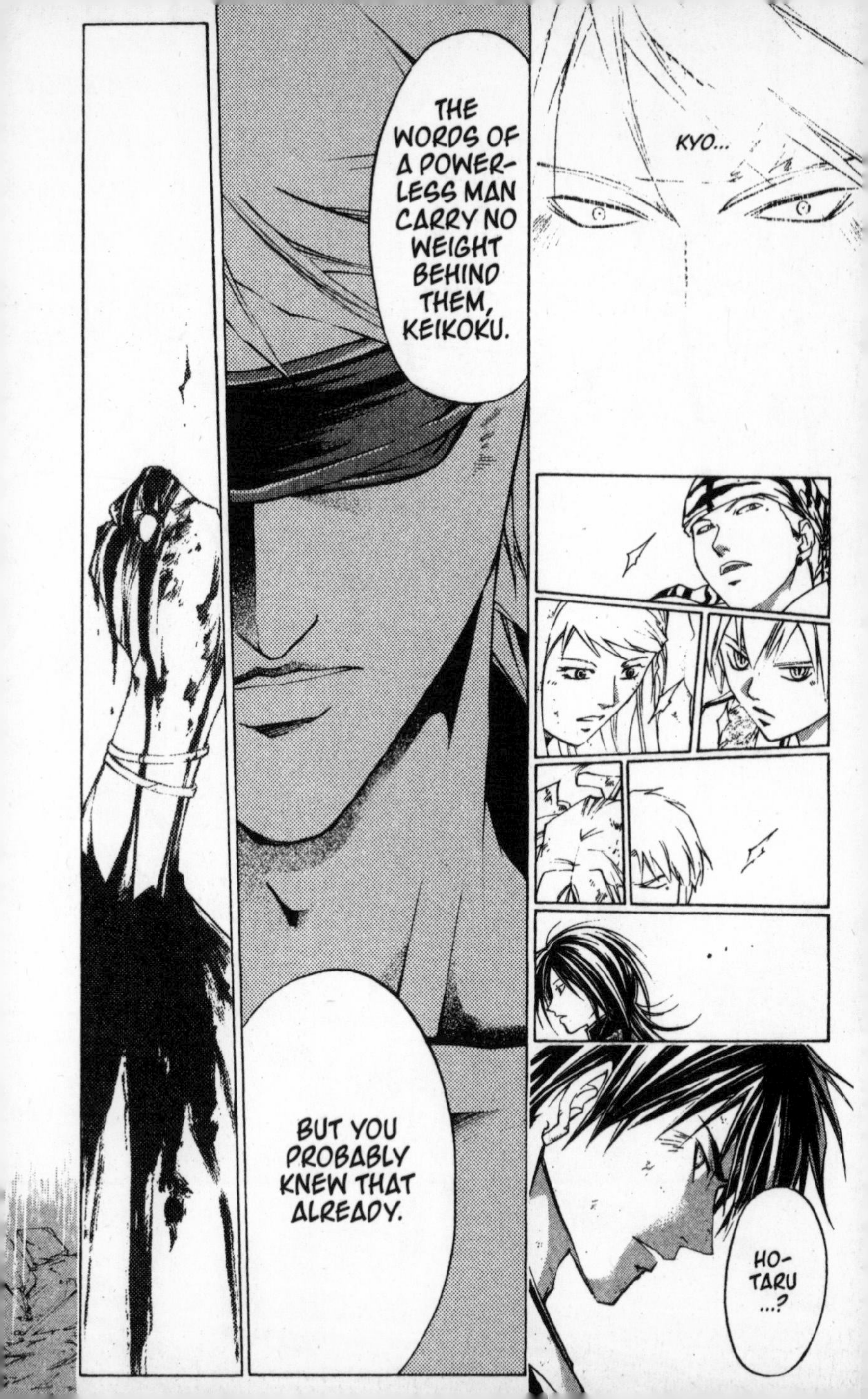
KYO...
HO-TARU ...?
THE WORDS OF A POWER-LESS MAN CARRY NO WEIGHT BEHIND THEM, KEIKOKU.
BUT YOU PROBABLY KNEW THAT ALREADY.

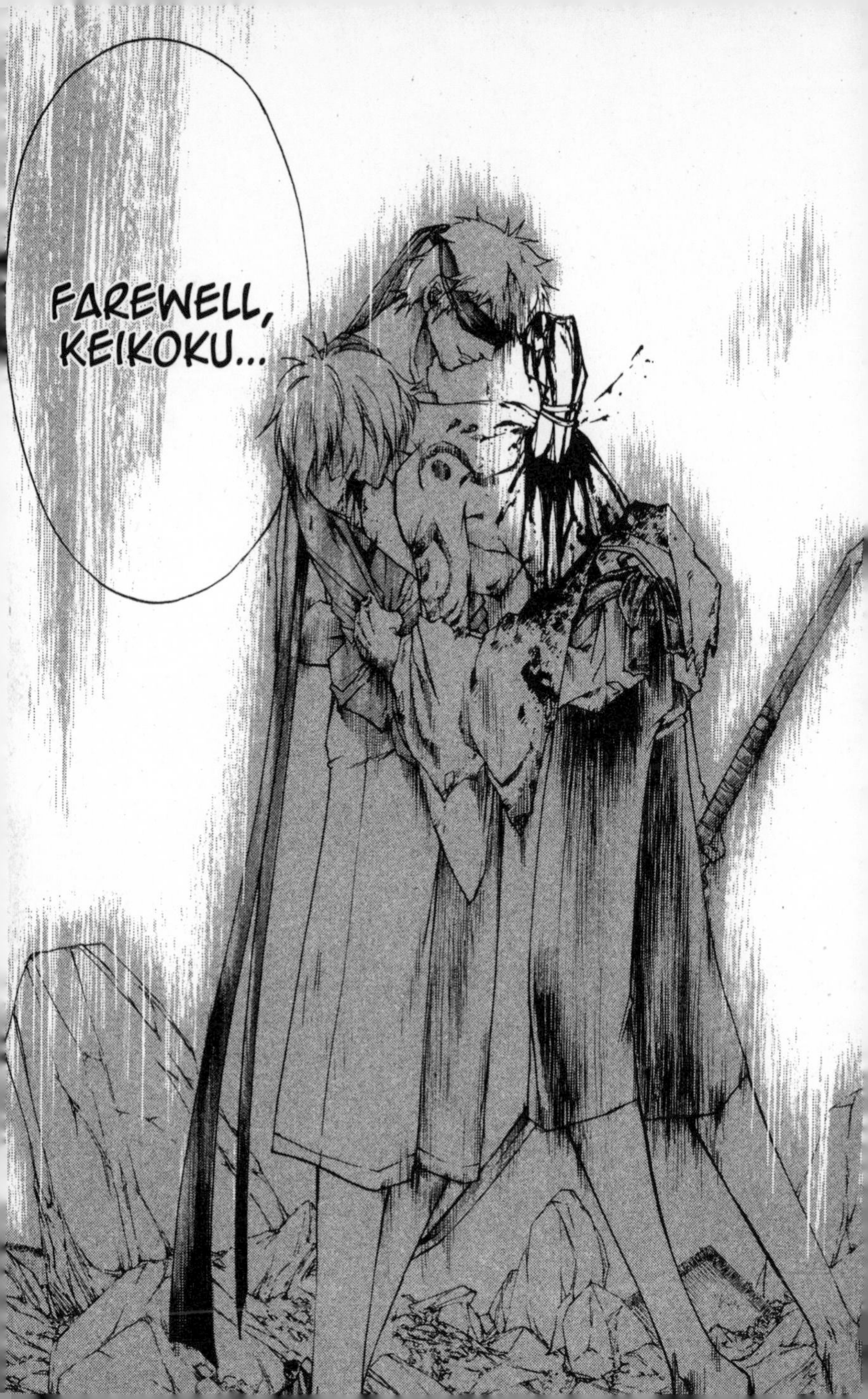
FAREWELL, KEIKOKU...

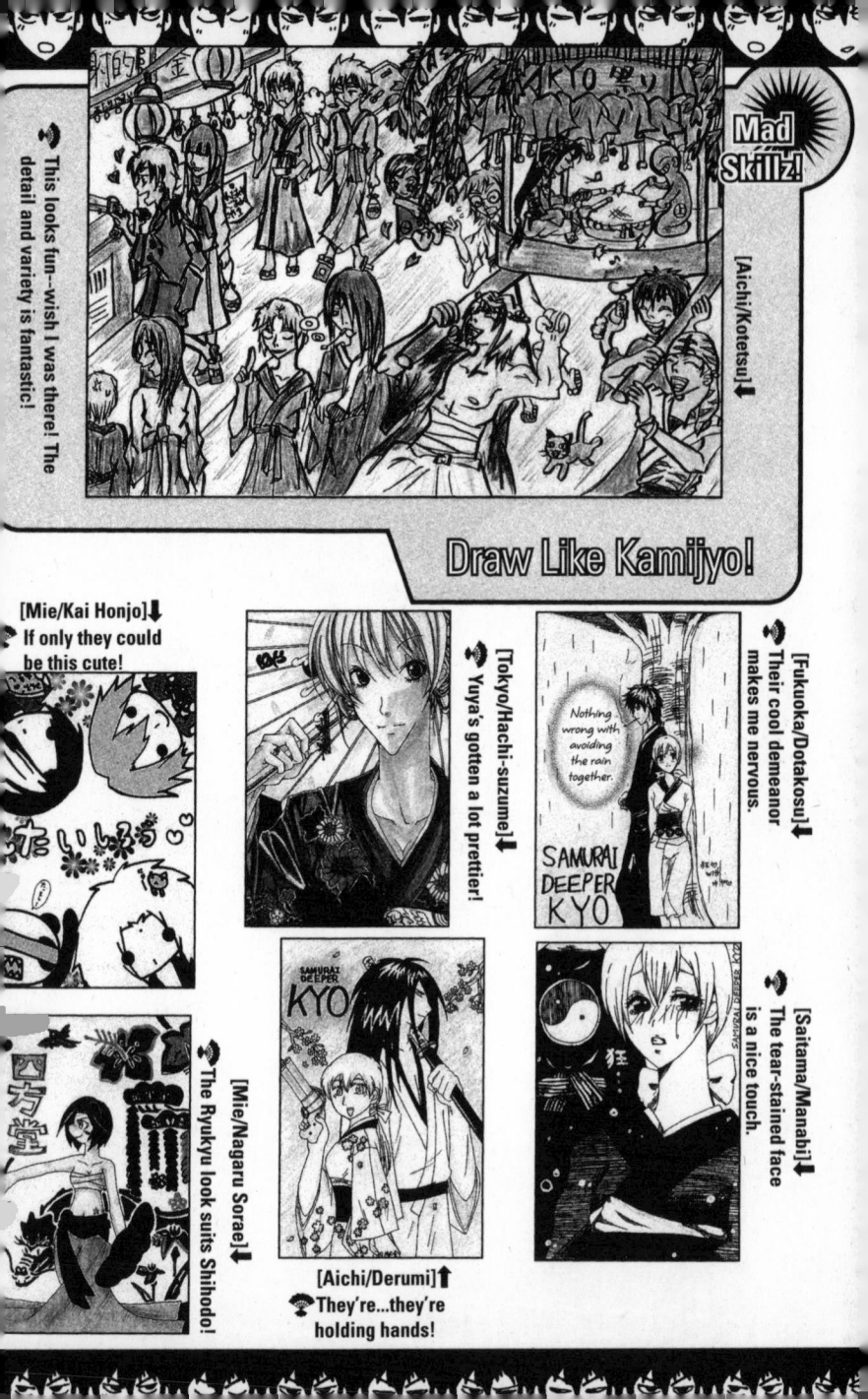

Draw Like Kamijyo!

[Aichi/Kotetsu]⬇

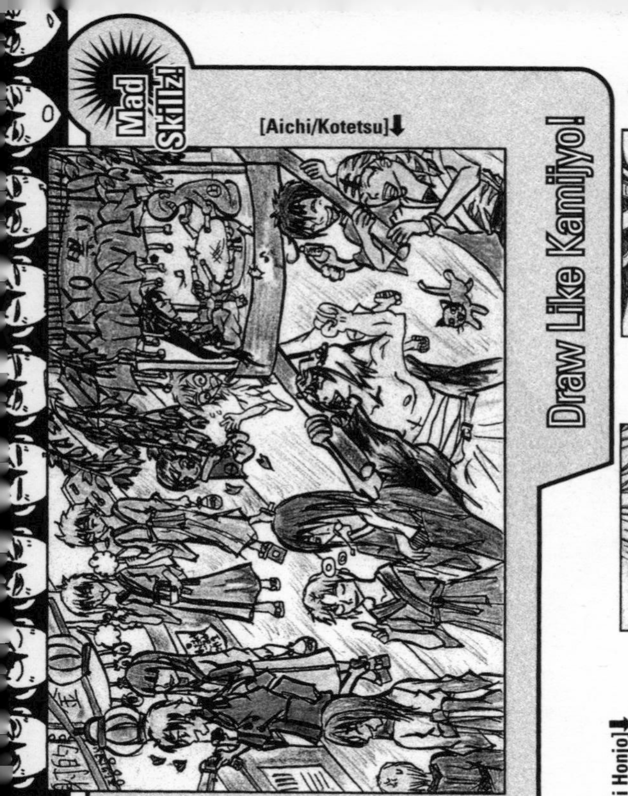

This looks fun--wish I was there! The detail and variety is fantastic!

[Fukuoka/Dotakosu]⬇

Their cool demeanor makes me nervous.

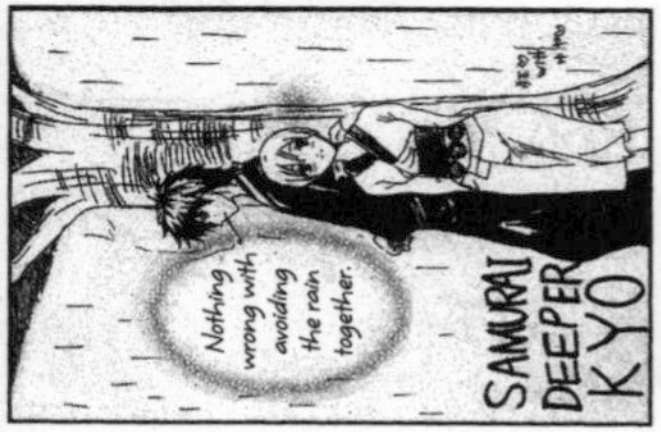
Nothing wrong with avoiding the rain together.
SAMURAI DEEPER KYO

[Saitama/Manabi]⬇

The tear-stained face is a nice touch.

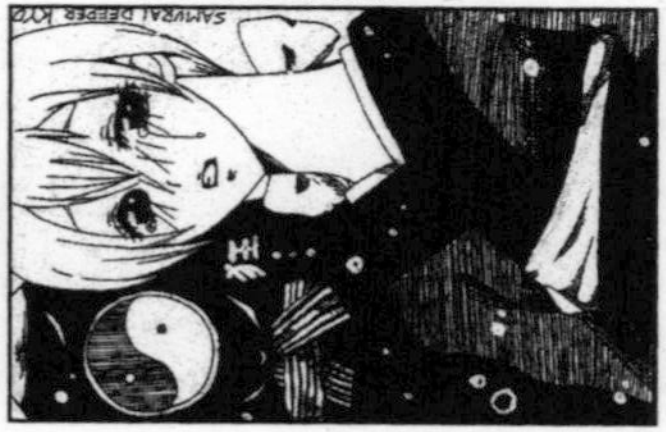

[Tokyo/Hachi-suzume]⬇

Yuya's gotten a lot prettier!

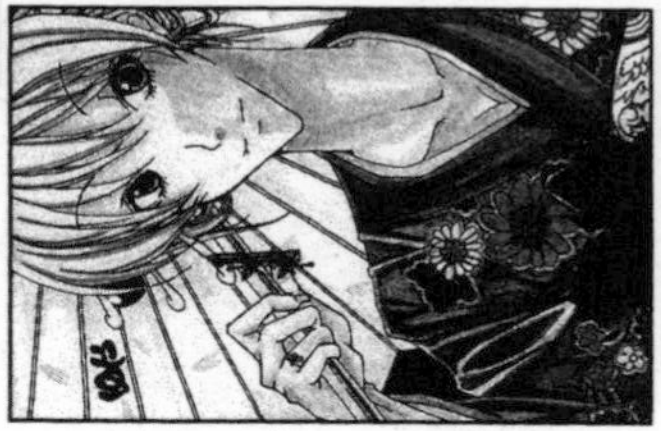

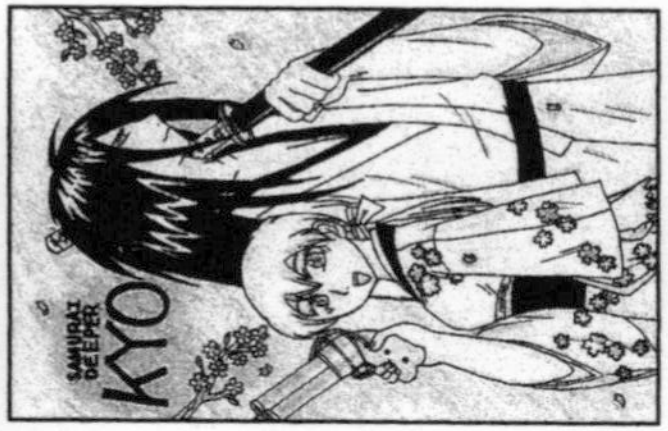
SAMURAI DEEPER KYO

[Aichi/Derumi]⬆

They're...they're holding hands!

[Mie/Kai Honjo]➡

If only they could be this cute!

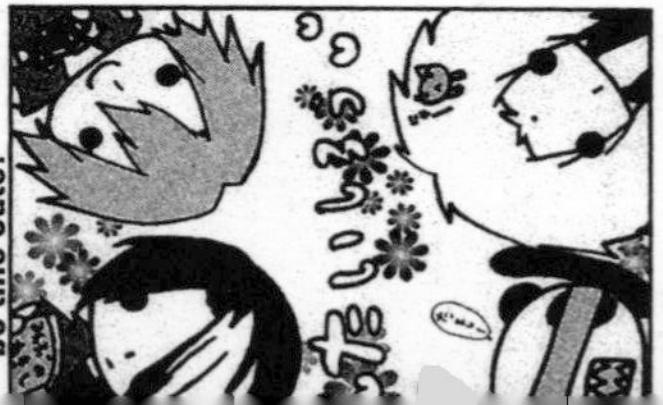

[Mie/Nagaru Sorae]⬇

The Ryukyu look suits Shihodo!

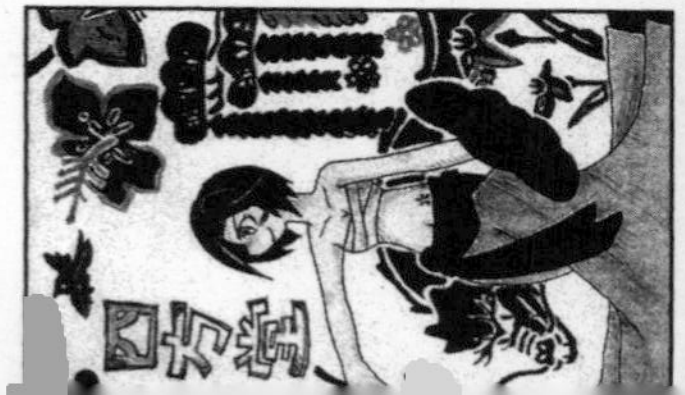

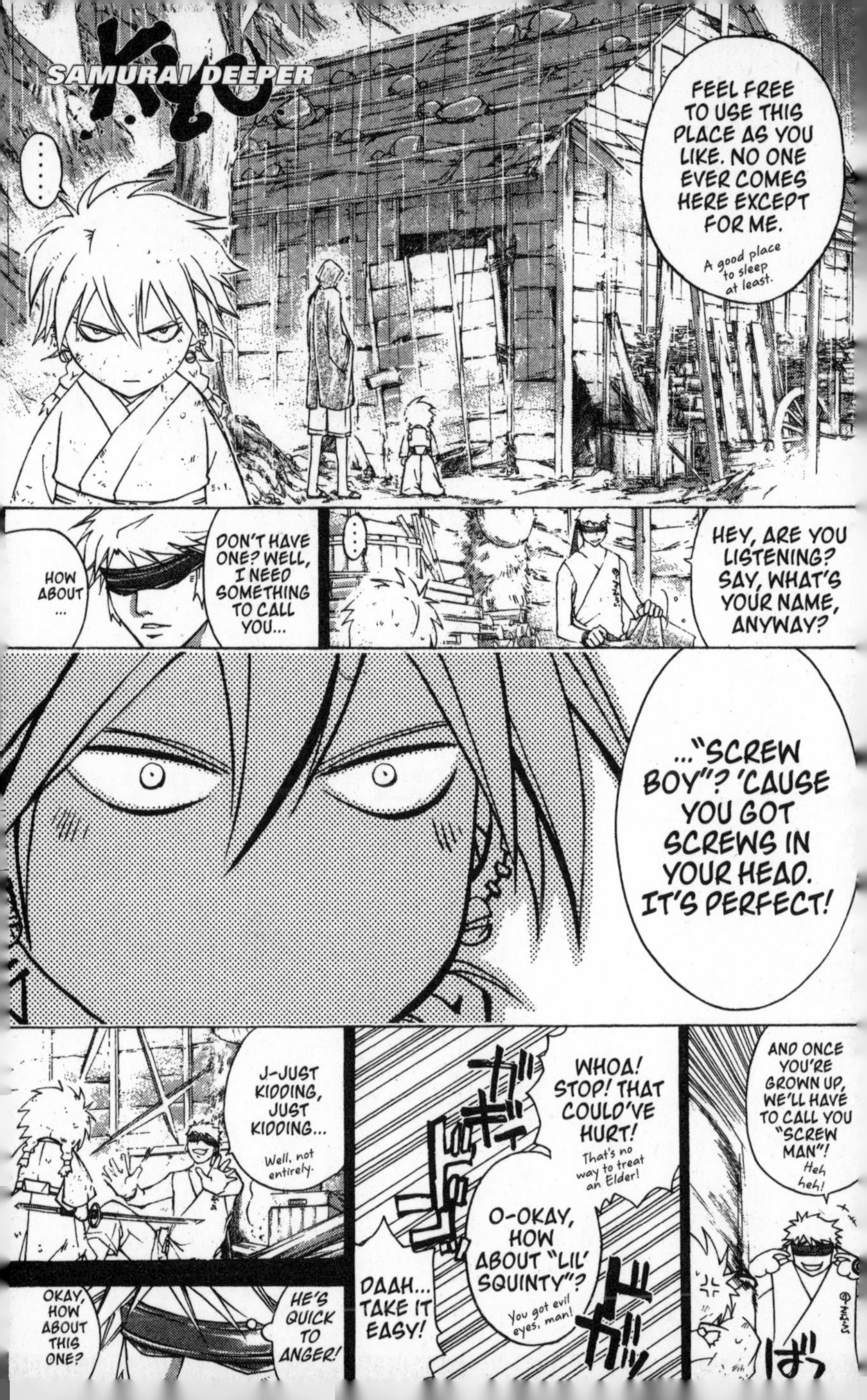
SAMURAI DEEPER KYO
FEEL FREE TO USE THIS PLACE AS YOU LIKE. NO ONE EVER COMES HERE EXCEPT FOR ME.
A good place to sleep at least.
......
HEY, ARE YOU LISTENING? SAY, WHAT'S YOUR NAME, ANYWAY?
...
DON'T HAVE ONE? WELL, I NEED SOMETHING TO CALL YOU...
HOW ABOUT ...
..."SCREW BOY"? 'CAUSE YOU GOT SCREWS IN YOUR HEAD. IT'S PERFECT!
AND ONCE YOU'RE GROWN UP, WE'LL HAVE TO CALL YOU "SCREW MAN"!
Heh heh!
ぱっ
WHOA! STOP! THAT COULD'VE HURT!
That's no way to treat an Elder!
ガギィ
O-OKAY, HOW ABOUT "LIL' SQUINTY"?
You got evil eyes, man!
ドガッ
DAAH... TAKE IT EASY!
J-JUST KIDDING, JUST KIDDING...
Well, not entirely.
HE'S QUICK TO ANGER!
OKAY, HOW ABOUT THIS ONE?

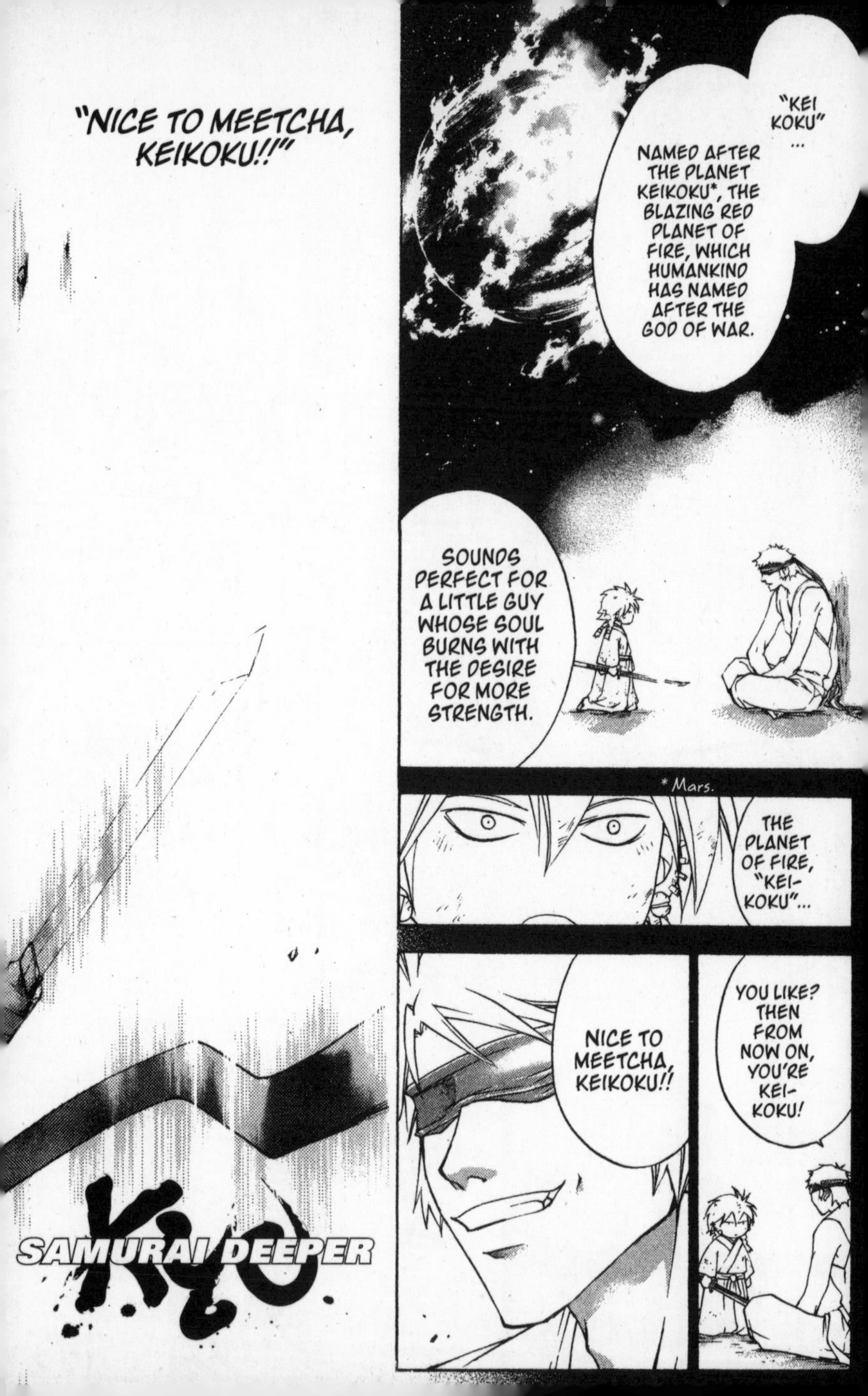
"KEI KOKU" ...
NAMED AFTER THE PLANET KEIKOKU*, THE BLAZING RED PLANET OF FIRE, WHICH HUMANKIND HAS NAMED AFTER THE GOD OF WAR.
SOUNDS PERFECT FOR A LITTLE GUY WHOSE SOUL BURNS WITH THE DESIRE FOR MORE STRENGTH.
* Mars.
THE PLANET OF FIRE, "KEI-KOKU"...
YOU LIKE? THEN FROM NOW ON, YOU'RE KEI-KOKU!
NICE TO MEETCHA, KEIKOKU!!
"NICE TO MEETCHA, KEIKOKU!!"
SAMURAI DEEPER KYO

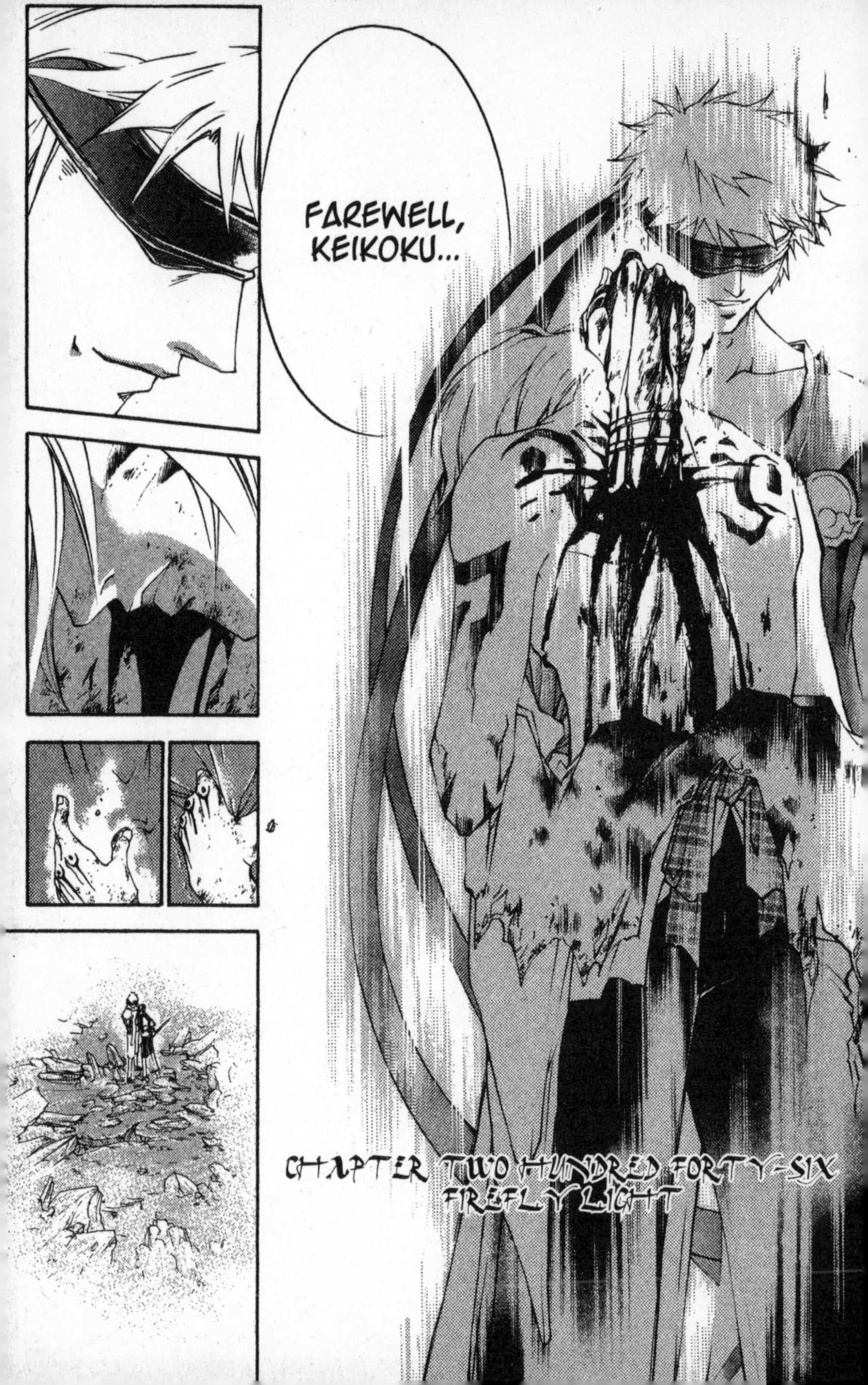
FAREWELL, KEIKOKU...
CHAPTER TWO HUNDRED FORTY-SIX
FIREFLY LIGHT

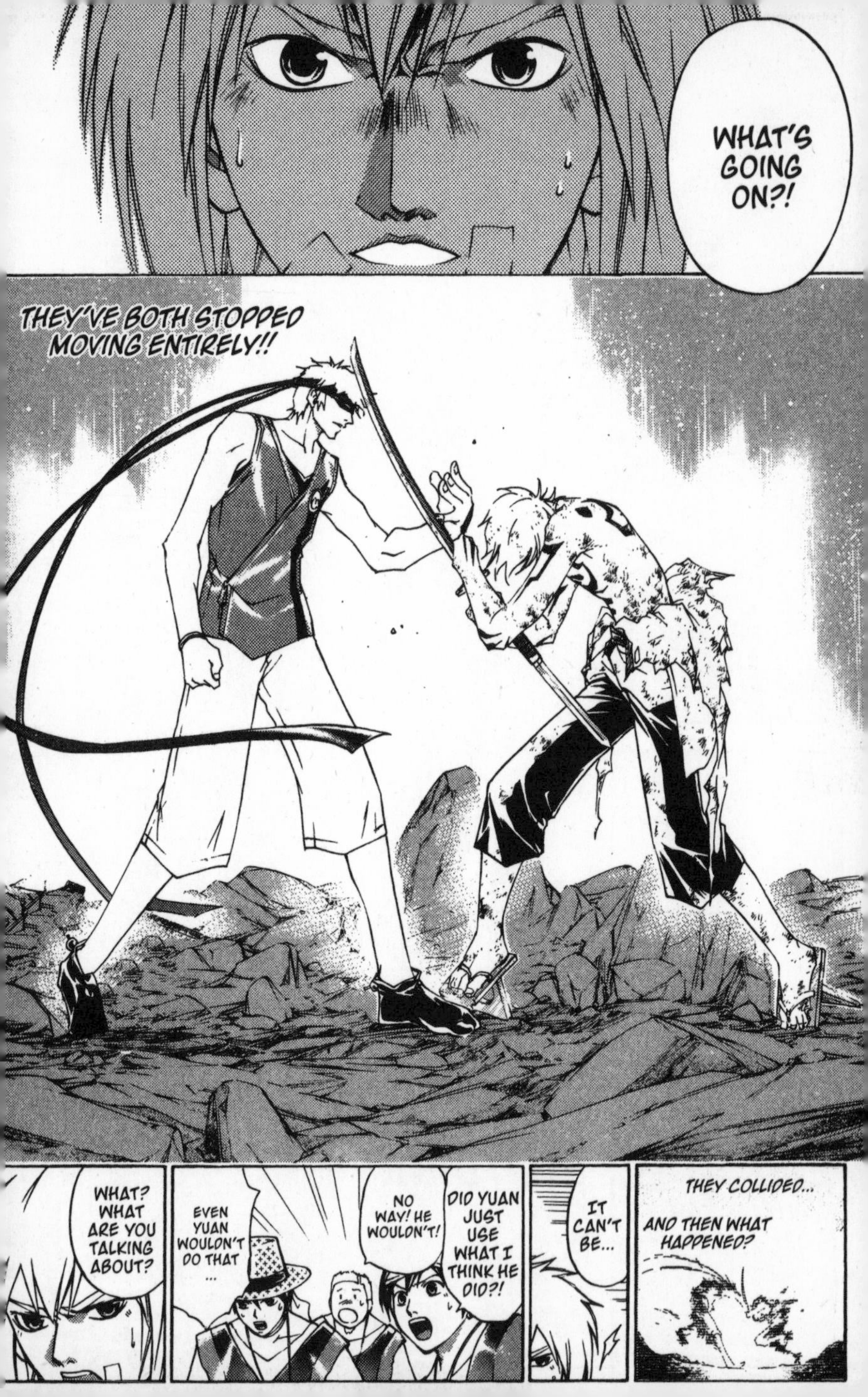
WHAT'S GOING ON?!
THEY'VE BOTH STOPPED MOVING ENTIRELY!!
THEY COLLIDED...
AND THEN WHAT HAPPENED?
IT CAN'T BE...
DID YUAN JUST USE WHAT I THINK HE DID?!
NO WAY! HE WOULDN'T!
EVEN YUAN WOULDN'T DO THAT ...
WHAT? WHAT ARE YOU TALKING ABOUT?

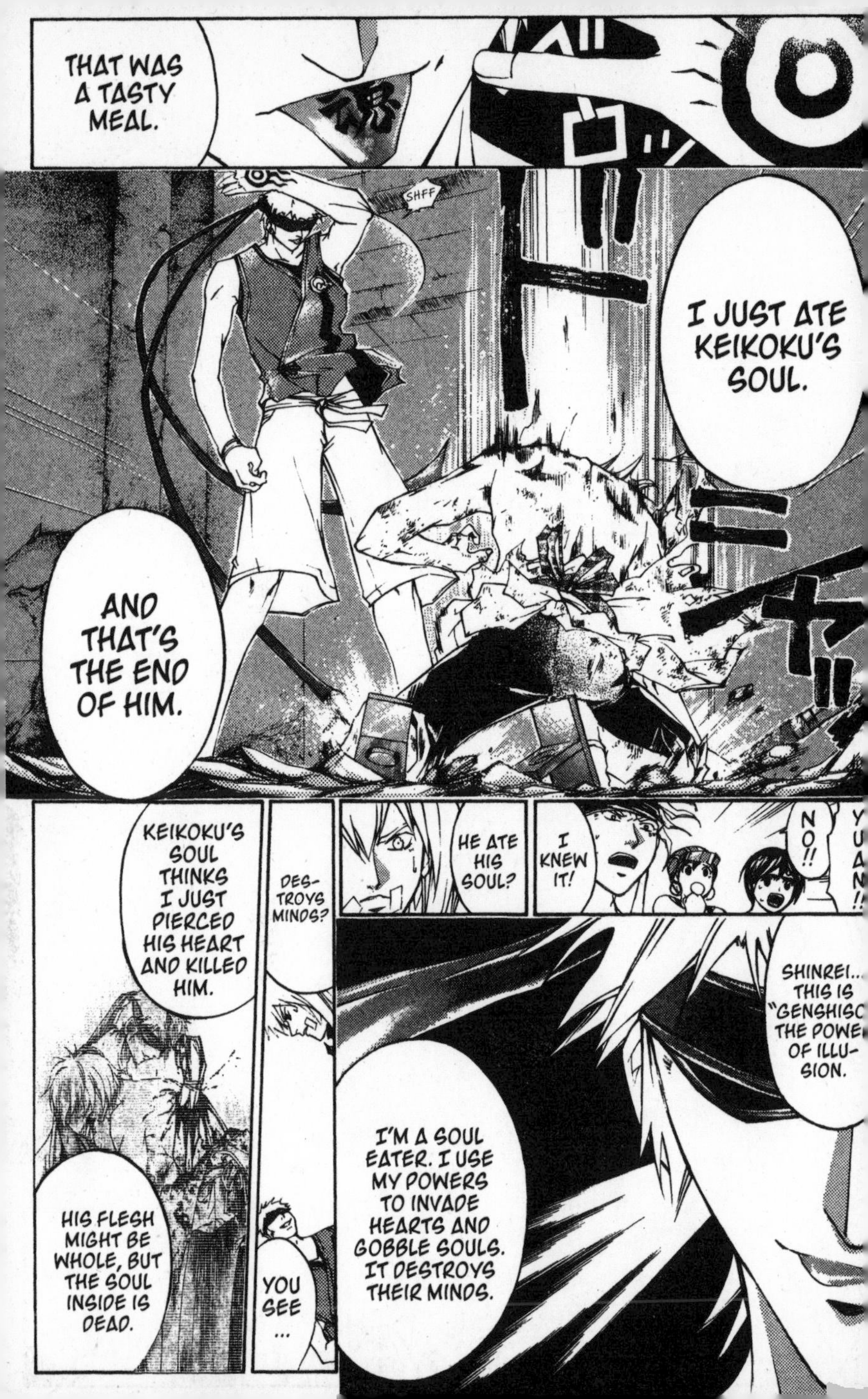
THAT WAS A TASTY MEAL.
I JUST ATE KEIKOKU'S SOUL.
SHFF
AND THAT'S THE END OF HIM.
YUAN!!
NO!!
I KNEW IT!
HE ATE HIS SOUL?
SHINREI... THIS IS "GENSHISO THE POWE OF ILLU-SION.
I'M A SOUL EATER. I USE MY POWERS TO INVADE HEARTS AND GOBBLE SOULS. IT DESTROYS THEIR MINDS.
DES-TROYS MINDS?
YOU SEE ...
KEIKOKU'S SOUL THINKS I JUST PIERCED HIS HEART AND KILLED HIM.
HIS FLESH MIGHT BE WHOLE, BUT THE SOUL INSIDE IS DEAD.

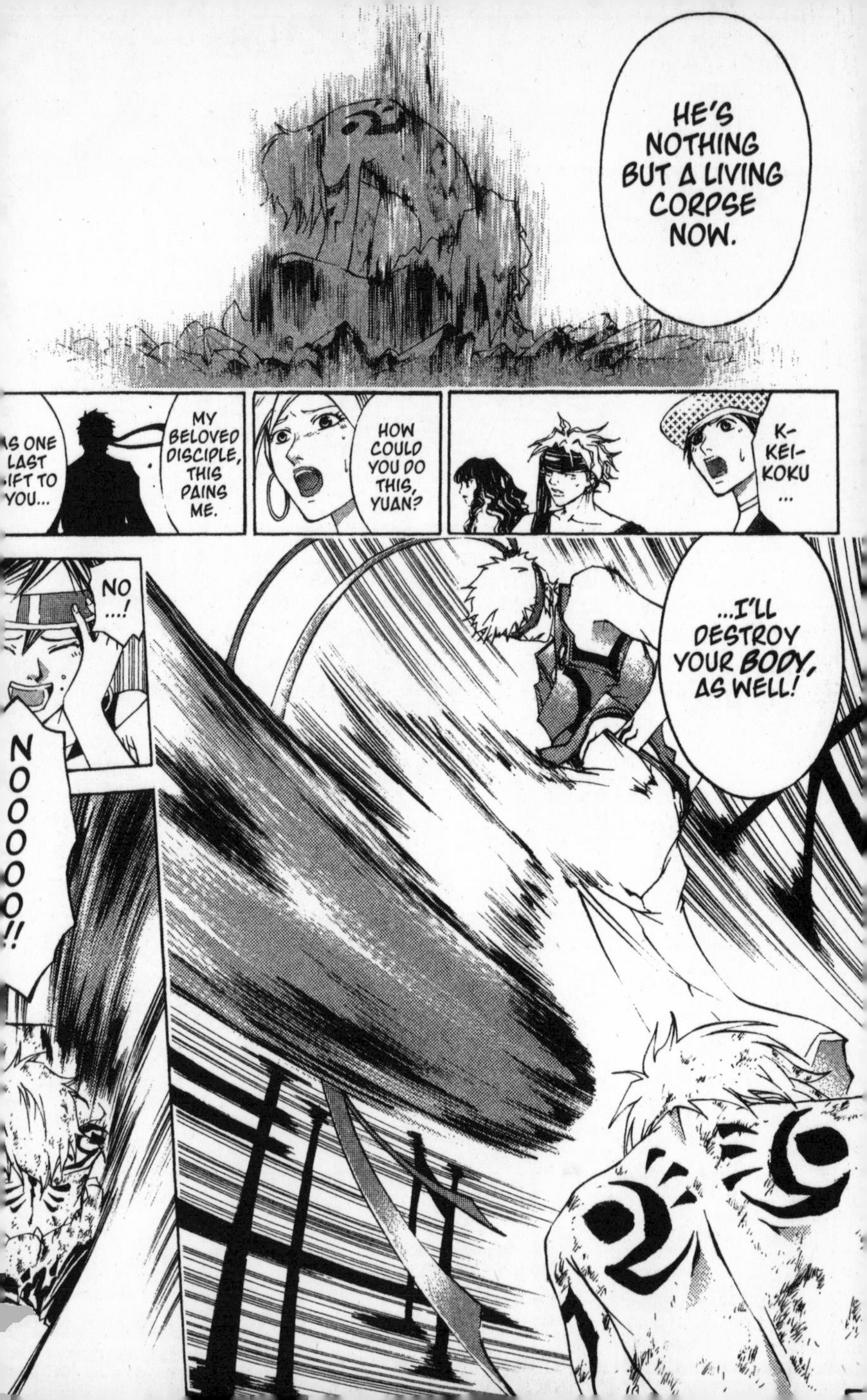
HE'S NOTHING BUT A LIVING CORPSE NOW.
K-KEI-KOKU...
HOW COULD YOU DO THIS, YUAN?
MY BELOVED DISCIPLE, THIS PAINS ME.
S ONE LAST IFT TO YOU...
...I'LL DESTROY YOUR BODY, AS WELL!
NO...!
NOOOOOOO!!

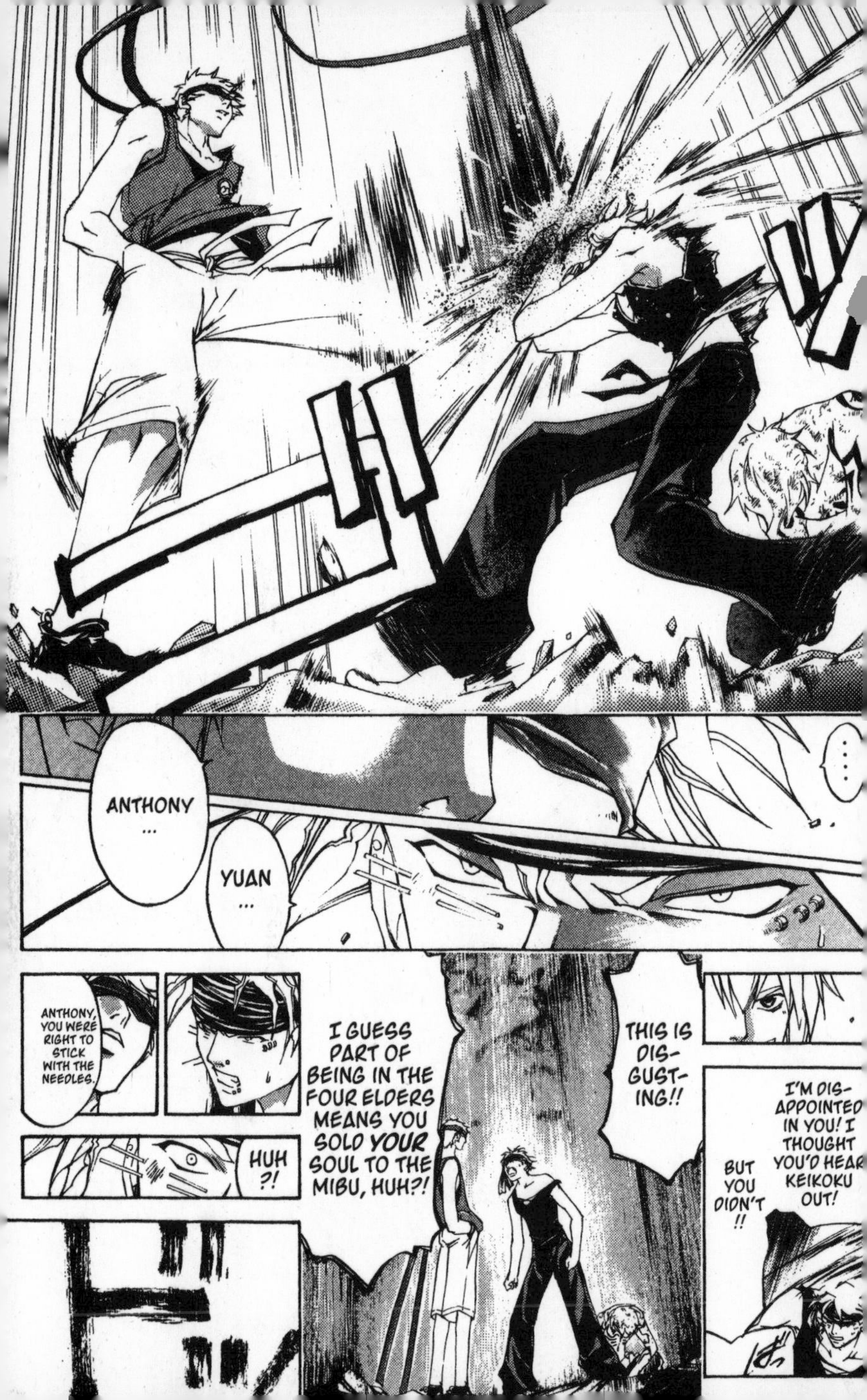
....
ANTHONY ...
YUAN ...
I'M DIS-APPOINTED IN YOU! I THOUGHT YOU'D HEAR KEIKOKU OUT!
BUT YOU DIDN'T !!
THIS IS DIS-GUST-ING!!
I GUESS PART OF BEING IN THE FOUR ELDERS MEANS YOU SOLD YOUR SOUL TO THE MIBU, HUH?!
ANTHONY, YOU WERE RIGHT TO STICK WITH THE NEEDLES.
HUH ?!

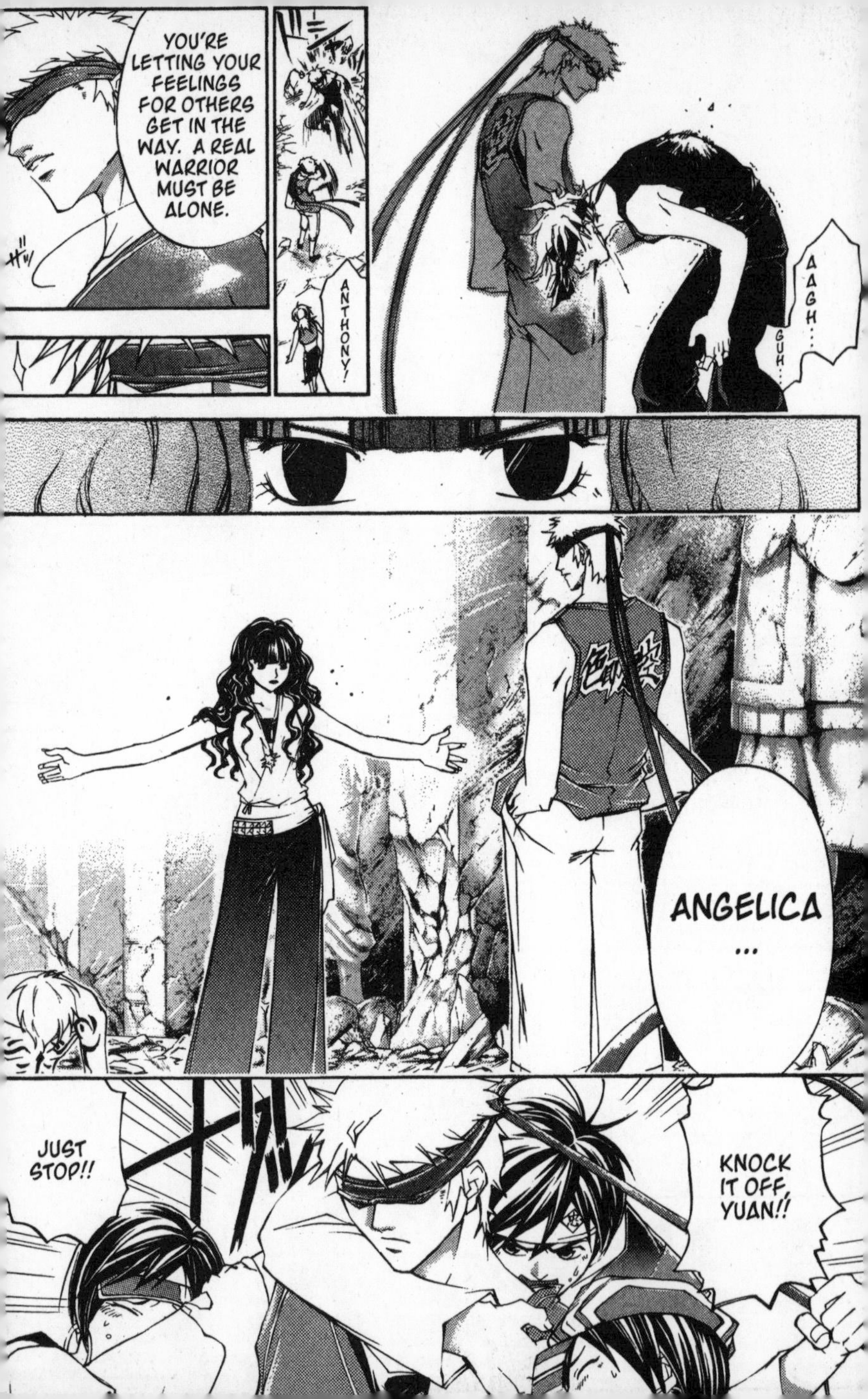
AAGH...
GUH...
ANTHONY!
YOU'RE LETTING YOUR FEELINGS FOR OTHERS GET IN THE WAY. A REAL WARRIOR MUST BE ALONE.
ANGELICA ...
KNOCK IT OFF, YUAN!!
JUST STOP!!

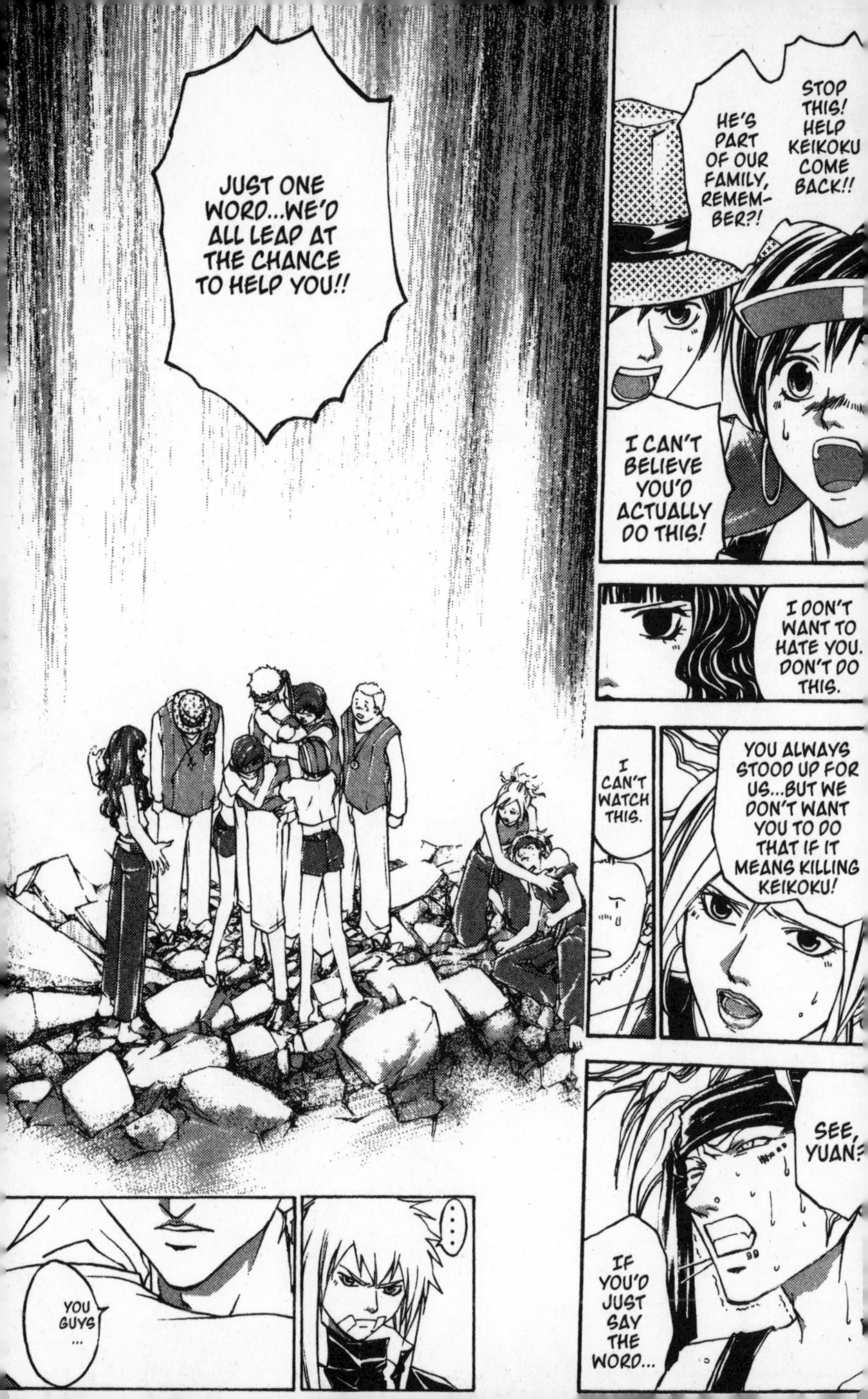
STOP THIS! HELP KEIKOKU COME BACK!!
HE'S PART OF OUR FAMILY, REMEMBER?!
I CAN'T BELIEVE YOU'D ACTUALLY DO THIS!
I DON'T WANT TO HATE YOU. DON'T DO THIS.
YOU ALWAYS STOOD UP FOR US...BUT WE DON'T WANT YOU TO DO THAT IF IT MEANS KILLING KEIKOKU!
I CAN'T WATCH THIS.
SEE, YUAN?
IF YOU'D JUST SAY THE WORD...
JUST ONE WORD...WE'D ALL LEAP AT THE CHANCE TO HELP YOU!!
...
YOU GUYS ...

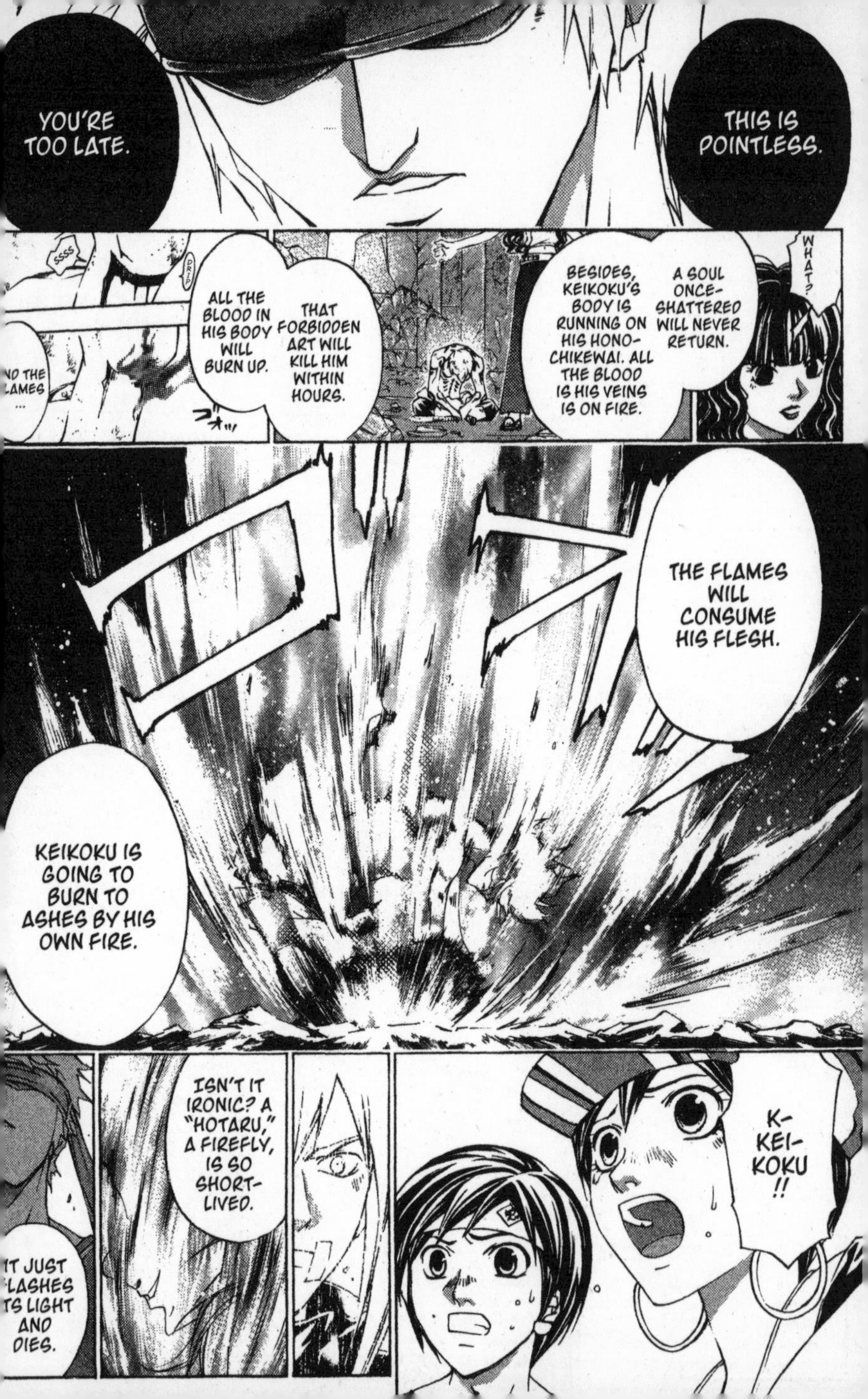
THIS IS POINTLESS.
YOU'RE TOO LATE.
WHAT?
A SOUL ONCE-SHATTERED WILL NEVER RETURN.
BESIDES, KEIKOKU'S BODY IS RUNNING ON HIS HONO-CHIKEWAI. ALL THE BLOOD IS HIS VEINS IS ON FIRE.
THAT FORBIDDEN ART WILL KILL HIM WITHIN HOURS.
ALL THE BLOOD IN HIS BODY WILL BURN UP.
DRIP
SSSS
THE FLAMES WILL CONSUME HIS FLESH.
KEIKOKU IS GOING TO BURN TO ASHES BY HIS OWN FIRE.
K-KEI-KOKU!!
ISN'T IT IRONIC? A "HOTARU," A FIREFLY, IS SO SHORT-LIVED.
IT JUST FLASHES ITS LIGHT AND DIES.

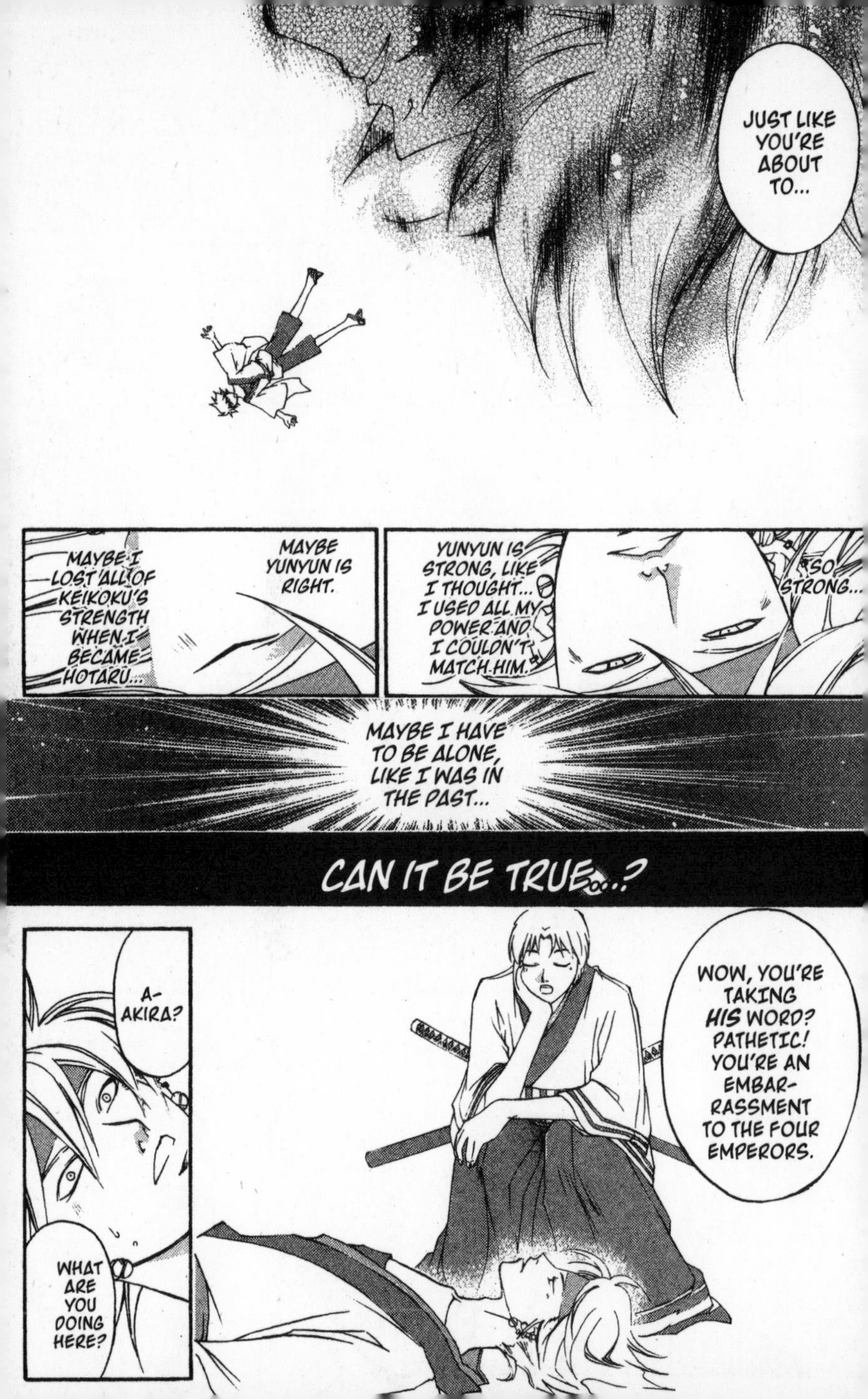
JUST LIKE YOU'RE ABOUT TO...
SO STRONG...
YUNYUN IS STRONG, LIKE I THOUGHT... I USED ALL MY POWER AND I COULDN'T MATCH HIM.
MAYBE YUNYUN IS RIGHT.
MAYBE I LOST ALL OF KEIKOKU'S STRENGTH WHEN I BECAME HOTARU...
MAYBE I HAVE TO BE ALONE, LIKE I WAS IN THE PAST...
CAN IT BE TRUE...?
WOW, YOU'RE TAKING HIS WORD? PATHETIC! YOU'RE AN EMBAR-RASSMENT TO THE FOUR EMPERORS.
A-AKIRA?
WHAT ARE YOU DOING HERE?

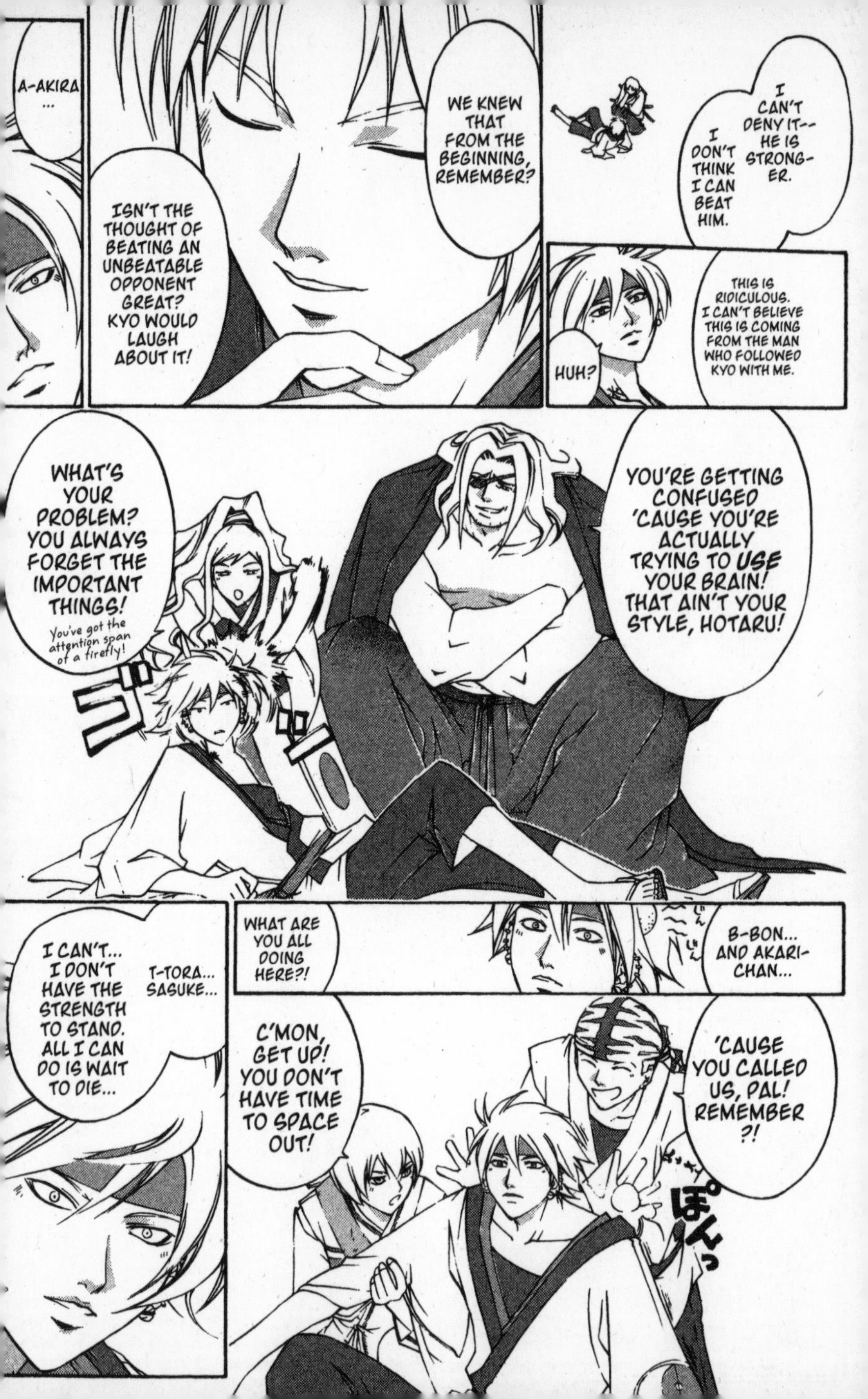
I CAN'T DENY IT-- HE IS STRONGER.
I DON'T THINK I CAN BEAT HIM.
THIS IS RIDICULOUS. I CAN'T BELIEVE THIS IS COMING FROM THE MAN WHO FOLLOWED KYO WITH ME.
HUH?
WE KNEW THAT FROM THE BEGINNING, REMEMBER?
ISN'T THE THOUGHT OF BEATING AN UNBEATABLE OPPONENT GREAT? KYO WOULD LAUGH ABOUT IT!
A-AKIRA...
YOU'RE GETTING CONFUSED 'CAUSE YOU'RE ACTUALLY TRYING TO USE YOUR BRAIN! THAT AIN'T YOUR STYLE, HOTARU!
WHAT'S YOUR PROBLEM? YOU ALWAYS FORGET THE IMPORTANT THINGS!
You've got the attention span of a firefly!
B-BON... AND AKARI-CHAN...
WHAT ARE YOU ALL DOING HERE?!
'CAUSE YOU CALLED US, PAL! REMEMBER?!
ぽんっ
C'MON, GET UP! YOU DON'T HAVE TIME TO SPACE OUT!
T-TORA... SASUKE...
I CAN'T... I DON'T HAVE THE STRENGTH TO STAND. ALL I CAN DO IS WAIT TO DIE...

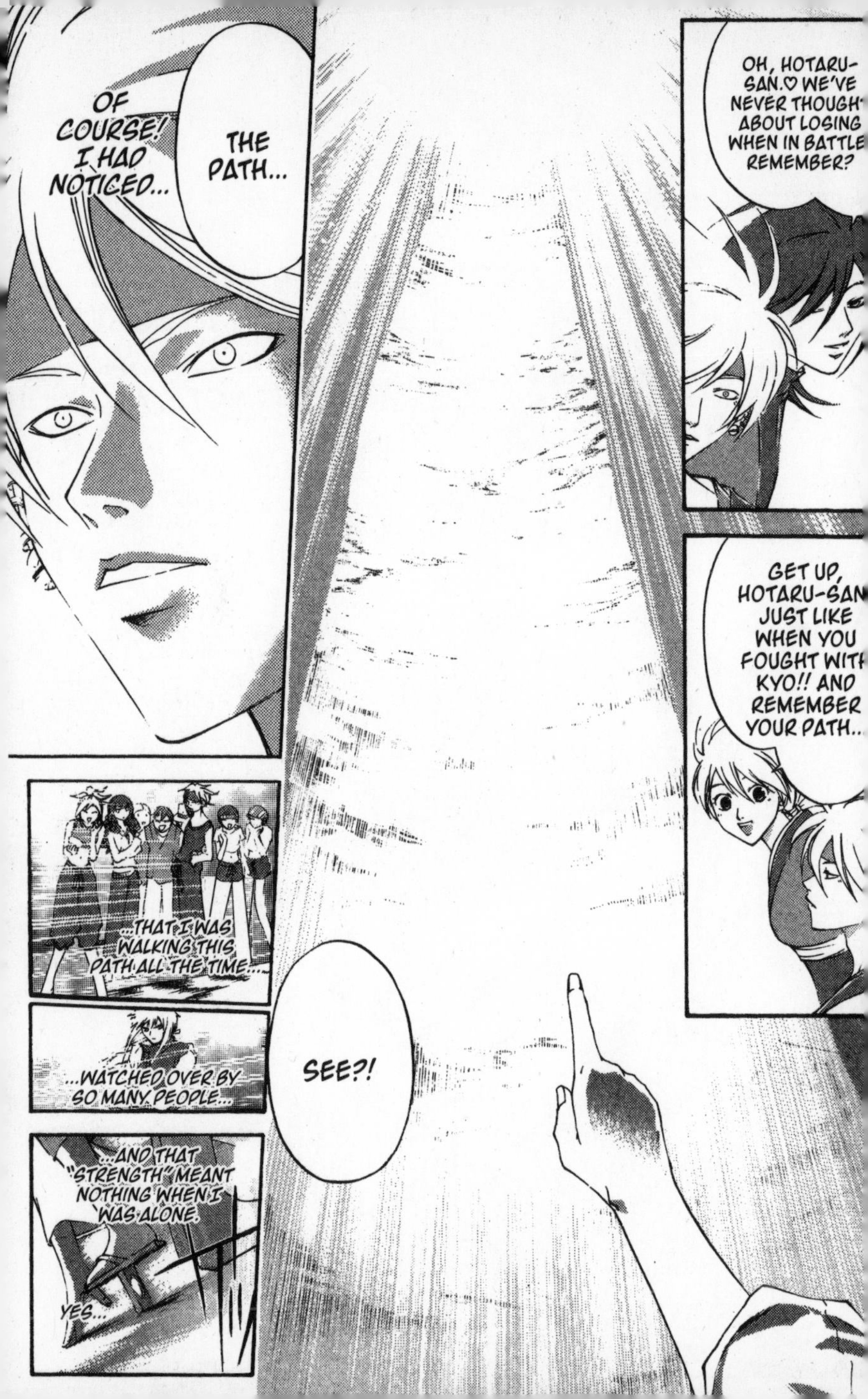
OH, HOTARU-SAN.♡ WE'VE NEVER THOUGH- ABOUT LOSING WHEN IN BATTLE REMEMBER?
GET UP, HOTARU-SAN JUST LIKE WHEN YOU FOUGHT WITH KYO!! AND REMEMBER YOUR PATH...
SEE?!
THE PATH...
OF COURSE! I HAD NOTICED...
...THAT I WAS WALKING THIS PATH ALL THE TIME...
...WATCHED OVER BY SO MANY PEOPLE...
...AND THAT "STRENGTH" MEANT NOTHING WHEN I WAS ALONE.
YES...

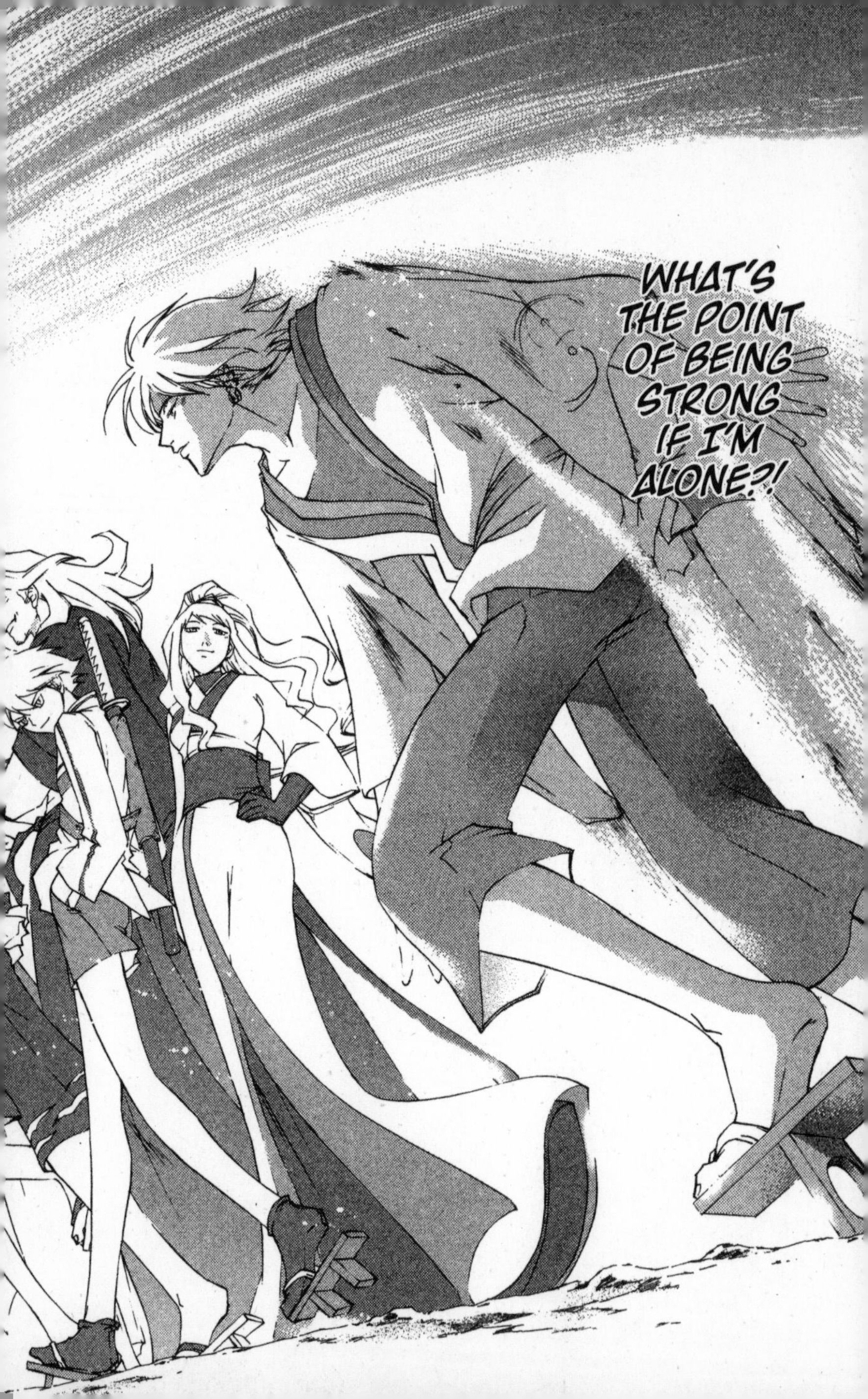
WHAT'S THE POINT OF BEING STRONG IF I'M ALONE?!

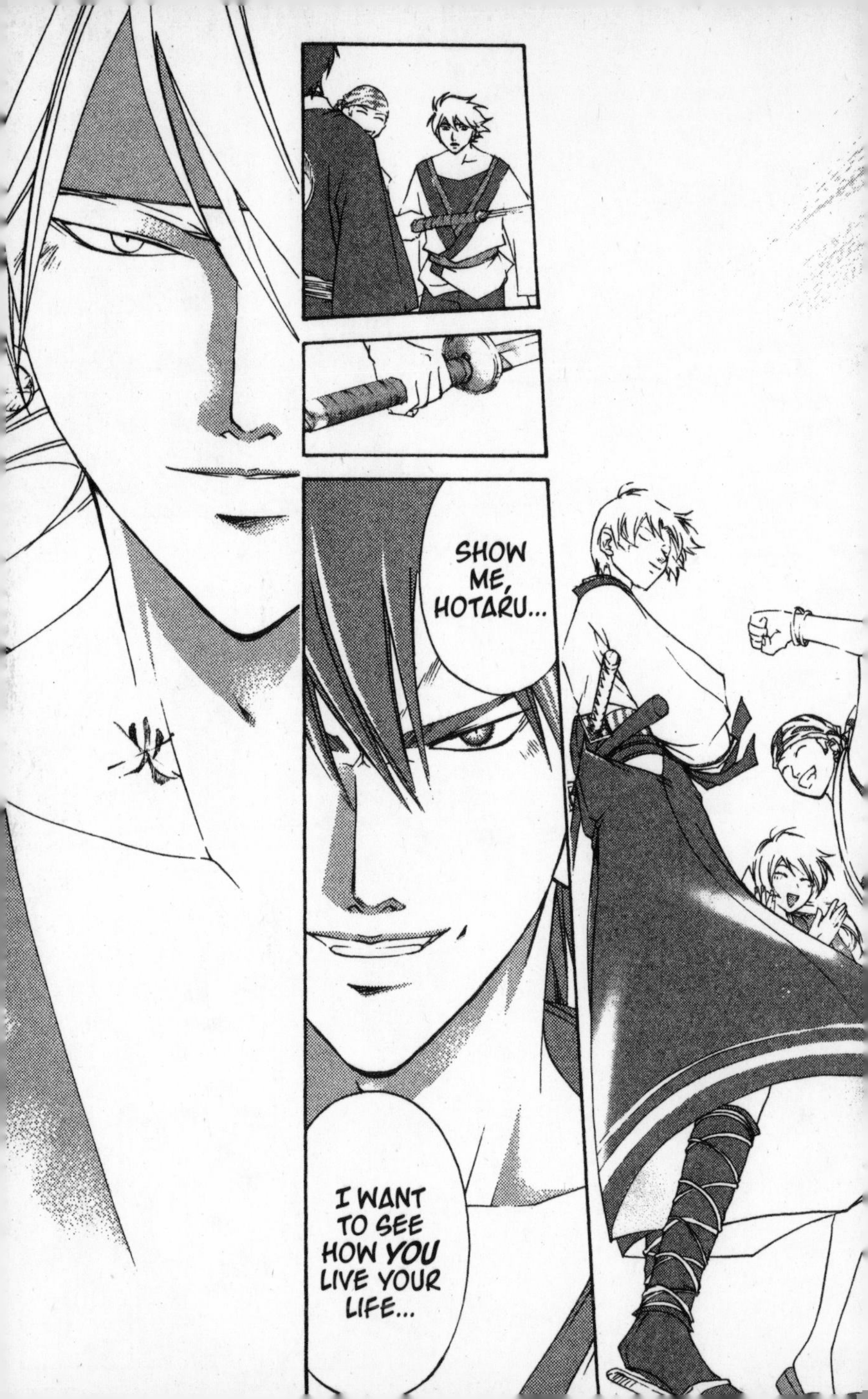
SHOW ME, HOTARU...
I WANT TO SEE HOW *YOU* LIVE YOUR LIFE...

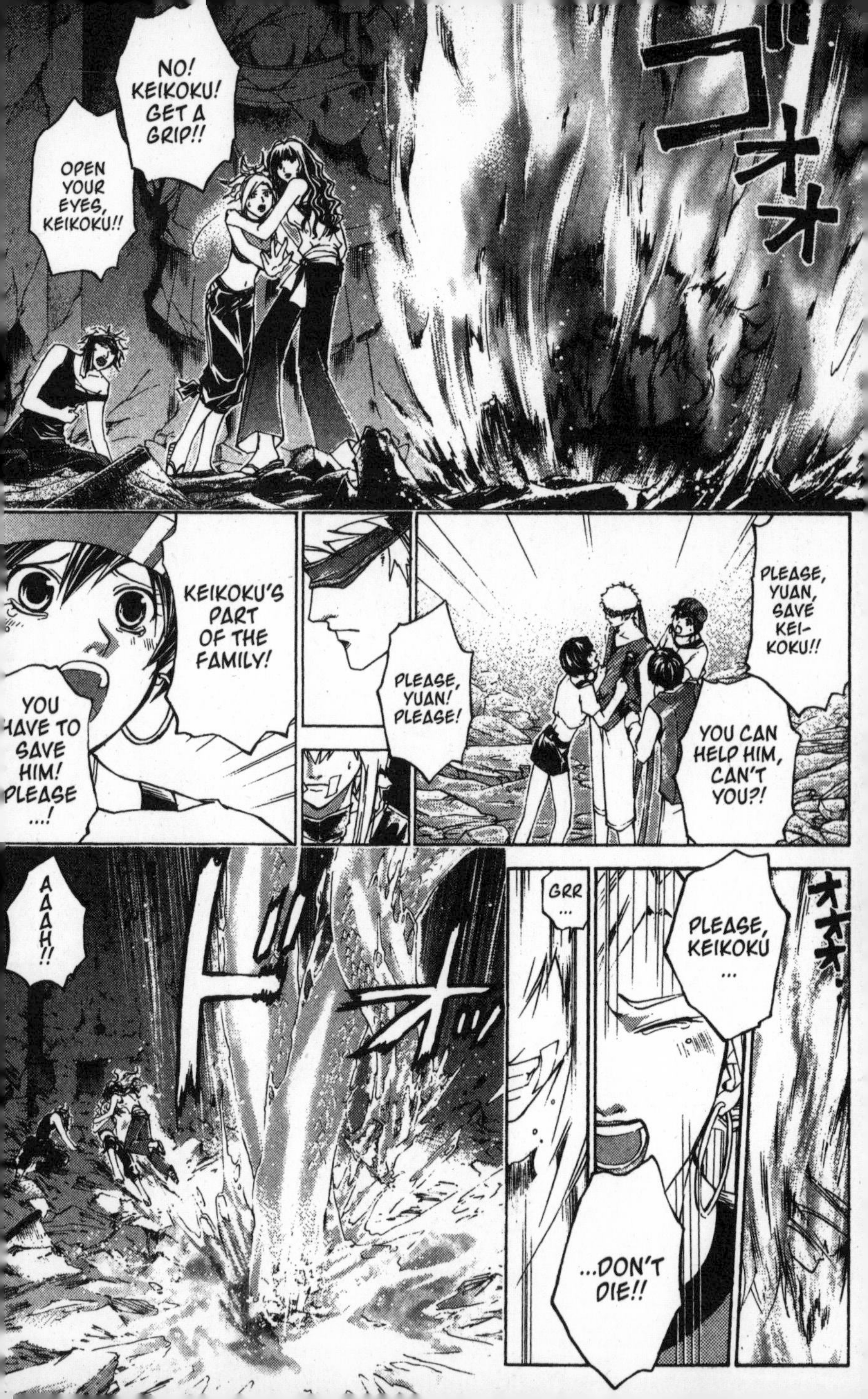
ゴオォ
NO! KEIKOKU! GET A GRIP!!
OPEN YOUR EYES, KEIKOKU!!
PLEASE, YUAN, SAVE KEI-KOKU!!
YOU CAN HELP HIM, CAN'T YOU?!
PLEASE, YUAN! PLEASE!
KEIKOKU'S PART OF THE FAMILY!
YOU HAVE TO SAVE HIM! PLEASE ...!
オォォ
PLEASE, KEIKOKU ...
GRR ...
...DON'T DIE!!
ドオッ
AAAAH!!

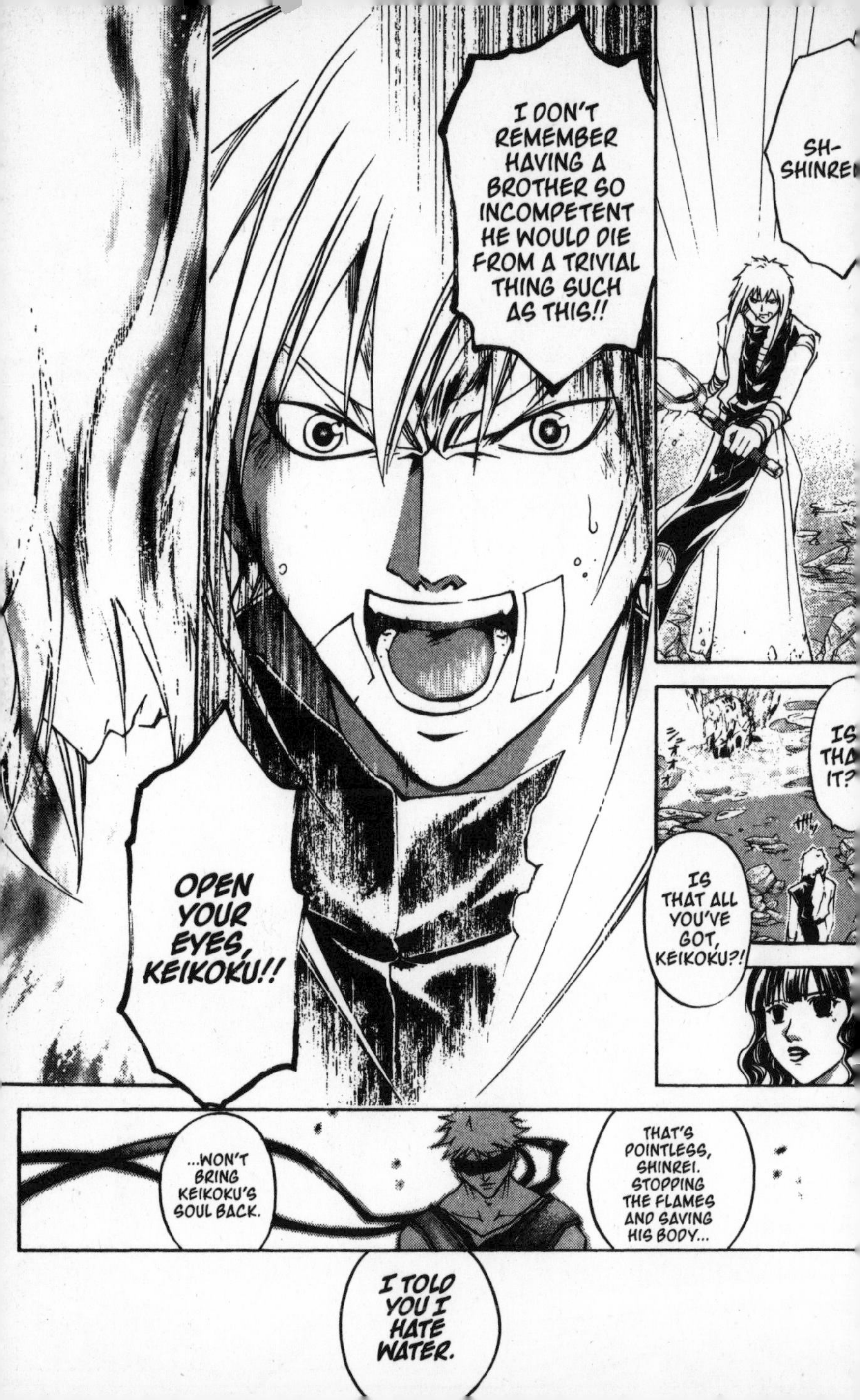
SH- SHINRE
IS THA IT?
IS THAT ALL YOU'VE GOT, KEIKOKU?!
I DON'T REMEMBER HAVING A BROTHER SO INCOMPETENT HE WOULD DIE FROM A TRIVIAL THING SUCH AS THIS!!
OPEN YOUR EYES, KEIKOKU!!
THAT'S POINTLESS, SHINREI. STOPPING THE FLAMES AND SAVING HIS BODY...
...WON'T BRING KEIKOKU'S SOUL BACK.
I TOLD YOU I HATE WATER.

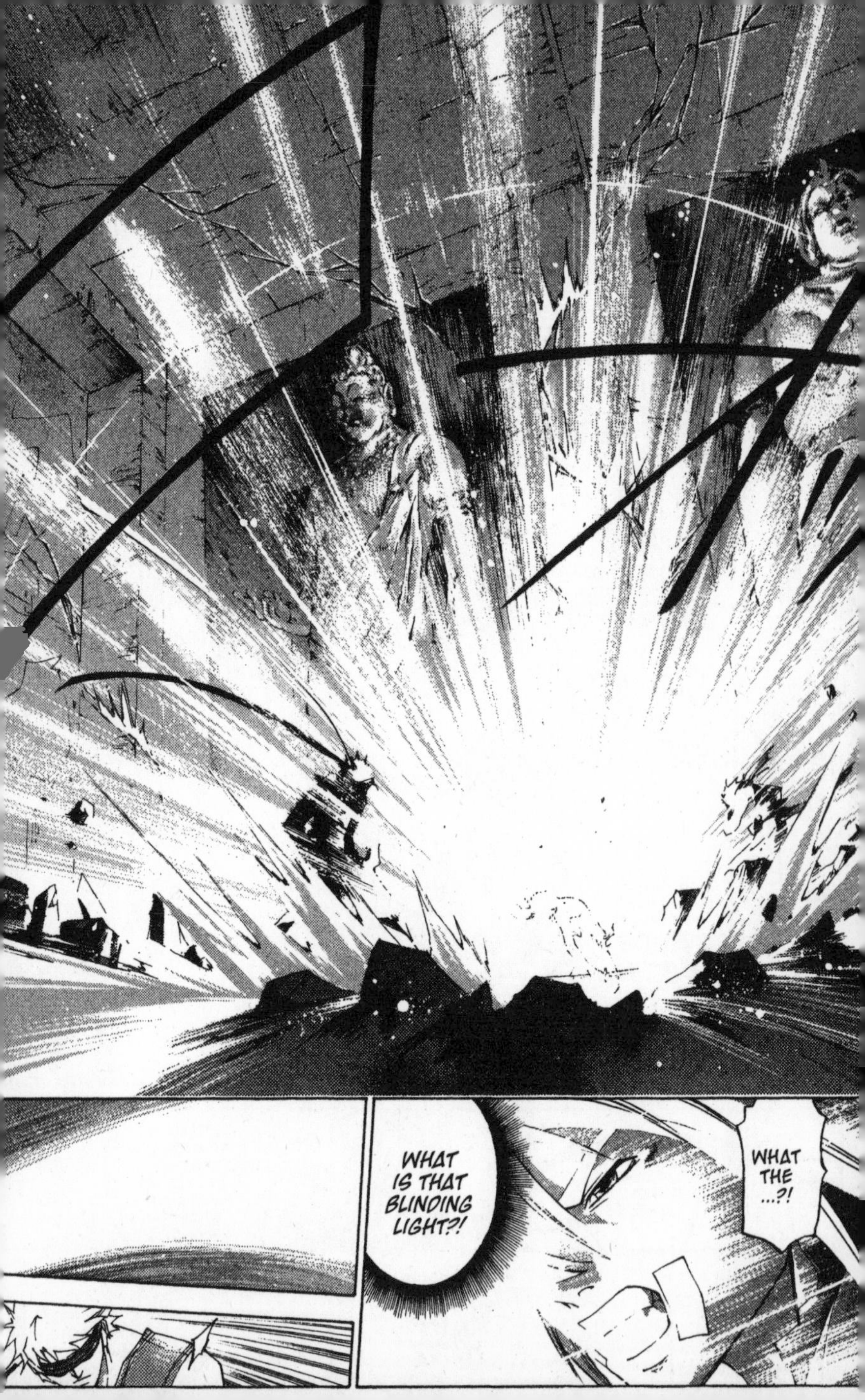
WHAT THE ...?!
WHAT IS THAT BLINDING LIGHT?!

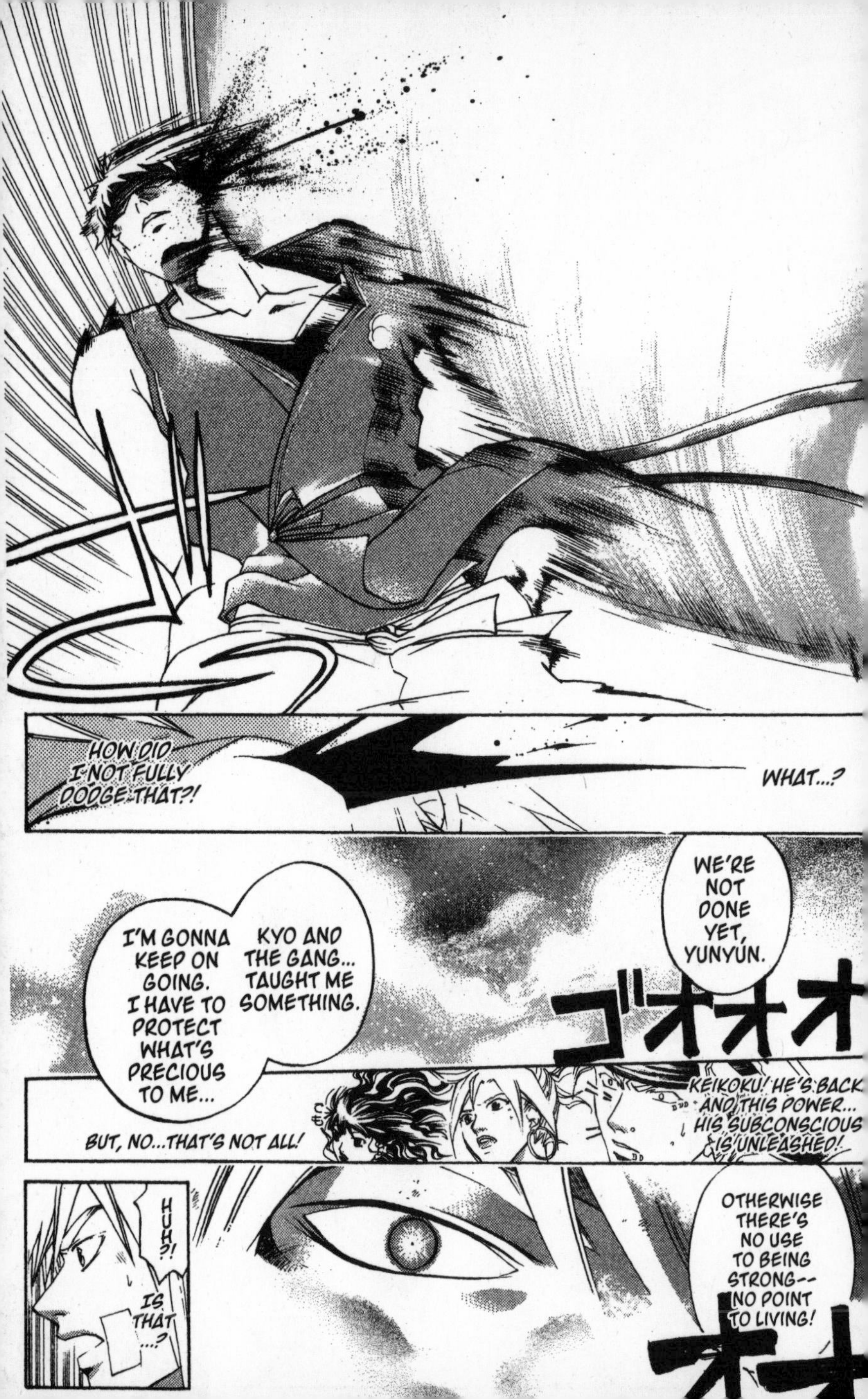
HOW DID I NOT FULLY DODGE THAT?!
WHAT...?
WE'RE NOT DONE YET, YUNYUN.
ゴオオオ
KYO AND THE GANG... TAUGHT ME SOMETHING.
I'M GONNA KEEP ON GOING. I HAVE TO PROTECT WHAT'S PRECIOUS TO ME...
KEIKOKU! HE'S BACK AND THIS POWER... HIS SUBCONSCIOUS IS UNLEASHED!
BUT, NO...THAT'S NOT ALL!
OTHERWISE THERE'S NO USE TO BEING STRONG--NO POINT TO LIVING!
オオ
HUH?!
IS THAT...?

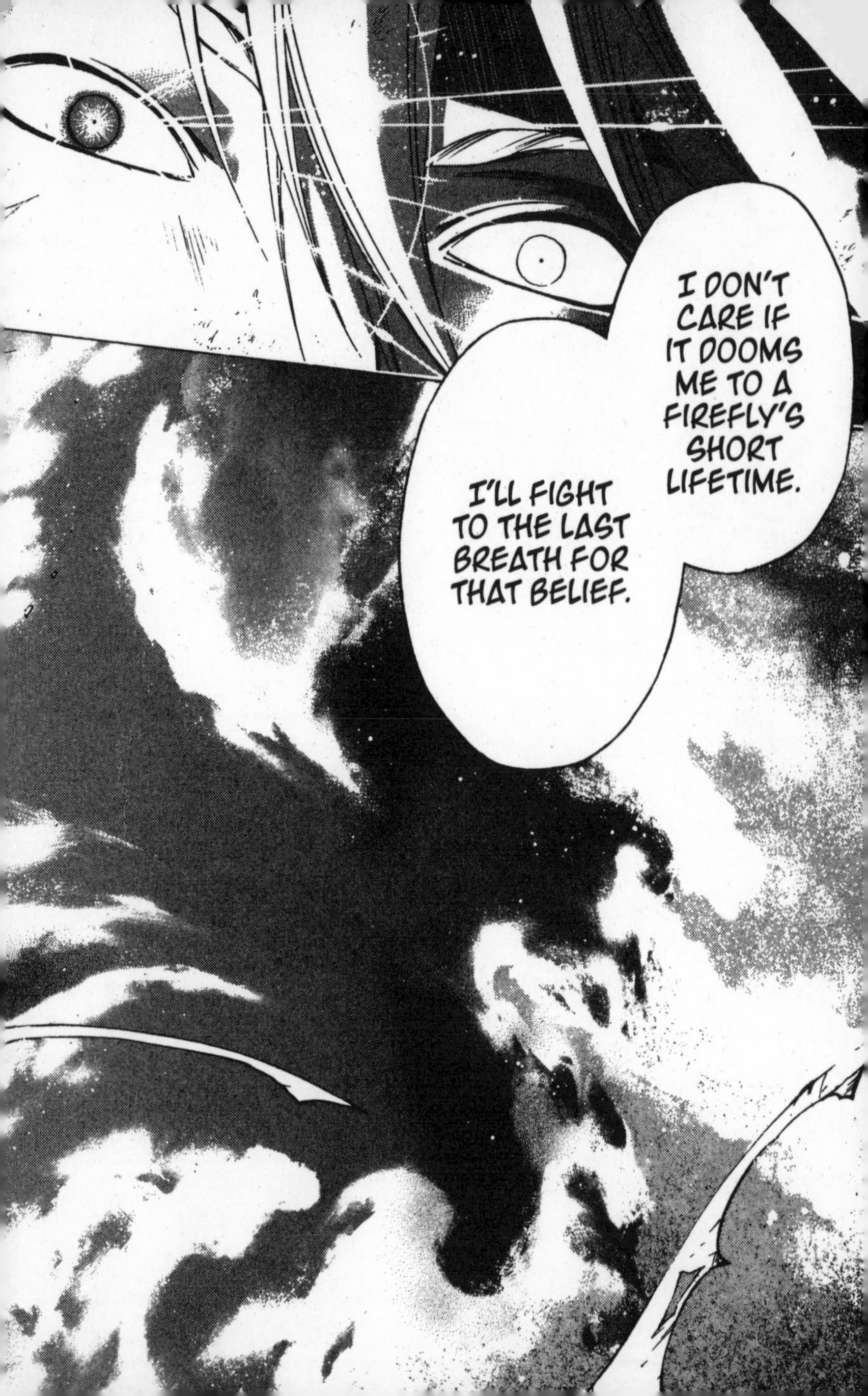
I DON'T CARE IF IT DOOMS ME TO A FIREFLY'S SHORT LIFETIME.
I'LL FIGHT TO THE LAST BREATH FOR THAT BELIEF.

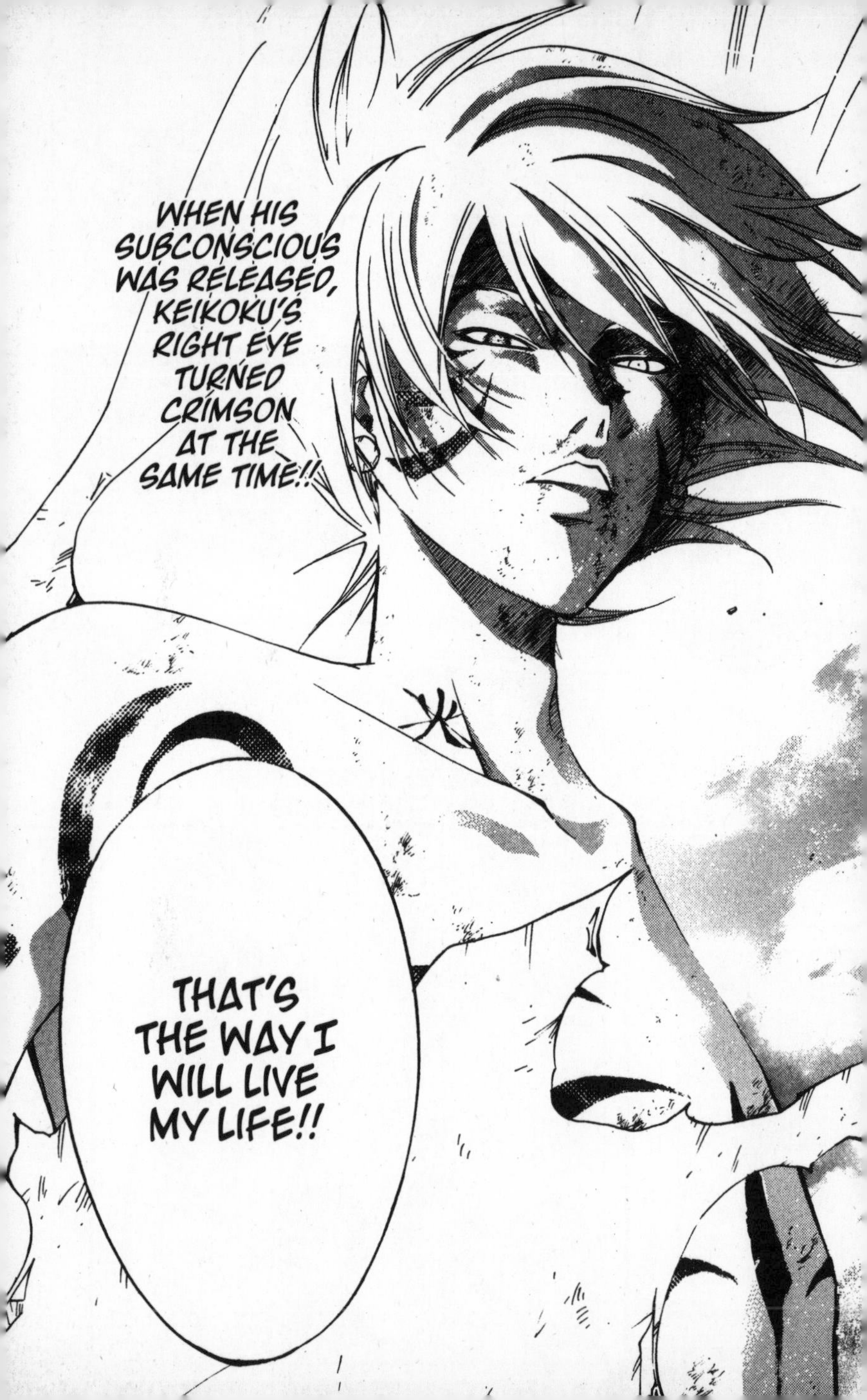
WHEN HIS SUBCONSCIOUS WAS RELEASED, KEIKOKU'S RIGHT EYE TURNED CRIMSON AT THE SAME TIME!!
THAT'S THE WAY I WILL LIVE MY LIFE!!

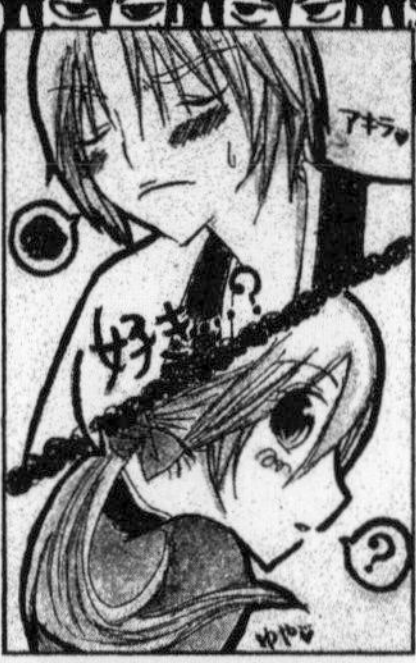
アキラ
好き

[Chiba/Yuu] ⬆
Akira's weakness?

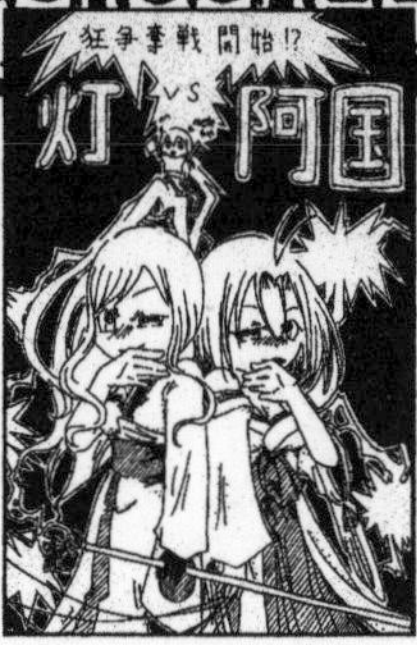
狂争事戦開始!?
灯 VS 阿国

[Fukuoka/Keiko Kendo]⬇
Y-yikes!

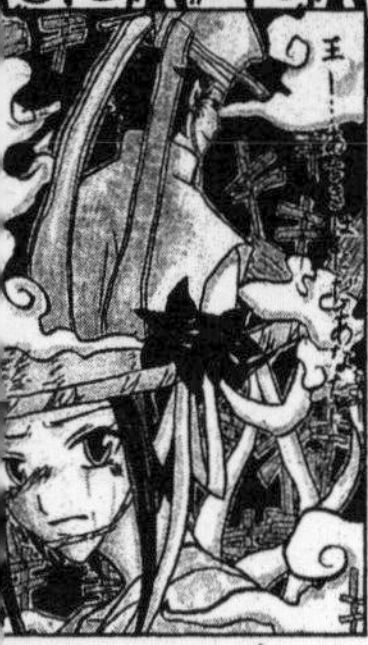

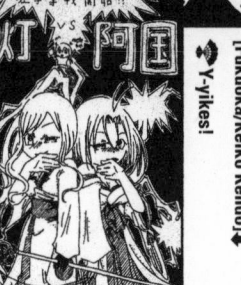

[Nagano/Azumi]⬆
The layout is fantastic!

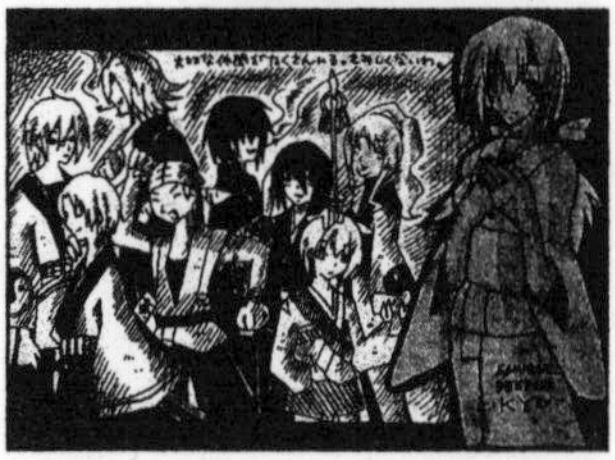

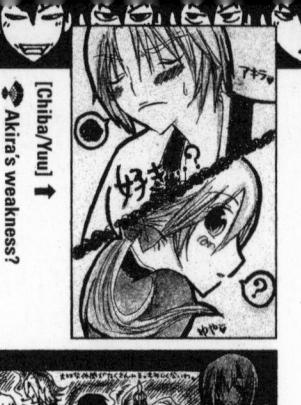

[Aomori/Rei.]➡
I love how Yuya is faded out.

New Years Card Exhibit!

Top of the Crop!

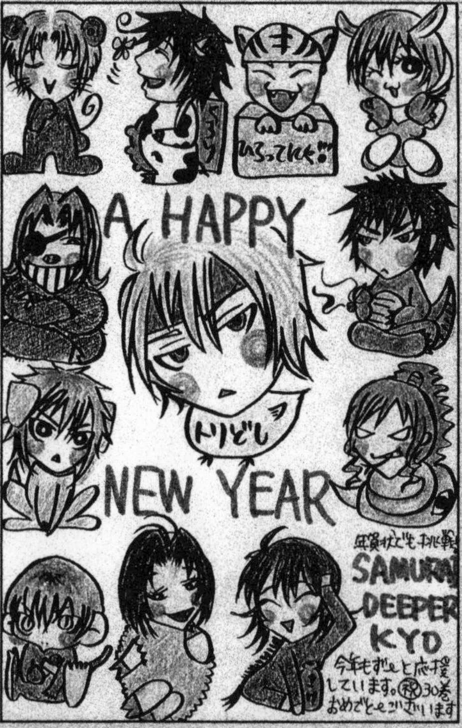
ひろってにゃ!!
A HAPPY
トリどし
NEW YEAR
SAMURAI DEEPER KYO
今年もずっと応援しています。㊗30巻おめでとーございます

[Kagawa/For Real?!] ⬇

What a surprise! Each character fits their Zodiac animal perfectly! Perfect choices!

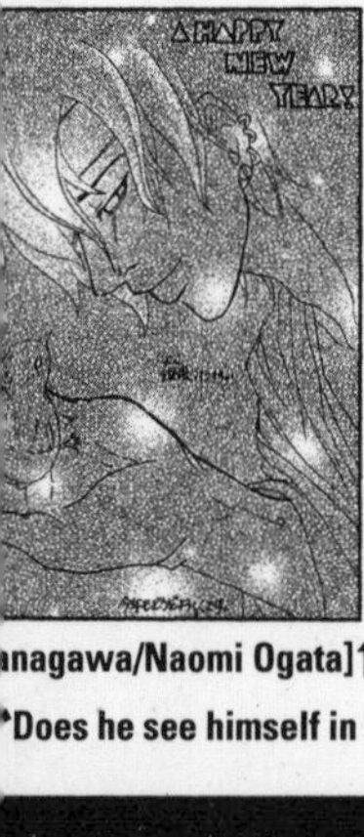
A HAPPY NEW YEAR!

[...anagawa/Naomi Ogata]⬆
Does he see himself in it?

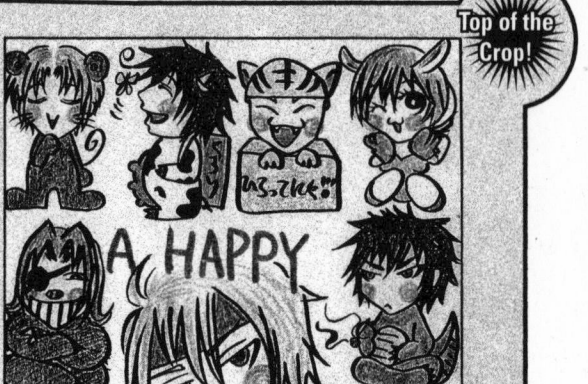

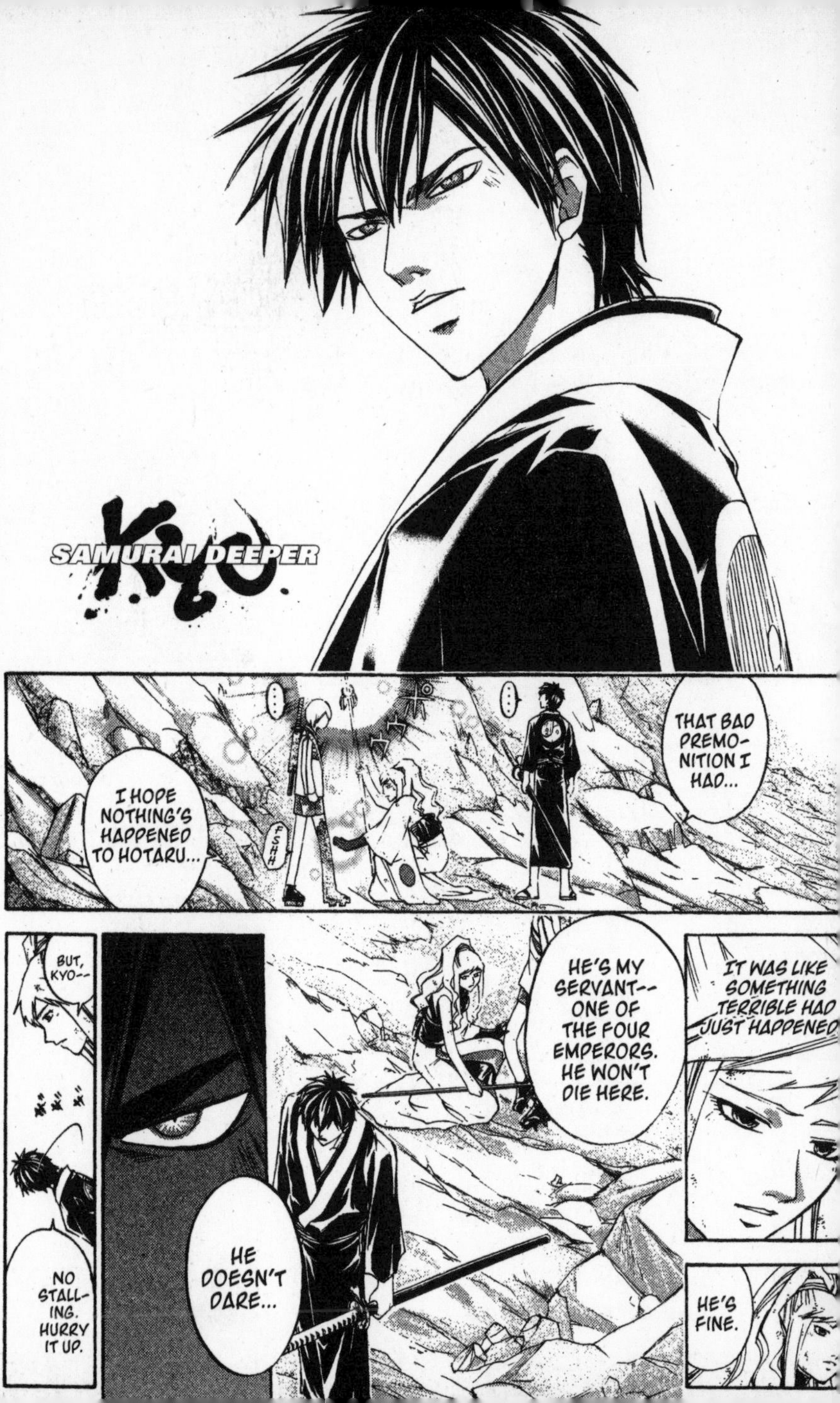
SAMURAI DEEPER KYO
THAT BAD PREMONITION I HAD...
...
...
FSHH
I HOPE NOTHING'S HAPPENED TO HOTARU...
IT WAS LIKE SOMETHING TERRIBLE HAD JUST HAPPENED
HE'S FINE.
HE'S MY SERVANT-- ONE OF THE FOUR EMPERORS. HE WON'T DIE HERE.
HE DOESN'T DARE...
BUT, KYO--
NO STALLING. HURRY IT UP.

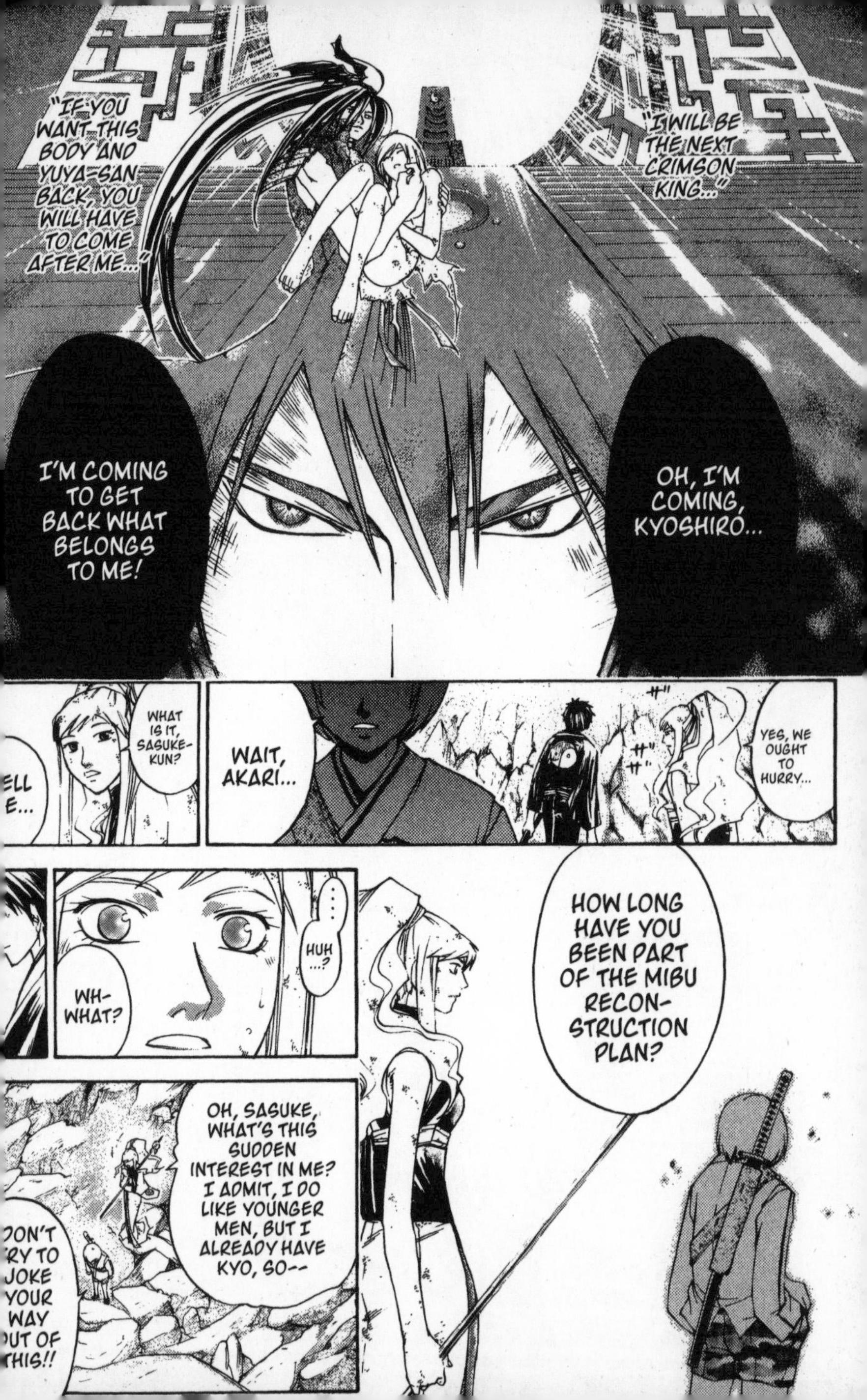
"I WILL BE THE NEXT CRIMSON KING..."
"IF YOU WANT THIS BODY AND YUYA-SAN BACK, YOU WILL HAVE TO COME AFTER ME..."
OH, I'M COMING, KYOSHIRO...
I'M COMING TO GET BACK WHAT BELONGS TO ME!
YES, WE OUGHT TO HURRY...
WAIT, AKARI...
WHAT IS IT, SASUKE-KUN?
HOW LONG HAVE YOU BEEN PART OF THE MIBU RECON-STRUCTION PLAN?
...
HUH ...?
WH-WHAT?
OH, SASUKE, WHAT'S THIS SUDDEN INTEREST IN ME? I ADMIT, I DO LIKE YOUNGER MEN, BUT I ALREADY HAVE KYO, SO--
ON'T RY TO JOKE YOUR WAY UT OF THIS!!

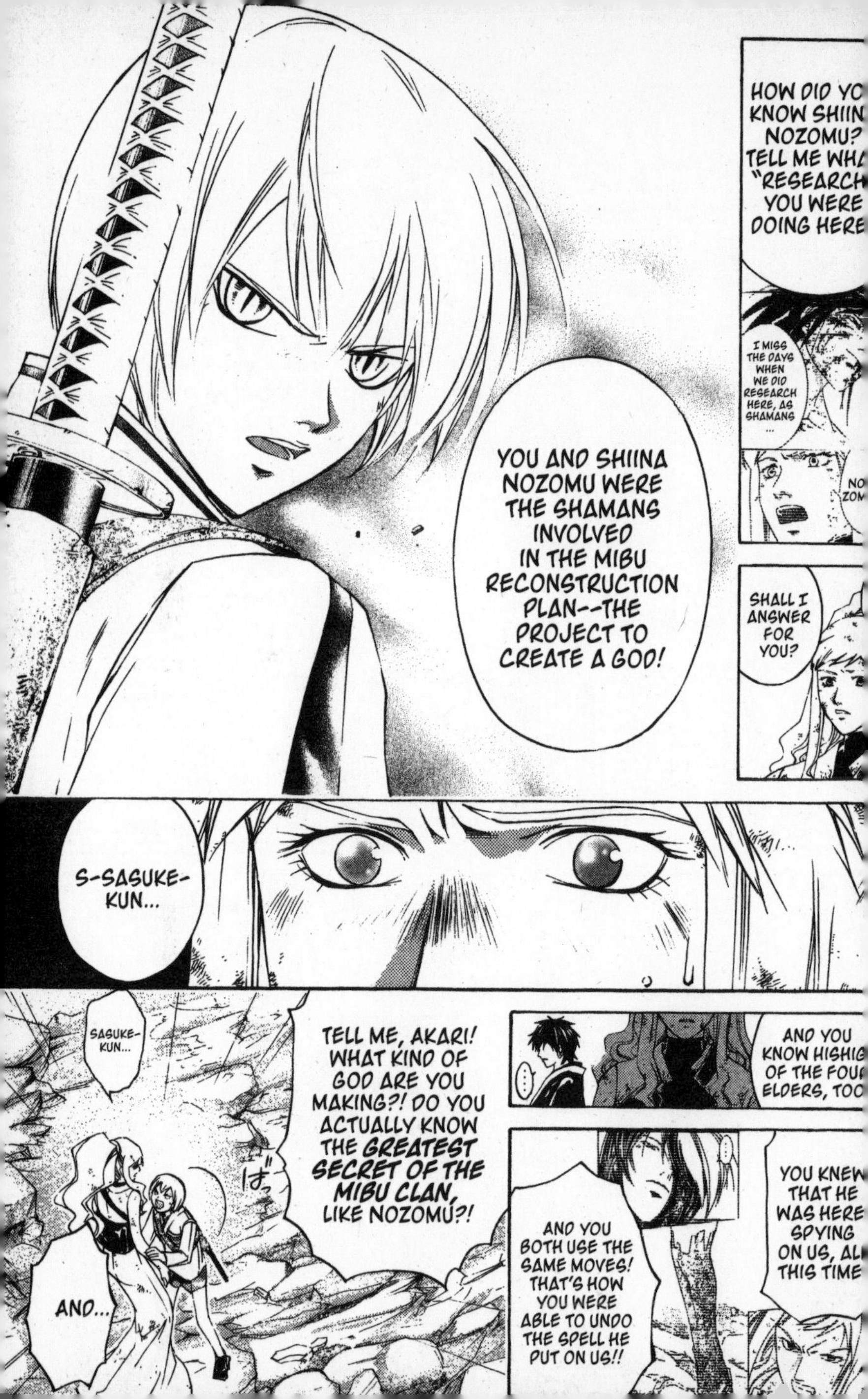
HOW DID YO KNOW SHIIN NOZOMU? TELL ME WHA "RESEARCH YOU WERE DOING HERE
I MISS THE DAYS WHEN WE DID RESEARCH HERE, AS SHAMANS ...
NO ZOM
SHALL I ANSWER FOR YOU?
YOU AND SHIINA NOZOMU WERE THE SHAMANS INVOLVED IN THE MIBU RECONSTRUCTION PLAN--THE PROJECT TO CREATE A GOD!
S-SASUKE-KUN...
AND YOU KNOW HISHIG OF THE FOU ELDERS, TOO
...
YOU KNEW THAT HE WAS HERE SPYING ON US, AL THIS TIME
...
AND YOU BOTH USE THE SAME MOVES! THAT'S HOW YOU WERE ABLE TO UNDO THE SPELL HE PUT ON US!!
TELL ME, AKARI! WHAT KIND OF GOD ARE YOU MAKING?! DO YOU ACTUALLY KNOW THE ***GREATEST SECRET OF THE MIBU CLAN,*** LIKE NOZOMU?!
SASUKE-KUN...
AND...

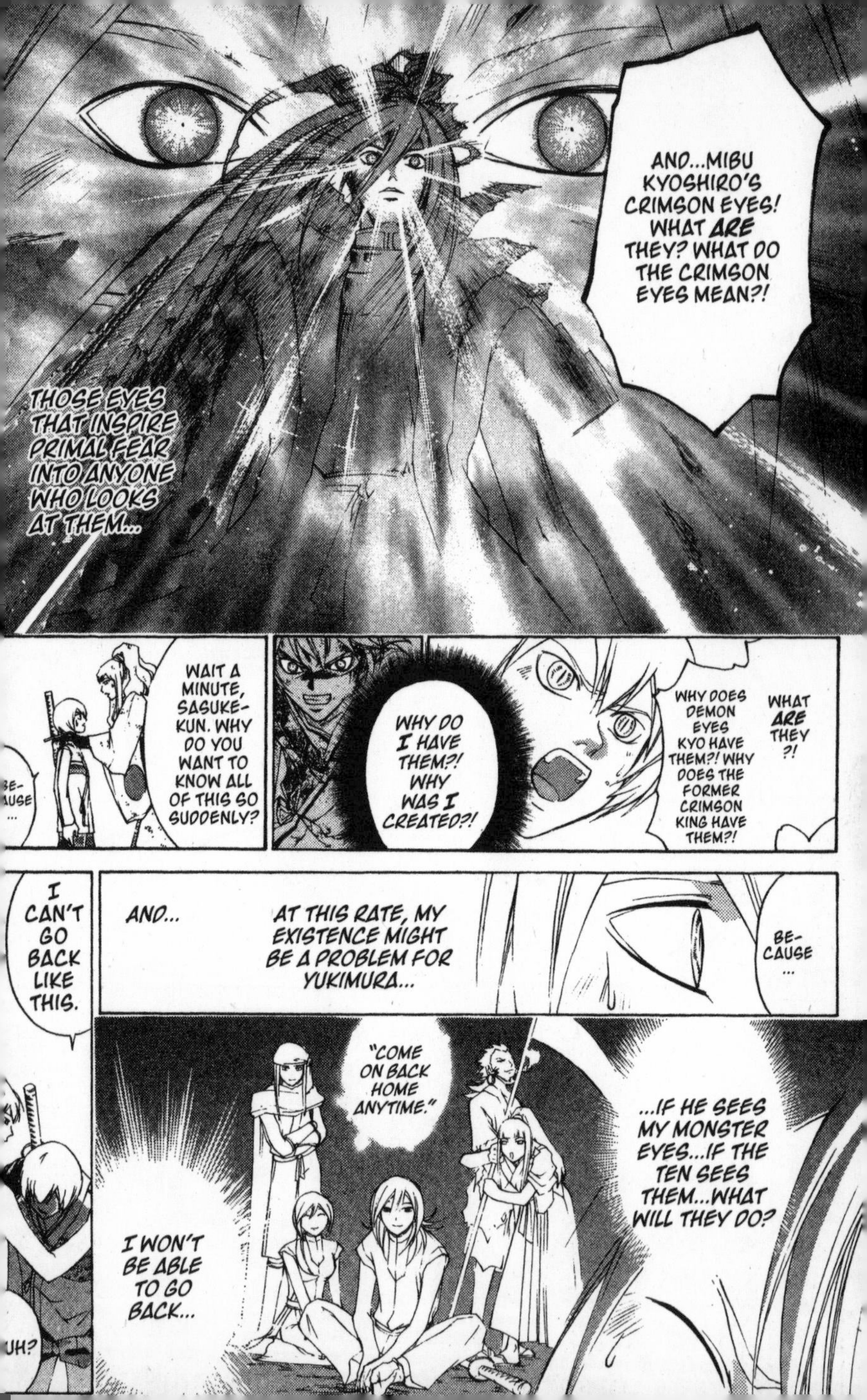
AND...MIBU KYOSHIRO'S CRIMSON EYES! WHAT ARE THEY? WHAT DO THE CRIMSON EYES MEAN?!
THOSE EYES THAT INSPIRE PRIMAL FEAR INTO ANYONE WHO LOOKS AT THEM...
WHAT ARE THEY ?!
WHY DOES DEMON EYES KYO HAVE THEM?! WHY DOES THE FORMER CRIMSON KING HAVE THEM?!
WHY DO I HAVE THEM?! WHY WAS I CREATED?!
WAIT A MINUTE, SASUKE-KUN. WHY DO YOU WANT TO KNOW ALL OF THIS SO SUDDENLY?
BE-CAUSE ...
BE-CAUSE ...
AT THIS RATE, MY EXISTENCE MIGHT BE A PROBLEM FOR YUKIMURA...
AND...
I CAN'T GO BACK LIKE THIS.
...IF HE SEES MY MONSTER EYES...IF THE TEN SEES THEM...WHAT WILL THEY DO?
"COME ON BACK HOME ANYTIME."
I WON'T BE ABLE TO GO BACK...
UH?

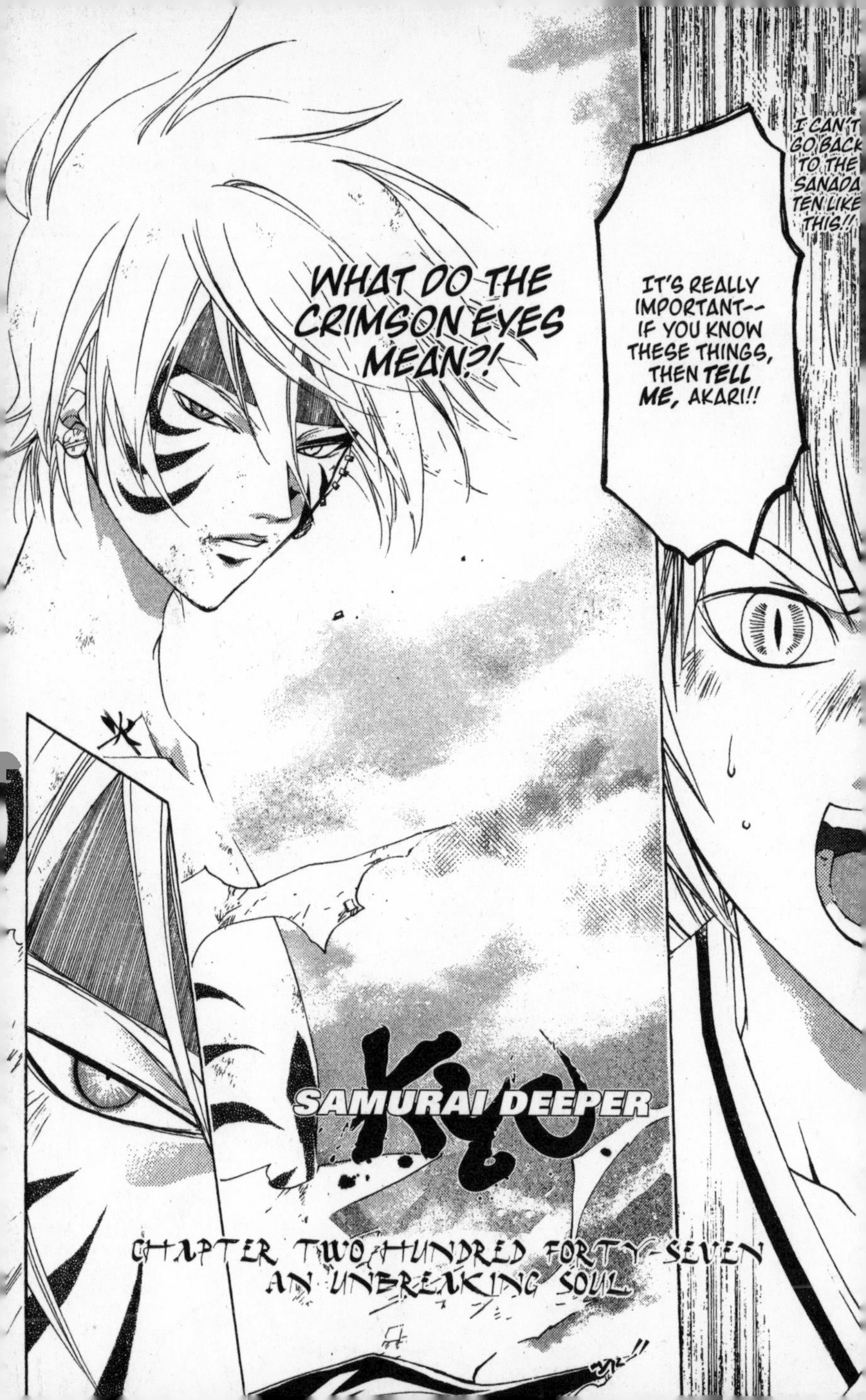
I CAN'T GO BACK TO THE SANADA TEN LIKE THIS!!
IT'S REALLY IMPORTANT-- IF YOU KNOW THESE THINGS, THEN TELL ME, AKARI!!
WHAT DO THE CRIMSON EYES MEAN?!
SAMURAI DEEPER KYO
CHAPTER TWO HUNDRED FORTY-SEVEN
AN UNBREAKING SOUL

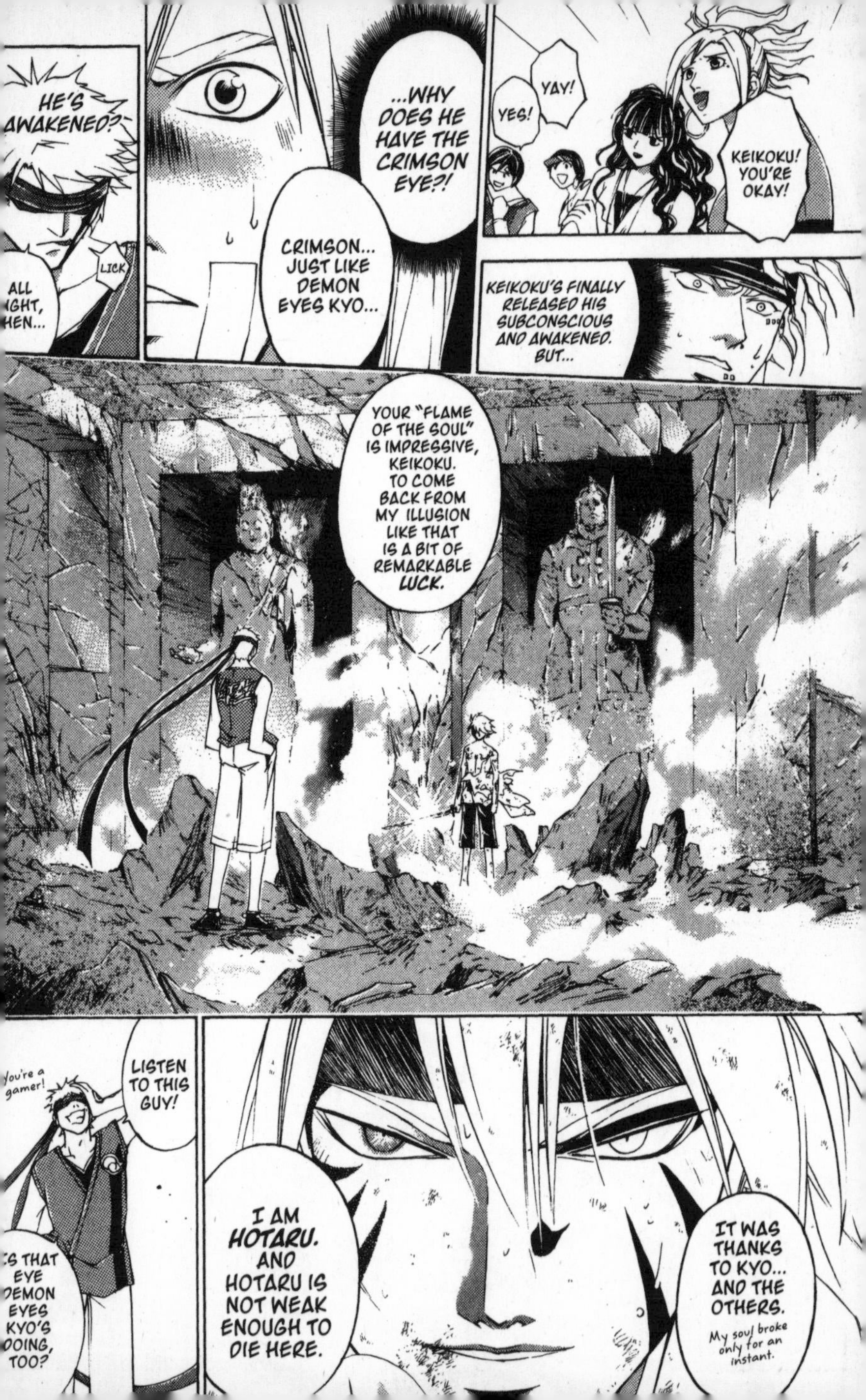
KEIKOKU! YOU'RE OKAY!
YES!
YAY!
KEIKOKU'S FINALLY RELEASED HIS SUBCONSCIOUS AND AWAKENED. BUT...
...WHY DOES HE HAVE THE CRIMSON EYE?!
CRIMSON... JUST LIKE DEMON EYES KYO...
HE'S AWAKENED?!
LICK
ALL RIGHT, THEN...
YOUR "FLAME OF THE SOUL" IS IMPRESSIVE, KEIKOKU. TO COME BACK FROM MY ILLUSION LIKE THAT IS A BIT OF REMARKABLE LUCK.
IT WAS THANKS TO KYO... AND THE OTHERS.
My soul broke only for an instant.
I AM HOTARU. AND HOTARU IS NOT WEAK ENOUGH TO DIE HERE.
LISTEN TO THIS GUY!
You're a gamer!
'S THAT EYE DEMON EYES KYO'S DOING, TOO?

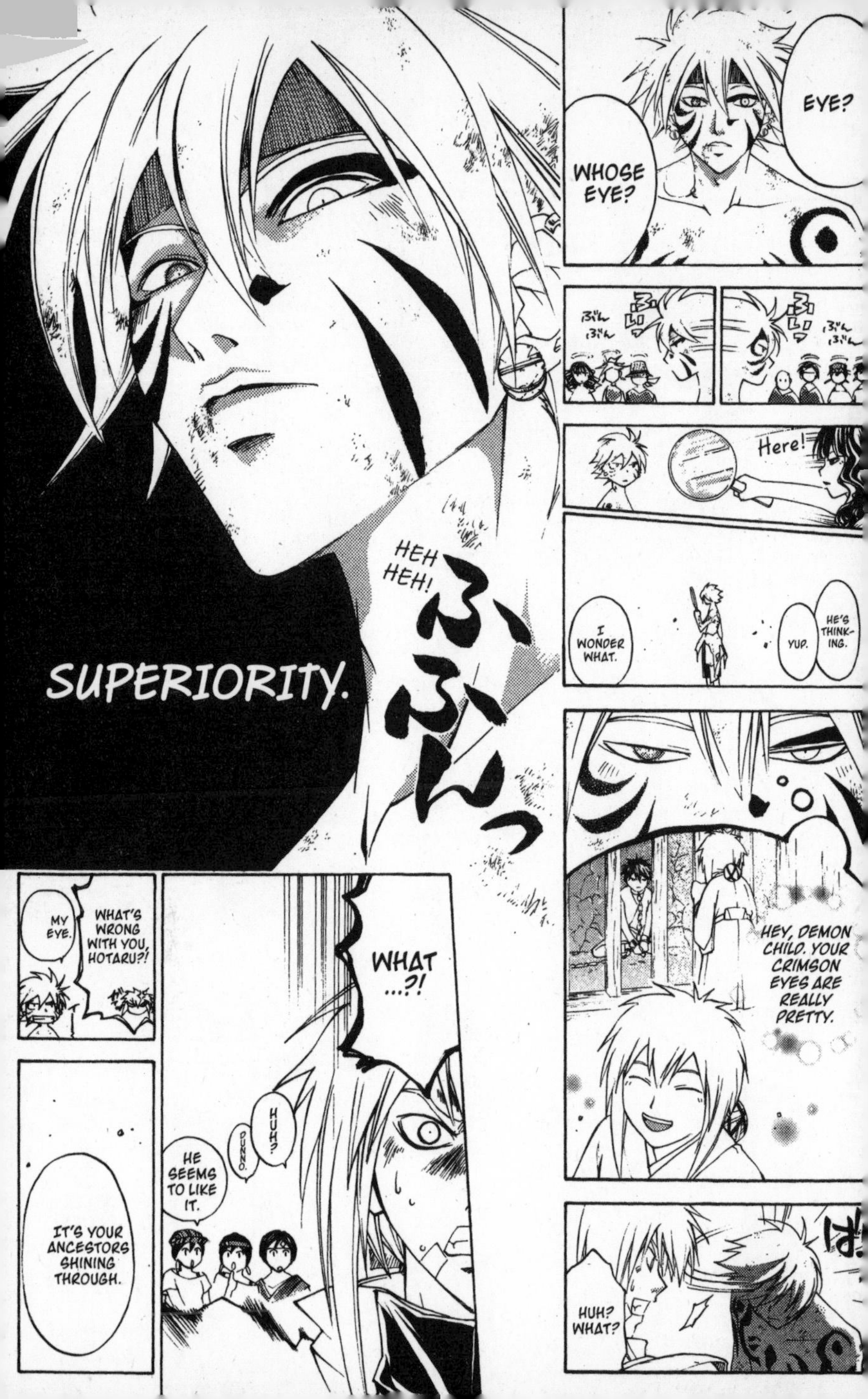
EYE?
WHOSE EYE?
ぶん ぶん
ぶん ぶん
Here!
HE'S THINK-ING.
YUP.
I WONDER WHAT.
HEY, DEMON CHILD. YOUR CRIMSON EYES ARE REALLY PRETTY.
HUH? WHAT?
HEH HEH!
ふふんっ
SUPERIORITY.
WHAT ...?!
HUH?
DUNNO.
HE SEEMS TO LIKE IT.
WHAT'S WRONG WITH YOU, HOTARU?!
MY EYE.
IT'S YOUR ANCESTORS SHINING THROUGH.

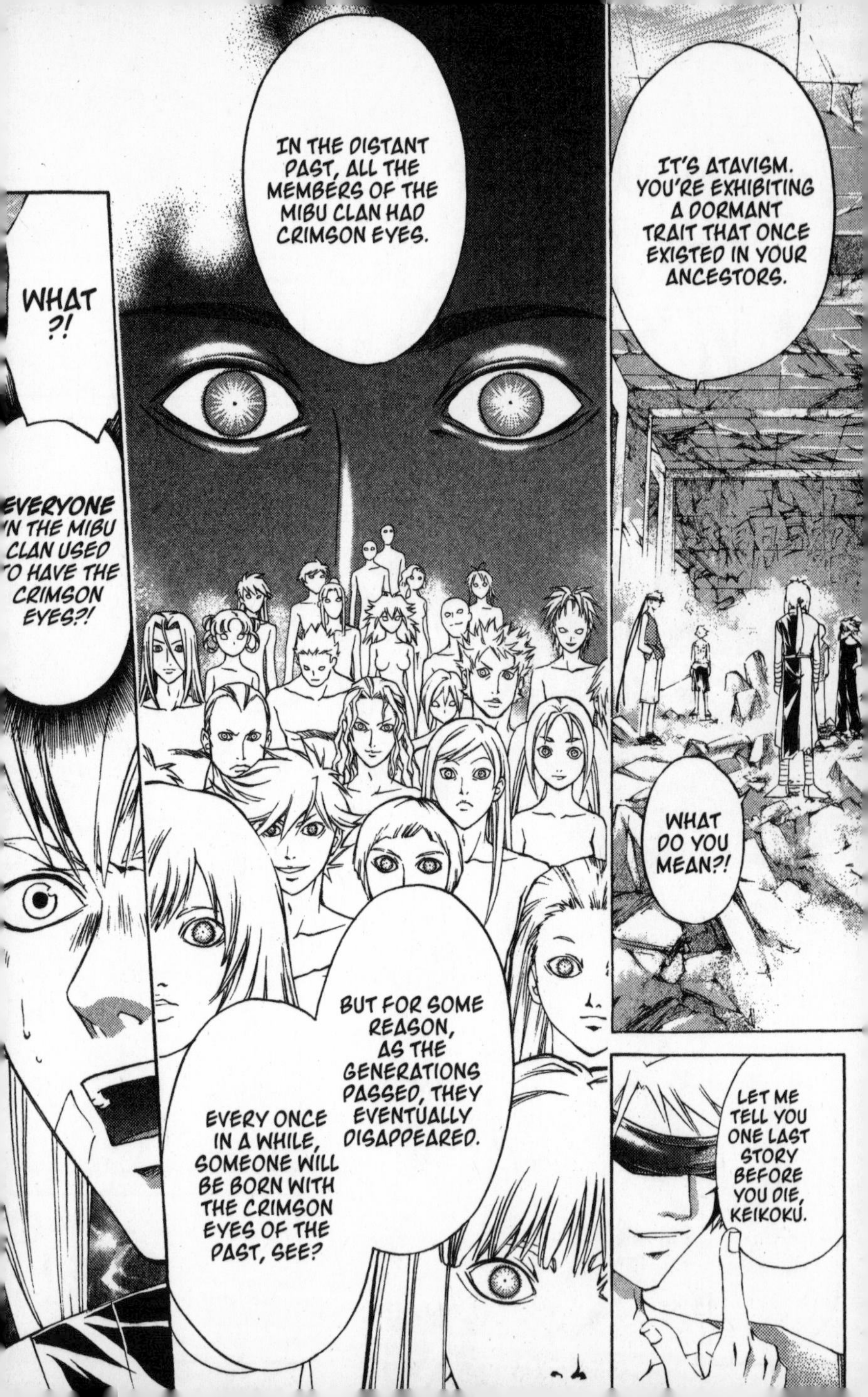
IT'S ATAVISM. YOU'RE EXHIBITING A DORMANT TRAIT THAT ONCE EXISTED IN YOUR ANCESTORS.
WHAT DO YOU MEAN?!
LET ME TELL YOU ONE LAST STORY BEFORE YOU DIE, KEIKOKU.
IN THE DISTANT PAST, ALL THE MEMBERS OF THE MIBU CLAN HAD CRIMSON EYES.
BUT FOR SOME REASON, AS THE GENERATIONS PASSED, THEY EVENTUALLY DISAPPEARED.
EVERY ONCE IN A WHILE, SOMEONE WILL BE BORN WITH THE CRIMSON EYES OF THE PAST, SEE?
WHAT ?!
EVERYONE IN THE MIBU CLAN USED TO HAVE THE CRIMSON EYES?!

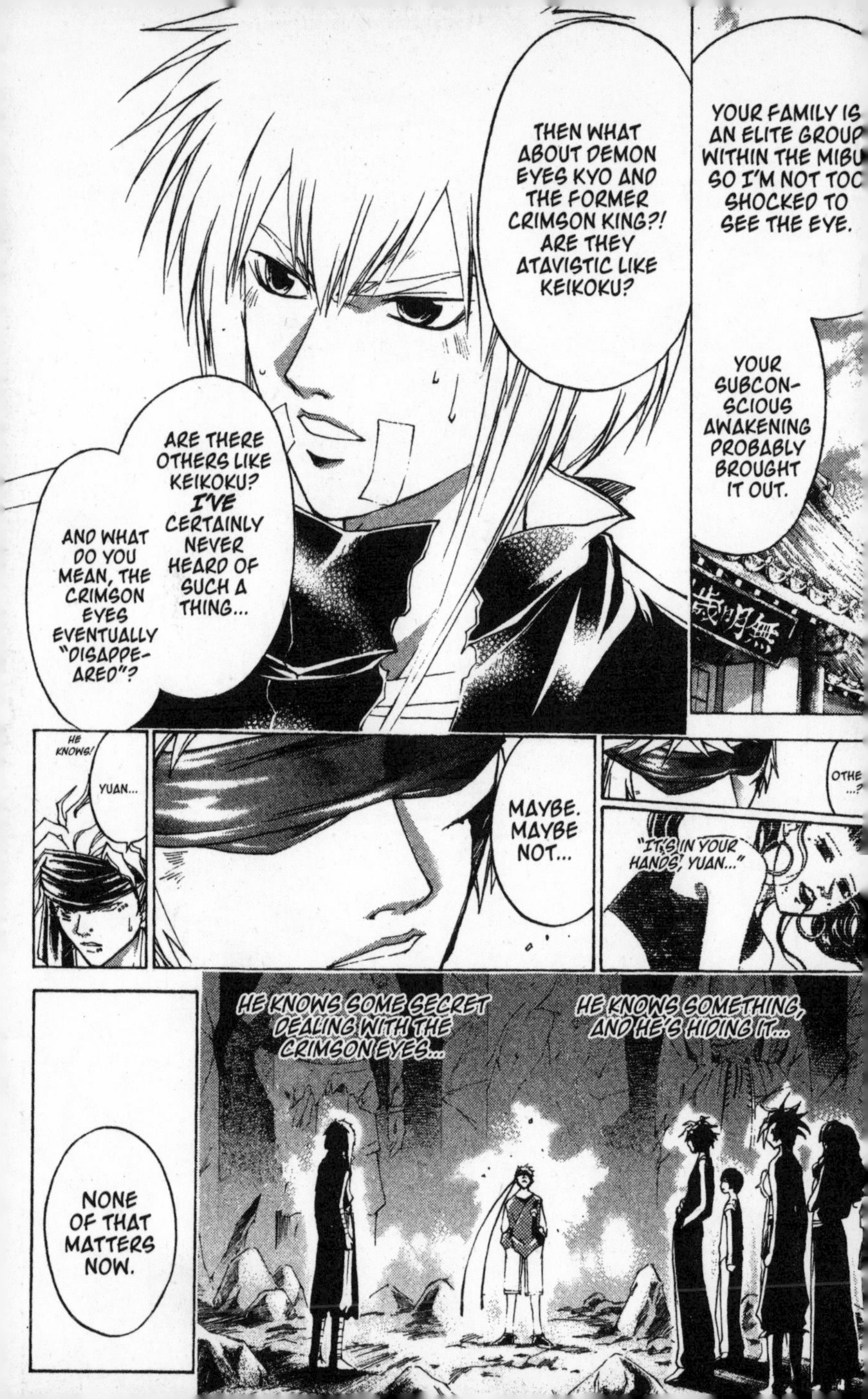
YOUR FAMILY IS AN ELITE GROUP WITHIN THE MIBU SO I'M NOT TOO SHOCKED TO SEE THE EYE.
YOUR SUBCON-SCIOUS AWAKENING PROBABLY BROUGHT IT OUT.
THEN WHAT ABOUT DEMON EYES KYO AND THE FORMER CRIMSON KING?! ARE THEY ATAVISTIC LIKE KEIKOKU?
ARE THERE OTHERS LIKE KEIKOKU? I'VE CERTAINLY NEVER HEARD OF SUCH A THING...
AND WHAT DO YOU MEAN, THE CRIMSON EYES EVENTUALLY "DISAPPE-ARED"?
OTHE ...?
"IT'S IN YOUR HANDS, YUAN..."
MAYBE. MAYBE NOT...
YUAN...
HE KNOWS!
HE KNOWS SOMETHING, AND HE'S HIDING IT...
HE KNOWS SOME SECRET DEALING WITH THE CRIMSON EYES...
NONE OF THAT MATTERS NOW.

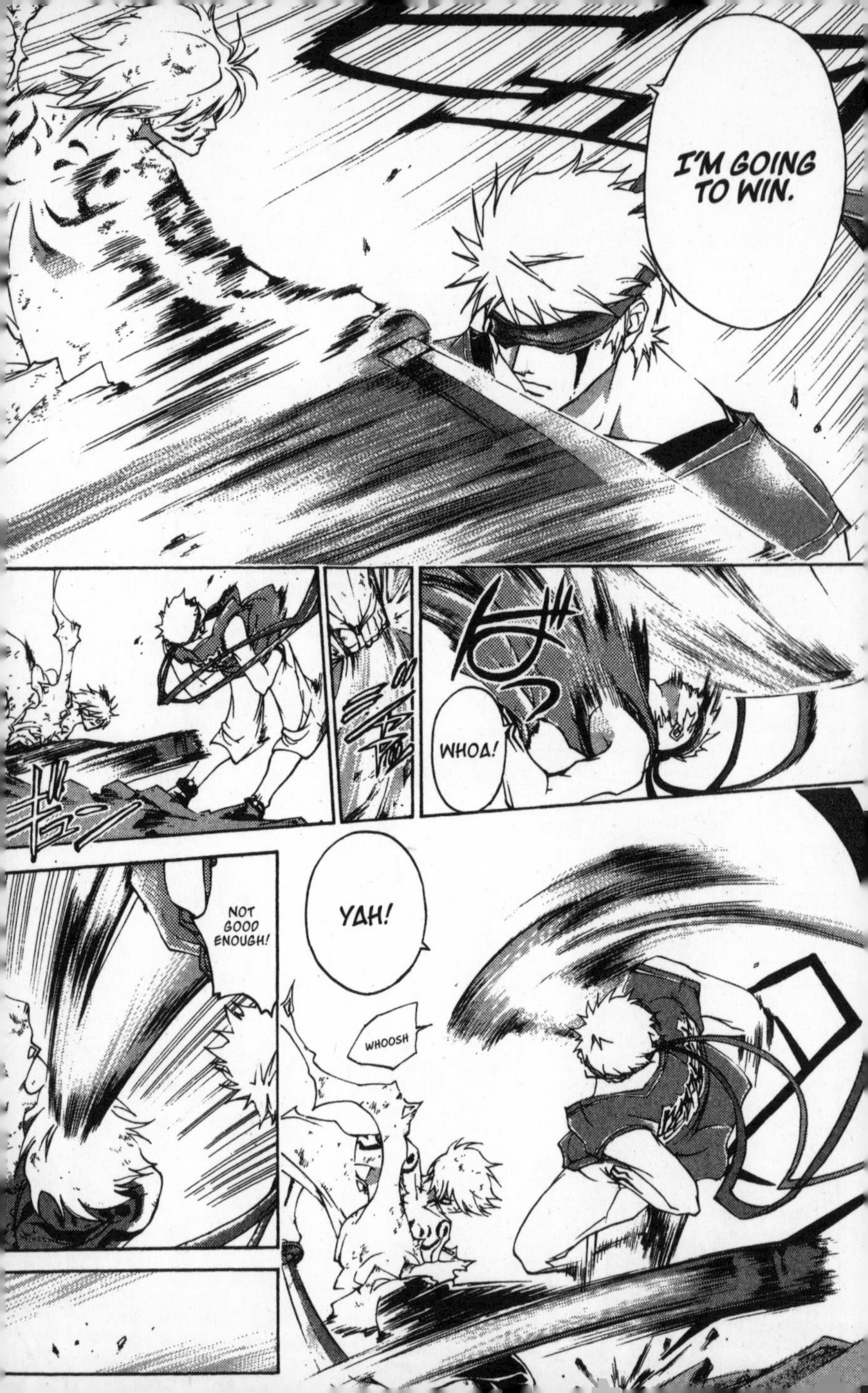
I'M GOING TO WIN.
WHOA!
YAH!
WHOOSH
NOT GOOD ENOUGH!

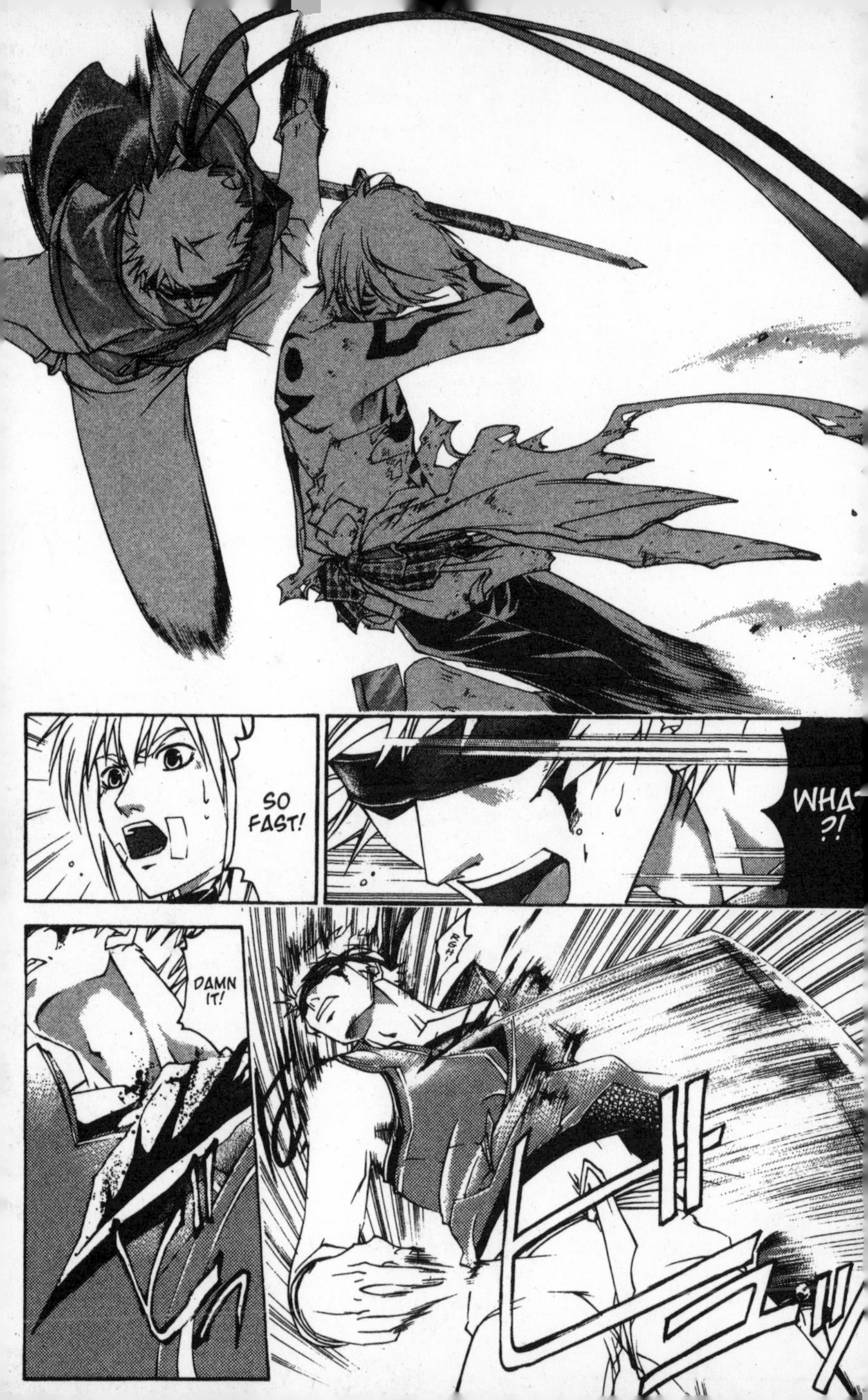
WHA-?!
SO FAST!
RGH!
DAMN IT!

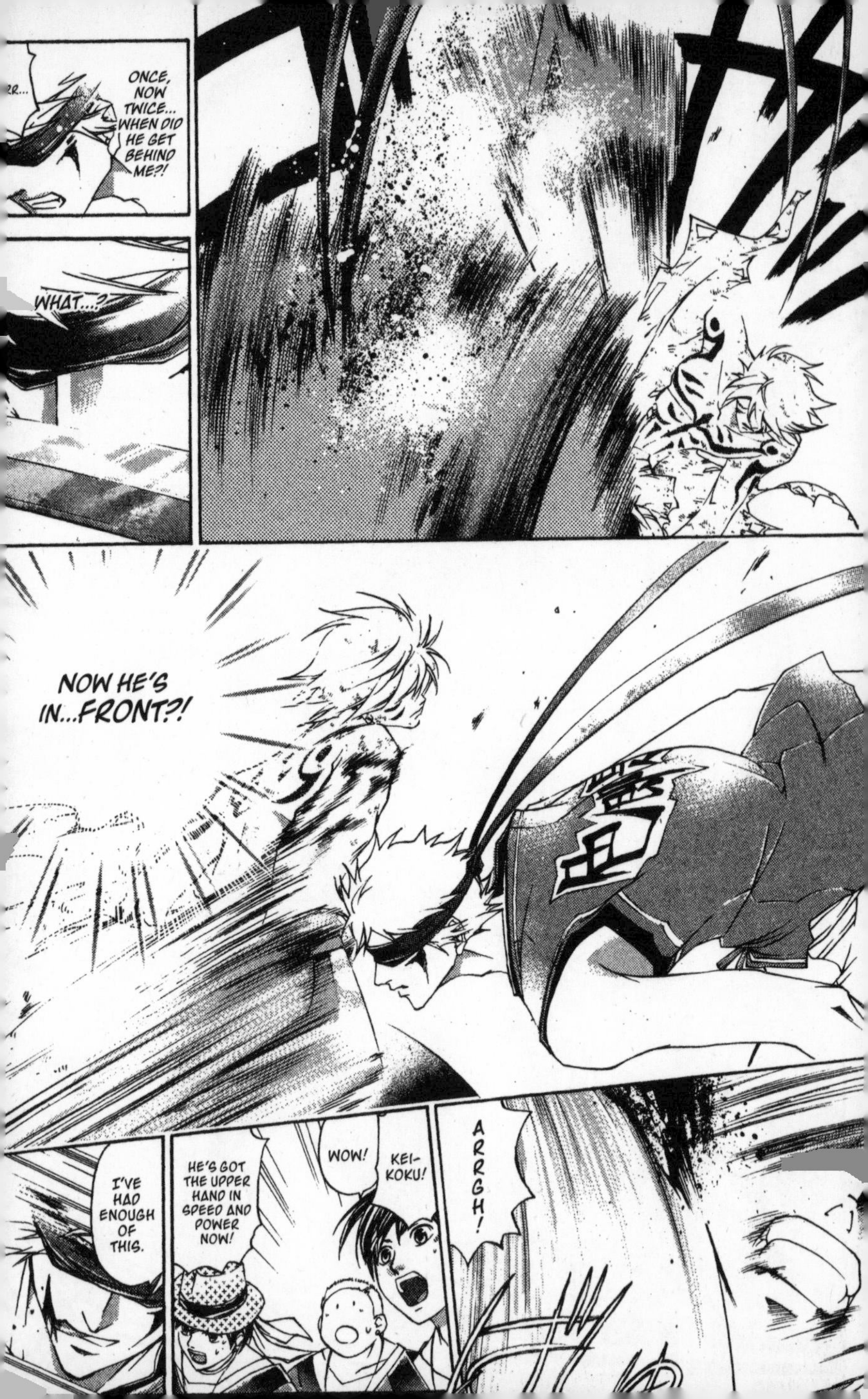
ONCE, NOW TWICE... WHEN DID HE GET BEHIND ME?!
WHAT...?
NOW HE'S IN...FRONT?!
ARRGH!
KEI-KOKU!
WOW!
HE'S GOT THE UPPER HAND IN SPEED AND POWER NOW!
I'VE HAD ENOUGH OF THIS.

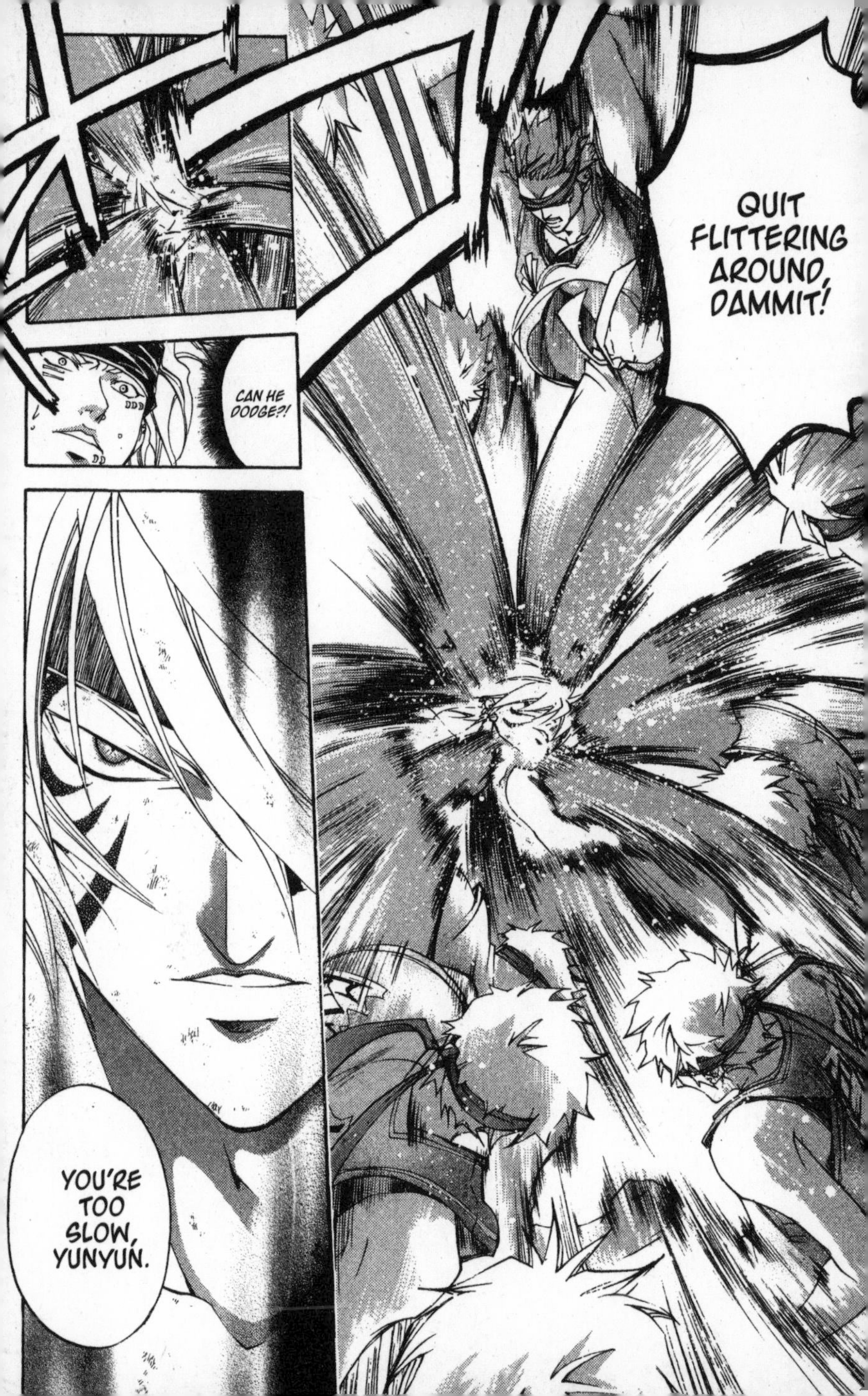
QUIT FLITTERING AROUND, DAMMIT!
CAN HE DODGE?!
YOU'RE TOO SLOW, YUNYUN.

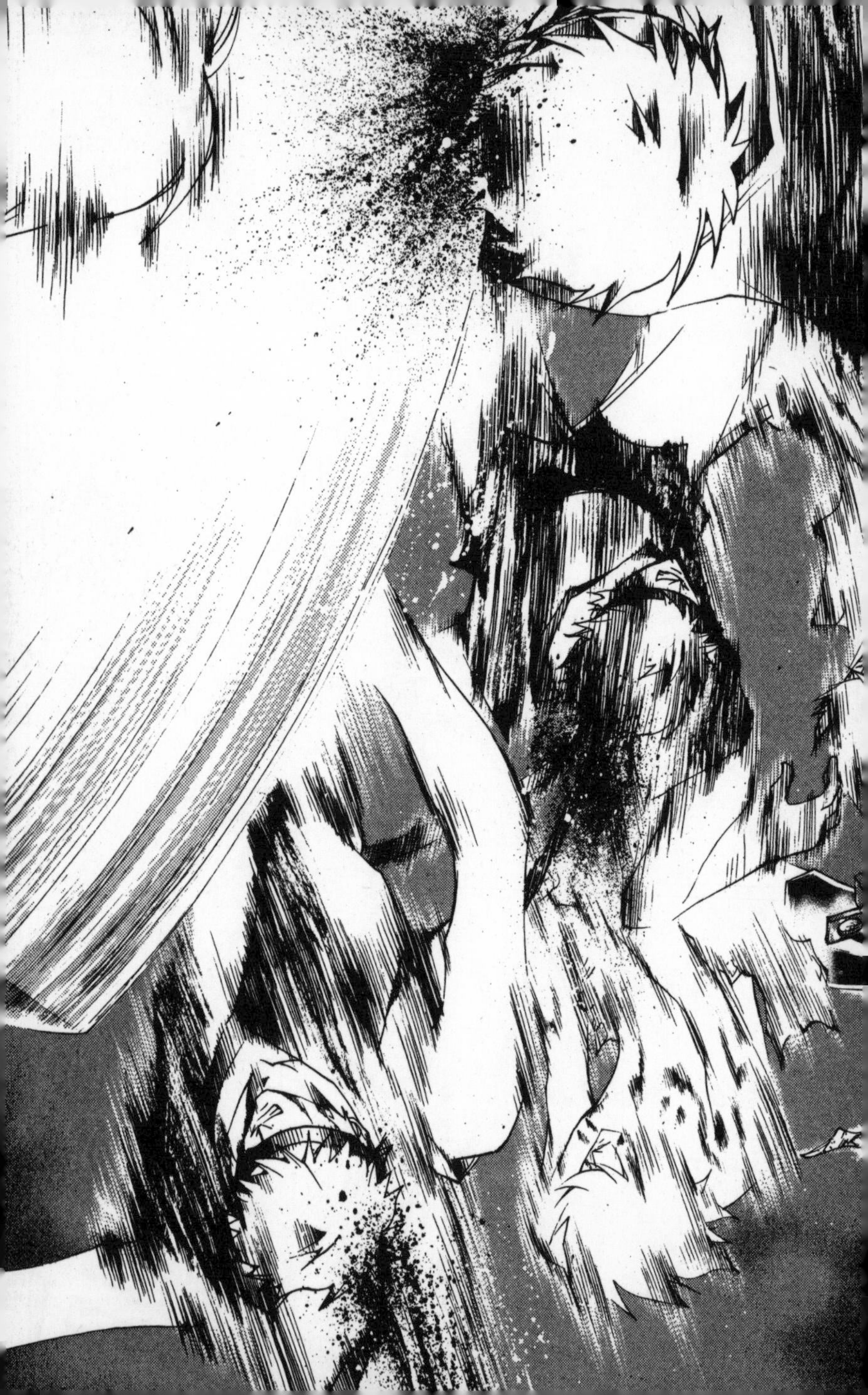

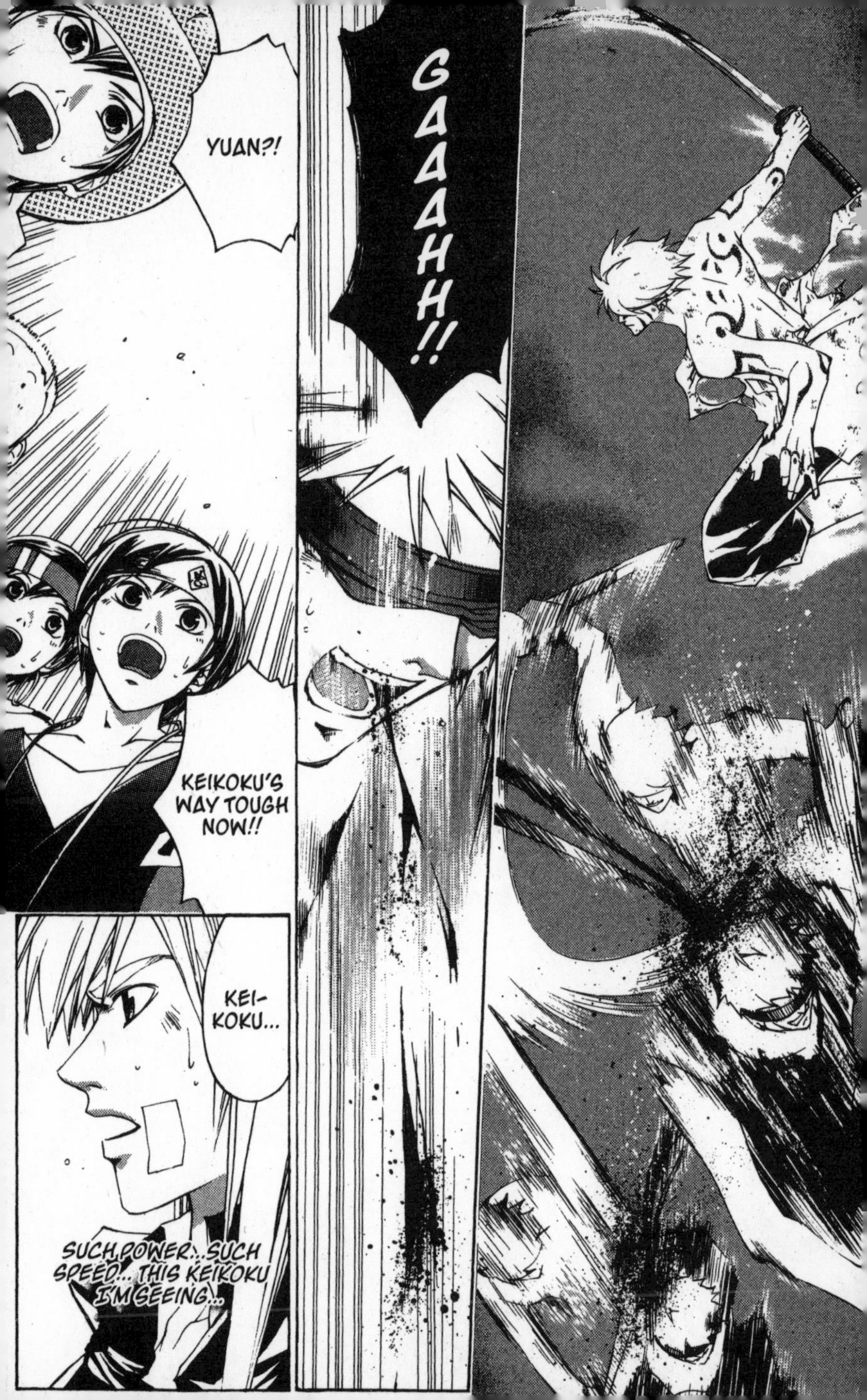
GAAAAHH!!
YUAN?!
KEIKOKU'S WAY TOUGH NOW!!
KEI-KOKU...
SUCH POWER... SUCH SPEED... THIS KEIKOKU I'M SEEING...

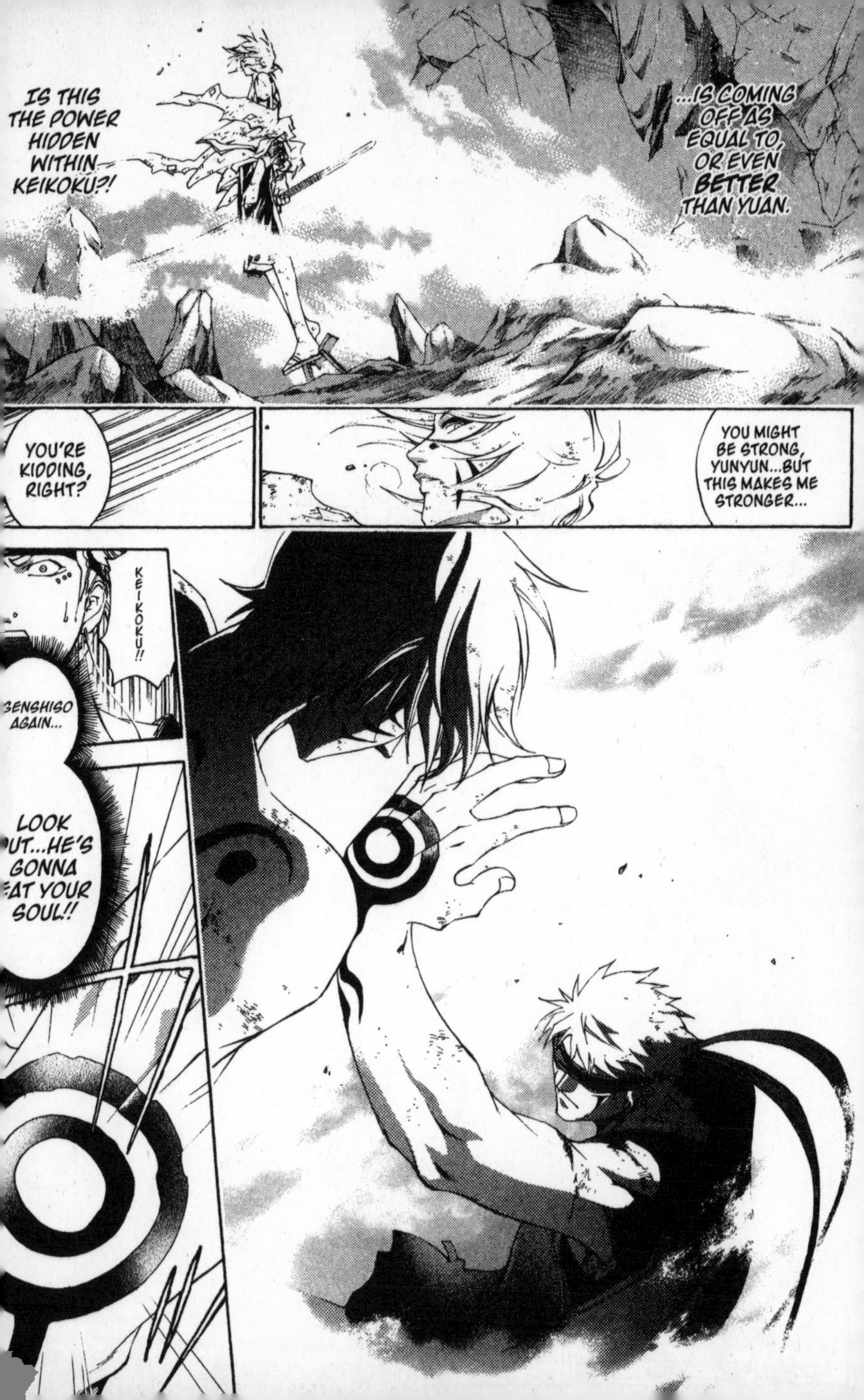
...IS COMING OFF AS EQUAL TO, OR EVEN BETTER THAN YUAN.
IS THIS THE POWER HIDDEN WITHIN KEIKOKU?!
YOU MIGHT BE STRONG, YUNYUN...BUT THIS MAKES ME STRONGER...
YOU'RE KIDDING, RIGHT?
KEIKOKU!!
SENSHISO AGAIN...
LOOK OUT...HE'S GONNA EAT YOUR SOUL!!

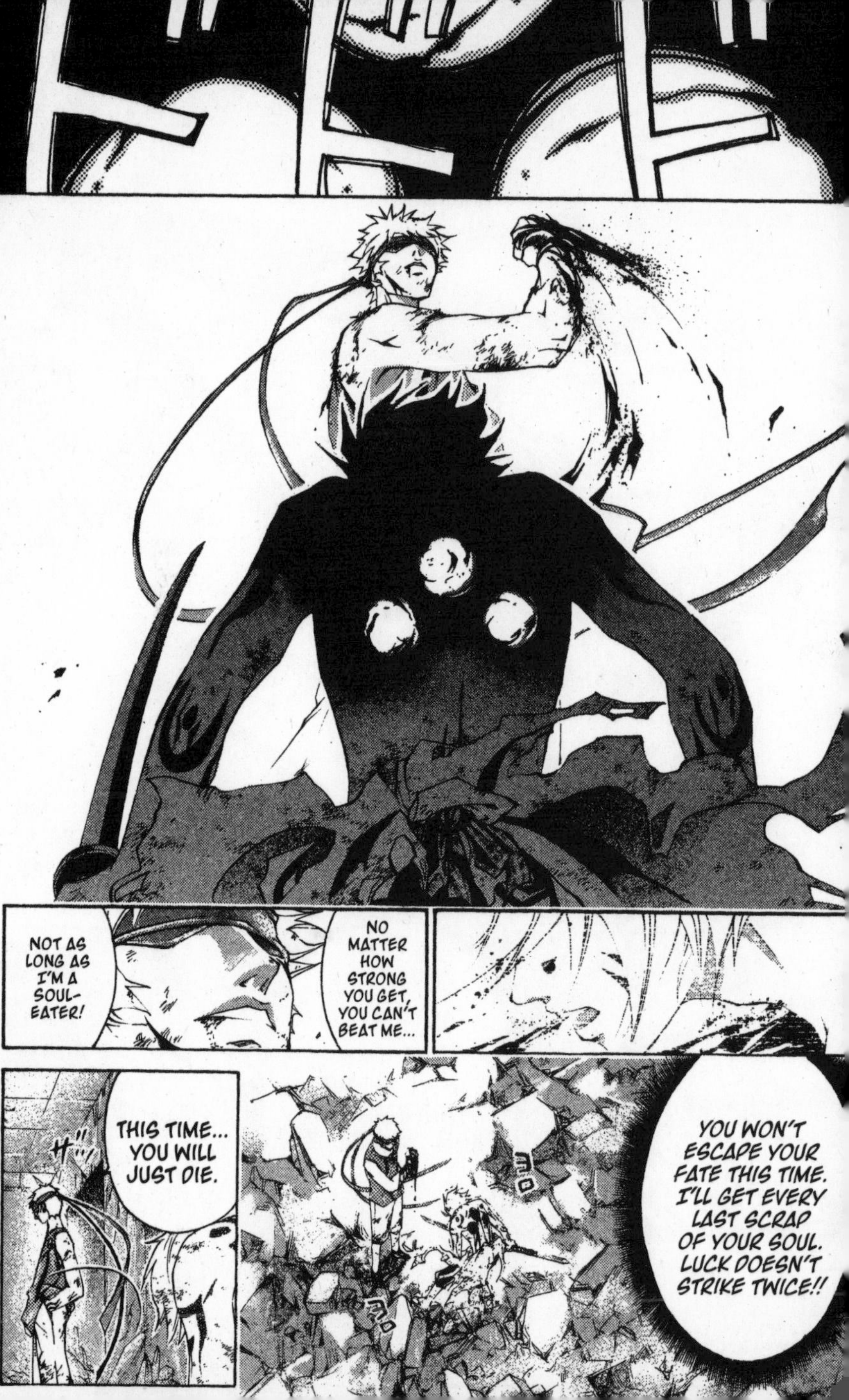
NO MATTER HOW STRONG YOU GET, YOU CAN'T BEAT ME...
NOT AS LONG AS I'M A SOUL-EATER!
YOU WON'T ESCAPE YOUR FATE THIS TIME. I'LL GET EVERY LAST SCRAP OF YOUR SOUL. LUCK DOESN'T STRIKE TWICE!!
THIS TIME... YOU WILL JUST DIE.

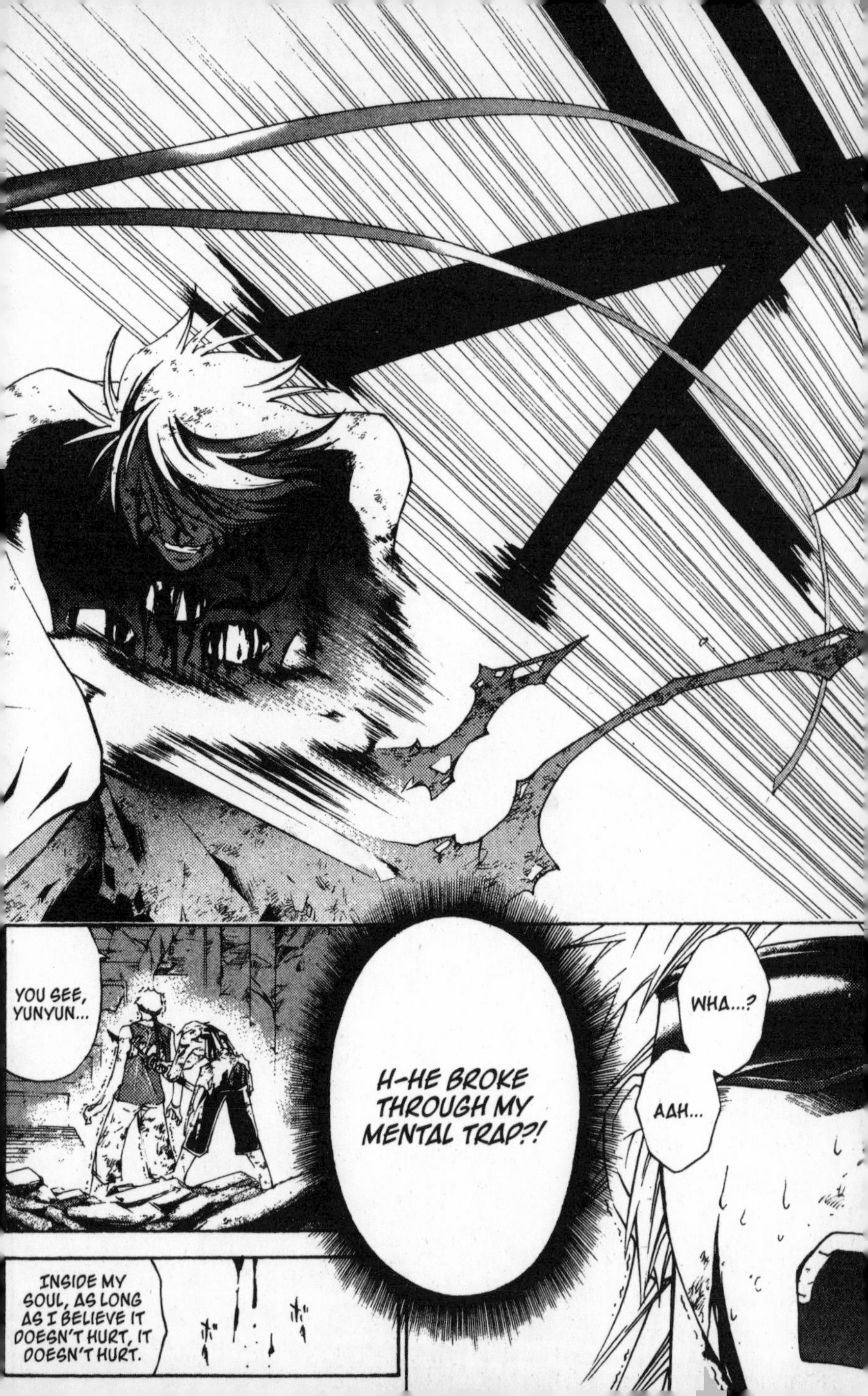
WHA...?
AAH...
H-HE BROKE THROUGH MY MENTAL TRAP?!
YOU SEE, YUNYUN...
INSIDE MY SOUL, AS LONG AS I BELIEVE IT DOESN'T HURT, IT DOESN'T HURT.

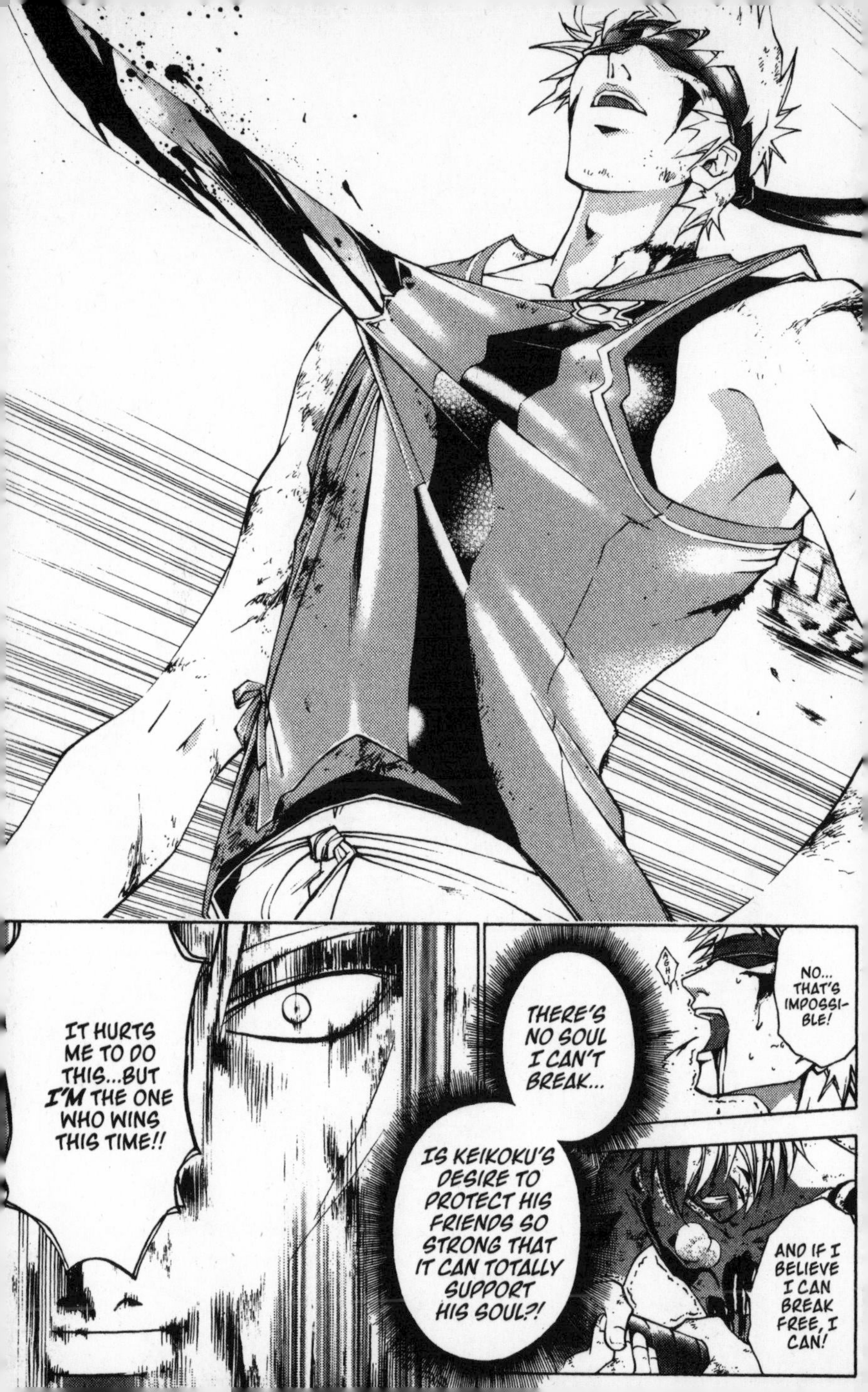
NO... THAT'S IMPOSSIBLE!
AGH!
THERE'S NO SOUL I CAN'T BREAK...
IS KEIKOKU'S DESIRE TO PROTECT HIS FRIENDS SO STRONG THAT IT CAN TOTALLY SUPPORT HIS SOUL?!
AND IF I BELIEVE I CAN BREAK FREE, I CAN!
IT HURTS ME TO DO THIS...BUT *I'M* THE ONE WHO WINS THIS TIME!!

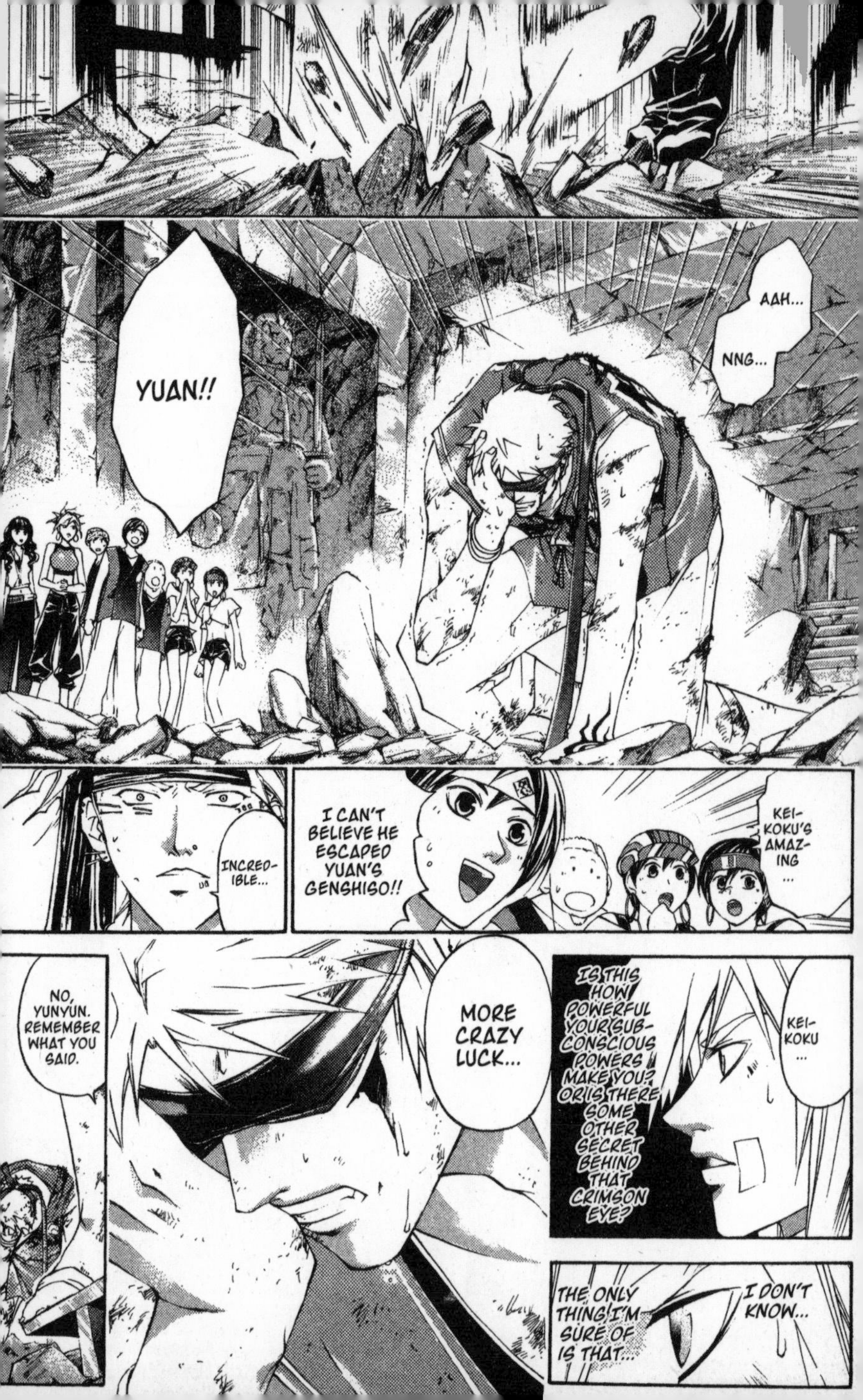
AAH...
NNG...
YUAN!!
KEI-KOKU'S AMAZ-ING ...
I CAN'T BELIEVE HE ESCAPED YUAN'S GENSHISO!!
INCRED-IBLE...
KEI-KOKU ...
IS THIS HOW POWERFUL YOUR SUB-CONSCIOUS POWERS MAKE YOU? OR IS THERE SOME OTHER SECRET BEHIND THAT CRIMSON EYE?
I DON'T KNOW...
THE ONLY THING I'M SURE OF IS THAT...
MORE CRAZY LUCK...
NO, YUNYUN. REMEMBER WHAT YOU SAID.

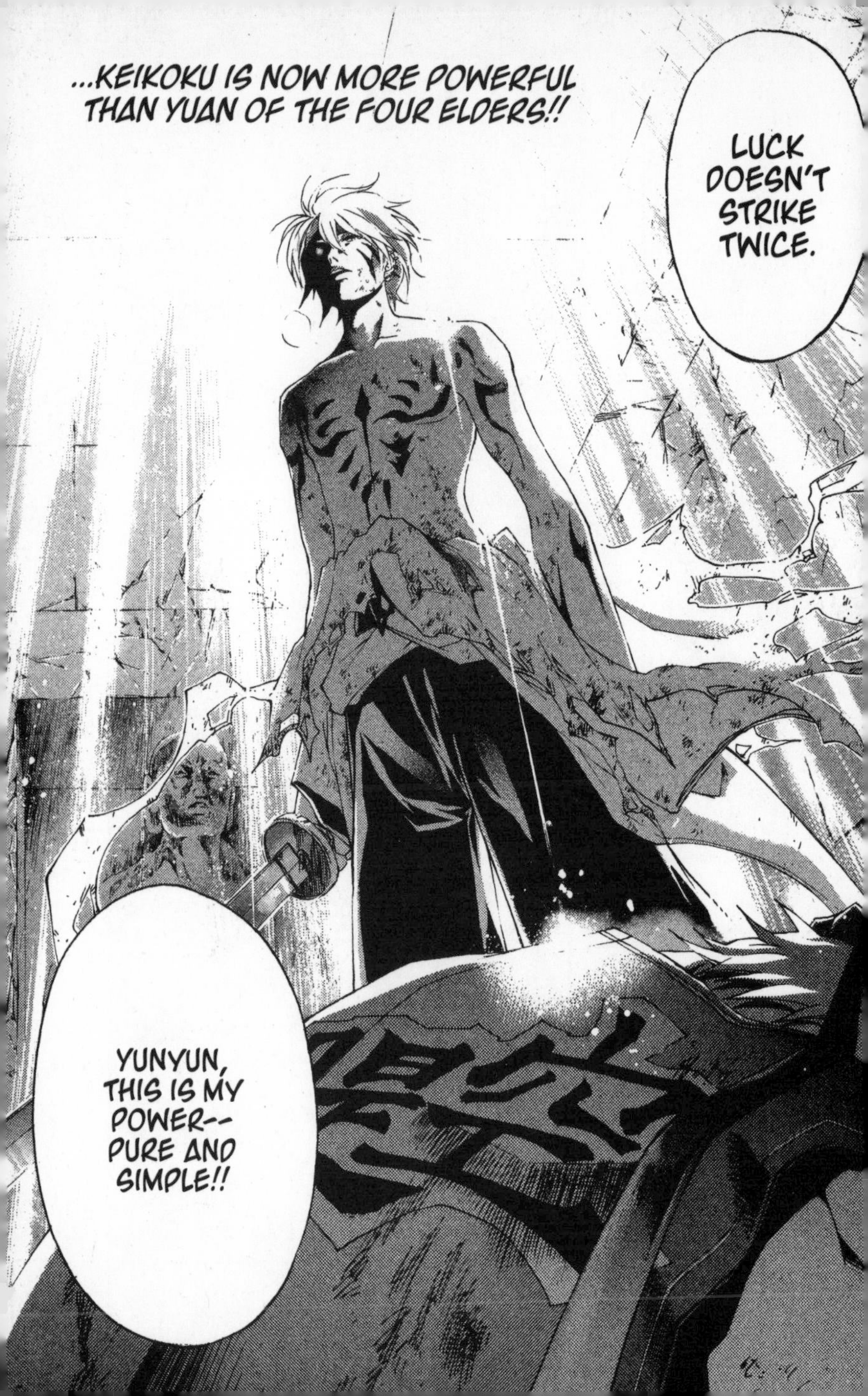
LUCK DOESN'T STRIKE TWICE.
...KEIKOKU IS NOW MORE POWERFUL THAN YUAN OF THE FOUR ELDERS!!
YUNYUN, THIS IS MY POWER--PURE AND SIMPLE!!

New Years Cards!

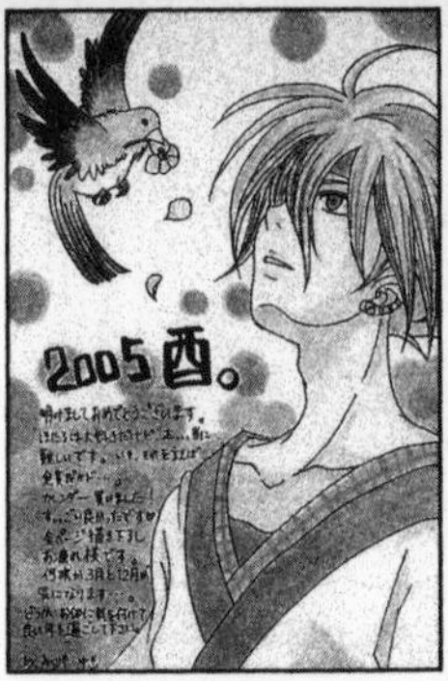
2005酉。

[Ibaraki/Yuki Mikuriya]⬆

Will this bird bring happiness?

[Mie/Mio Tsusaka]⬇

Black wings fit Tokito perfectly.

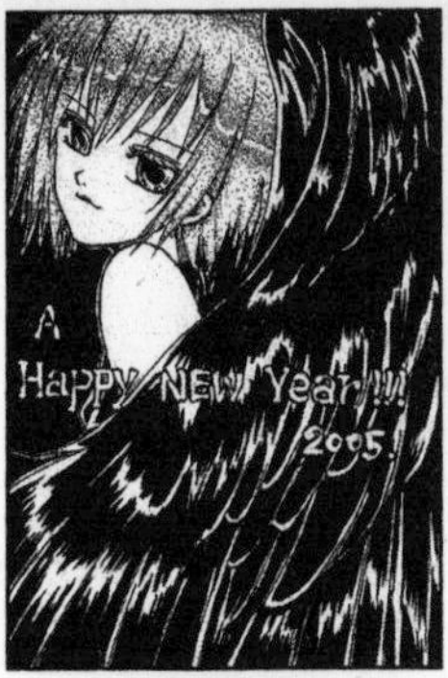
A Happy New Year!!!
2005!

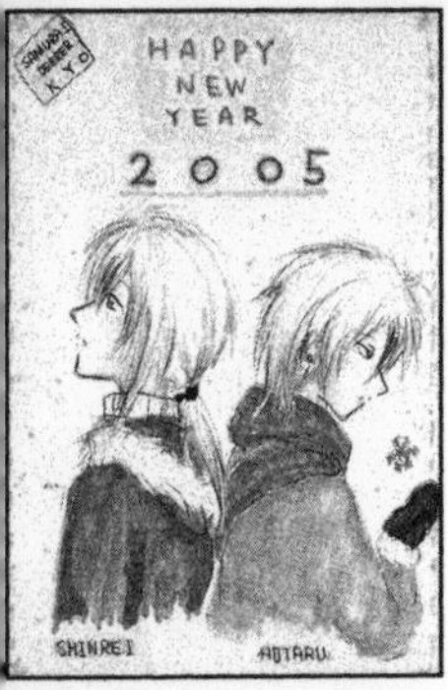
HAPPY NEW YEAR
2005
SHINREI
HOTARU

[Chiba/Tomo]⬆

Two boys on a snowy day.

[Yamaguchi/Ai Itonaga]⬇

How many of their New Year's Resolutions will come true, I wonder?

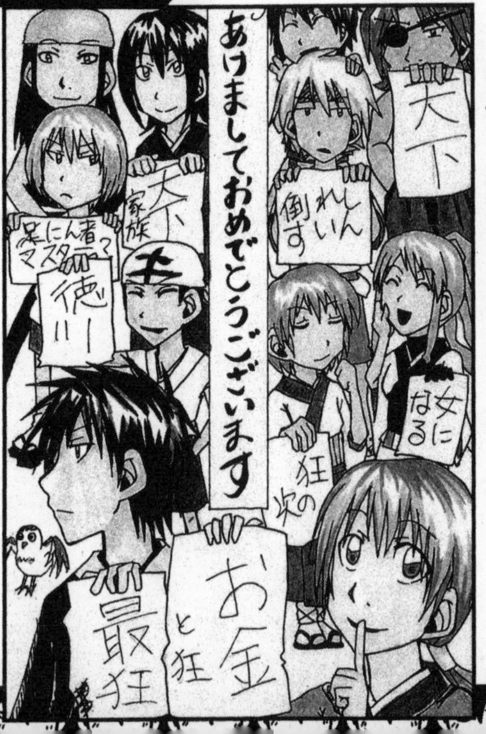
あけましておめでとうございます
天下
女になる
徳川

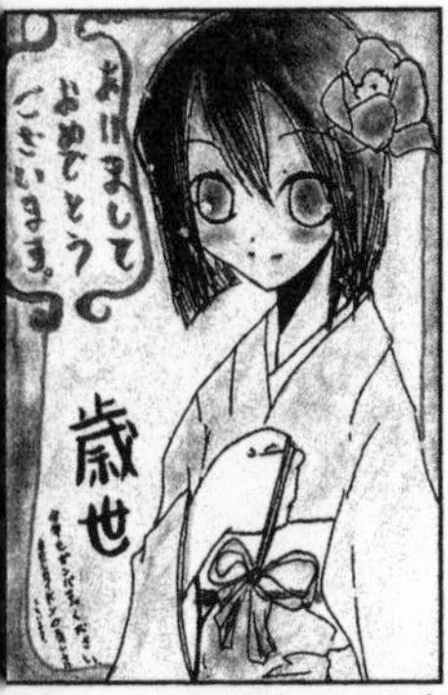
あけましておめでとうございます。

[Saitama/Rikako Watanabe]⬆

It's so...cute...

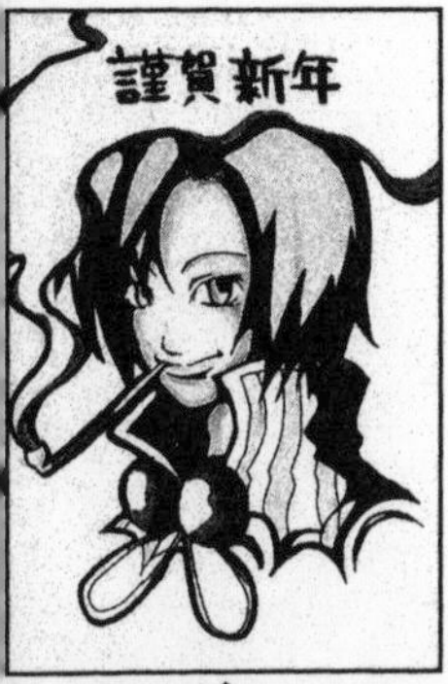
謹賀新年

[Hyogo/Nyonko]⬆

The thickness of those lines is really cool!

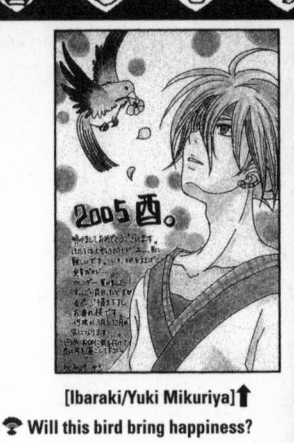

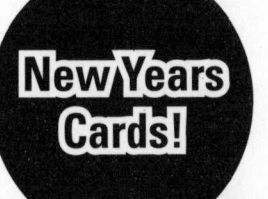

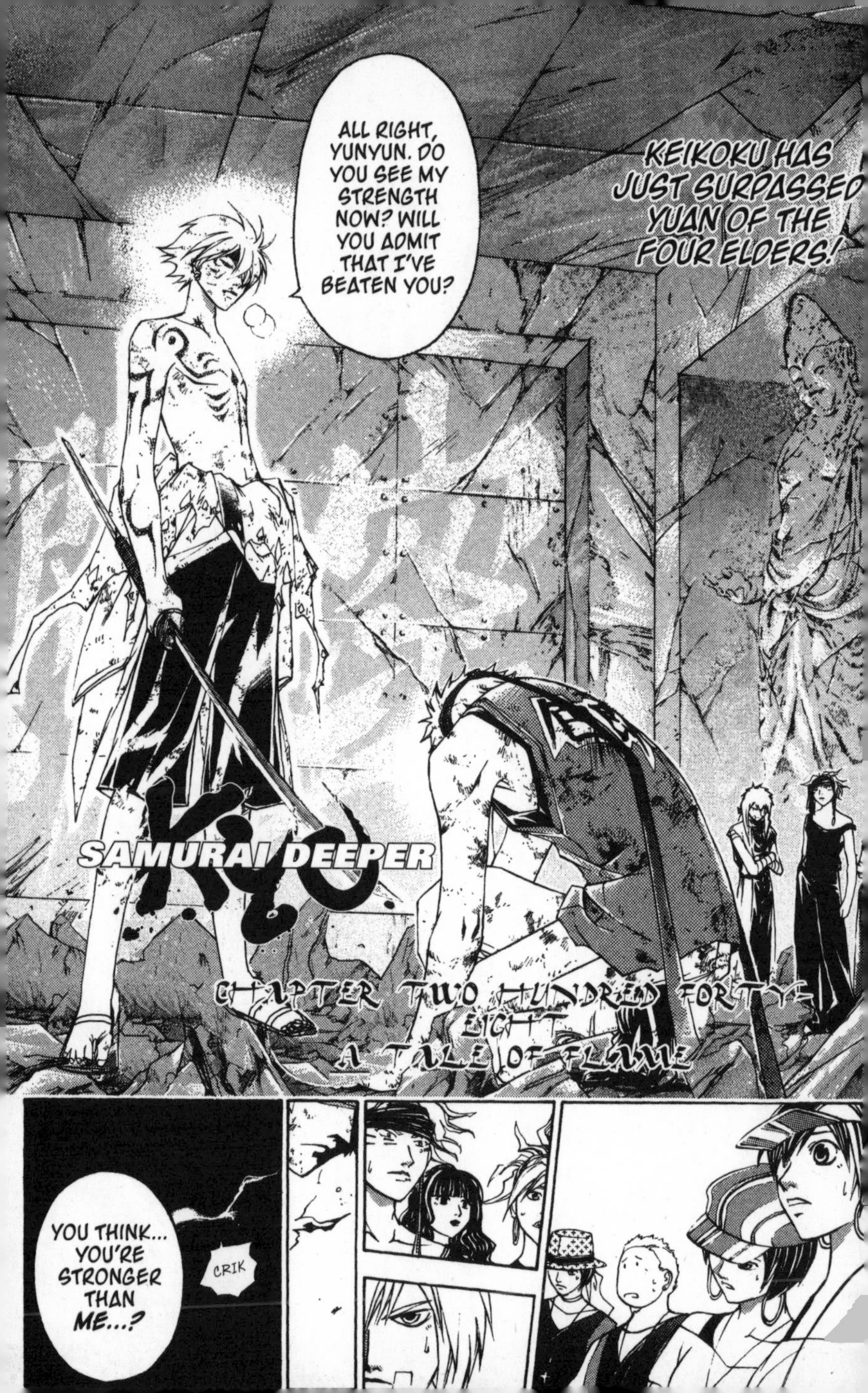
KEIKOKU HAS JUST SURPASSED YUAN OF THE FOUR ELDERS!
ALL RIGHT, YUNYUN. DO YOU SEE MY STRENGTH NOW? WILL YOU ADMIT THAT I'VE BEATEN YOU?
SAMURAI DEEPER KYO
CHAPTER TWO HUNDRED FORTY-EIGHT
A TALE OF FLAME
CRIK
YOU THINK... YOU'RE STRONGER THAN ME...?

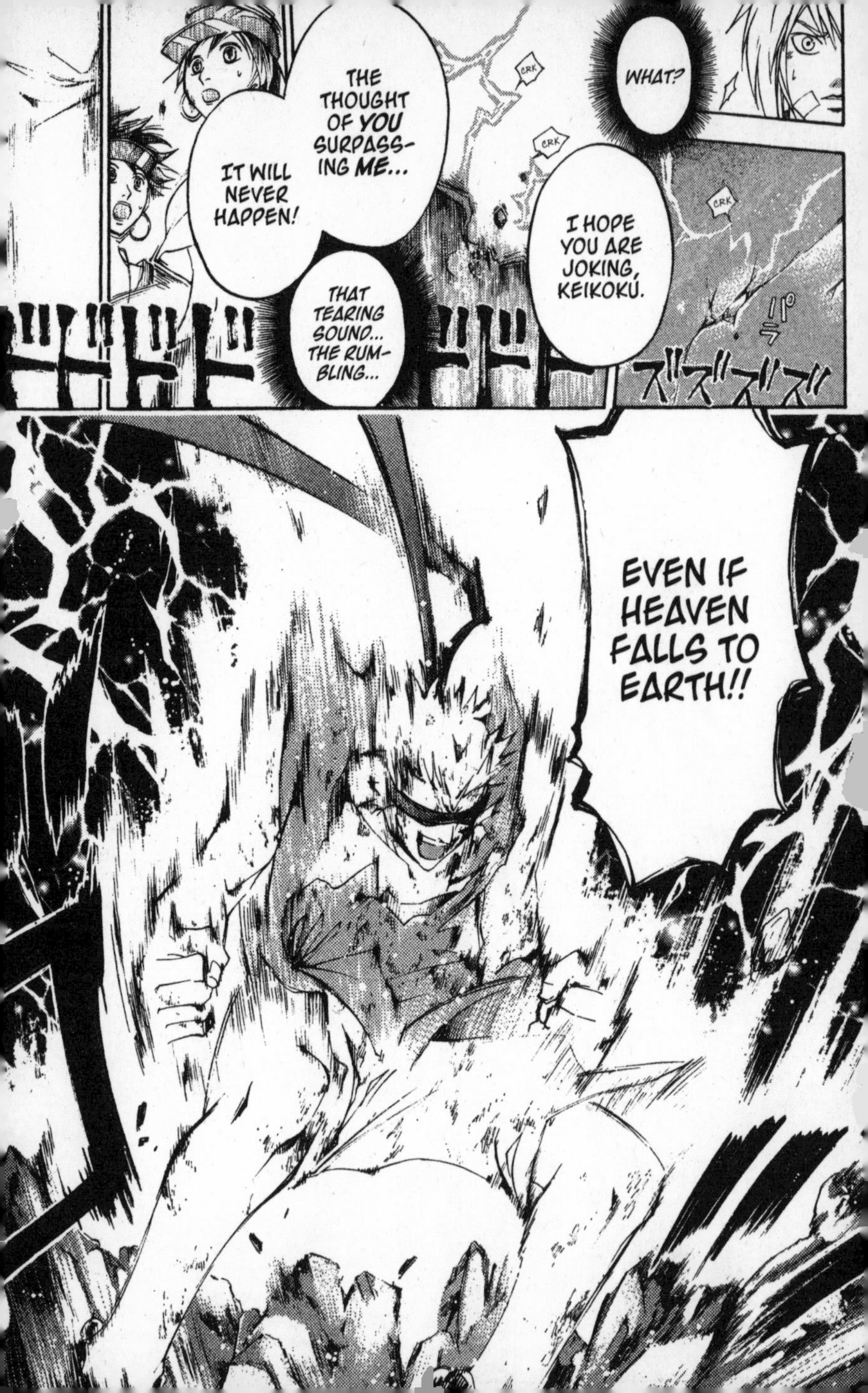
WHAT?
CRK
CRK
CRK
I HOPE YOU ARE JOKING, KEIKOKU.
パラ
ズズズズ
THE THOUGHT OF YOU SURPASSING ME...
IT WILL NEVER HAPPEN!
THAT TEARING SOUND... THE RUMBLING...
ドドドド
EVEN IF HEAVEN FALLS TO EARTH!!

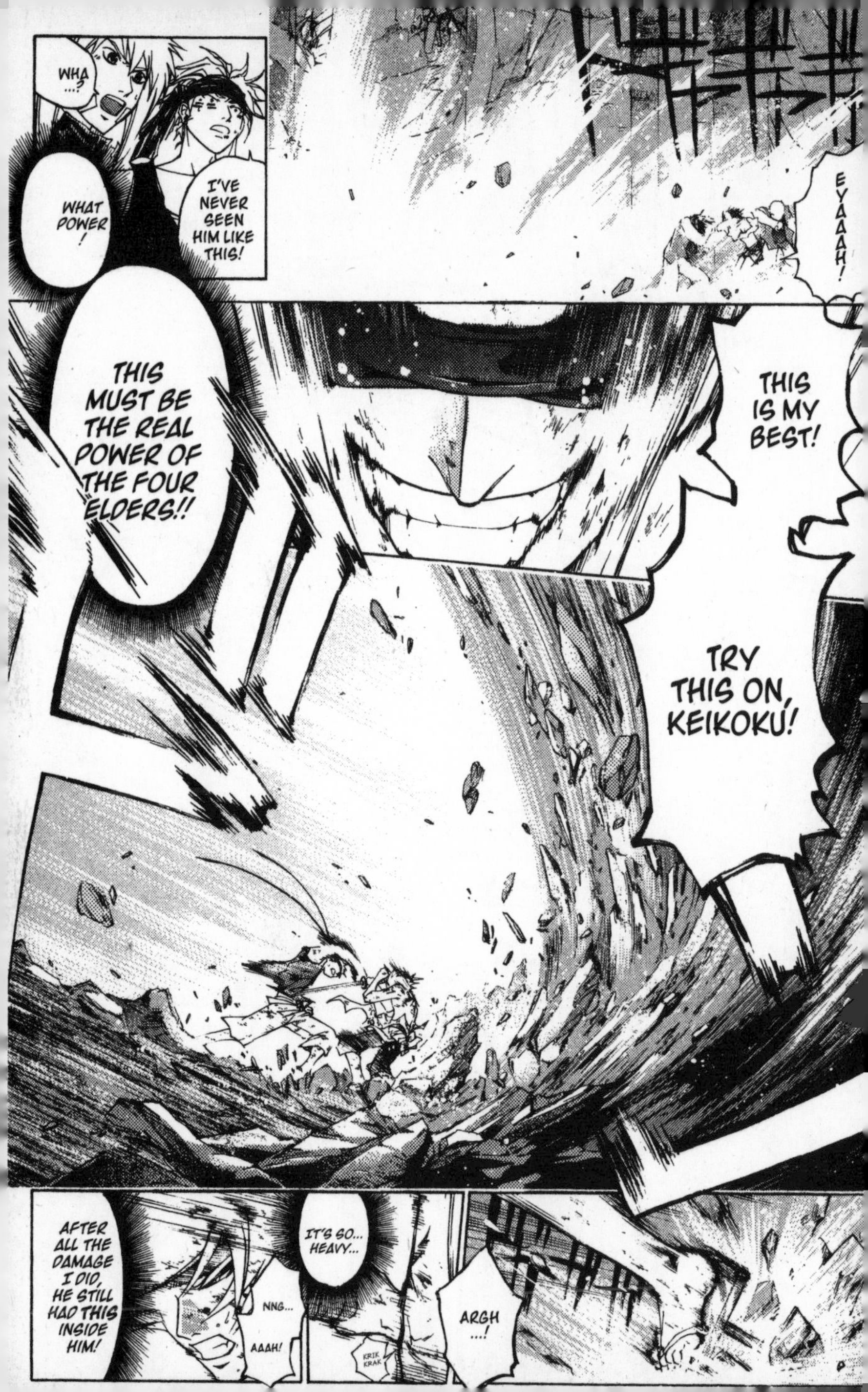
EYAAAH!
WHA ...?
I'VE NEVER SEEN HIM LIKE THIS!
WHAT POWER!
THIS IS MY BEST!
THIS MUST BE THE REAL POWER OF THE FOUR ELDERS!!
TRY THIS ON, KEIKOKU!
ARGH ...!
IT'S SO... HEAVY...
KRIK KRAK
NNG...
AAAH!
AFTER ALL THE DAMAGE I DID, HE STILL HAD THIS INSIDE HIM!

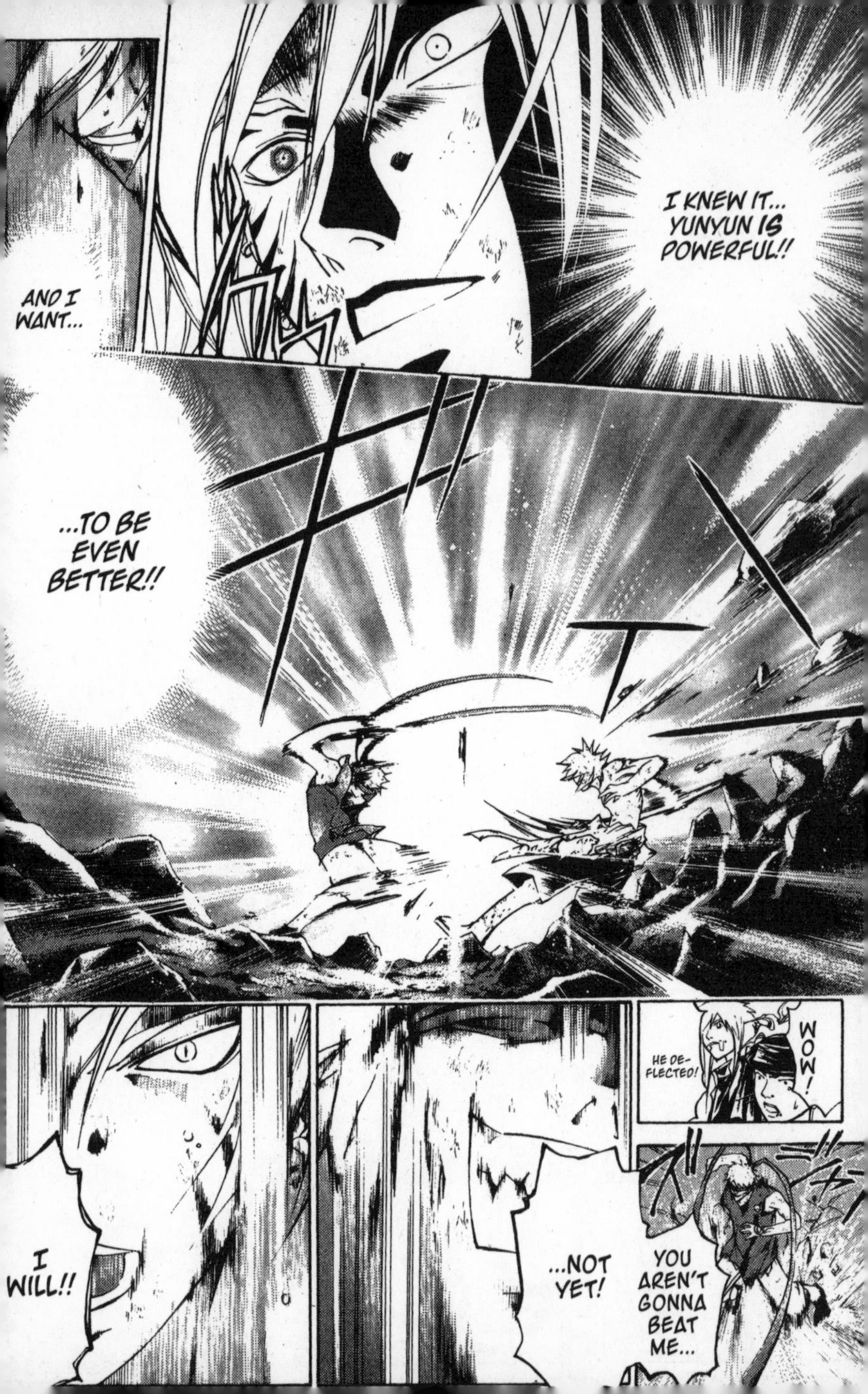
I KNEW IT... YUNYUN IS POWERFUL!!
AND I WANT...
...TO BE EVEN BETTER!!
WOW!
HE DE-FLECTED!
YOU AREN'T GONNA BEAT ME...
...NOT YET!
I WILL!!

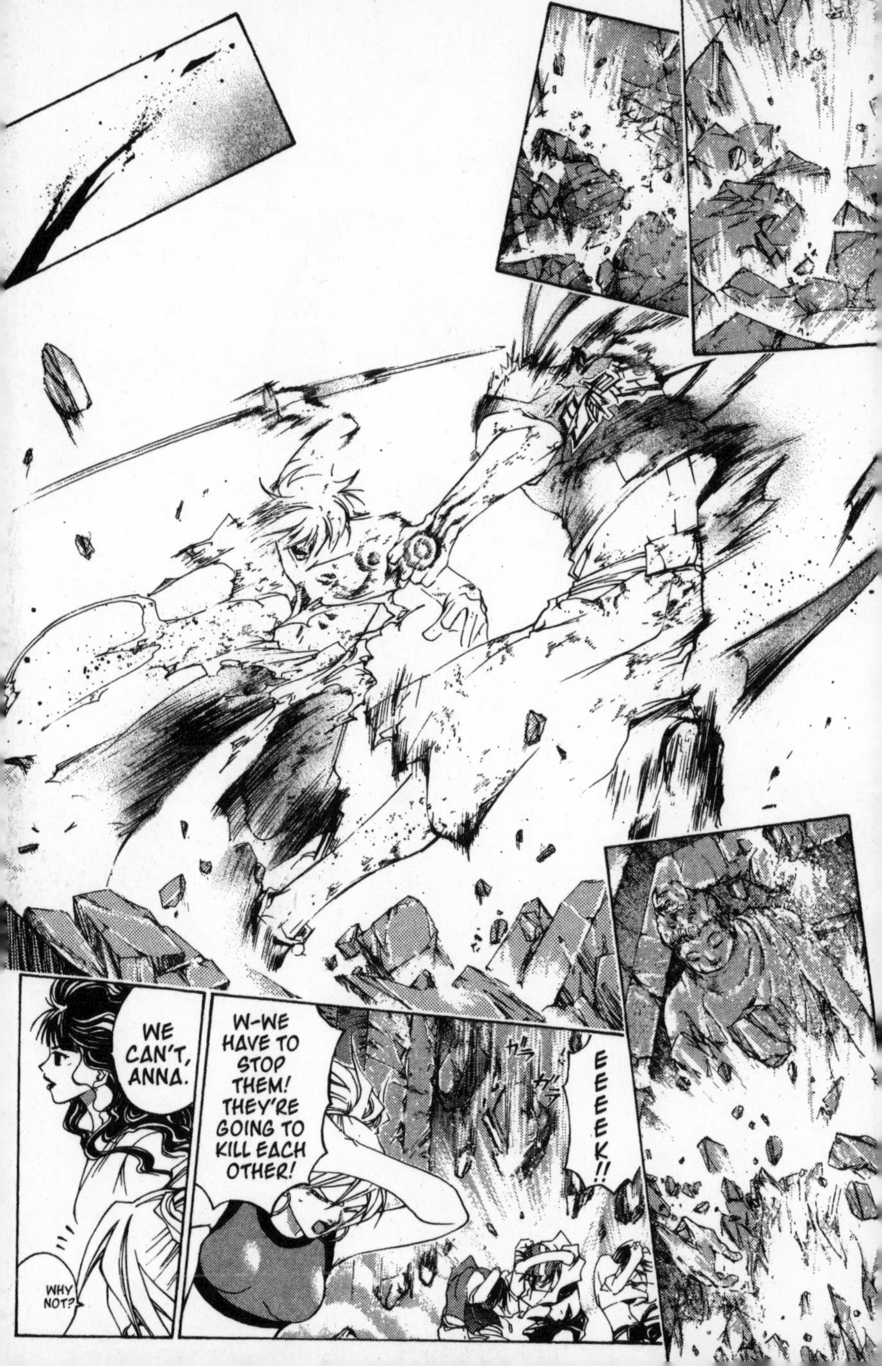
EEEEEK!!
W-WE HAVE TO STOP THEM! THEY'RE GOING TO KILL EACH OTHER!
WE CAN'T, ANNA.
...!
WHY NOT?

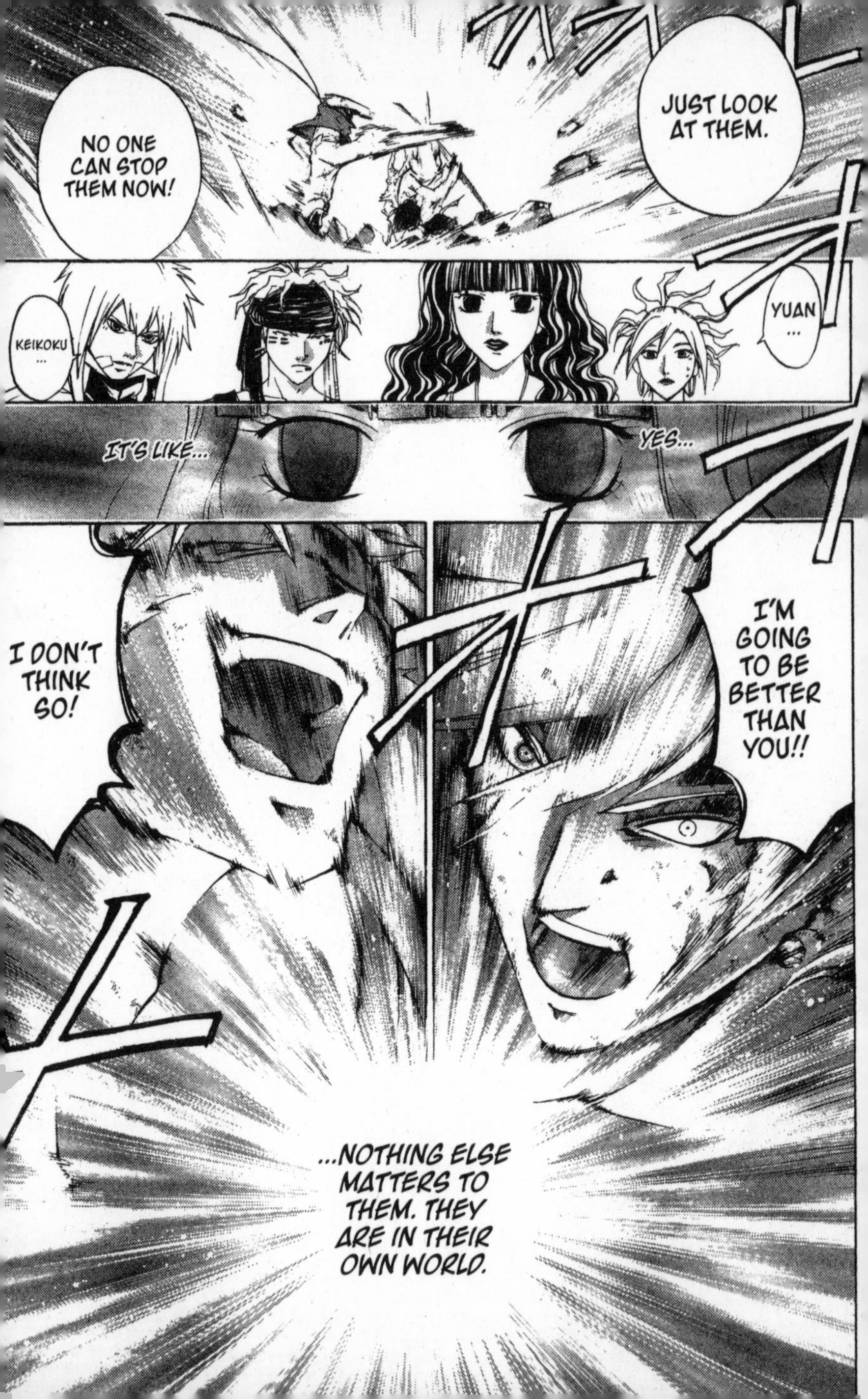
JUST LOOK AT THEM.
NO ONE CAN STOP THEM NOW!
YUAN ...
KEIKOKU ...
YES...
IT'S LIKE...
I'M GOING TO BE BETTER THAN YOU!!
I DON'T THINK SO!
...NOTHING ELSE MATTERS TO THEM. THEY ARE IN THEIR OWN WORLD.

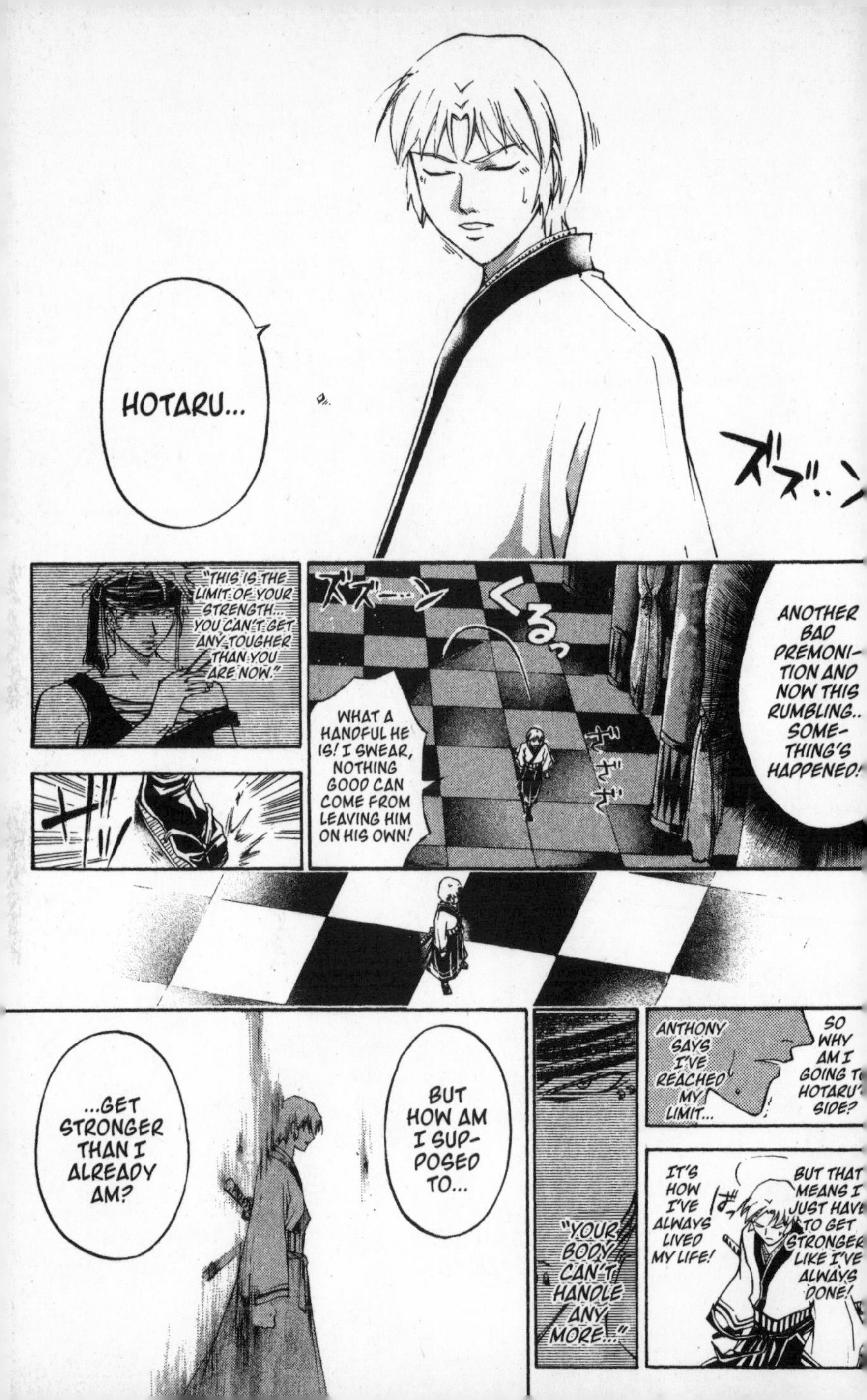
ズズ‥ン
HOTARU...
ANOTHER BAD PREMONITION AND NOW THIS RUMBLING... SOMETHING'S HAPPENED!
ズズー‥ン
くるっ
WHAT A HANDFUL HE IS! I SWEAR, NOTHING GOOD CAN COME FROM LEAVING HIM ON HIS OWN!
ざざざ
"THIS IS THE LIMIT OF YOUR STRENGTH... YOU CAN'T GET ANY TOUGHER THAN YOU ARE NOW."
SO WHY AM I GOING T HOTARU' SIDE?
ANTHONY SAYS I'VE REACHED MY LIMIT...
BUT THAT MEANS I JUST HAVE TO GET STRONGER LIKE I'VE ALWAYS DONE!
ばっ
IT'S HOW I'VE ALWAYS LIVED MY LIFE!
"YOUR BODY CAN'T HANDLE ANY MORE..."
BUT HOW AM I SUP-POSED TO...
...GET STRONGER THAN I ALREADY AM?

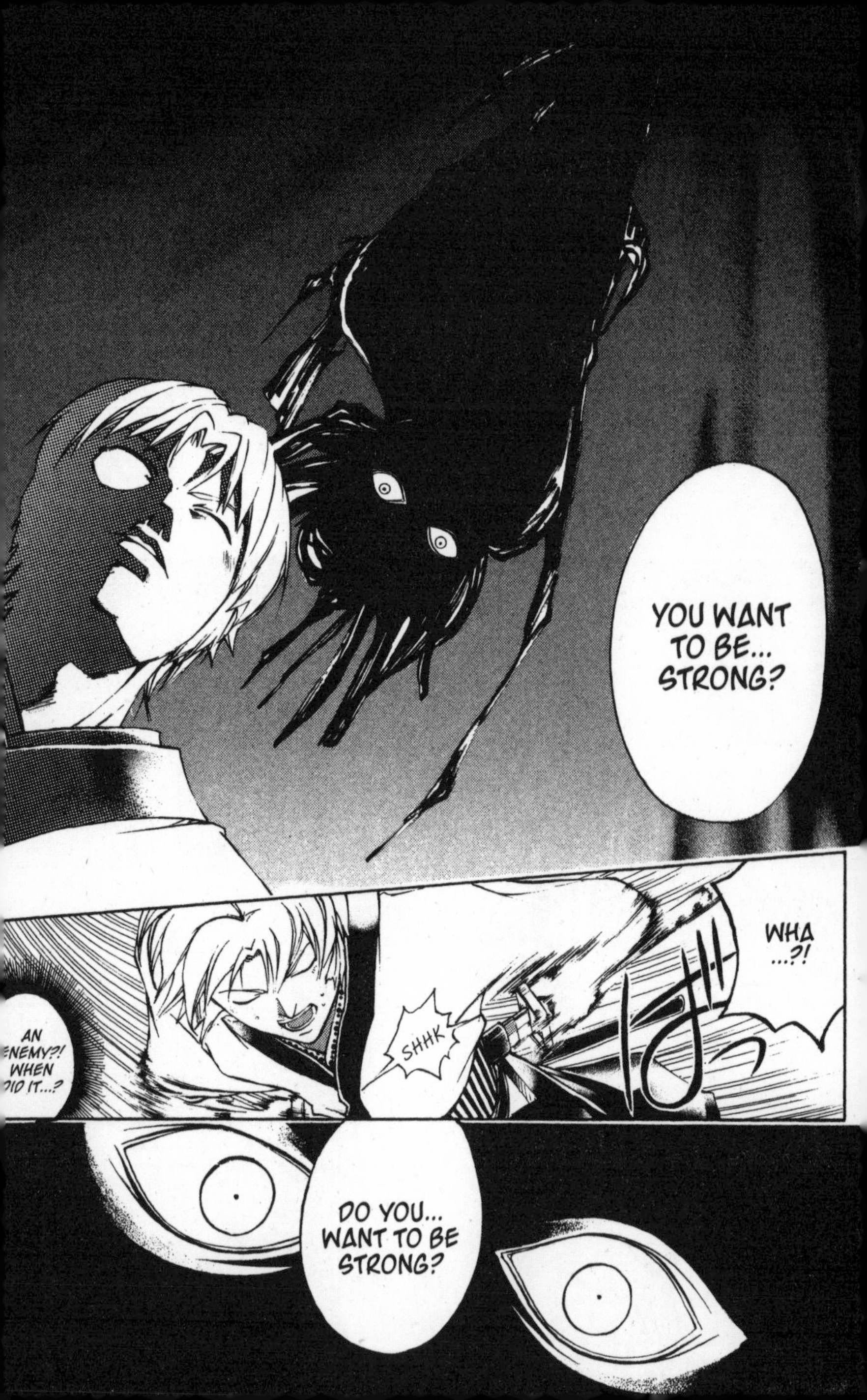
YOU WANT TO BE... STRONG?
WHA ...?!
SHHK
AN ENEMY?! WHEN DID IT...?
DO YOU... WANT TO BE STRONG?

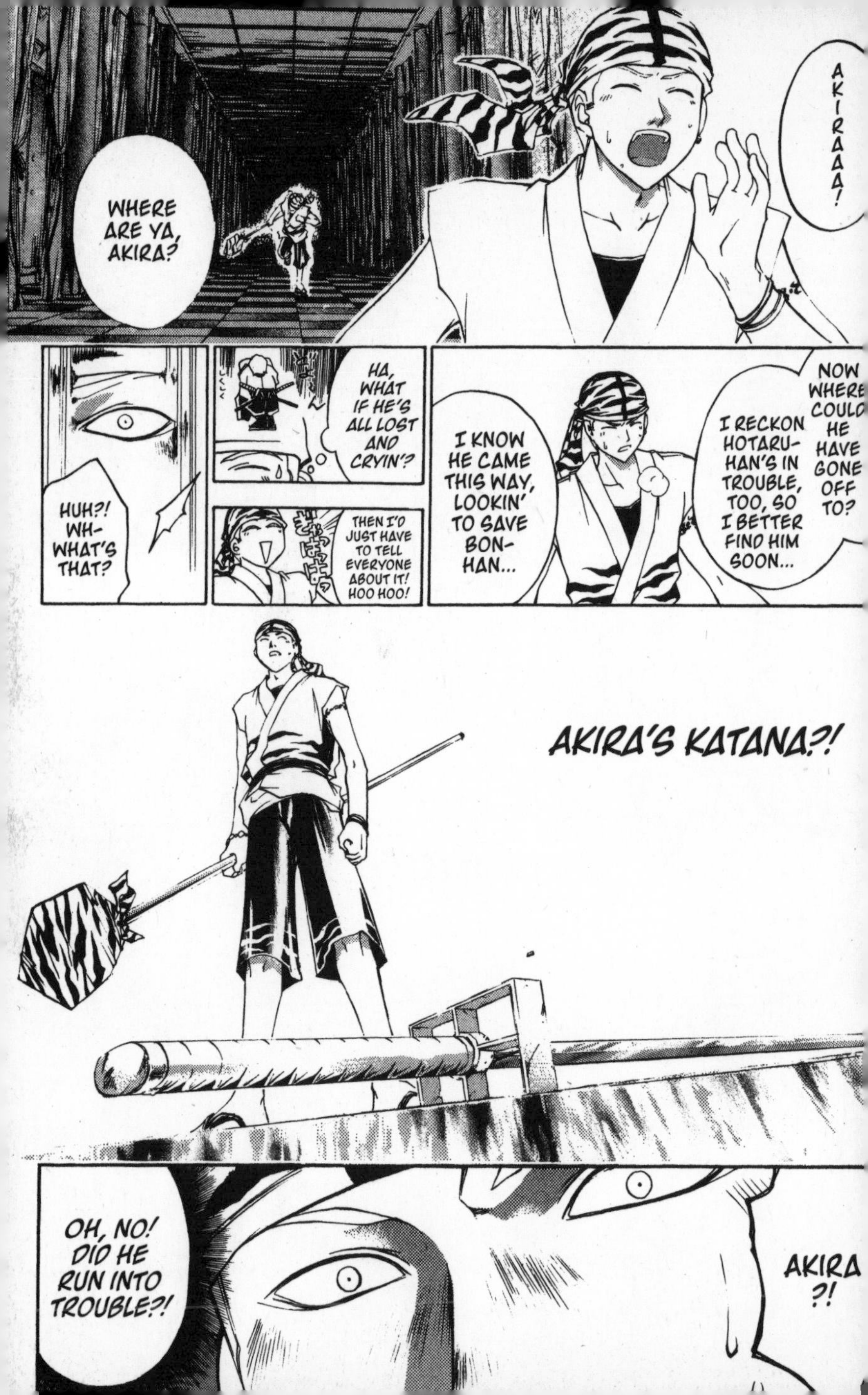
AKIRAAAA!
WHERE ARE YA, AKIRA?
NOW WHERE COULD HE HAVE GONE OFF TO?
I RECKON HOTARU-HAN'S IN TROUBLE, TOO, SO I BETTER FIND HIM SOON...
I KNOW HE CAME THIS WAY, LOOKIN' TO SAVE BON-HAN...
HA, WHAT IF HE'S ALL LOST AND CRYIN'?
THEN I'D JUST HAVE TO TELL EVERYONE ABOUT IT! HOO HOO!
HUH?! WH-WHAT'S THAT?
AKIRA'S KATANA?!
AKIRA ?!
OH, NO! DID HE RUN INTO TROUBLE?!

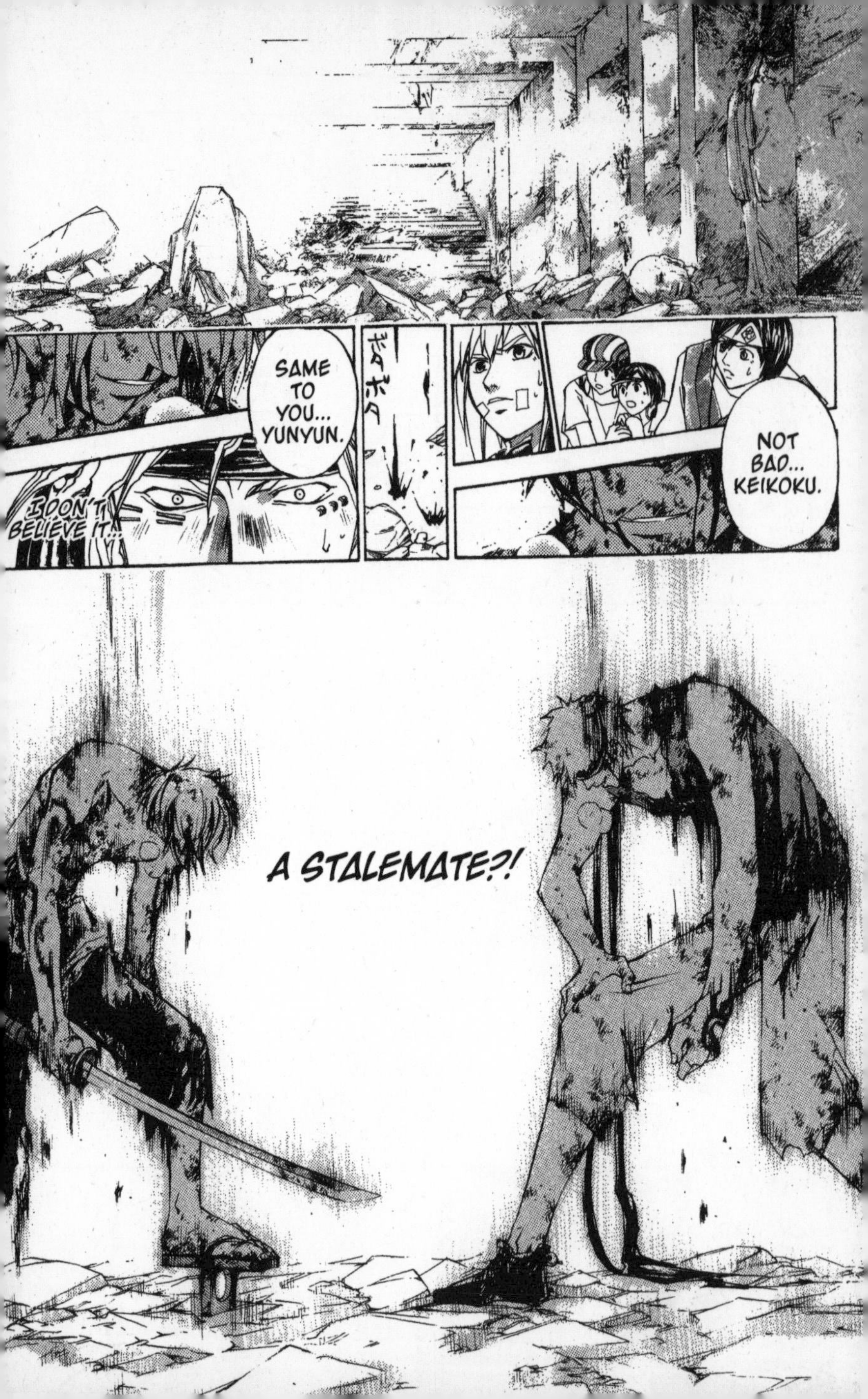
NOT BAD... KEIKOKU.
ボタボタ
SAME TO YOU... YUNYUN.
I DON'T BELIEVE IT...
A STALEMATE?!

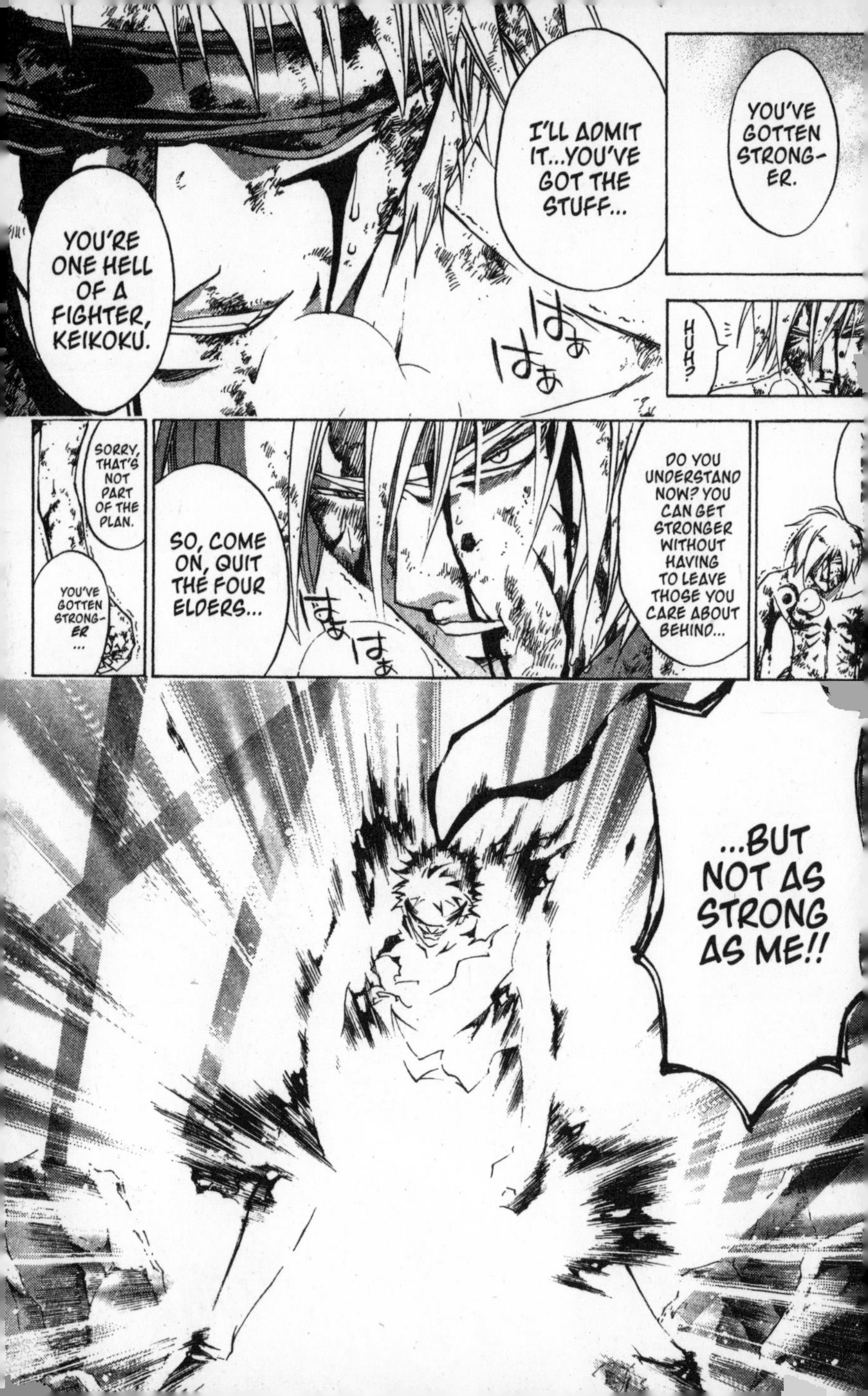
YOU'VE GOTTEN STRONG-ER.
HUH?
I'LL ADMIT IT...YOU'VE GOT THE STUFF...
はあ はあ
YOU'RE ONE HELL OF A FIGHTER, KEIKOKU.
DO YOU UNDERSTAND NOW? YOU CAN GET STRONGER WITHOUT HAVING TO LEAVE THOSE YOU CARE ABOUT BEHIND...
SO, COME ON, QUIT THE FOUR ELDERS...
はあ はあ
SORRY, THAT'S NOT PART OF THE PLAN.
YOU'VE GOTTEN STRONG-ER...
...BUT NOT AS STRONG AS ME!!

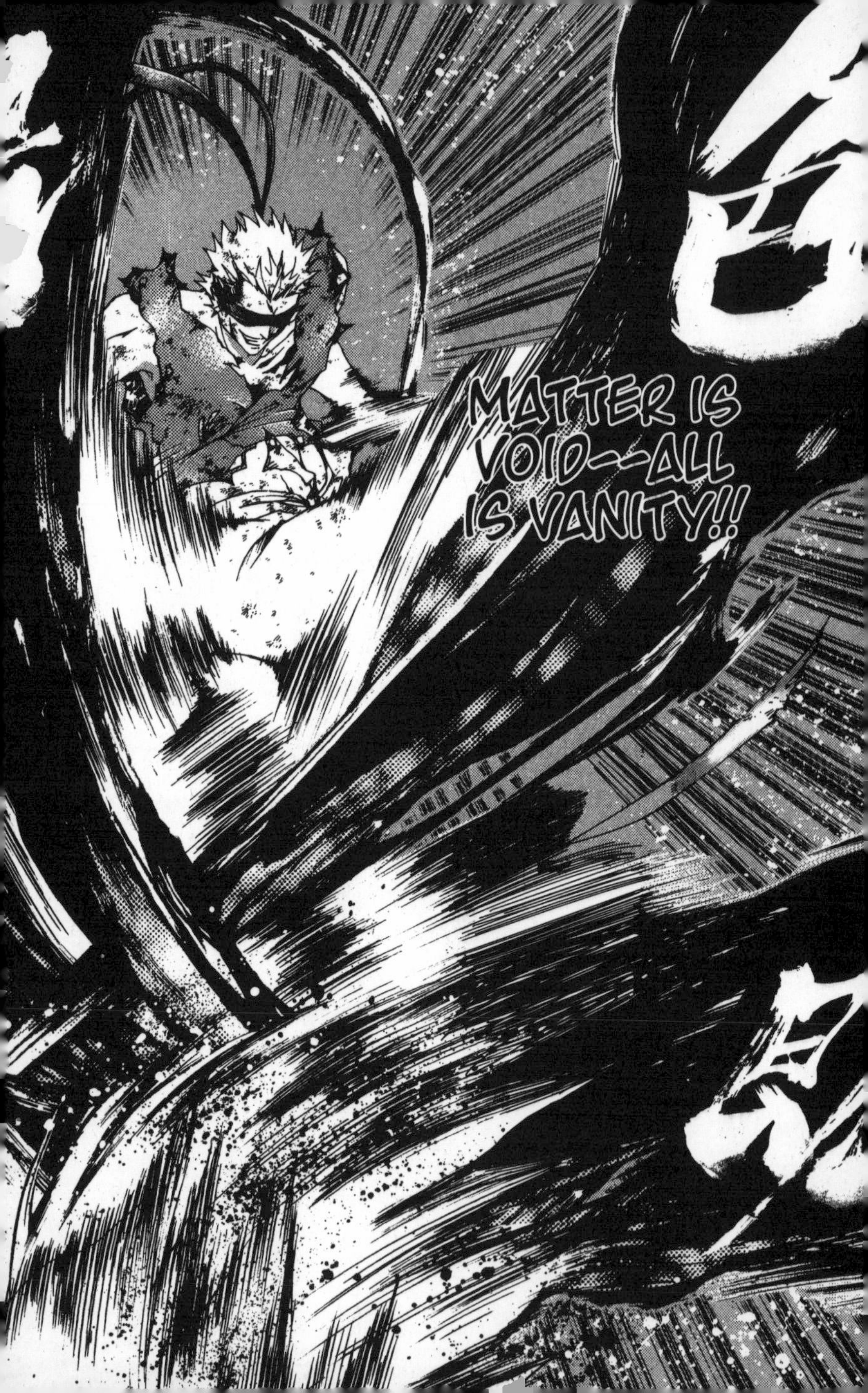
MATTER IS VOID--ALL IS VANITY!!

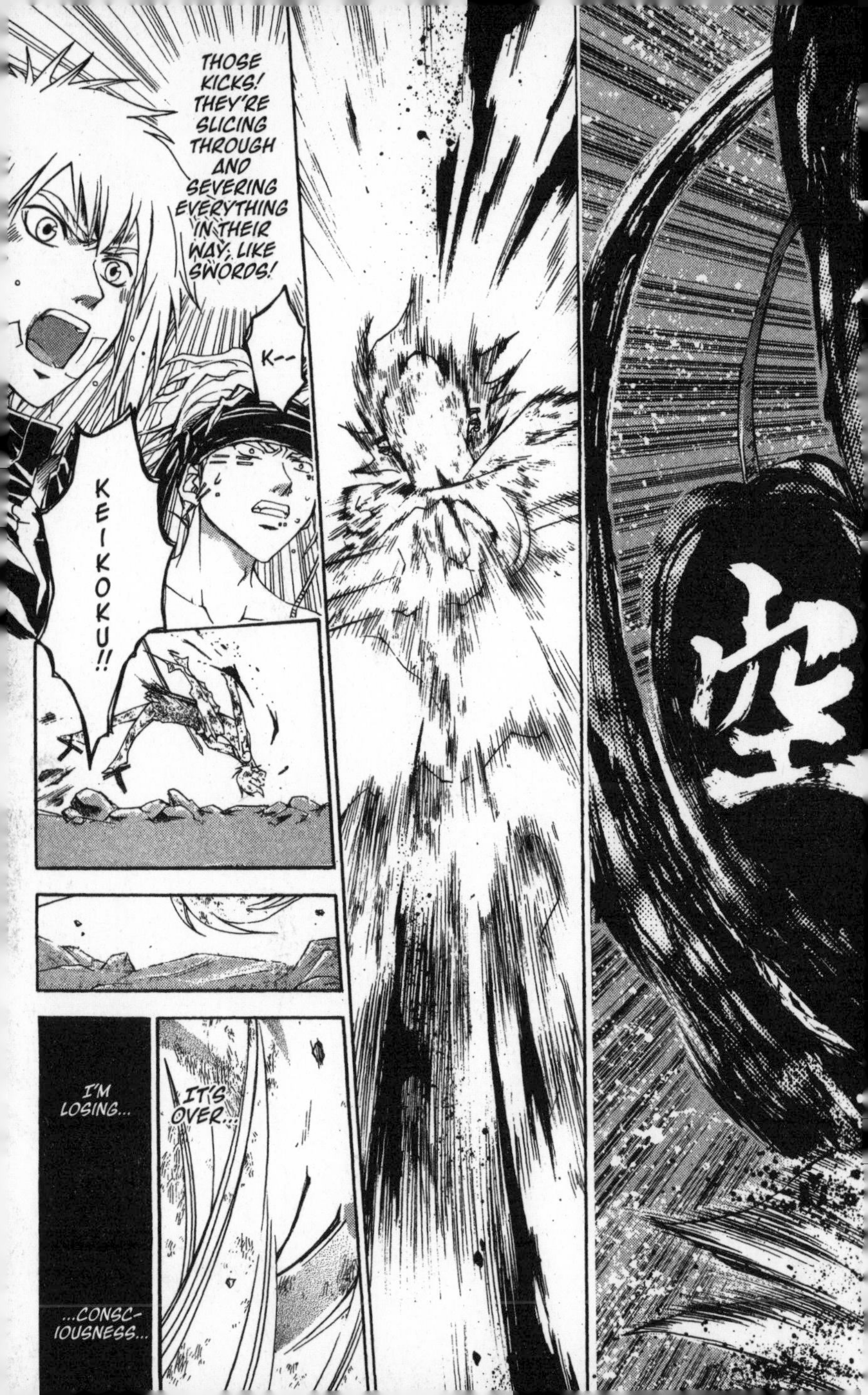
THOSE KICKS! THEY'RE SLICING THROUGH AND SEVERING EVERYTHING IN THEIR WAY, LIKE SWORDS!
K--
KEIKOKU!!
I'M LOSING...
IT'S OVER...
...CONSCIOUSNESS...

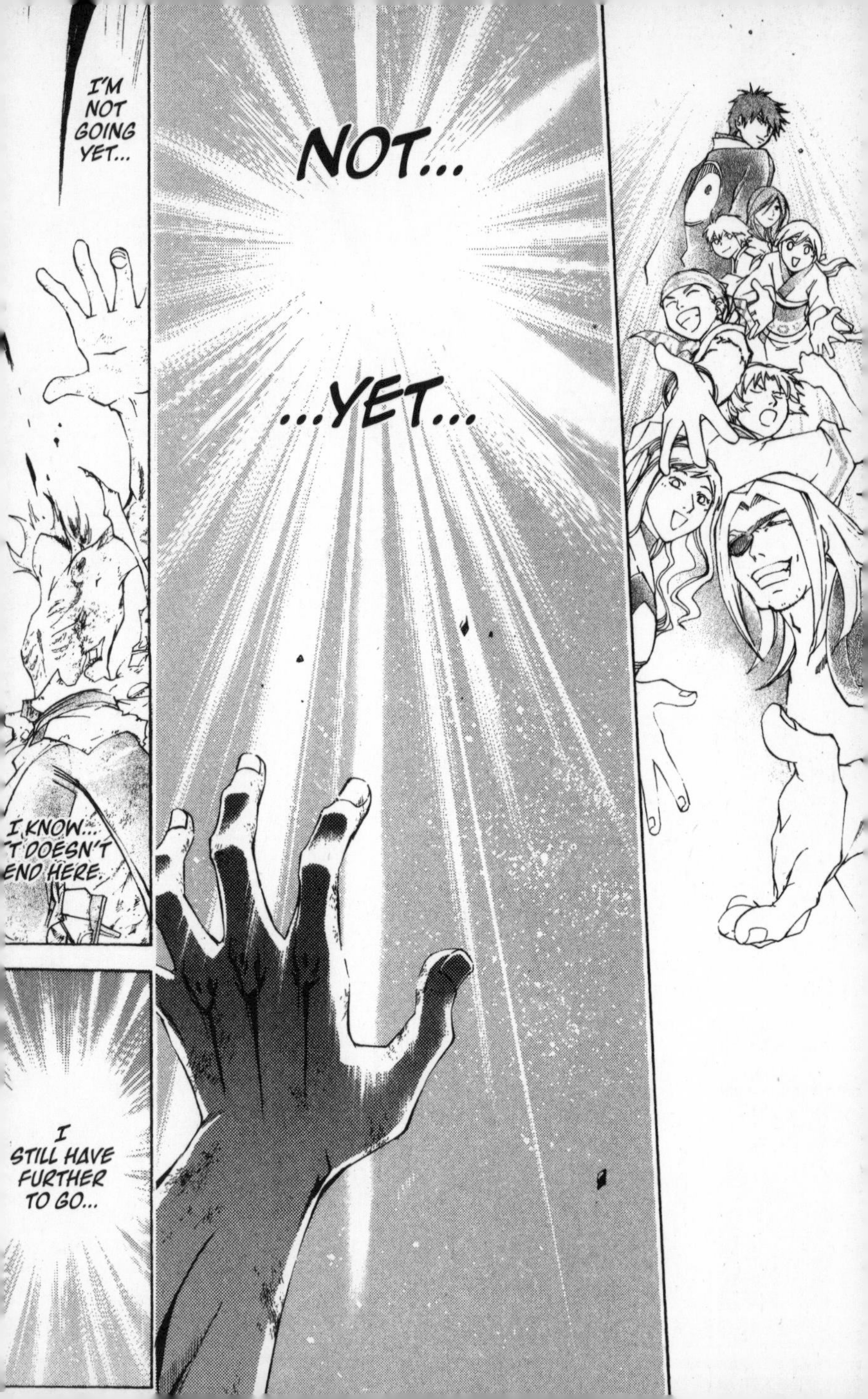
NOT...
...YET...
I'M NOT GOING YET...
I KNOW... 'T DOESN'T END HERE.
I STILL HAVE FURTHER TO GO...

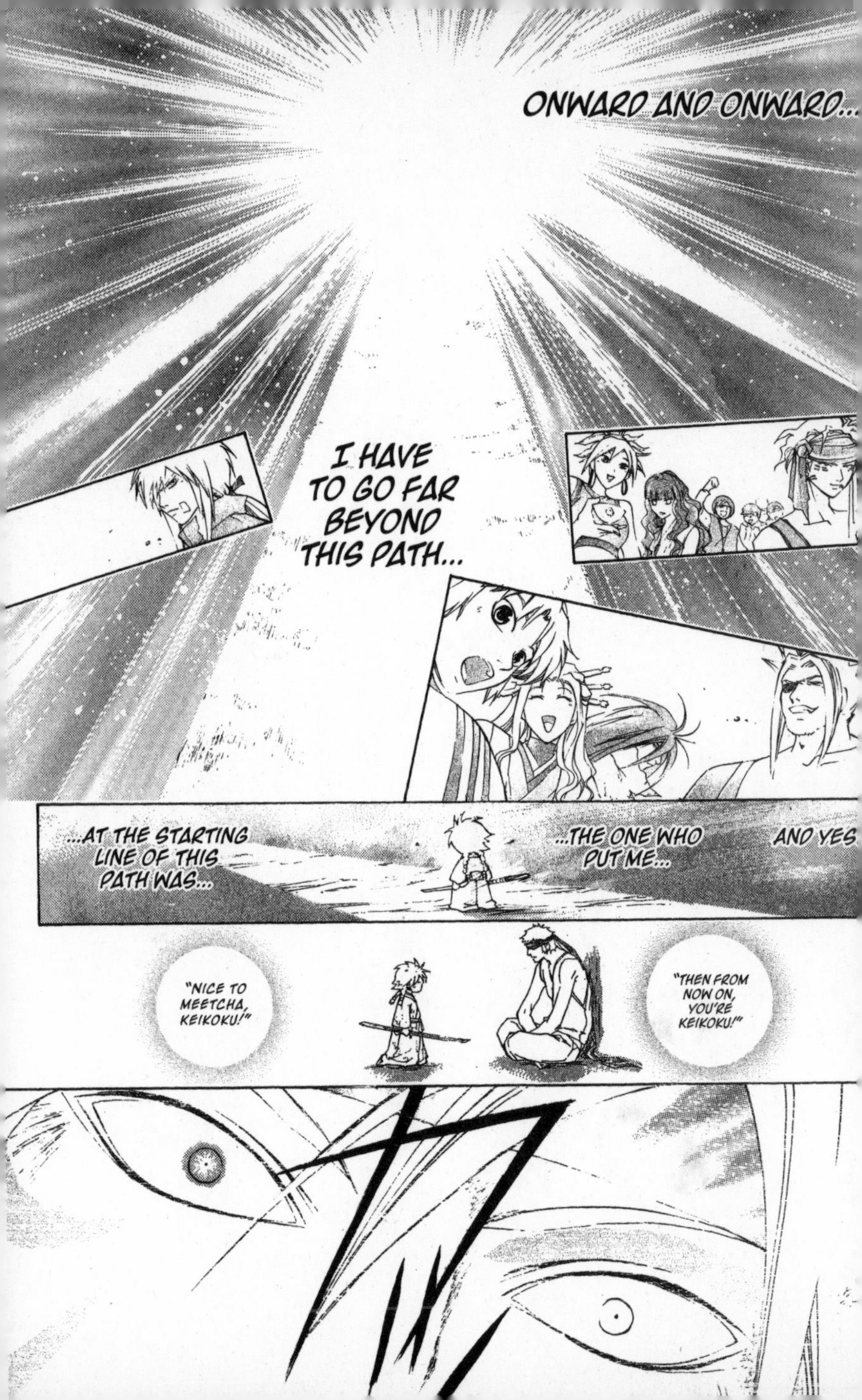
ONWARD AND ONWARD...
I HAVE TO GO FAR BEYOND THIS PATH...
AND YES
...THE ONE WHO PUT ME...
...AT THE STARTING LINE OF THIS PATH WAS...
"THEN FROM NOW ON, YOU'RE KEIKOKU!"
"NICE TO MEETCHA, KEIKOKU!"

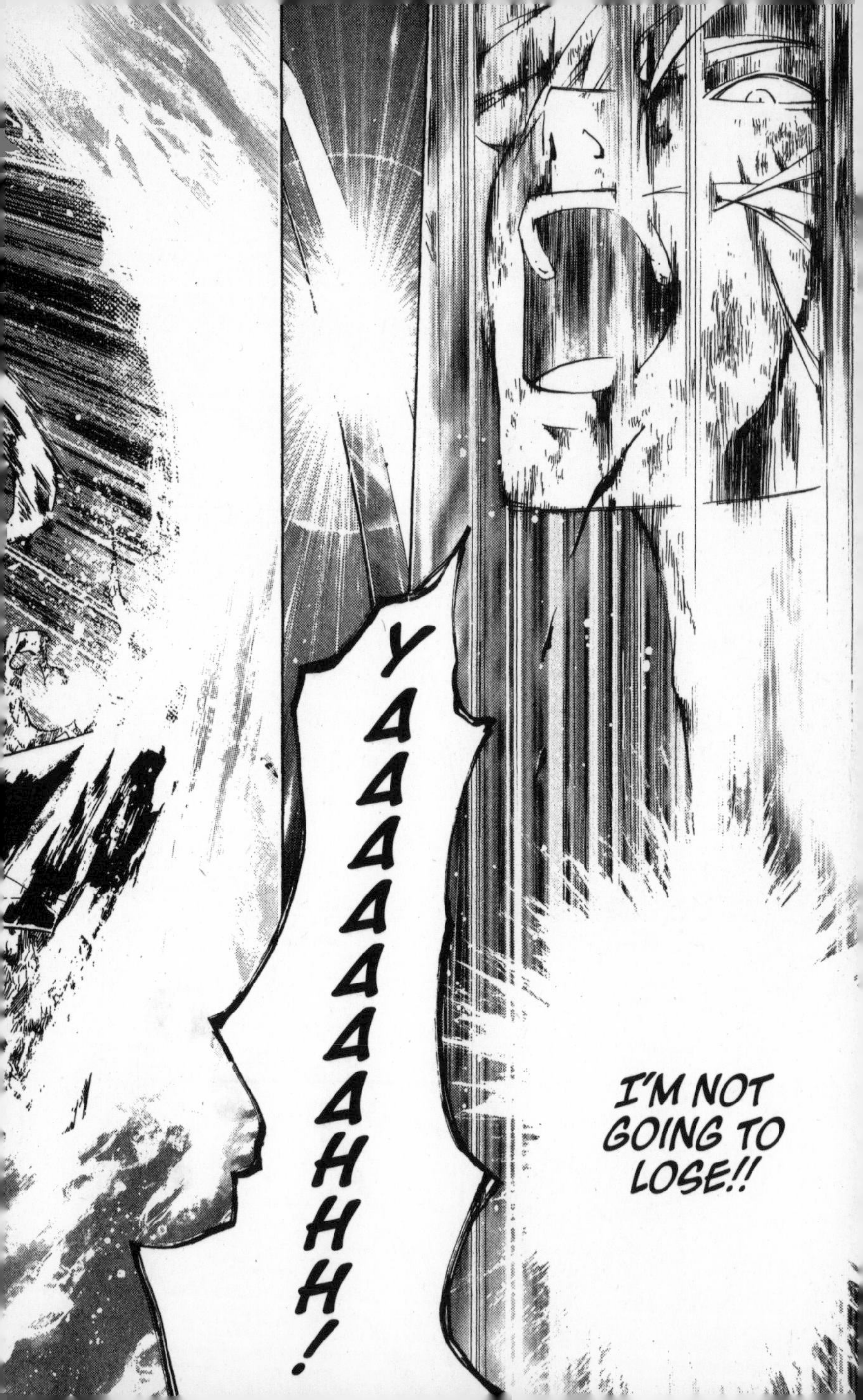
YAAAAAAAHHHH!
I'M NOT GOING TO LOSE!!

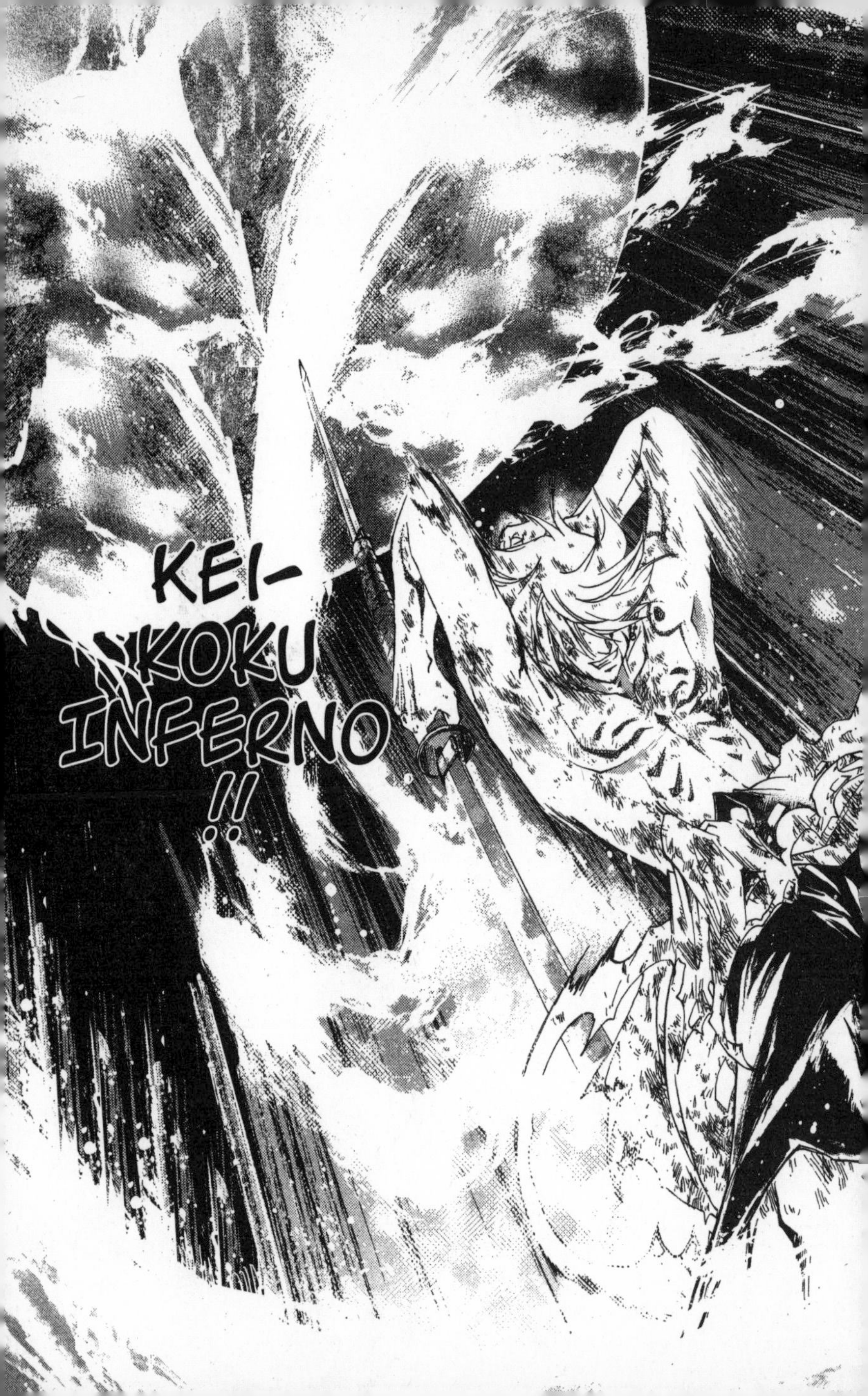
KEI-
KOKU
INFERNO
!!

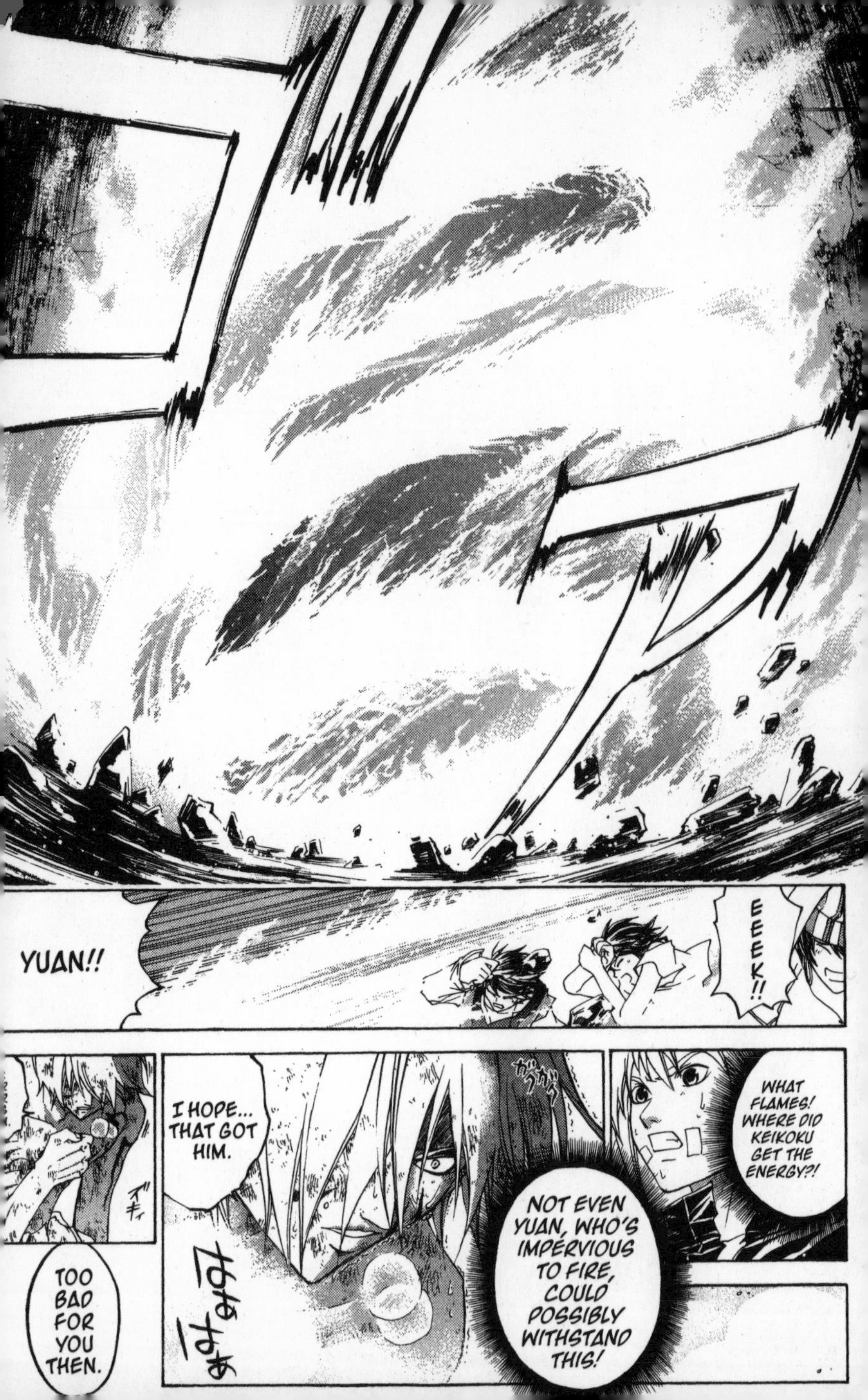
EEEEK!!
YUAN!!
WHAT FLAMES! WHERE DID KEIKOKU GET THE ENERGY?!
NOT EVEN YUAN, WHO'S IMPERVIOUS TO FIRE, COULD POSSIBLY WITHSTAND THIS!
I HOPE... THAT GOT HIM.
TOO BAD FOR YOU THEN.

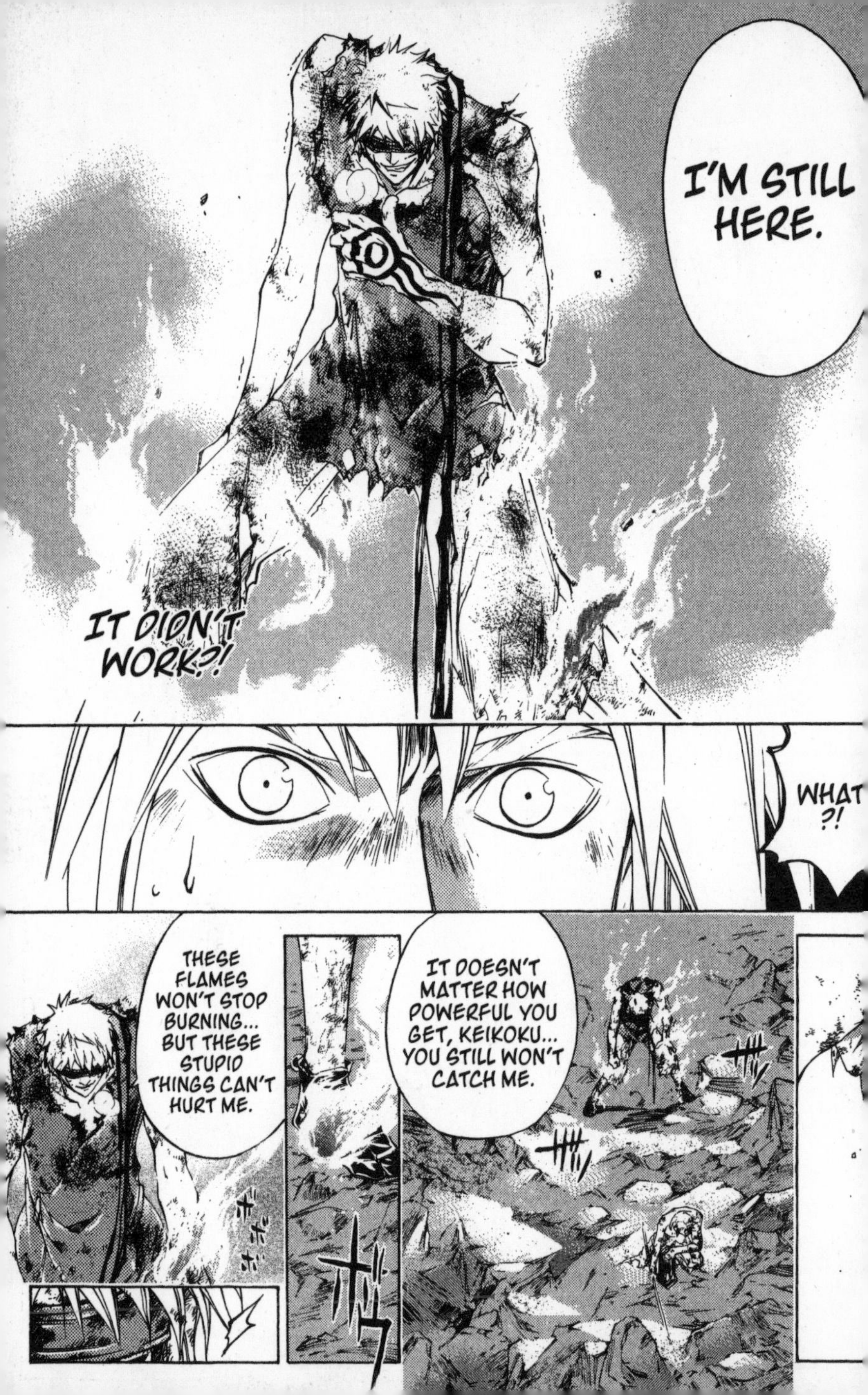
I'M STILL HERE.
IT DIDN'T WORK?!
WHAT ?!
IT DOESN'T MATTER HOW POWERFUL YOU GET, KEIKOKU... YOU STILL WON'T CATCH ME.
THESE FLAMES WON'T STOP BURNING... BUT THESE STUPID THINGS CAN'T HURT ME.

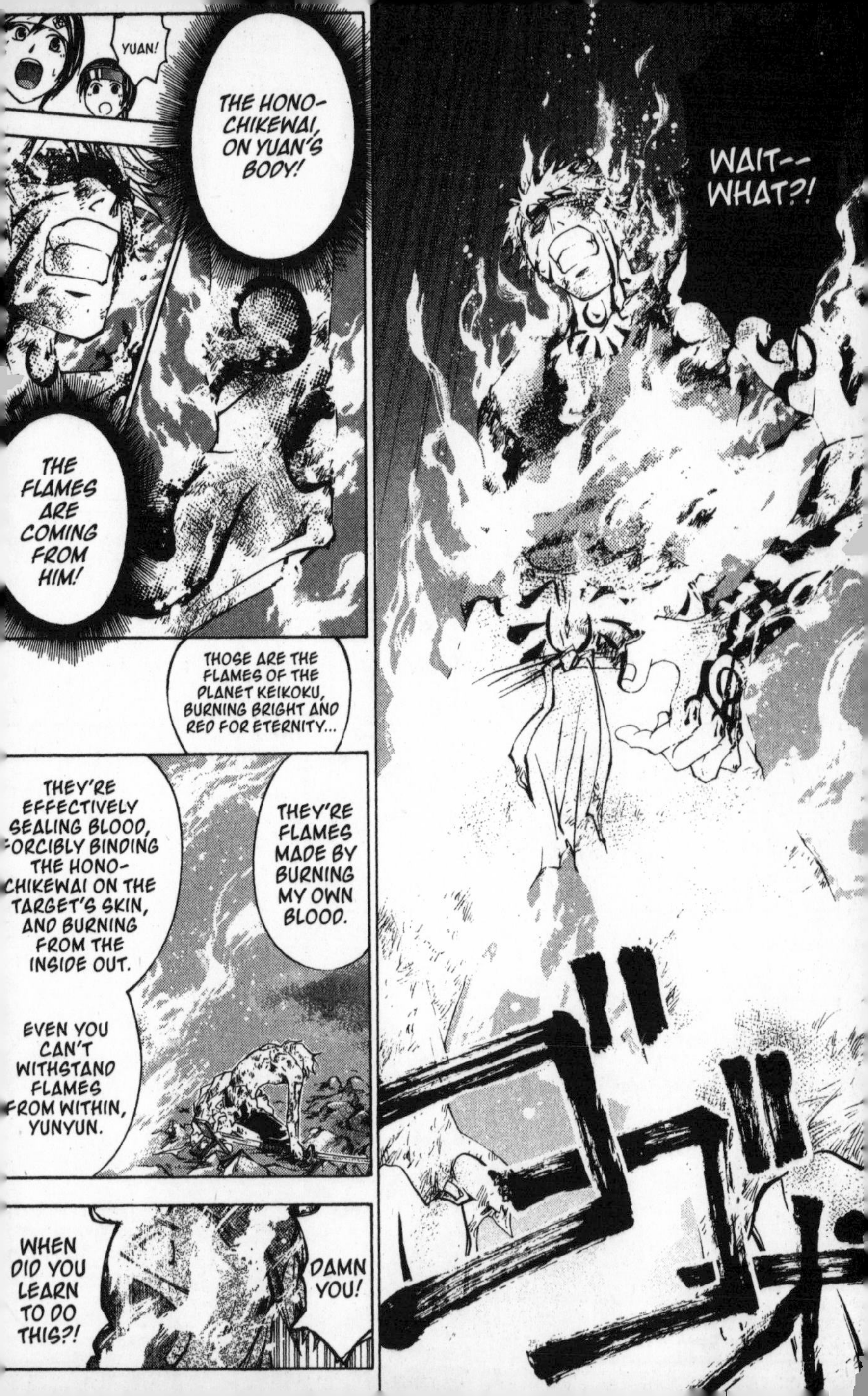
WAIT--
WHAT?!
YUAN!
THE HONO-CHIKEWAI, ON YUAN'S BODY!
THE FLAMES ARE COMING FROM HIM!
THOSE ARE THE FLAMES OF THE PLANET KEIKOKU, BURNING BRIGHT AND RED FOR ETERNITY...
THEY'RE FLAMES MADE BY BURNING MY OWN BLOOD.
THEY'RE EFFECTIVELY SEALING BLOOD, FORCIBLY BINDING THE HONO-CHIKEWAI ON THE TARGET'S SKIN, AND BURNING FROM THE INSIDE OUT.
EVEN YOU CAN'T WITHSTAND FLAMES FROM WITHIN, YUNYUN.
DAMN YOU!
WHEN DID YOU LEARN TO DO THIS?!

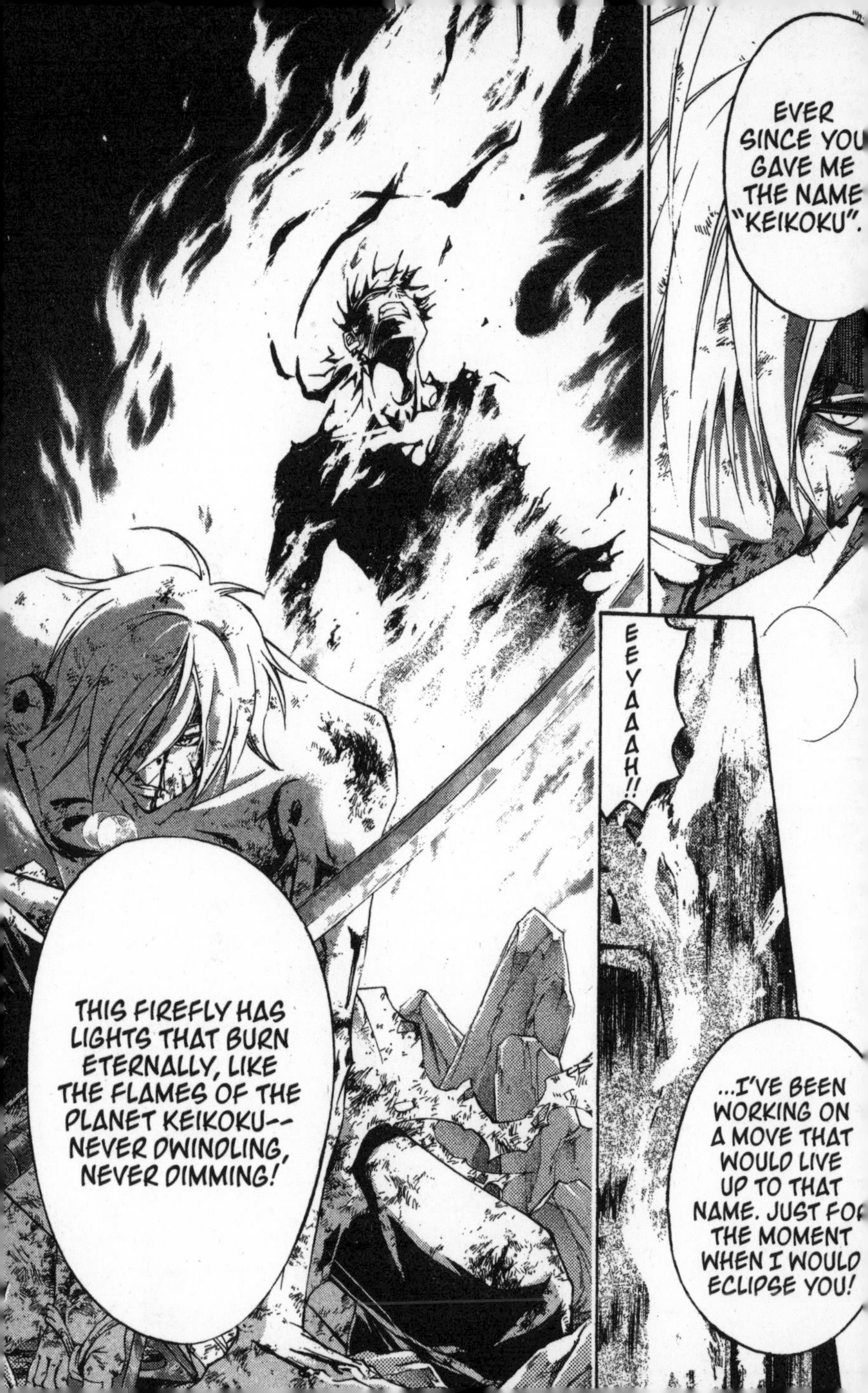
EVER SINCE YOU GAVE ME THE NAME "KEIKOKU".
...I'VE BEEN WORKING ON A MOVE THAT WOULD LIVE UP TO THAT NAME. JUST FOR THE MOMENT WHEN I WOULD ECLIPSE YOU!
EEYAAAAH!!
THIS FIREFLY HAS LIGHTS THAT BURN ETERNALLY, LIKE THE FLAMES OF THE PLANET KEIKOKU-- NEVER DWINDLING, NEVER DIMMING!

Character Collection: Shiina Nozomu

[Hiroshima/Atsushi]⬇

Big Brother is one of the stars now!

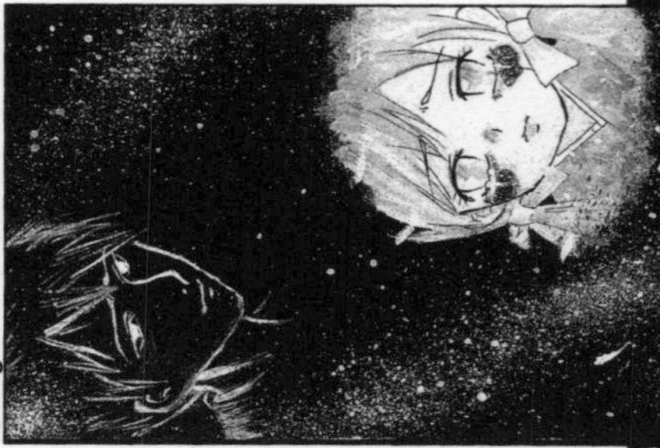

[Aomori/Saki Masuda]⬇

The images really come across!

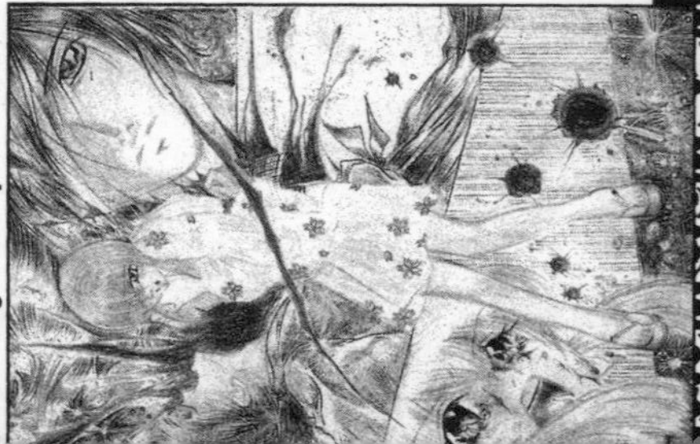

[Fukuoka/Azure Water Clock]⬇

Cutting-edge design!

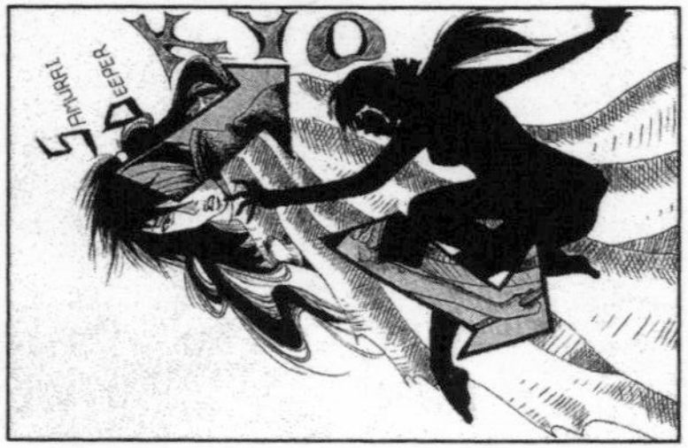
SAMURAI DEEPER
KYO

[Aichi/Akira]⬇

I love the atmosphere!

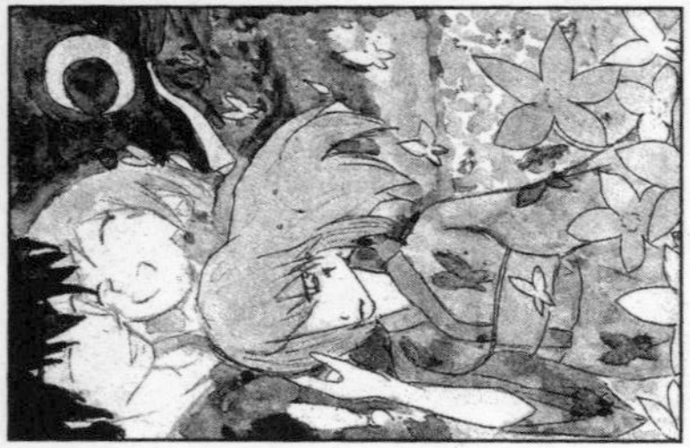

[Hiroshima/Nasu2]⬇

What a gentle smile.

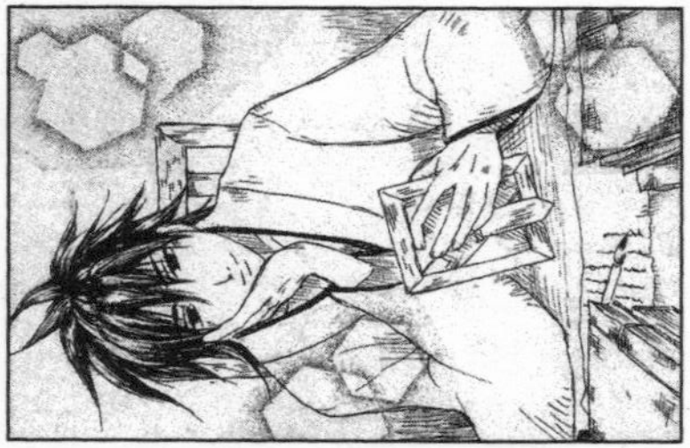

[Saitama/Kanna Ryu]⬇

Here's a cheeky Yuya-chan!

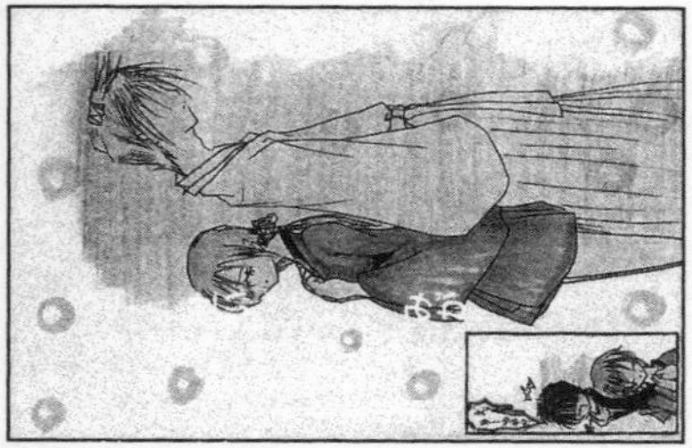

Thanks for all the illustrations, especially the New Year's cards!

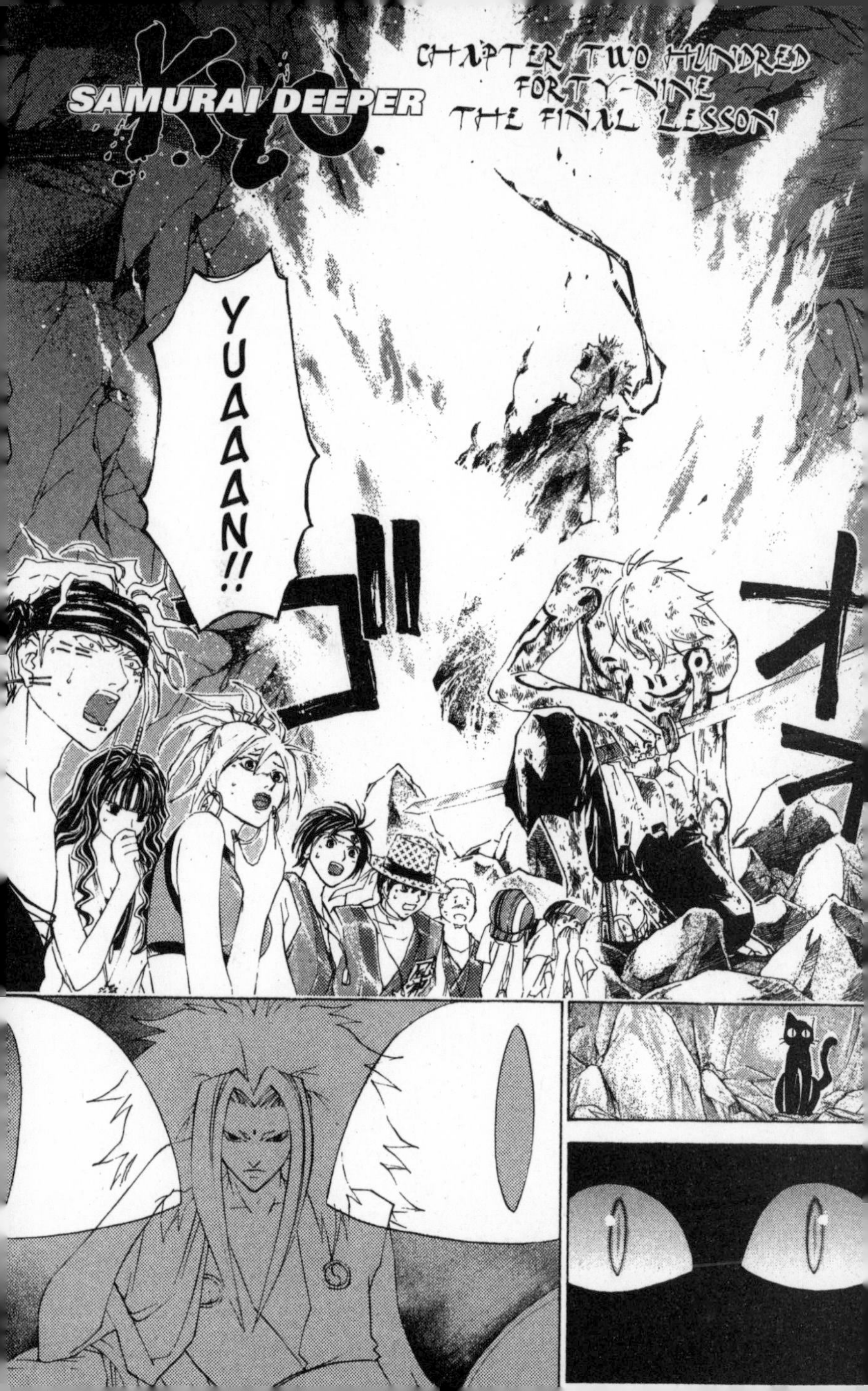
SAMURAI DEEPER KYO
CHAPTER TWO HUNDRED FORTY-NINE
THE FINAL LESSON
YUAAAAN!!
ゴ
オ

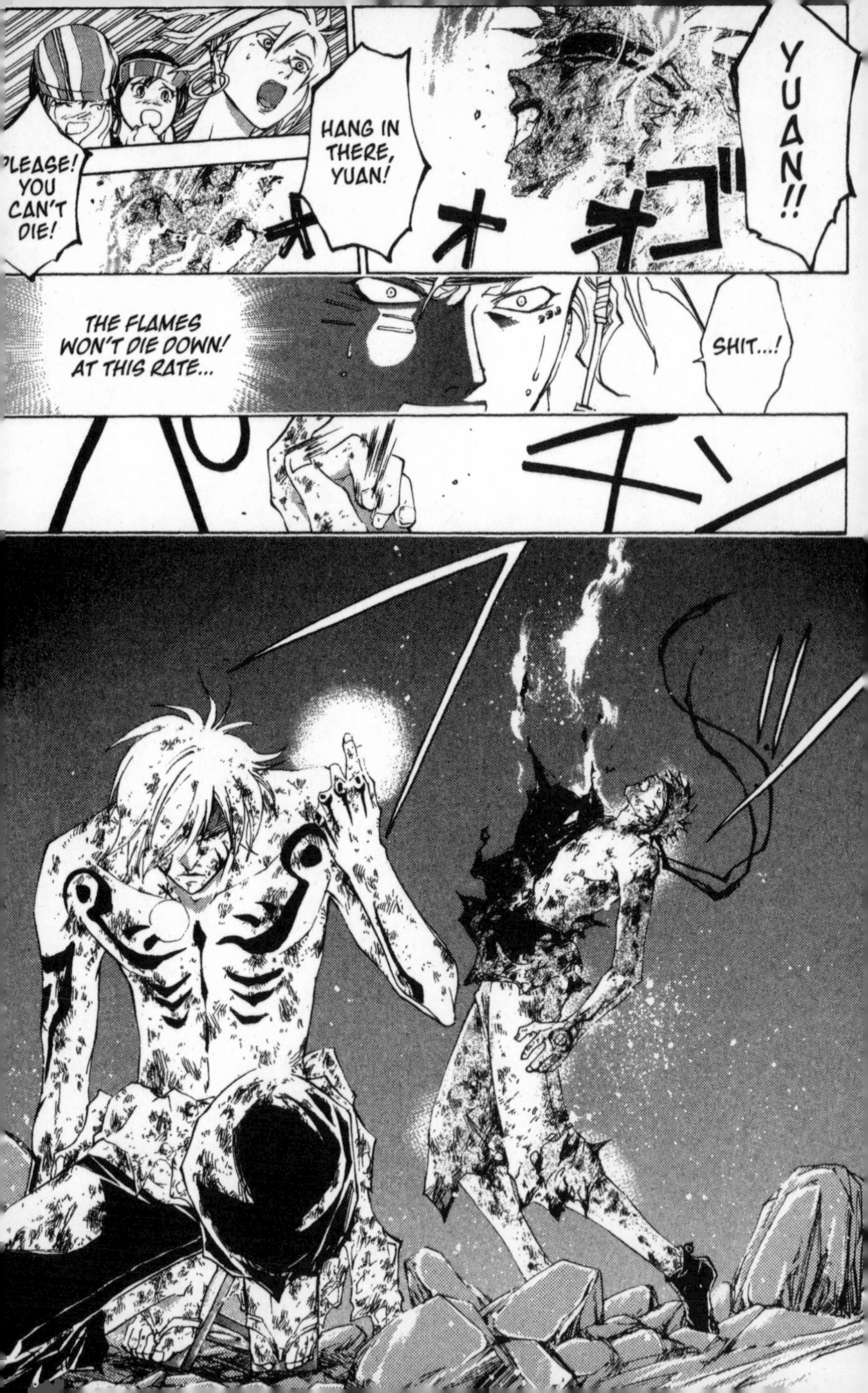
YUAN!!
HANG IN THERE, YUAN!
PLEASE! YOU CAN'T DIE!
SHIT...!
THE FLAMES WON'T DIE DOWN! AT THIS RATE...

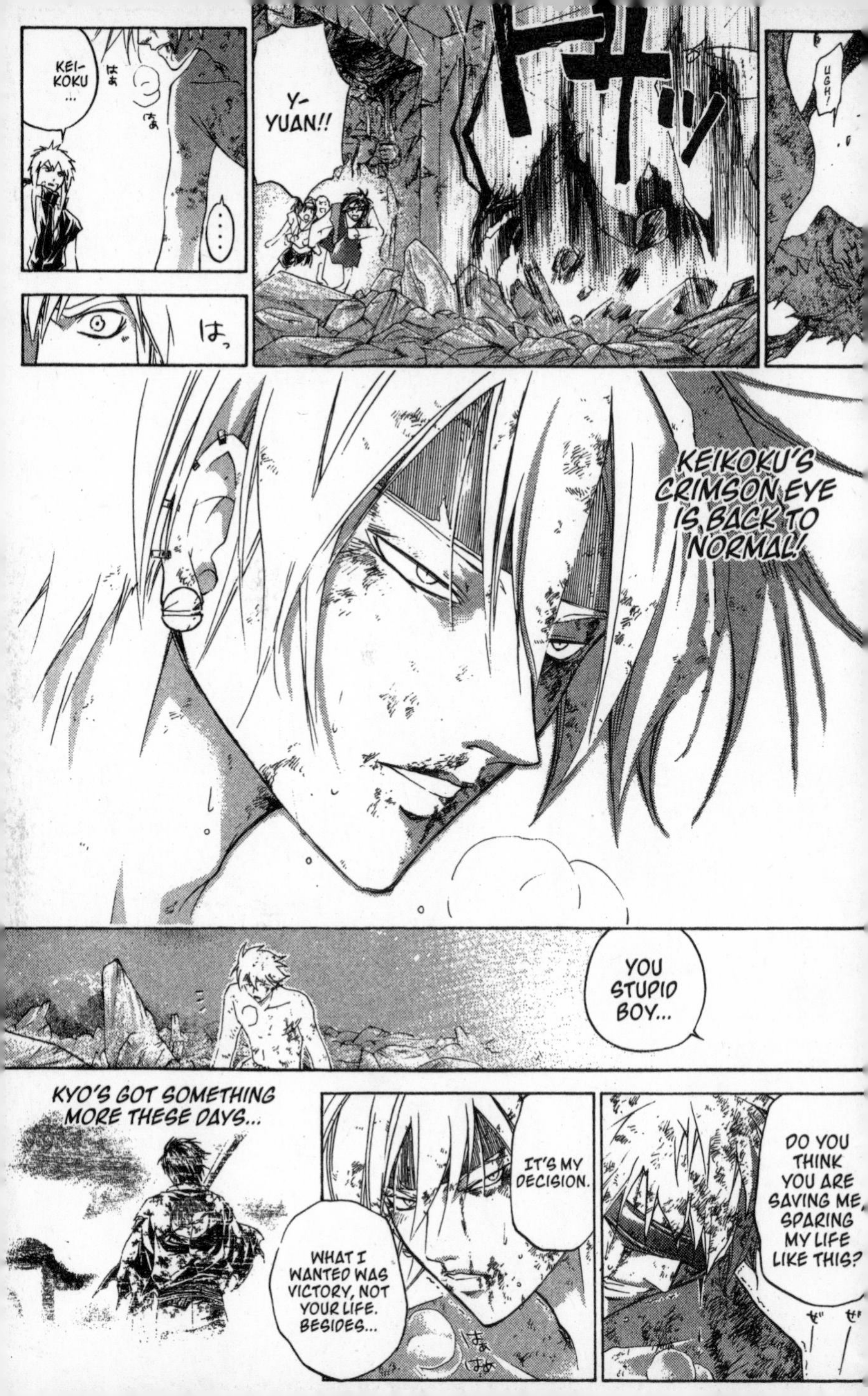
UGH!
ドガッ
Y-YUAN!!
KEI-KOKU...
はぁ
はぁ
....
はっ
KEIKOKU'S CRIMSON EYE IS BACK TO NORMAL!
YOU STUPID BOY...
DO YOU THINK YOU ARE SAVING ME, SPARING MY LIFE LIKE THIS?
ぜー
ぜー
IT'S MY DECISION.
WHAT I WANTED WAS VICTORY, NOT YOUR LIFE. BESIDES...
はぁ
はぁ
KYO'S GOT SOMETHING MORE THESE DAYS...

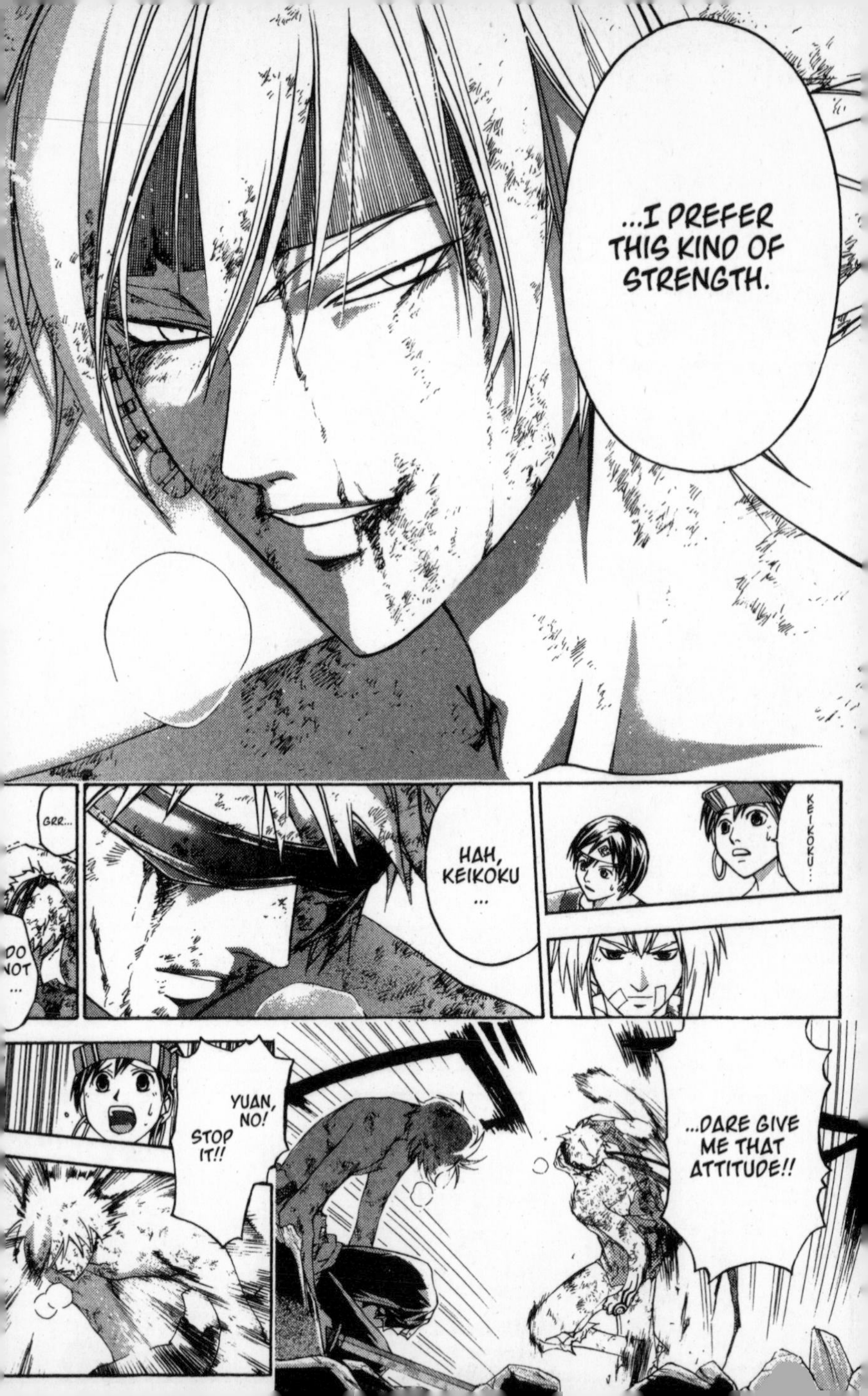
...I PREFER THIS KIND OF STRENGTH.
KEIKOKU...
HAH, KEIKOKU ...
GRR...
DO NOT ...
...DARE GIVE ME THAT ATTITUDE!!
YUAN, NO! STOP IT!!

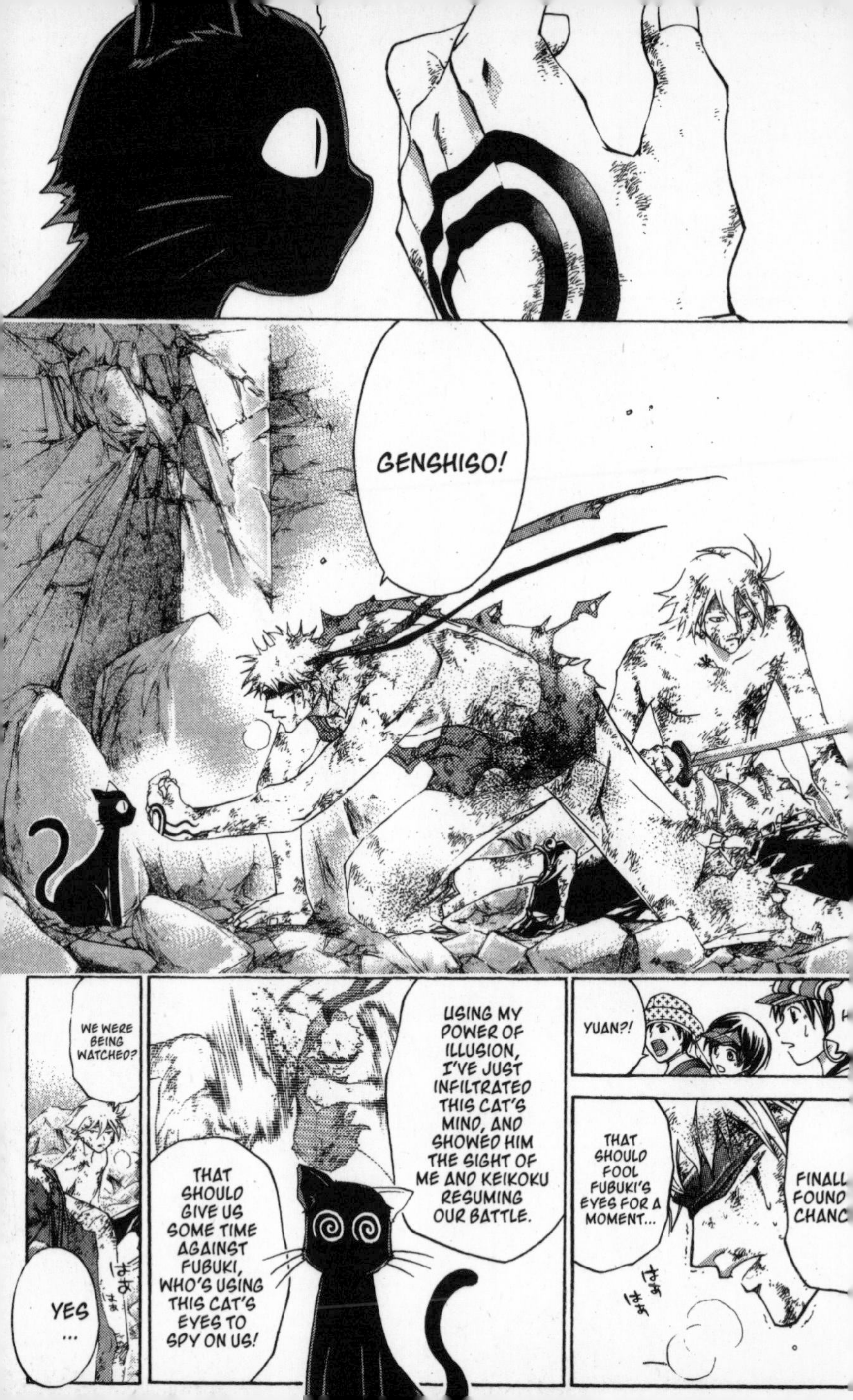
GENSHISO!
YUAN?!
THAT SHOULD FOOL FUBUKI'S EYES FOR A MOMENT...
FINALL FOUND CHANC
はあ はあ
USING MY POWER OF ILLUSION, I'VE JUST INFILTRATED THIS CAT'S MIND, AND SHOWED HIM THE SIGHT OF ME AND KEIKOKU RESUMING OUR BATTLE.
THAT SHOULD GIVE US SOME TIME AGAINST FUBUKI, WHO'S USING THIS CAT'S EYES TO SPY ON US!
WE WERE BEING WATCHED?
はあ はあ
YES ...

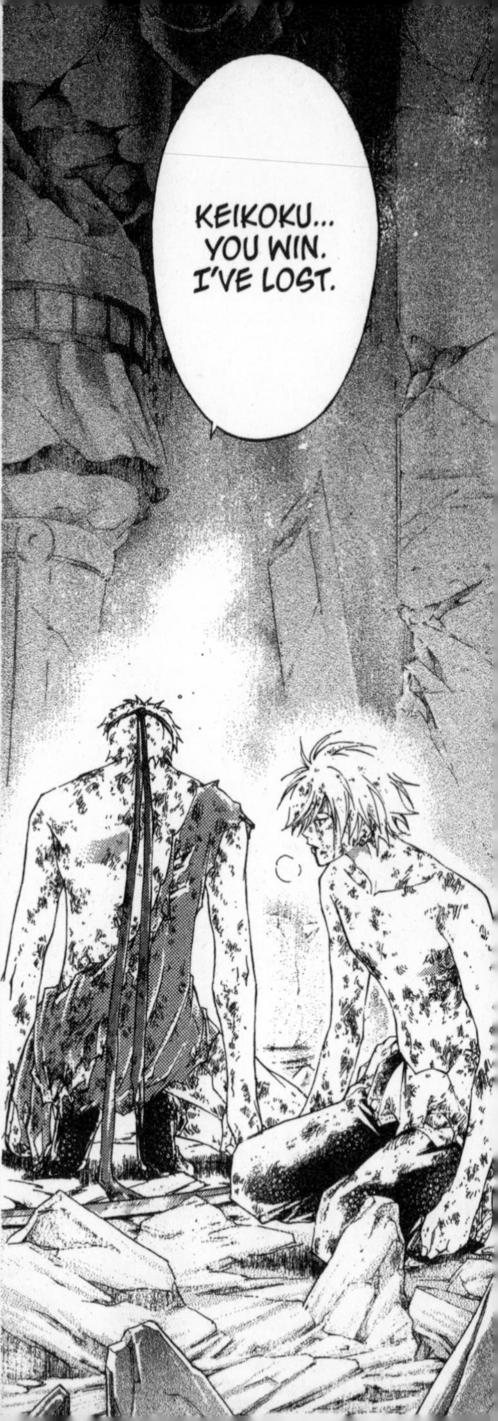
KEIKOKU... YOU WIN. I'VE LOST.

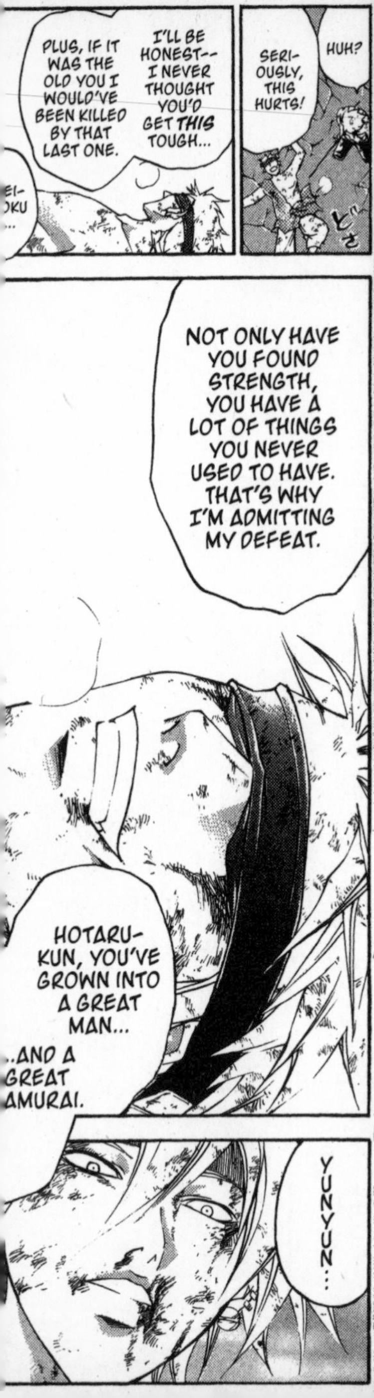
HUH?
SERIOUSLY, THIS HURTS!
I'LL BE HONEST-- I NEVER THOUGHT YOU'D GET **THIS** TOUGH...
PLUS, IF IT WAS THE OLD YOU I WOULD'VE BEEN KILLED BY THAT LAST ONE.
NOT ONLY HAVE YOU FOUND STRENGTH, YOU HAVE A LOT OF THINGS YOU NEVER USED TO HAVE. THAT'S WHY I'M ADMITTING MY DEFEAT.
HOTARU-KUN, YOU'VE GROWN INTO A GREAT MAN...
..AND A GREAT AMURAI.
YUNYUN...

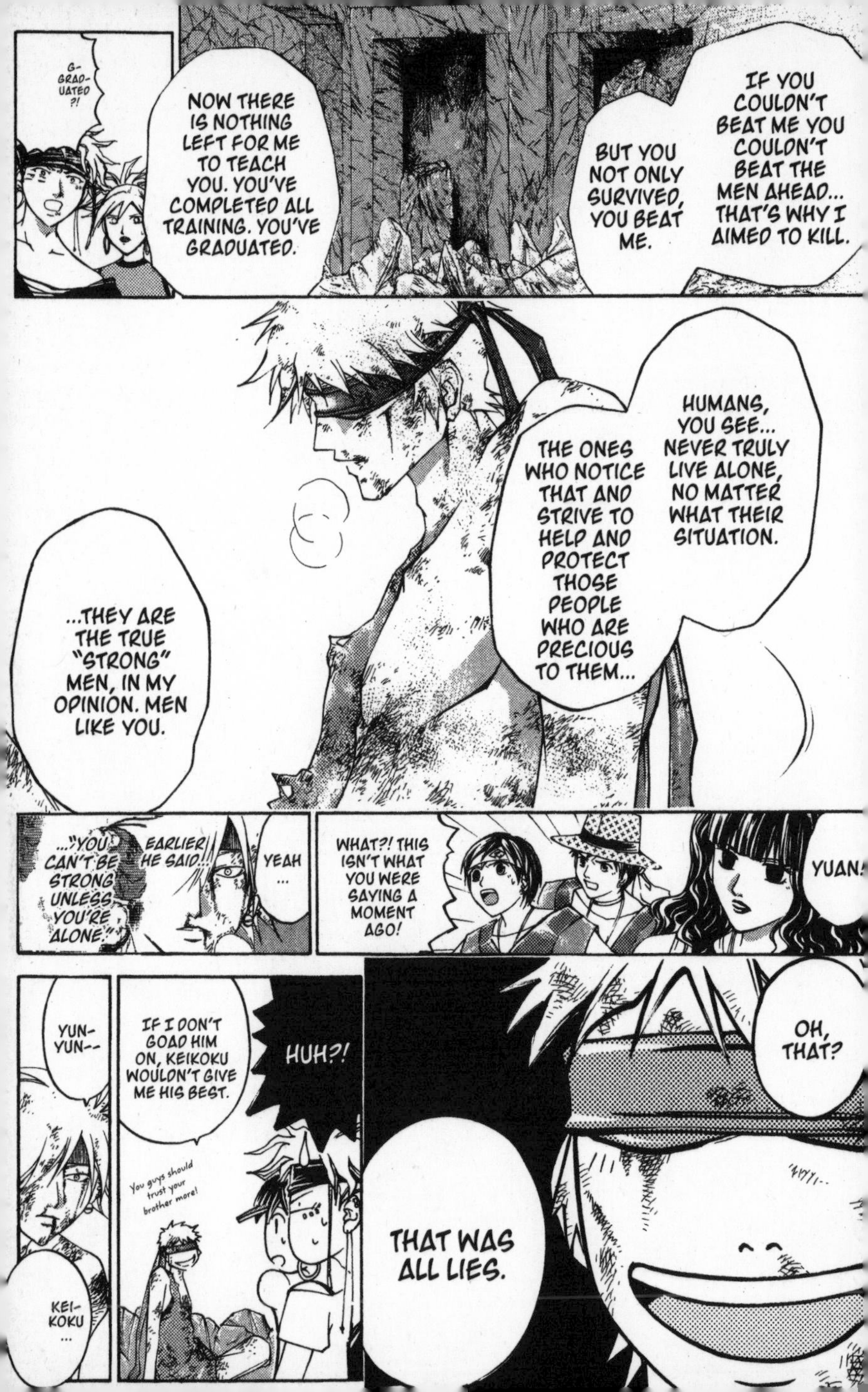
IF YOU COULDN'T BEAT ME YOU COULDN'T BEAT THE MEN AHEAD... THAT'S WHY I AIMED TO KILL.
BUT YOU NOT ONLY SURVIVED, YOU BEAT ME.
NOW THERE IS NOTHING LEFT FOR ME TO TEACH YOU. YOU'VE COMPLETED ALL TRAINING. YOU'VE GRADUATED.
G-GRADUATED?!
HUMANS, YOU SEE... NEVER TRULY LIVE ALONE, NO MATTER WHAT THEIR SITUATION.
THE ONES WHO NOTICE THAT AND STRIVE TO HELP AND PROTECT THOSE PEOPLE WHO ARE PRECIOUS TO THEM...
...THEY ARE THE TRUE "STRONG" MEN, IN MY OPINION. MEN LIKE YOU.
YUAN!
WHAT?! THIS ISN'T WHAT YOU WERE SAYING A MOMENT AGO!
YEAH ...
EARLIER HE SAID...
..."YOU CAN'T BE STRONG UNLESS YOU'RE ALONE."
OH, THAT?
THAT WAS ALL LIES.
HUH?!
IF I DON'T GOAD HIM ON, KEIKOKU WOULDN'T GIVE ME HIS BEST.
You guys should trust your brother more!
YUN-YUN--
KEI-KOKU ...

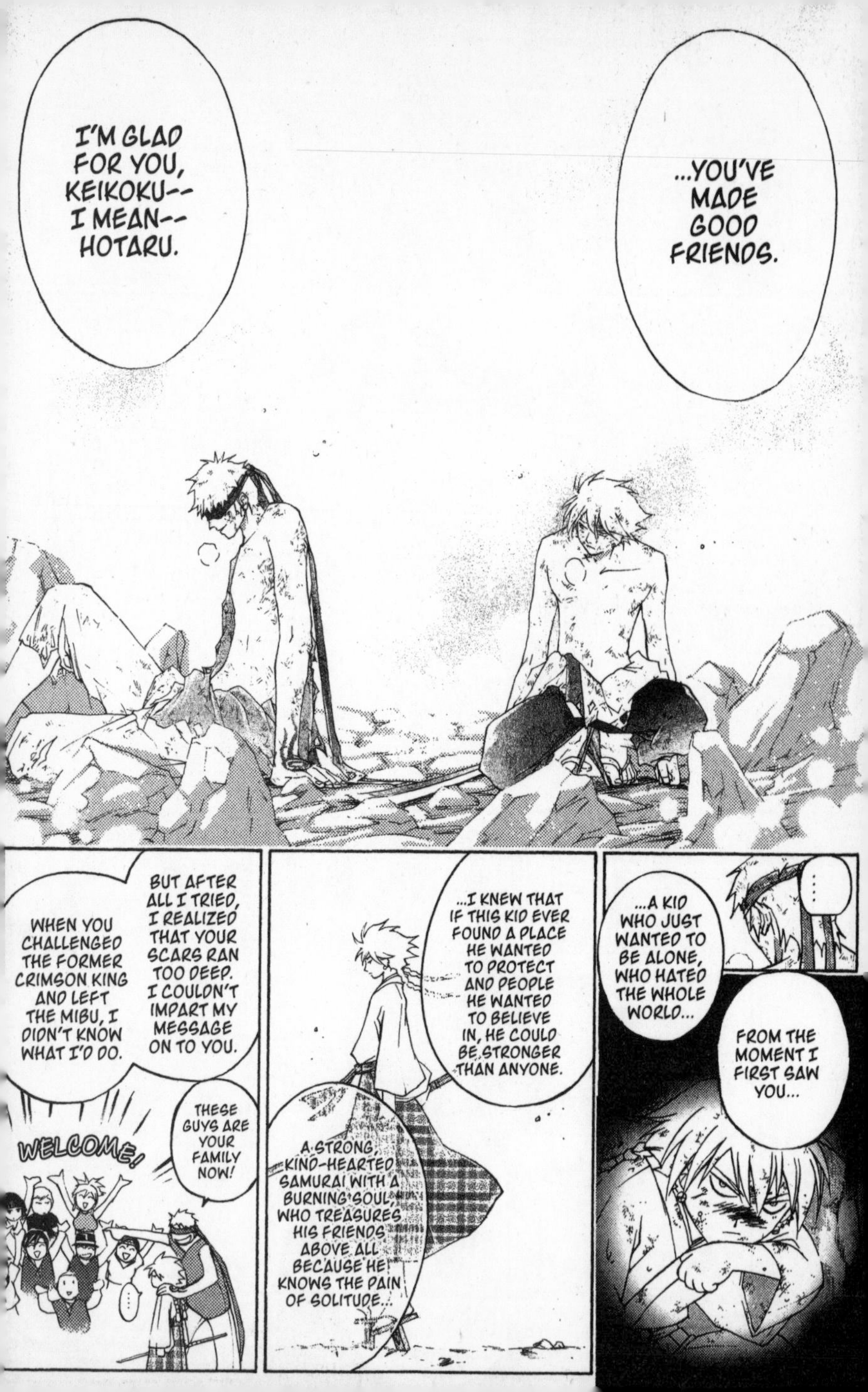
...YOU'VE MADE GOOD FRIENDS.
I'M GLAD FOR YOU, KEIKOKU-- I MEAN-- HOTARU.
...
...A KID WHO JUST WANTED TO BE ALONE, WHO HATED THE WHOLE WORLD...
FROM THE MOMENT I FIRST SAW YOU...
...I KNEW THAT IF THIS KID EVER FOUND A PLACE HE WANTED TO PROTECT AND PEOPLE HE WANTED TO BELIEVE IN, HE COULD BE STRONGER THAN ANYONE.
A STRONG, KIND-HEARTED SAMURAI WITH A BURNING SOUL, WHO TREASURES HIS FRIENDS ABOVE ALL BECAUSE HE KNOWS THE PAIN OF SOLITUDE...
BUT AFTER ALL I TRIED, I REALIZED THAT YOUR SCARS RAN TOO DEEP. I COULDN'T IMPART MY MESSAGE ON TO YOU.
WHEN YOU CHALLENGED THE FORMER CRIMSON KING AND LEFT THE MIBU, I DIDN'T KNOW WHAT I'D DO.
THESE GUYS ARE YOUR FAMILY NOW!
WELCOME!
...

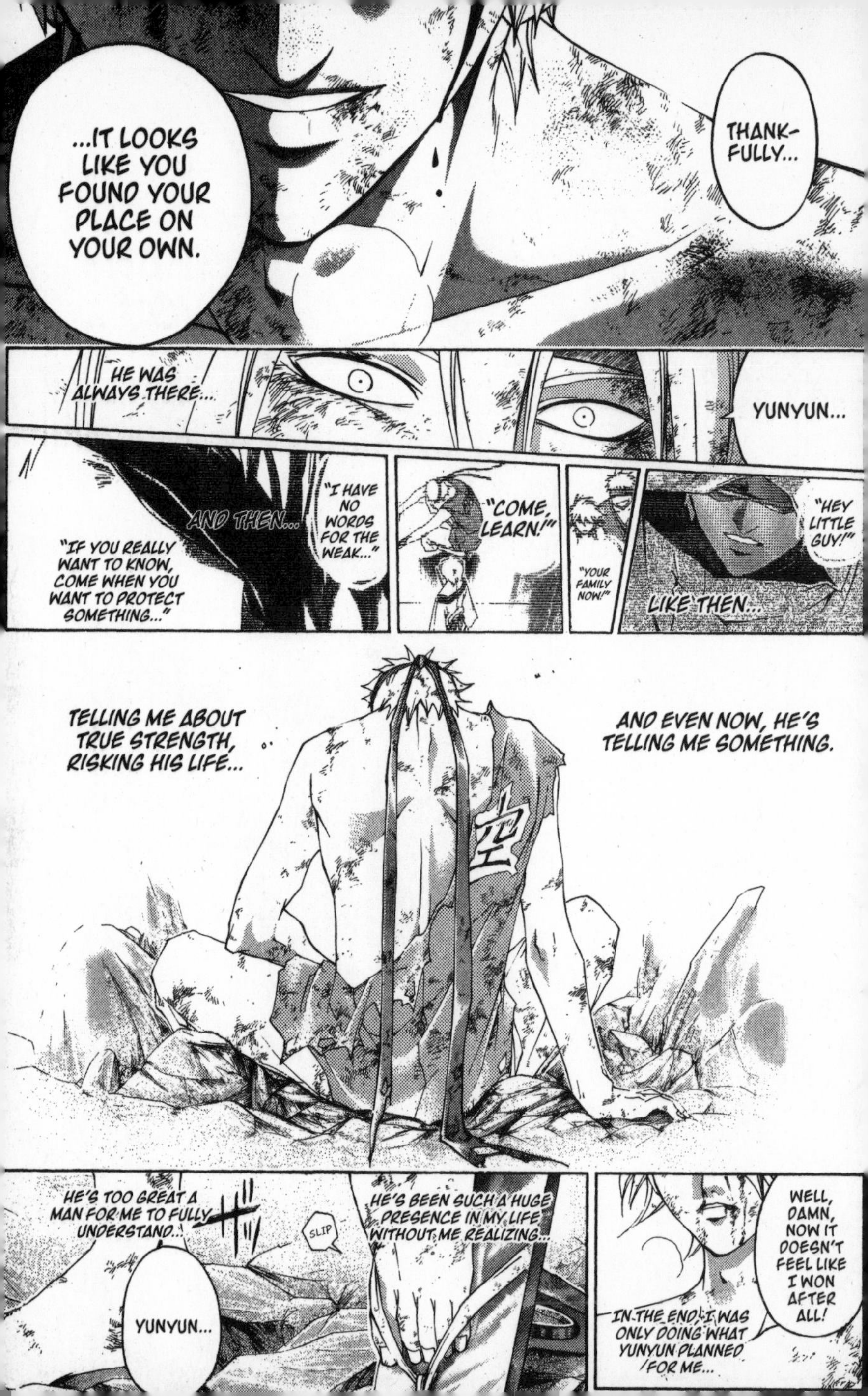
THANK-FULLY...
...IT LOOKS LIKE YOU FOUND YOUR PLACE ON YOUR OWN.
YUNYUN...
HE WAS ALWAYS THERE...
"HEY LITTLE GUY!"
LIKE THEN...
"YOUR FAMILY NOW!"
"COME, LEARN!"
"I HAVE NO WORDS FOR THE WEAK..."
AND THEN...
"IF YOU REALLY WANT TO KNOW, COME WHEN YOU WANT TO PROTECT SOMETHING..."
AND EVEN NOW, HE'S TELLING ME SOMETHING.
TELLING ME ABOUT TRUE STRENGTH, RISKING HIS LIFE...
WELL, DAMN, NOW IT DOESN'T FEEL LIKE I WON AFTER ALL!
IN THE END, I WAS ONLY DOING WHAT YUNYUN PLANNED FOR ME...
HE'S BEEN SUCH A HUGE PRESENCE IN MY LIFE WITHOUT ME REALIZING...
SLIP
HE'S TOO GREAT A MAN FOR ME TO FULLY UNDERSTAND...
YUNYUN...

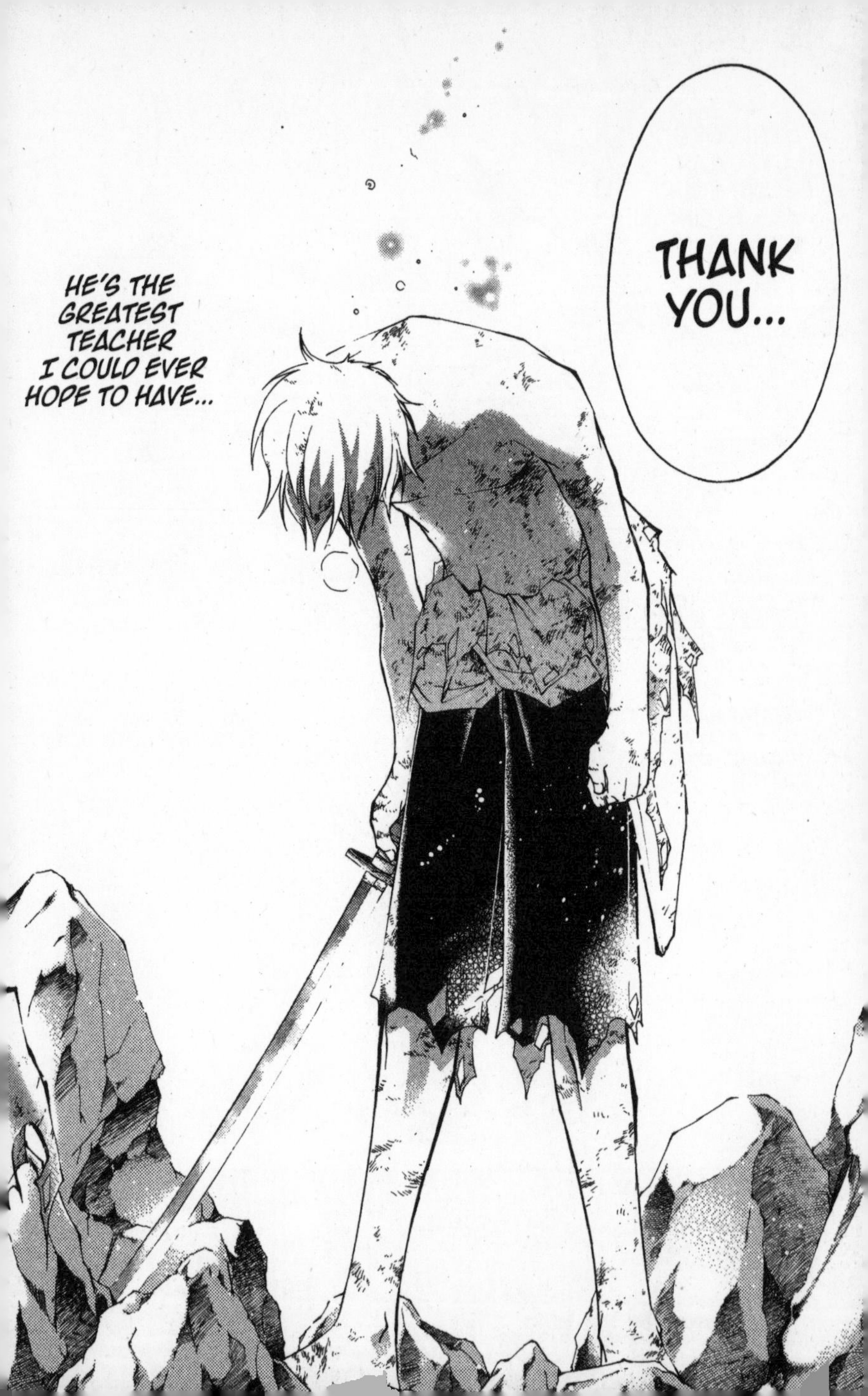
THANK YOU...
HE'S THE GREATEST TEACHER I COULD EVER HOPE TO HAVE...

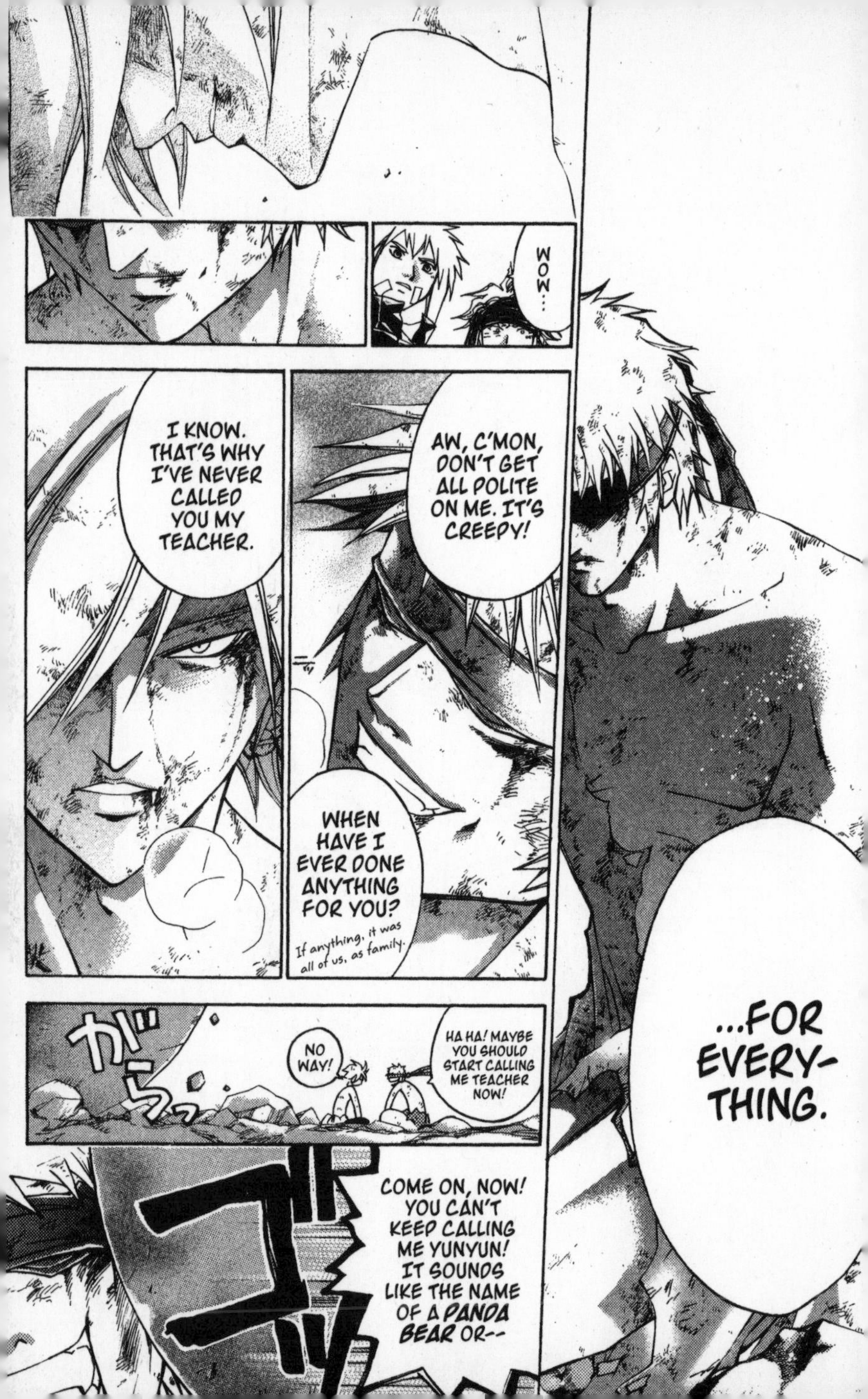
...FOR EVERY-THING.
WOW...
AW, C'MON, DON'T GET ALL POLITE ON ME. IT'S CREEPY!
WHEN HAVE I EVER DONE ANYTHING FOR YOU?
If anything, it was all of us, as family.
I KNOW. THAT'S WHY I'VE NEVER CALLED YOU MY TEACHER.
HA HA! MAYBE YOU SHOULD START CALLING ME TEACHER NOW!
NO WAY!
COME ON, NOW! YOU CAN'T KEEP CALLING ME YUNYUN! IT SOUNDS LIKE THE NAME OF A PANDA BEAR OR--

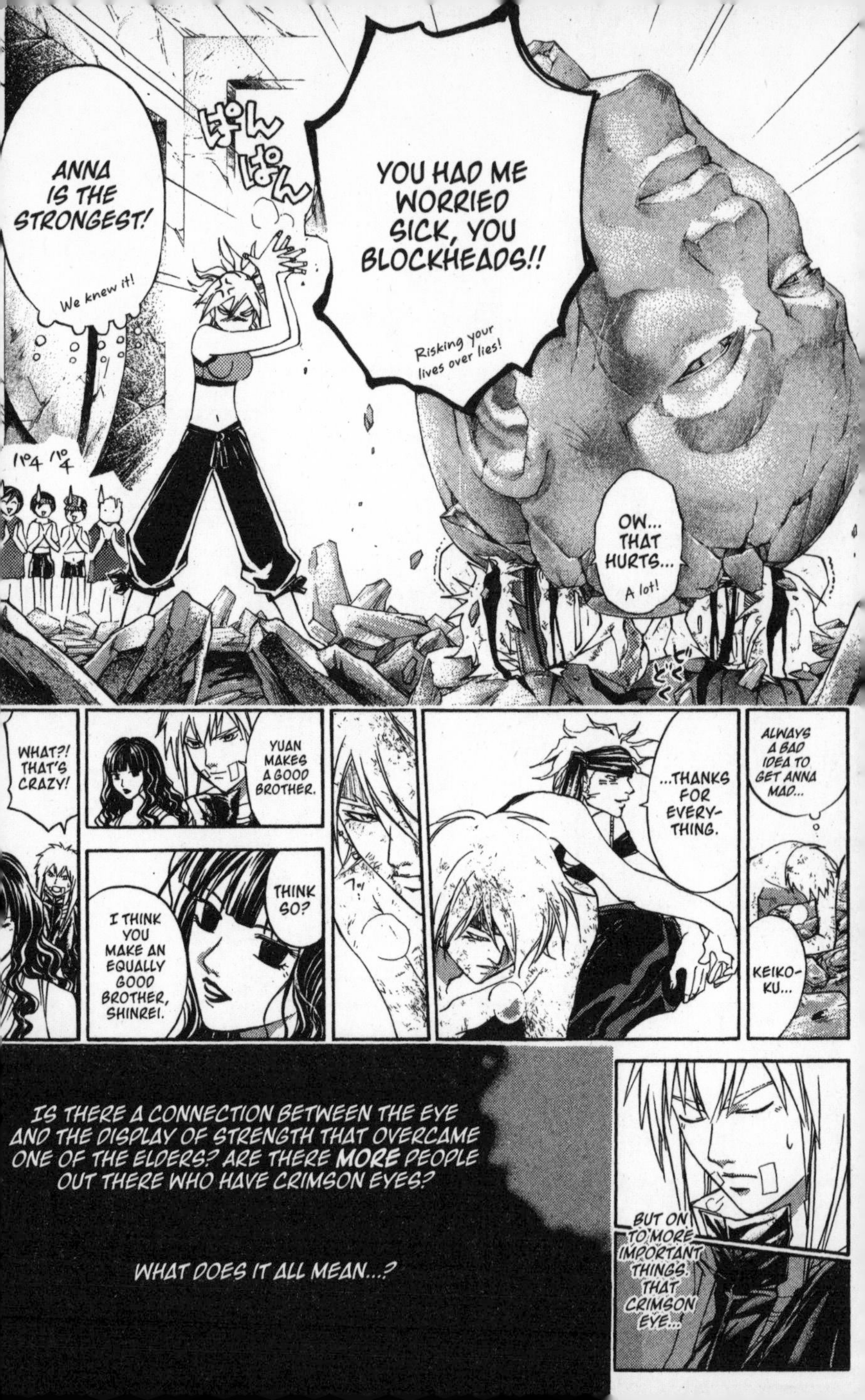
OW... THAT HURTS...
A lot!
YOU HAD ME WORRIED SICK, YOU BLOCKHEADS!!
Risking your lives over lies!
ぱんぱん
ANNA IS THE STRONGEST!
We knew it!
ALWAYS A BAD IDEA TO GET ANNA MAD...
KEIKO-KU...
...THANKS FOR EVERY-THING.
YUAN MAKES A GOOD BROTHER.
THINK SO?
I THINK YOU MAKE AN EQUALLY GOOD BROTHER, SHINREI.
WHAT?! THAT'S CRAZY!
BUT ON TO MORE IMPORTANT THINGS. THAT CRIMSON EYE...
IS THERE A CONNECTION BETWEEN THE EYE AND THE DISPLAY OF STRENGTH THAT OVERCAME ONE OF THE ELDERS? ARE THERE MORE PEOPLE OUT THERE WHO HAVE CRIMSON EYES?
WHAT DOES IT ALL MEAN...?

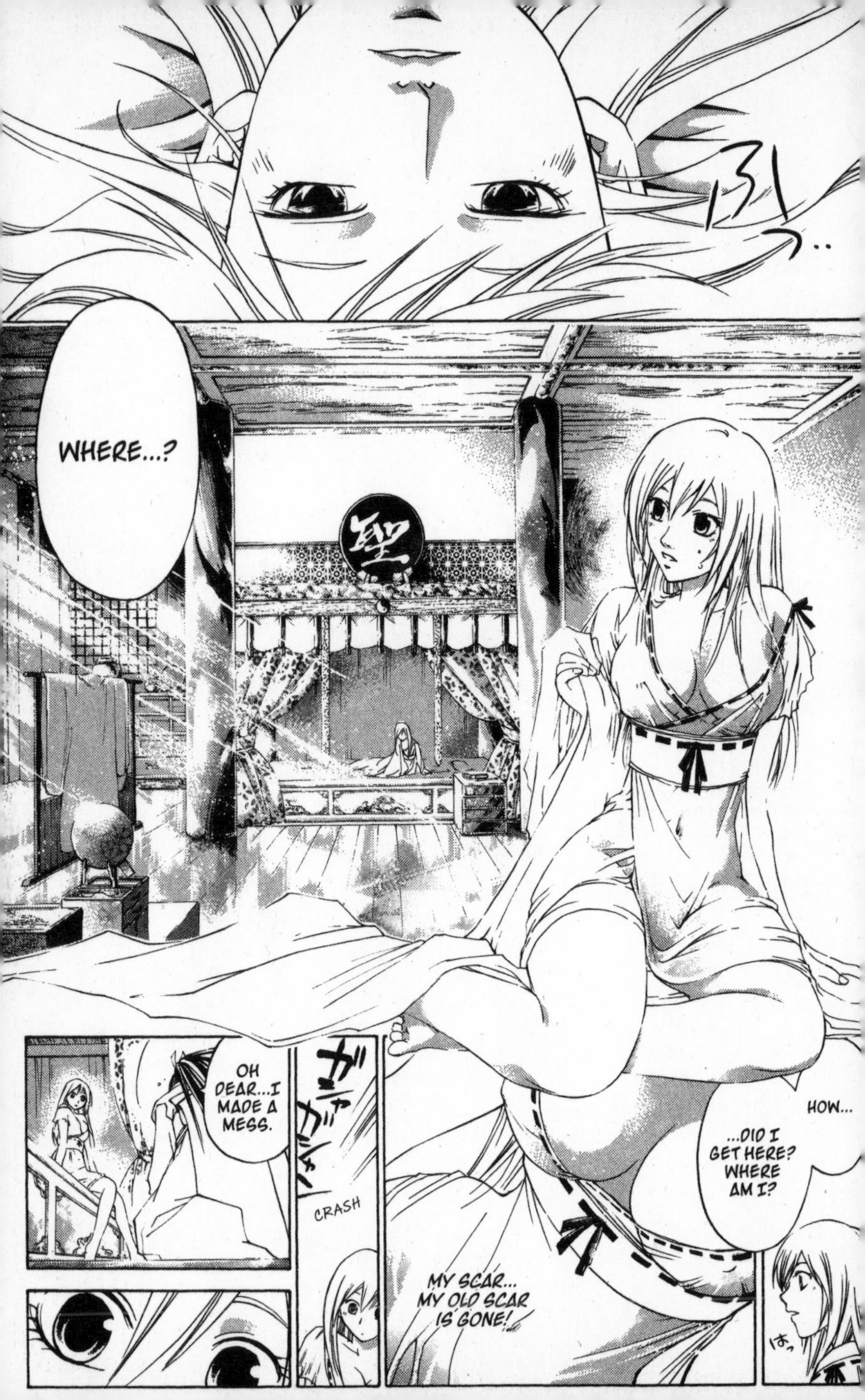
ふっ..
WHERE...?
HOW...
...DID I GET HERE? WHERE AM I?
はっ
MY SCAR... MY OLD SCAR IS GONE!
ガシャガシャン
CRASH
OH DEAR...I MADE A MESS.

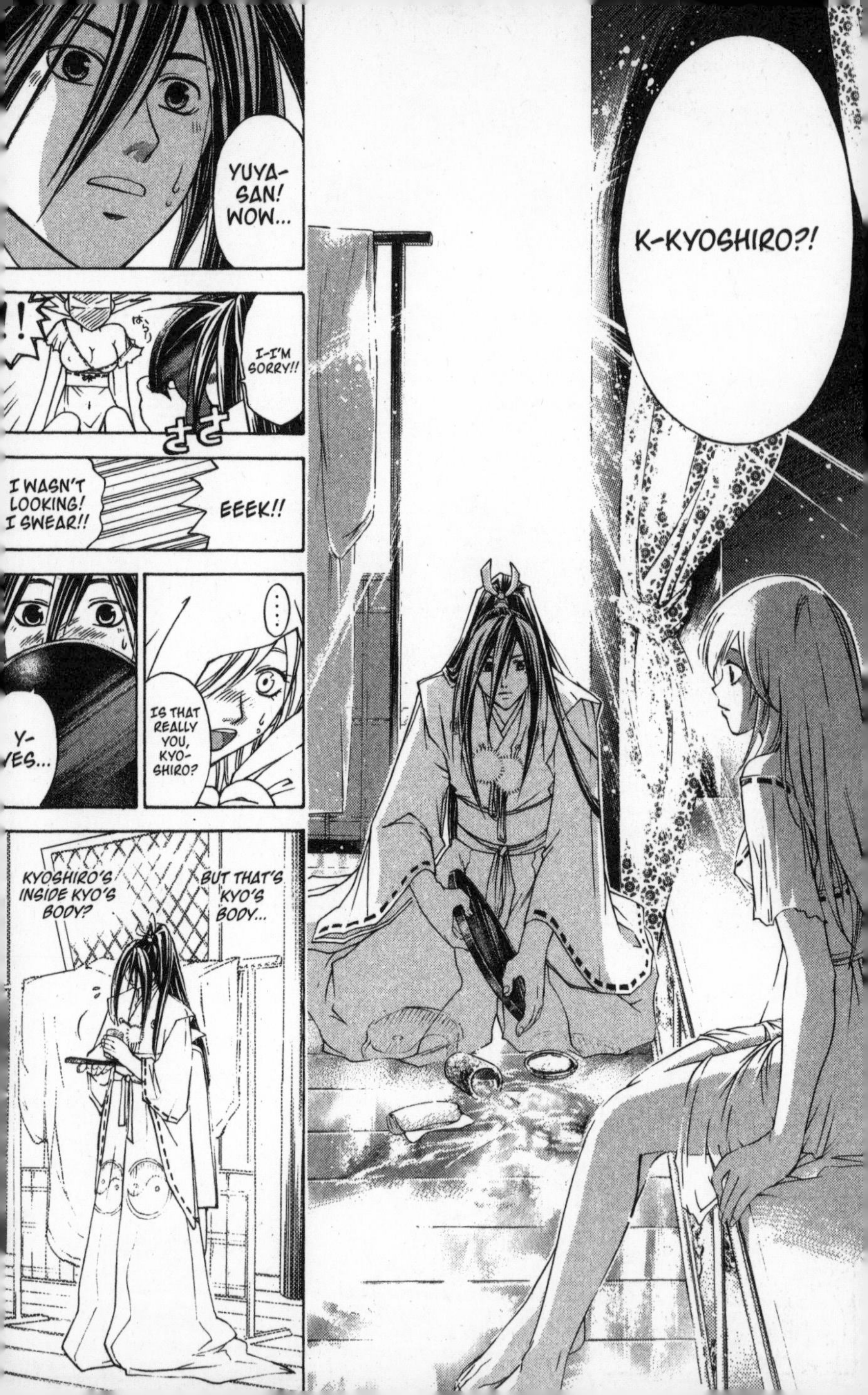
K-KYOSHIRO?!
YUYA-SAN! WOW...
!
I-I'M SORRY!!
I WASN'T LOOKING! I SWEAR!!
EEEK!!
...
IS THAT REALLY YOU, KYO-SHIRO?
Y-YES...
KYOSHIRO'S INSIDE KYO'S BODY?
BUT THAT'S KYO'S BODY...

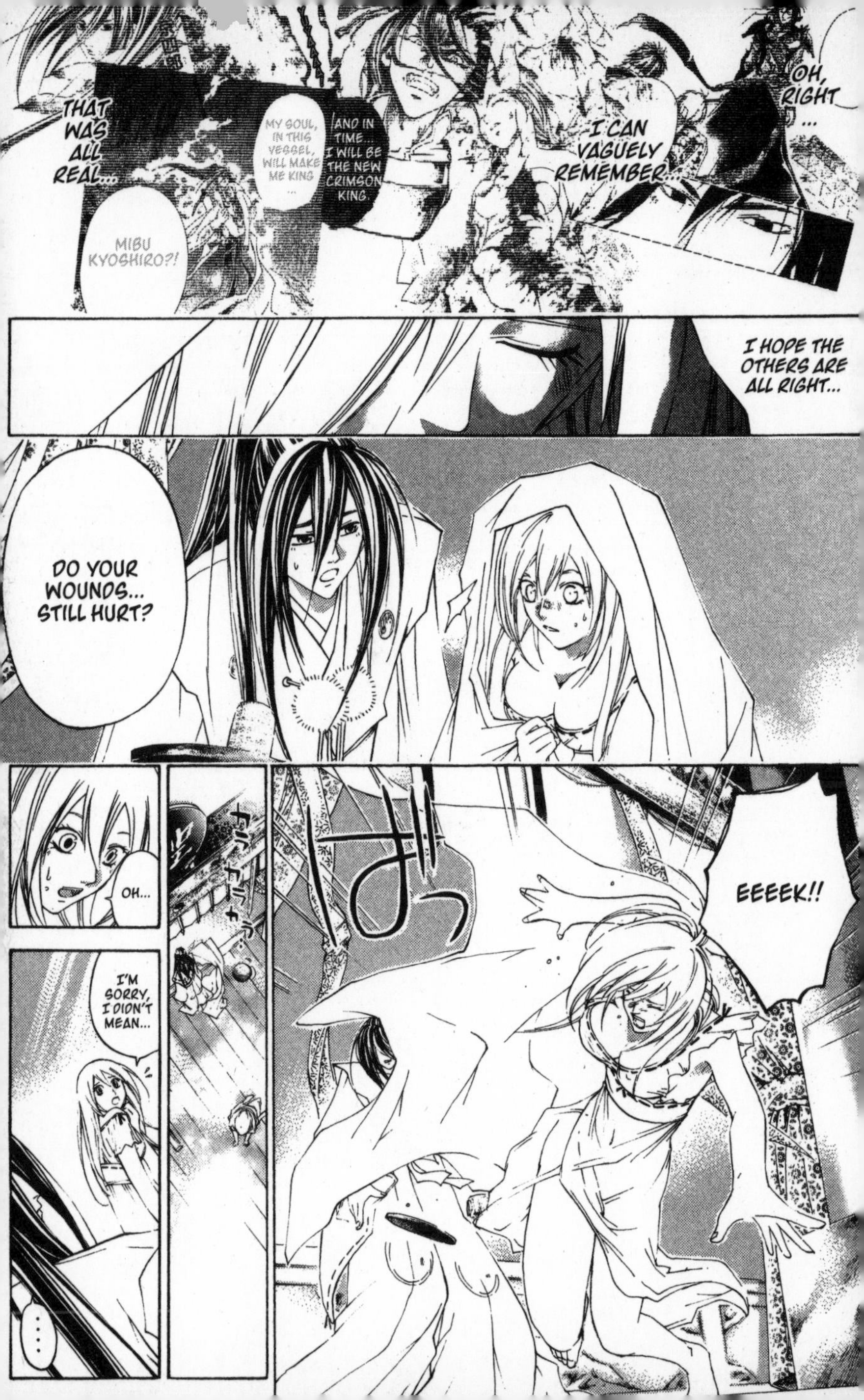
OH, RIGHT...
I CAN VAGUELY REMEMBER...
AND IN TIME... I WILL BE THE NEW CRIMSON KING.
MY SOUL, IN THIS VESSEL, WILL MAKE ME KING...
THAT WAS ALL REAL...
MIBU KYOSHIRO?!
I HOPE THE OTHERS ARE ALL RIGHT...
DO YOUR WOUNDS... STILL HURT?
EEEEK!!
OH...
I'M SORRY, I DIDN'T MEAN...
....

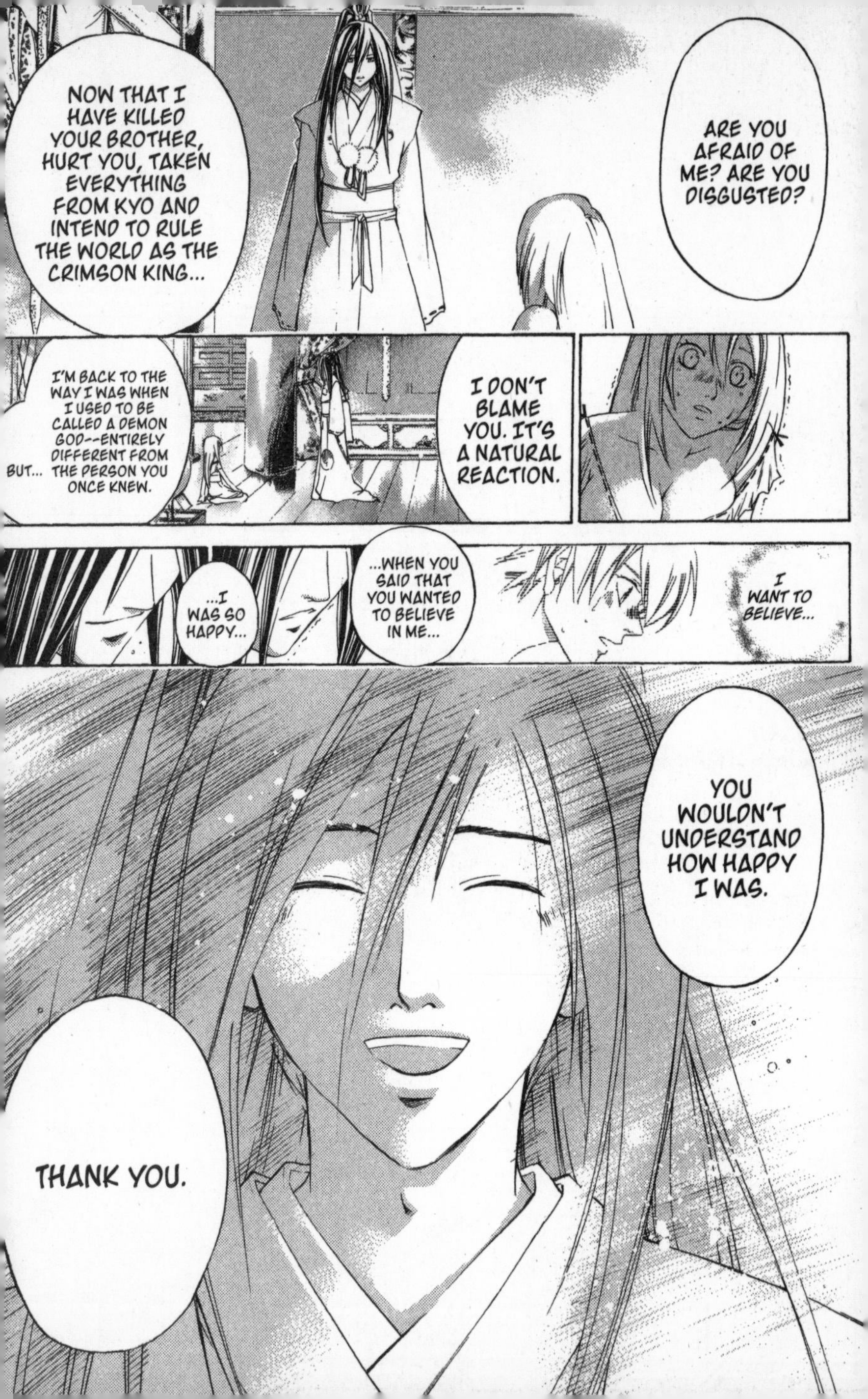
NOW THAT I HAVE KILLED YOUR BROTHER, HURT YOU, TAKEN EVERYTHING FROM KYO AND INTEND TO RULE THE WORLD AS THE CRIMSON KING...
ARE YOU AFRAID OF ME? ARE YOU DISGUSTED?
I DON'T BLAME YOU. IT'S A NATURAL REACTION.
I'M BACK TO THE WAY I WAS WHEN I USED TO BE CALLED A DEMON GOD--ENTIRELY DIFFERENT FROM THE PERSON YOU ONCE KNEW.
BUT...
I WANT TO BELIEVE...
...WHEN YOU SAID THAT YOU WANTED TO BELIEVE IN ME...
...I WAS SO HAPPY...
YOU WOULDN'T UNDERSTAND HOW HAPPY I WAS.
THANK YOU.

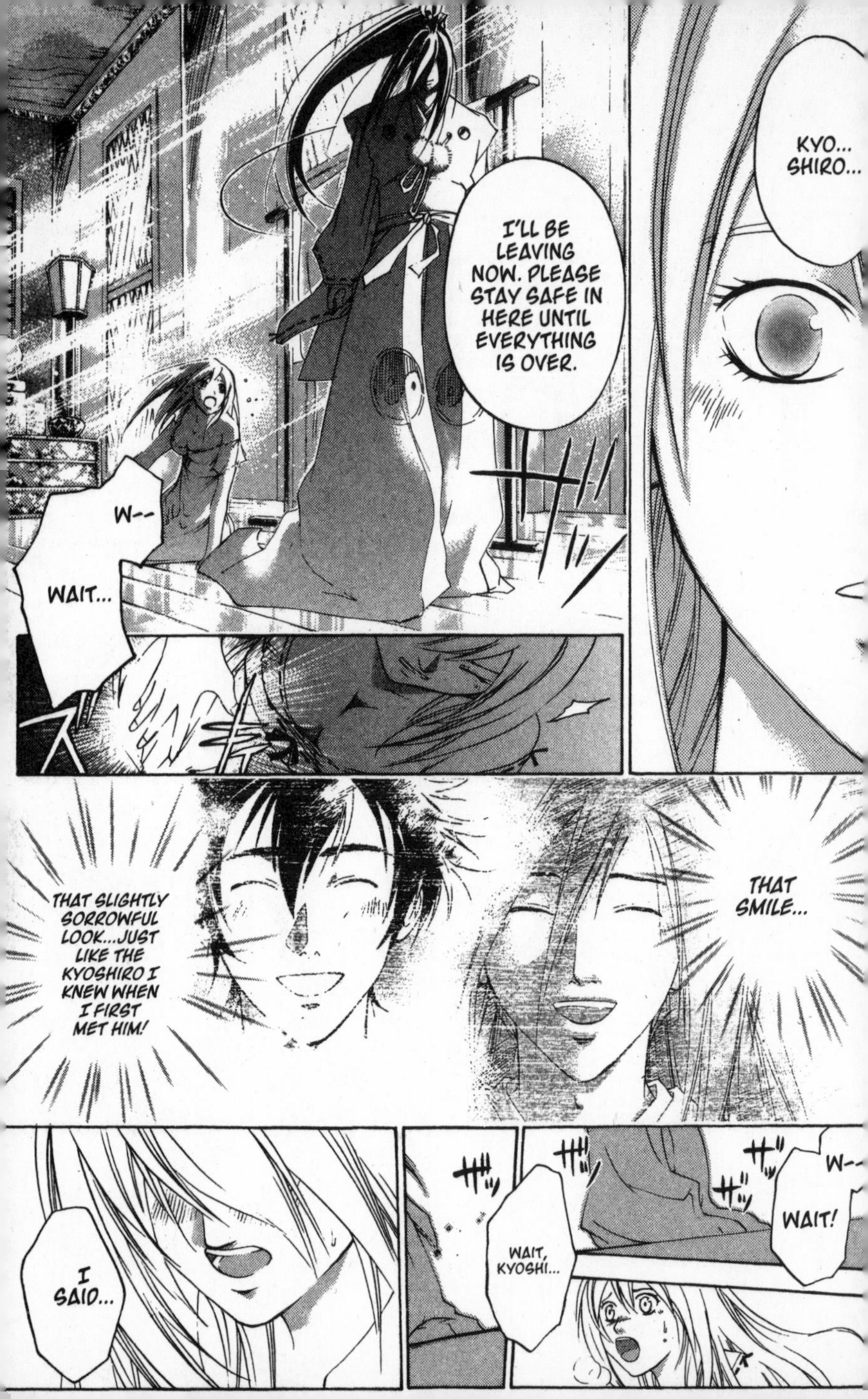
KYO... SHIRO...
I'LL BE LEAVING NOW. PLEASE STAY SAFE IN HERE UNTIL EVERYTHING IS OVER.
W--
WAIT...
THAT SMILE...
THAT SLIGHTLY SORROWFUL LOOK...JUST LIKE THE KYOSHIRO I KNEW WHEN I FIRST MET HIM!
W--
WAIT!
WAIT, KYOSHI...
I SAID...

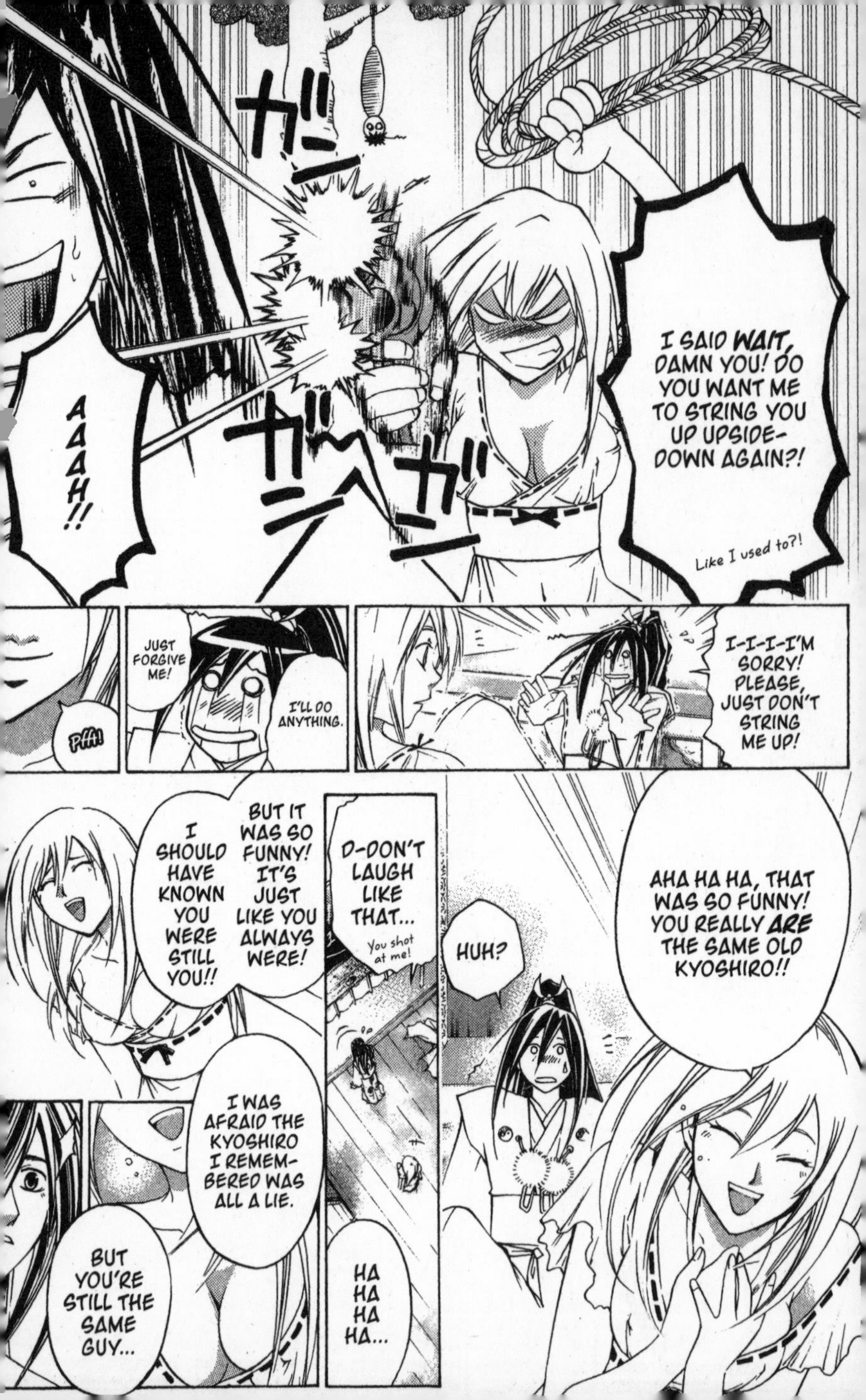
I SAID **WAIT**, DAMN YOU! DO YOU WANT ME TO STRING YOU UP UPSIDE-DOWN AGAIN?!
Like I used to?!
AAAAH!!
I-I-I-I'M SORRY! PLEASE, JUST DON'T STRING ME UP!
JUST FORGIVE ME!
I'LL DO ANYTHING.
PFFT!
AHA HA HA, THAT WAS SO FUNNY! YOU REALLY **ARE** THE SAME OLD KYOSHIRO!!
HUH?
D-DON'T LAUGH LIKE THAT...
You shot at me!
BUT IT WAS SO FUNNY! IT'S JUST LIKE YOU ALWAYS WERE!
I SHOULD HAVE KNOWN YOU WERE STILL YOU!!
HA HA HA HA...
I WAS AFRAID THE KYOSHIRO I REMEMBERED WAS ALL A LIE.
BUT YOU'RE STILL THE SAME GUY...

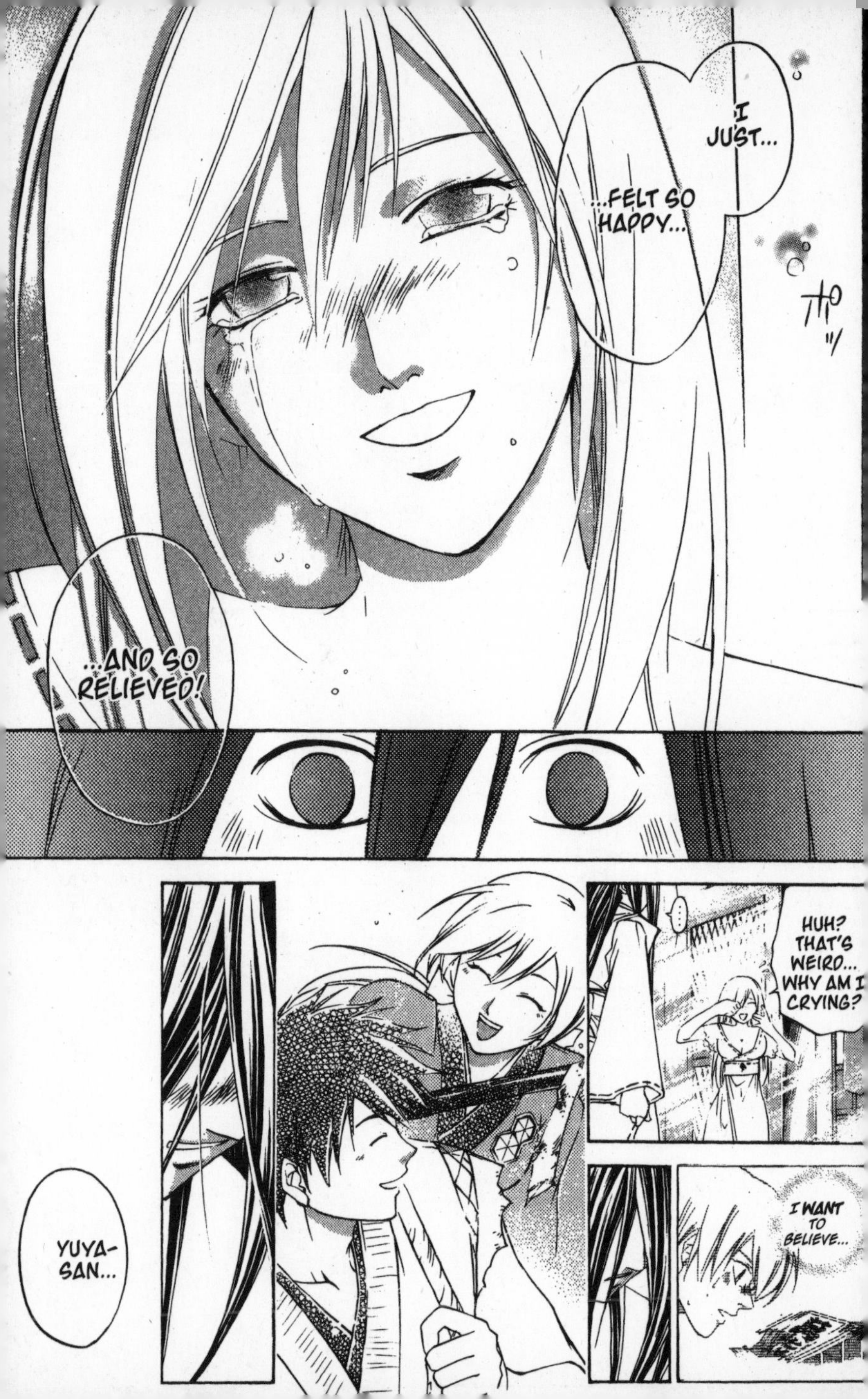
I JUST...
...FELT SO HAPPY...
...AND SO RELIEVED!
HUH? THAT'S WEIRD... WHY AM I CRYING?
...
I WANT TO BELIEVE...
YUYA-SAN...

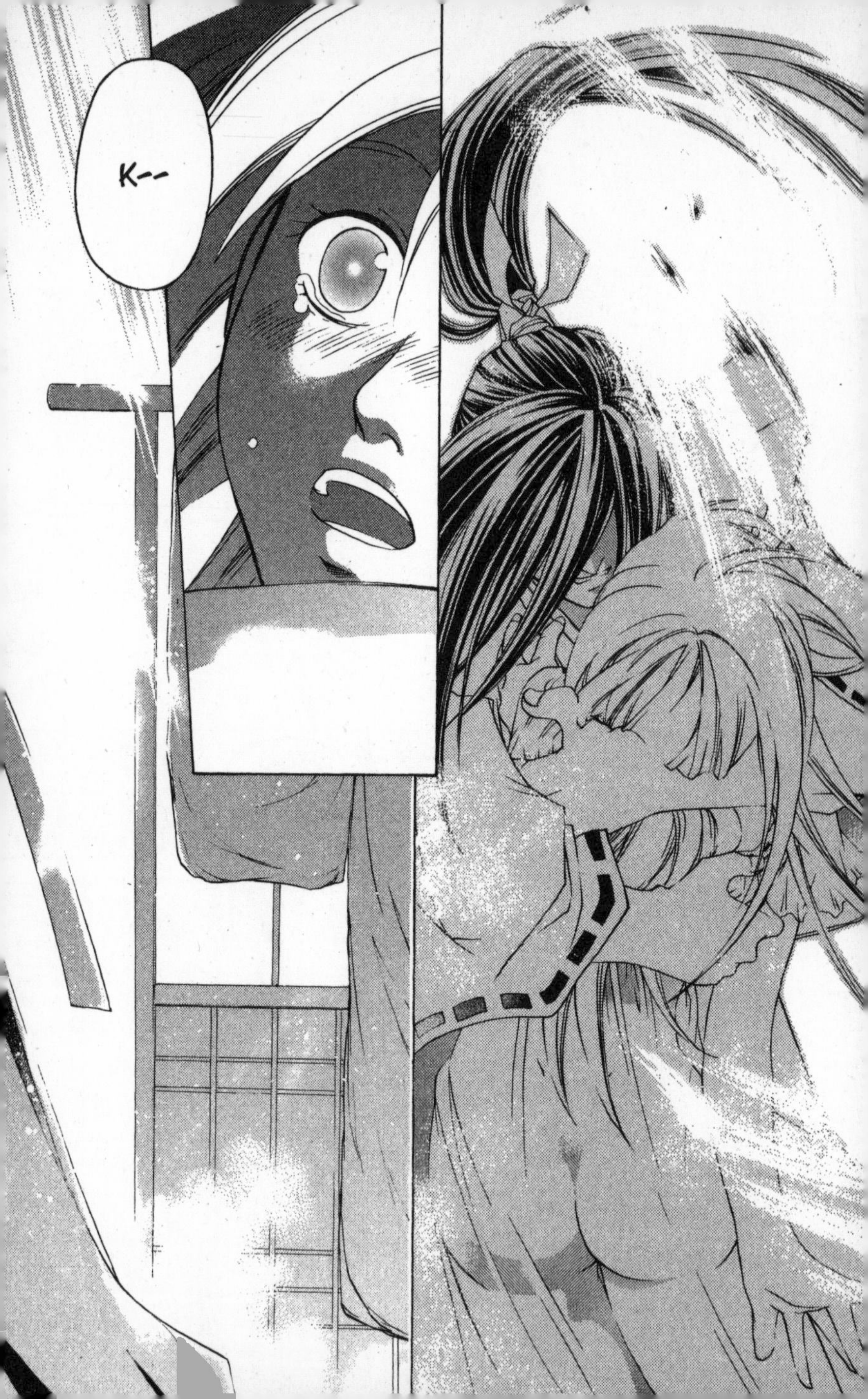
K--

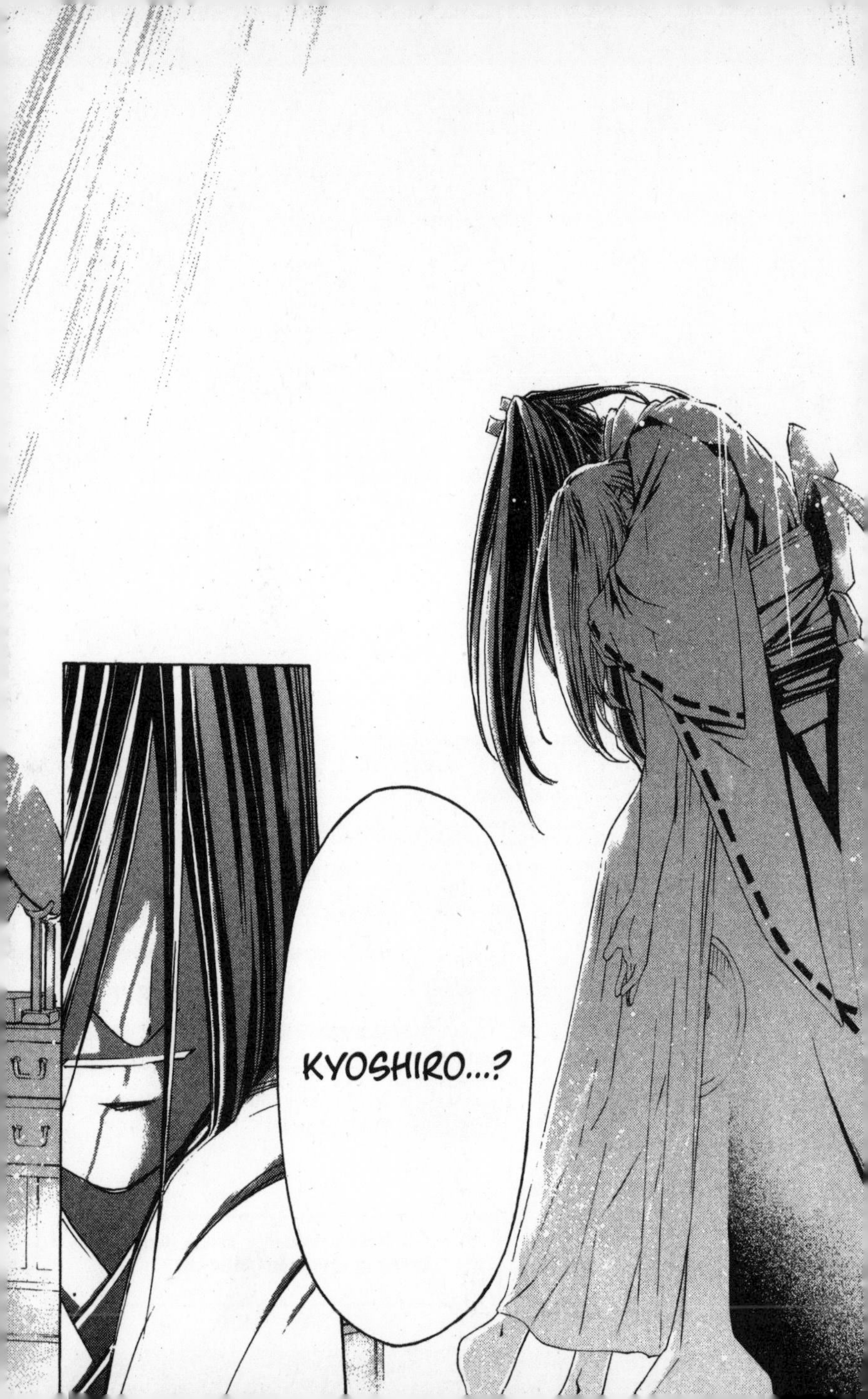
KYOSHIRO...?

兄様…ー
ずっと一緒だよ…
SAMURAI DEEPER KYO

[Kanagawa/Rain] ⬆
Nice memories...

KYO
兄様大好き
ありがとう
椎名望のぞむ

[Hokkaido/3 BLAB. ☆] ⬆
That's a positive brother!

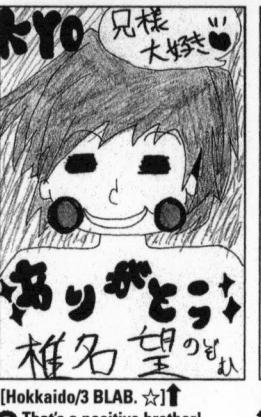

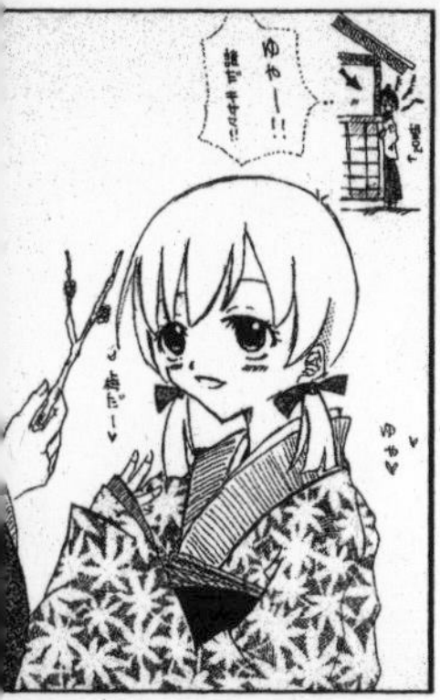

[Fukuoka/Yusura] ⬇
What a worrywart!

望兄様
ずっと見守っていて……

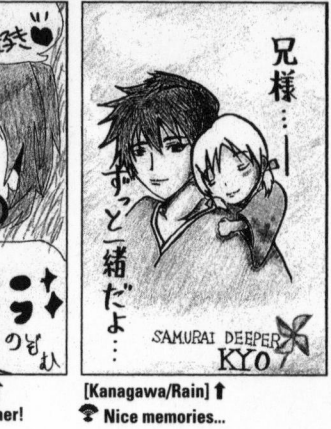

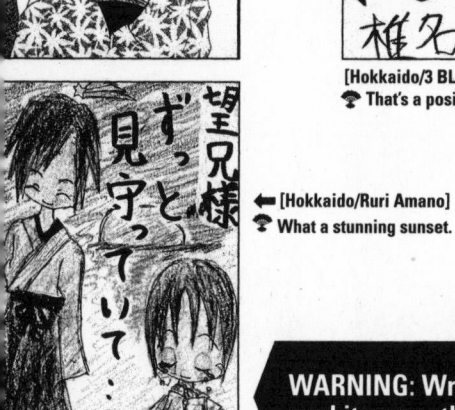

⬅ [Hokkaido/Ruri Amano]
What a stunning sunset.

WARNING: Write your name clearly. If we can't read it correctly, we can't print your name right!

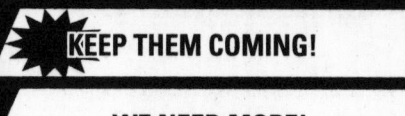

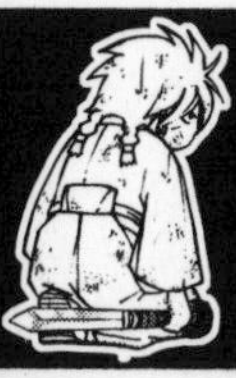

KEEP THEM COMING!

WE NEED MORE!

Samural Deeper Kyo Fanmail
c/o TOKYOPOP
5900 Wilshire Blvd. Ste. 2000
Los Angeles, CA 90036

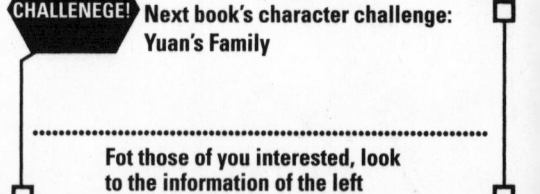

CHALLENEGE! Next book's character challenge:
Yuan's Family

Fot those of you interested, look to the information of the left

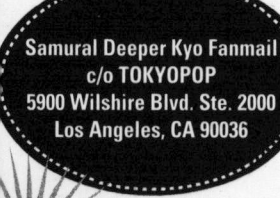

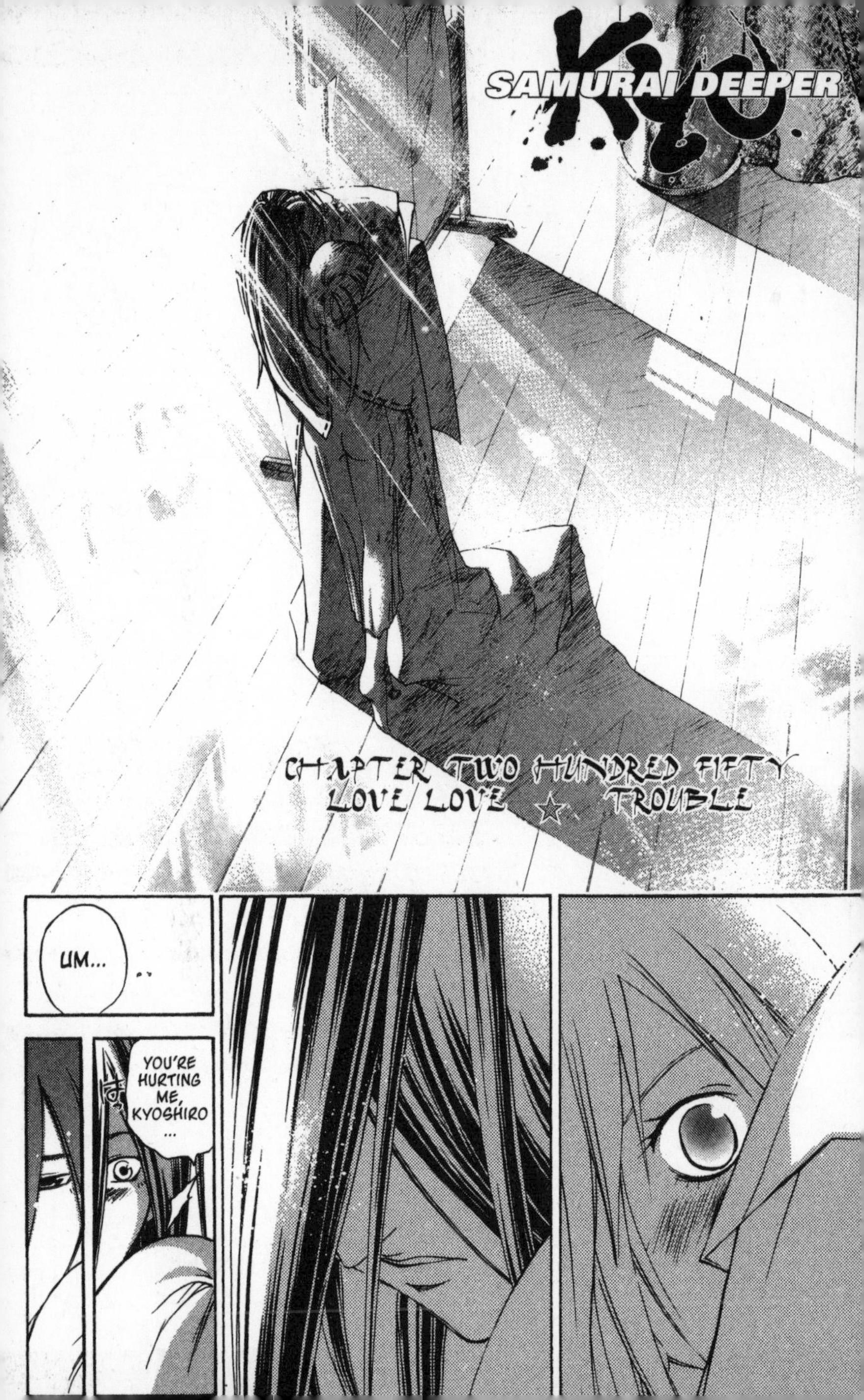
SAMURAI DEEPER KYO
CHAPTER TWO HUNDRED FIFTY
LOVE LOVE ☆ TROUBLE
UM...
YOU'RE HURTING ME, KYOSHIRO ...

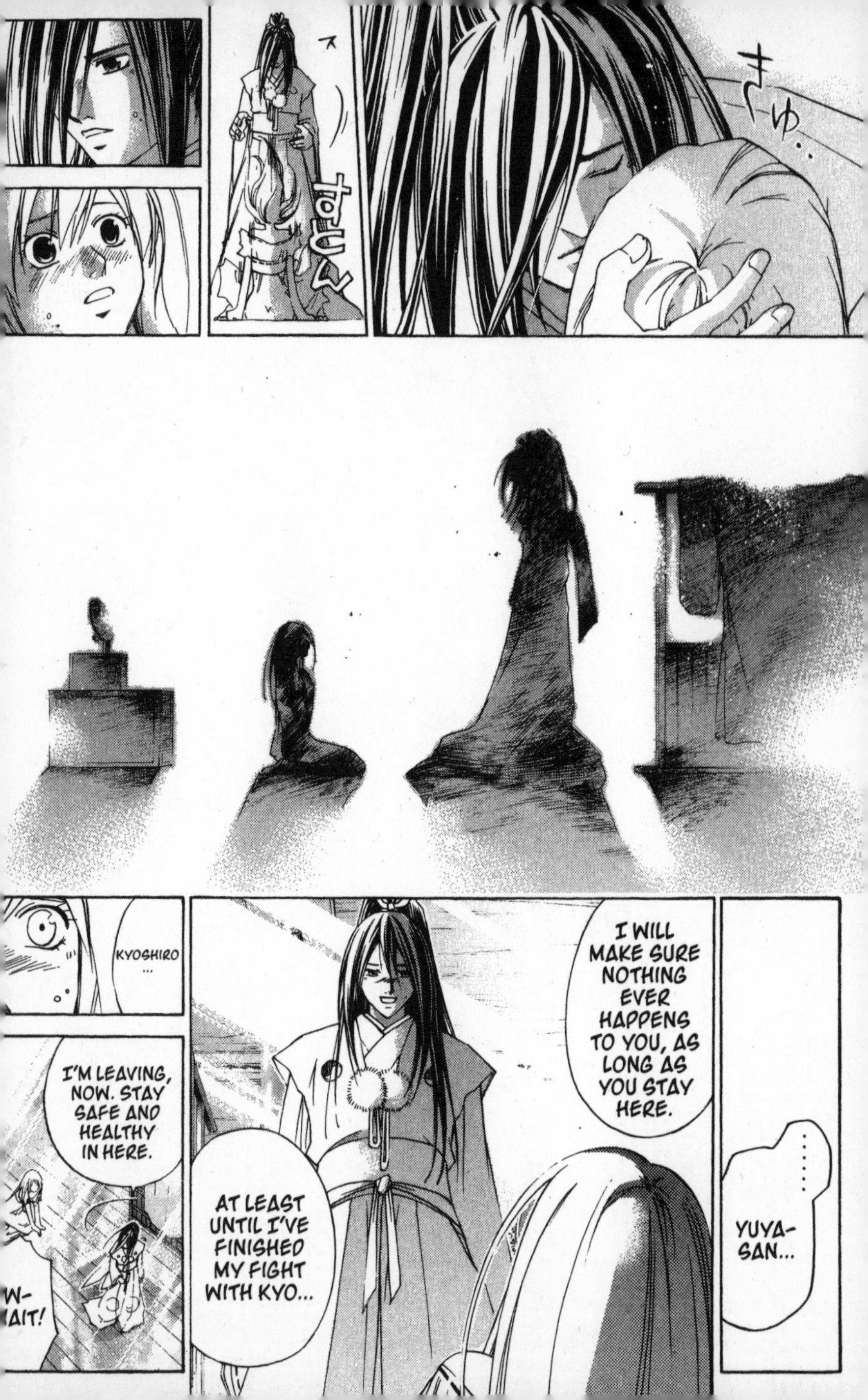
きゅ…
すとん
……
YUYA-SAN…
I WILL MAKE SURE NOTHING EVER HAPPENS TO YOU, AS LONG AS YOU STAY HERE.
AT LEAST UNTIL I'VE FINISHED MY FIGHT WITH KYO…
KYOSHIRO …
I'M LEAVING, NOW. STAY SAFE AND HEALTHY IN HERE.
W-WAIT!

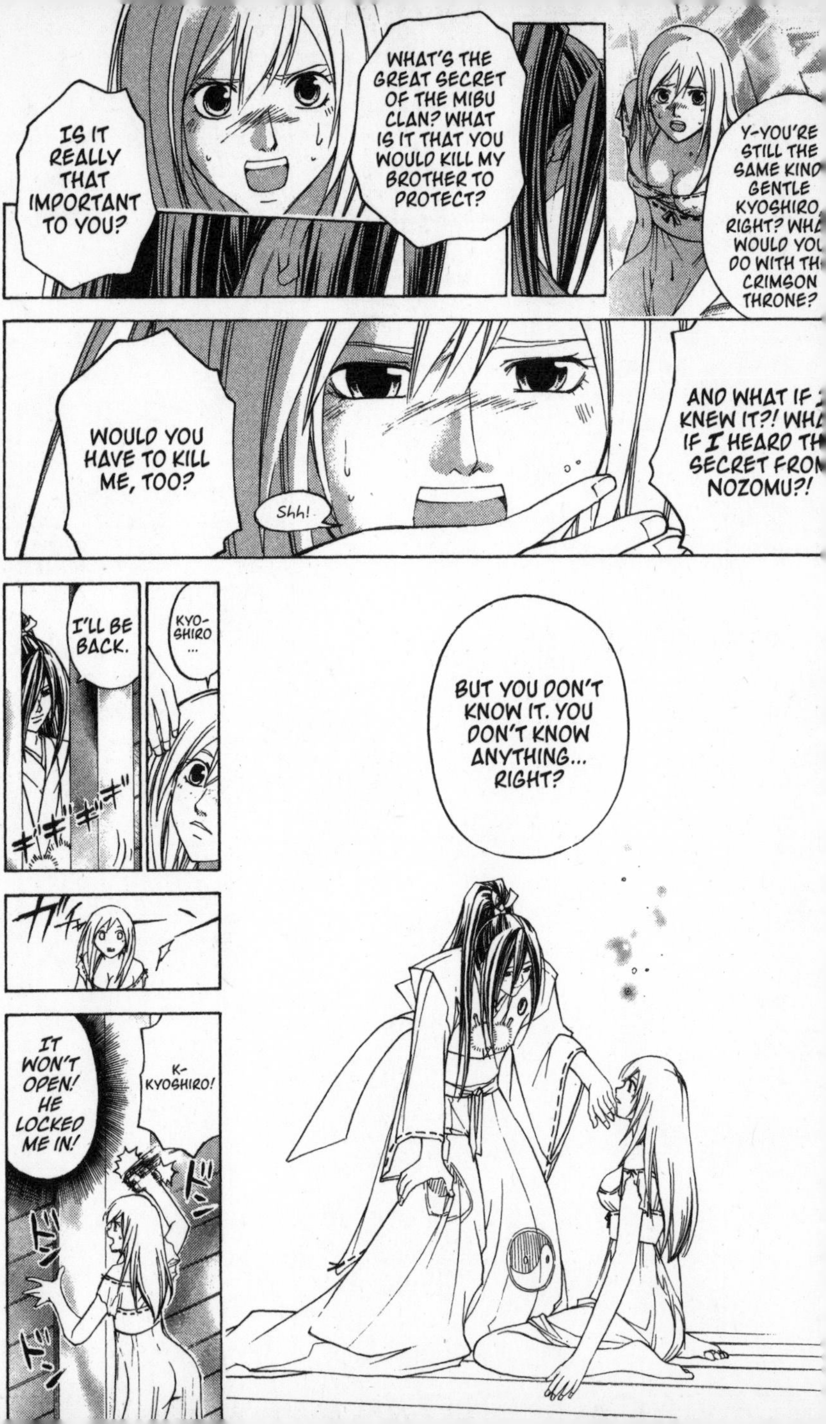
Y-YOU'RE STILL THE SAME KIND GENTLE KYOSHIRO, RIGHT? WHA WOULD YOU DO WITH TH CRIMSON THRONE?
WHAT'S THE GREAT SECRET OF THE MIBU CLAN? WHAT IS IT THAT YOU WOULD KILL MY BROTHER TO PROTECT?
IS IT REALLY THAT IMPORTANT TO YOU?
AND WHAT IF KNEW IT?! WHA IF I HEARD TH SECRET FRON NOZOMU?!
Shh!
WOULD YOU HAVE TO KILL ME, TOO?
BUT YOU DON'T KNOW IT. YOU DON'T KNOW ANYTHING... RIGHT?
KYO-SHIRO...
I'LL BE BACK.
ギギギギ
ガチャ
K-KYOSHIRO!
IT WON'T OPEN! HE LOCKED ME IN!
ドン
ドン

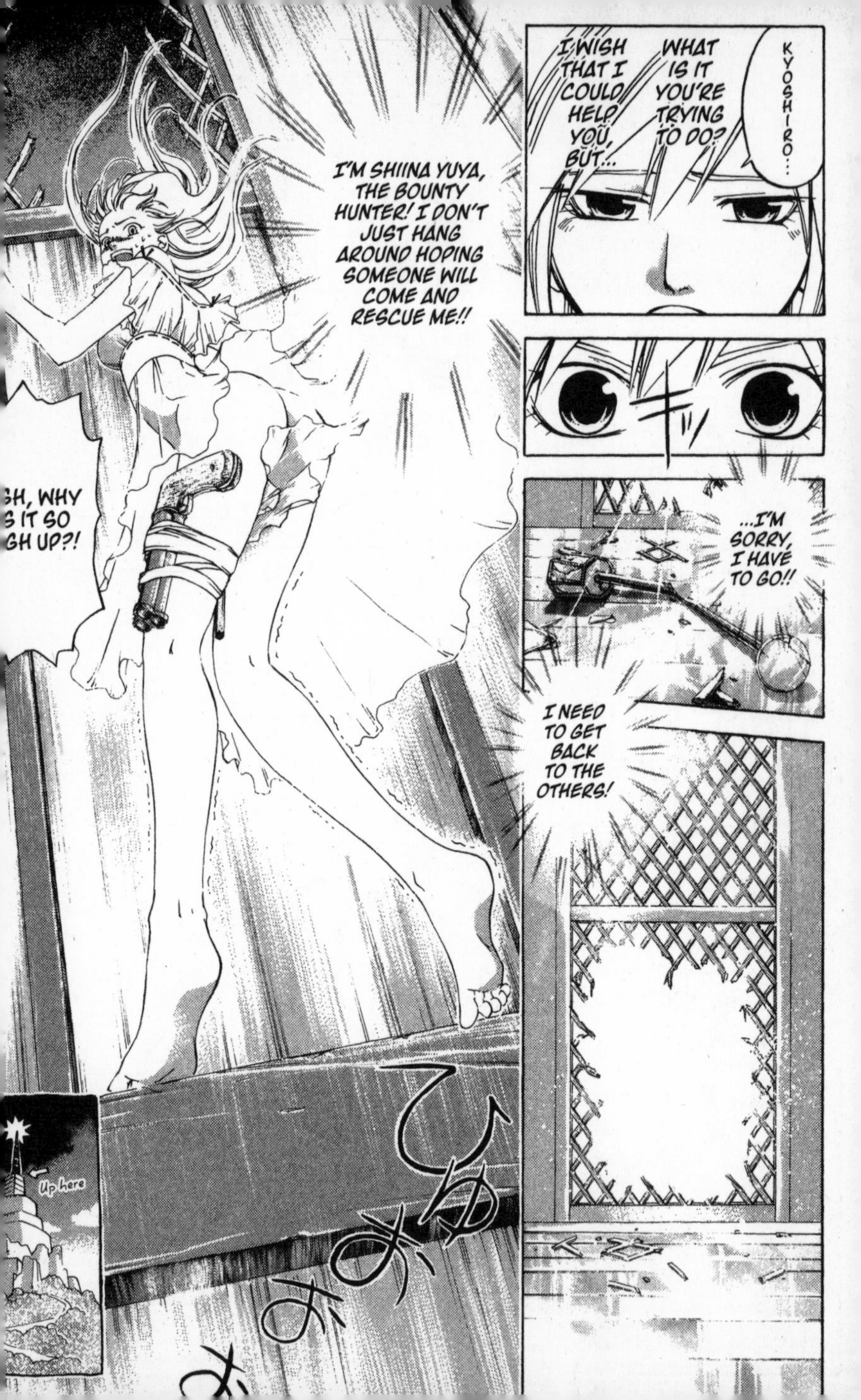
KYOSHIRO...
WHAT IS IT YOU'RE TRYING TO DO?
I WISH THAT I COULD HELP YOU, BUT...
...I'M SORRY, I HAVE TO GO!!
I NEED TO GET BACK TO THE OTHERS!
I'M SHIINA YUYA, THE BOUNTY HUNTER! I DON'T JUST HANG AROUND HOPING SOMEONE WILL COME AND RESCUE ME!!
Up here

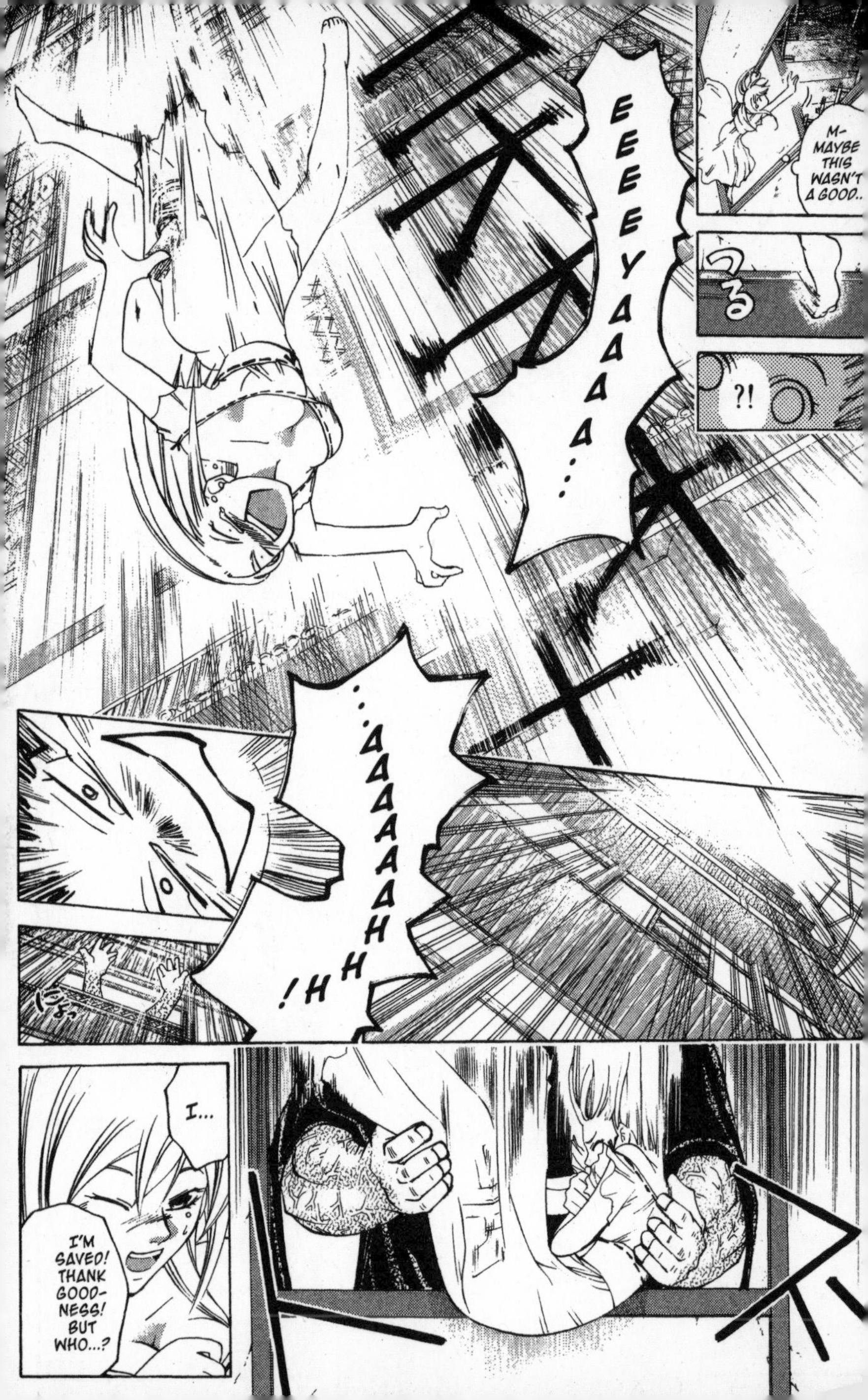
M-MAYBE THIS WASN'T A GOOD..
つる
?!
EEEEYAAAAA...
...AAAAAAAAHHH!
I...
I'M SAVED! THANK GOODNESS! BUT WHO...?

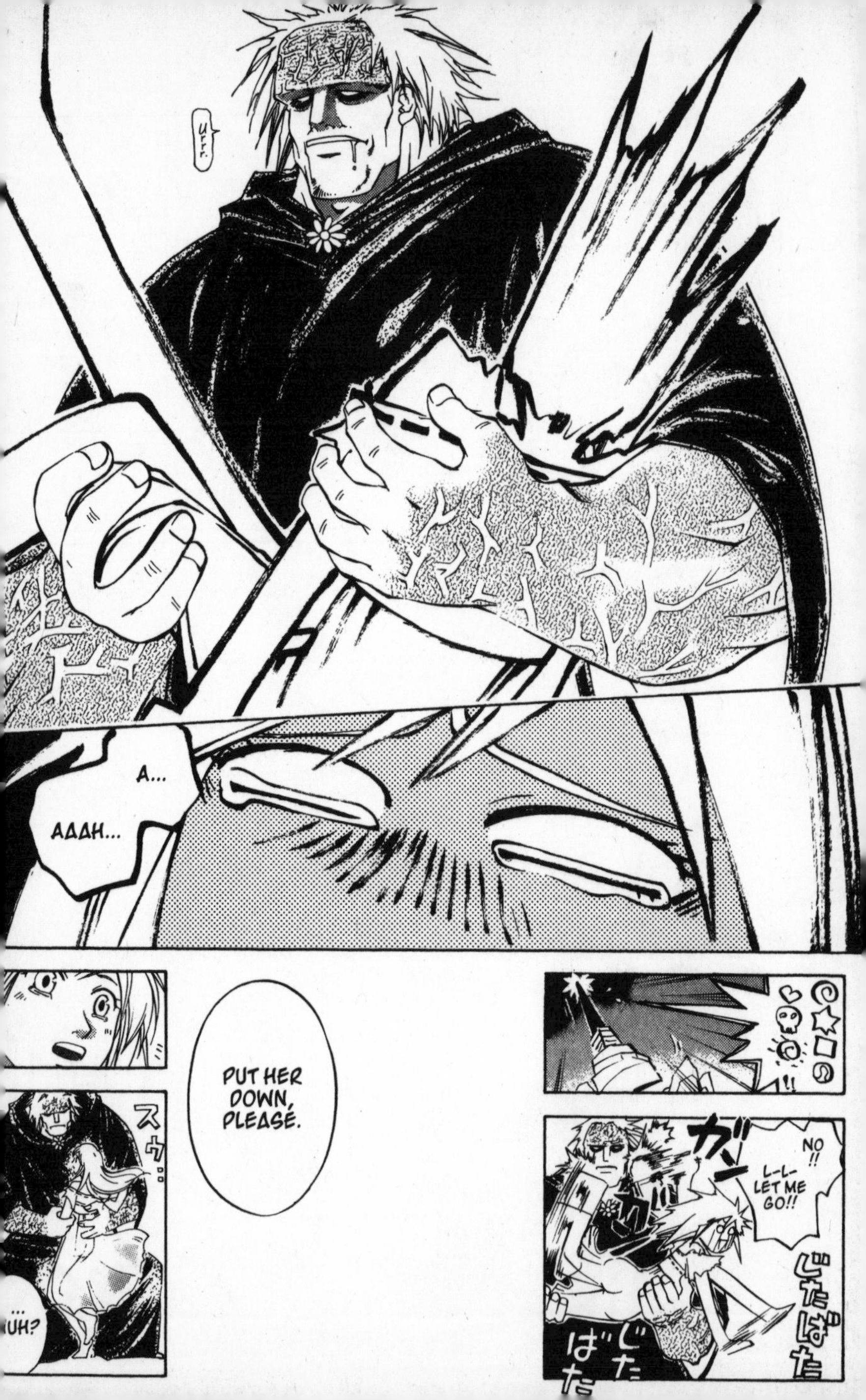
Urr.
A...
AAAH...
NO!!
L-L-LET ME GO!!
ガン
じたばた
じたばた
PUT HER DOWN, PLEASE.
スゥ…
...UH?

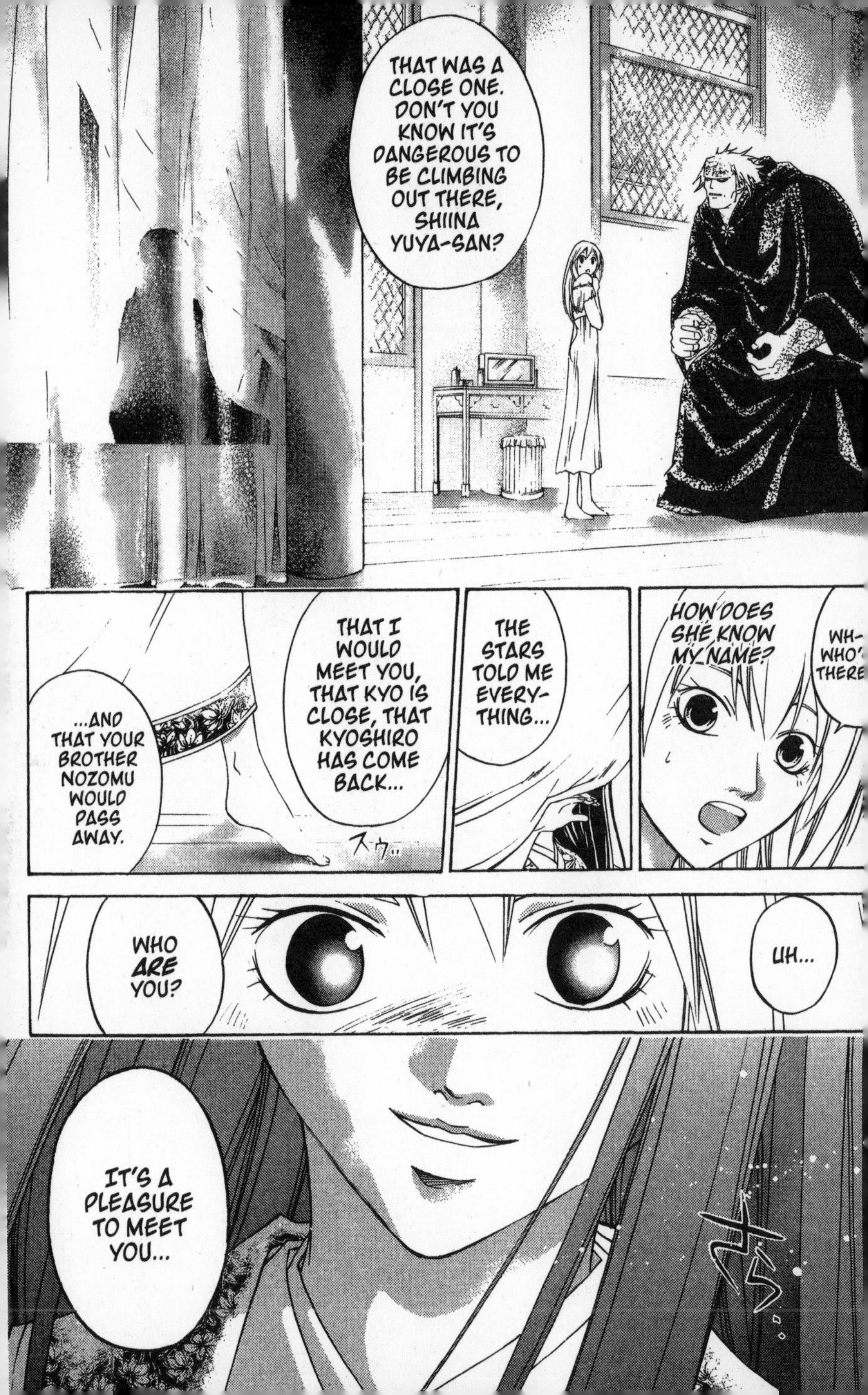
THAT WAS A CLOSE ONE. DON'T YOU KNOW IT'S DANGEROUS TO BE CLIMBING OUT THERE, SHIINA YUYA-SAN?
WH- WHO'S THERE
HOW DOES SHE KNOW MY NAME?
THE STARS TOLD ME EVERY-THING...
THAT I WOULD MEET YOU, THAT KYO IS CLOSE, THAT KYOSHIRO HAS COME BACK...
...AND THAT YOUR BROTHER NOZOMU WOULD PASS AWAY.
UH...
WHO ARE YOU?
IT'S A PLEASURE TO MEET YOU...

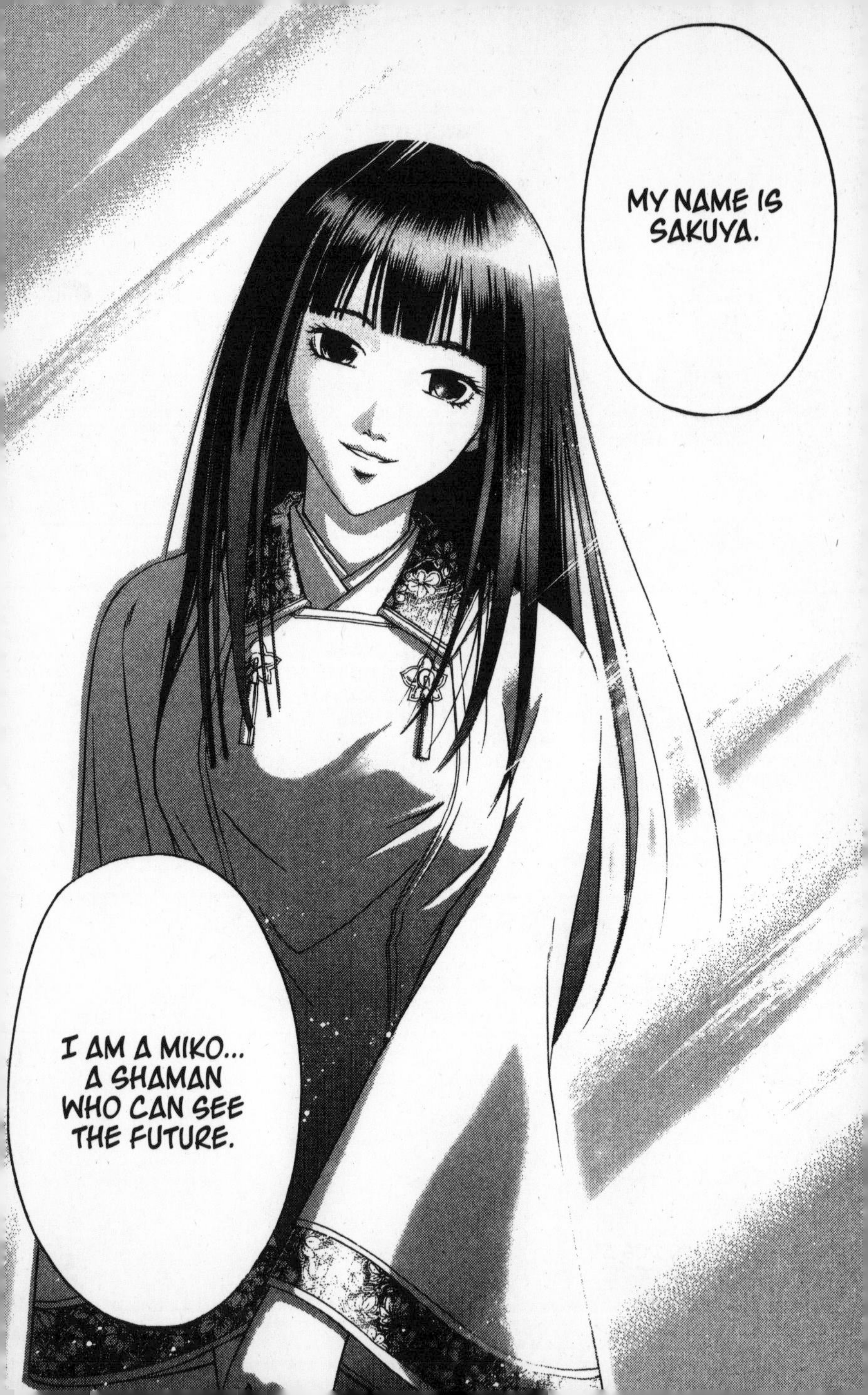
MY NAME IS SAKUYA.
I AM A MIKO... A SHAMAN WHO CAN SEE THE FUTURE.

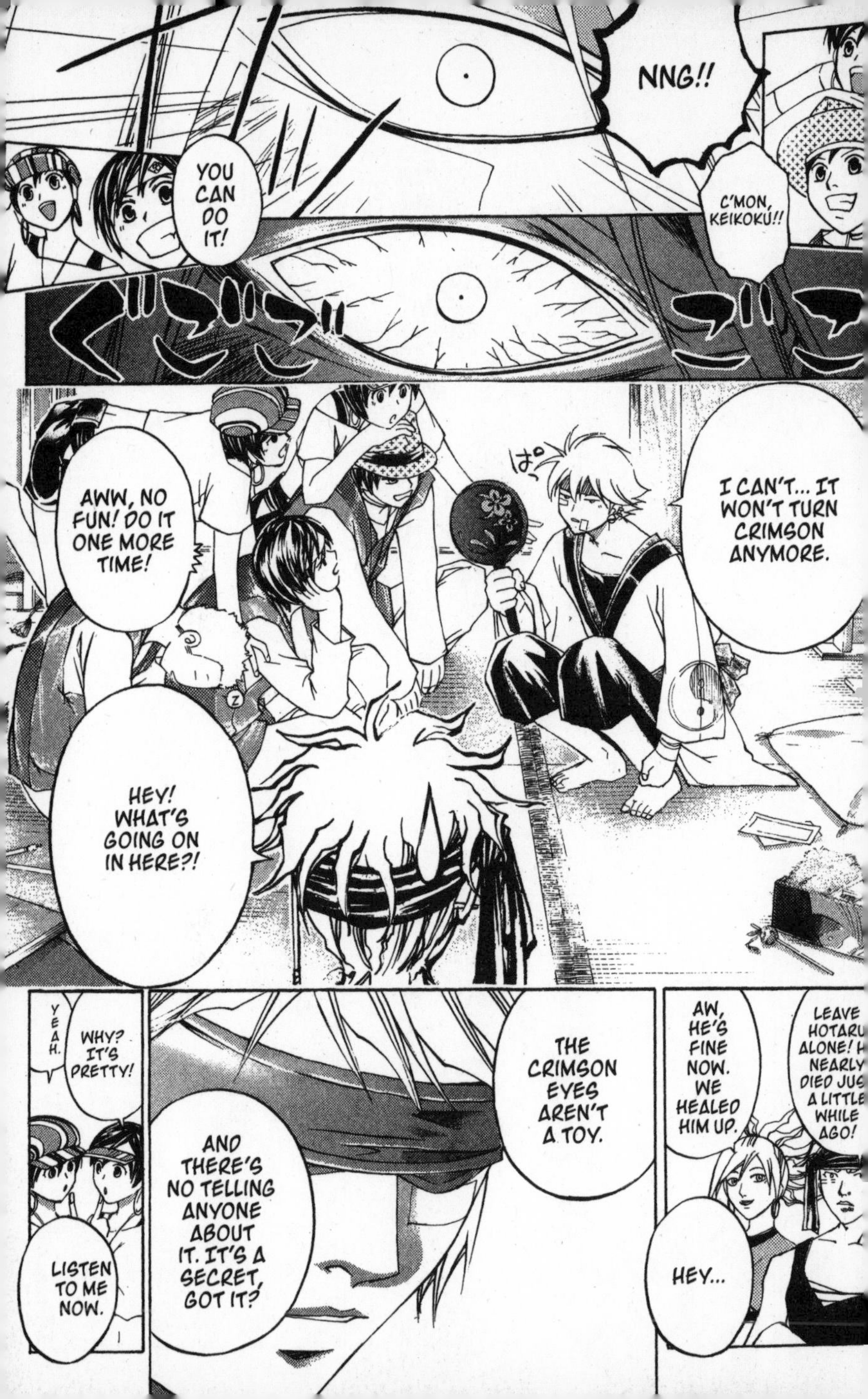
NNG!!
C'MON, KEIKOKU!!
YOU CAN DO IT!
I CAN'T... IT WON'T TURN CRIMSON ANYMORE.
AWW, NO FUN! DO IT ONE MORE TIME!
HEY! WHAT'S GOING ON IN HERE?!
LEAVE HOTARU ALONE! H NEARLY DIED JUS A LITTLE WHILE AGO!
AW, HE'S FINE NOW. WE HEALED HIM UP.
HEY...
THE CRIMSON EYES AREN'T A TOY.
AND THERE'S NO TELLING ANYONE ABOUT IT. IT'S A SECRET, GOT IT?
WHY? IT'S PRETTY!
YEAH.
LISTEN TO ME NOW.

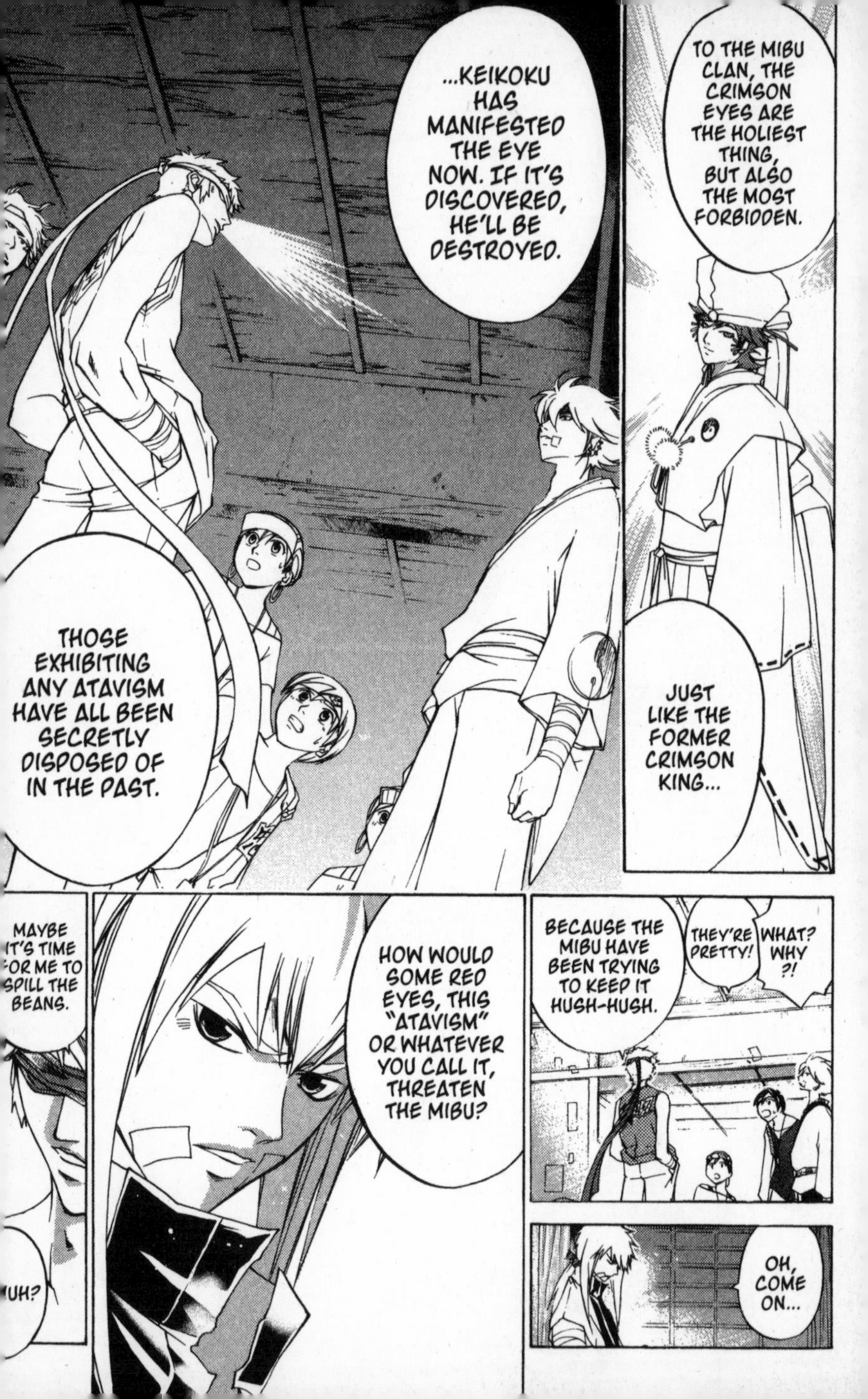
TO THE MIBU CLAN, THE CRIMSON EYES ARE THE HOLIEST THING, BUT ALSO THE MOST FORBIDDEN.
JUST LIKE THE FORMER CRIMSON KING...
...KEIKOKU HAS MANIFESTED THE EYE NOW. IF IT'S DISCOVERED, HE'LL BE DESTROYED.
THOSE EXHIBITING ANY ATAVISM HAVE ALL BEEN SECRETLY DISPOSED OF IN THE PAST.
WHAT? WHY ?!
THEY'RE PRETTY!
BECAUSE THE MIBU HAVE BEEN TRYING TO KEEP IT HUSH-HUSH.
OH, COME ON...
HOW WOULD SOME RED EYES, THIS "ATAVISM" OR WHATEVER YOU CALL IT, THREATEN THE MIBU?
MAYBE IT'S TIME FOR ME TO SPILL THE BEANS.
UH?

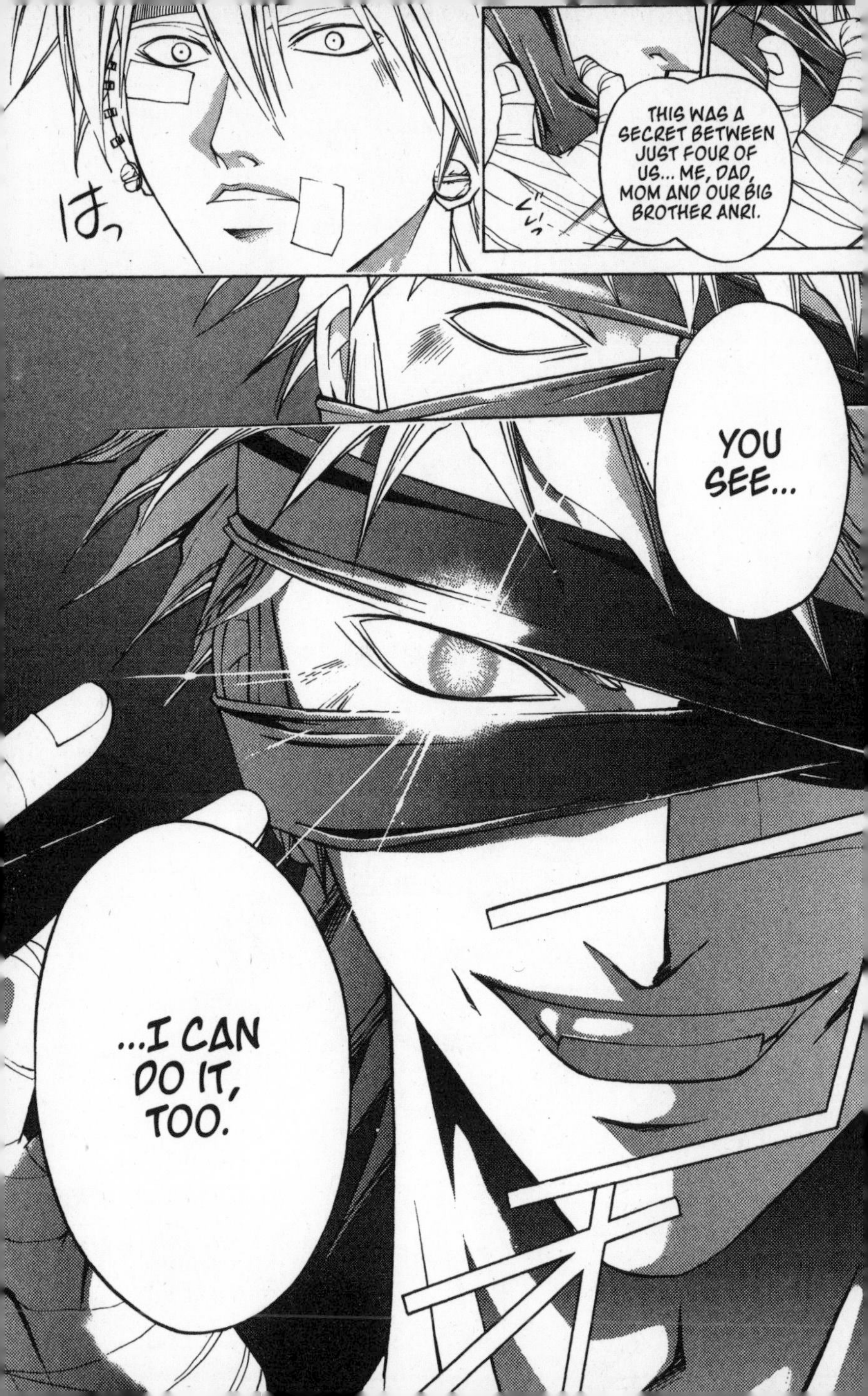
THIS WAS A SECRET BETWEEN JUST FOUR OF US... ME, DAD, MOM AND OUR BIG BROTHER ANRI.
ぐいっ
はっ
YOU SEE...
...I CAN DO IT, TOO.

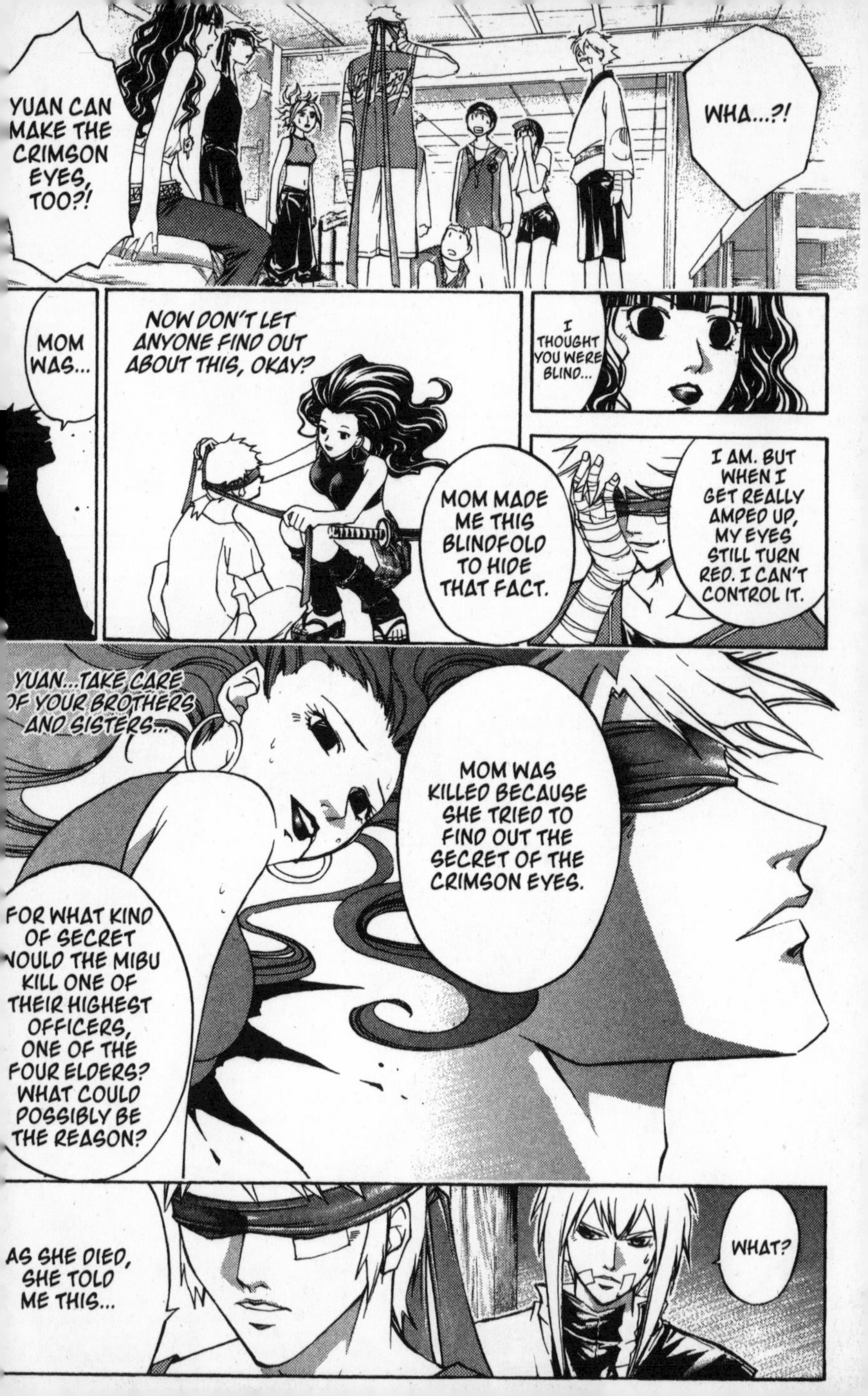
WHA...?!
YUAN CAN MAKE THE CRIMSON EYES, TOO?!
I THOUGHT YOU WERE BLIND...
I AM. BUT WHEN I GET REALLY AMPED UP, MY EYES STILL TURN RED. I CAN'T CONTROL IT.
MOM MADE ME THIS BLINDFOLD TO HIDE THAT FACT.
NOW DON'T LET ANYONE FIND OUT ABOUT THIS, OKAY?
MOM WAS...
MOM WAS KILLED BECAUSE SHE TRIED TO FIND OUT THE SECRET OF THE CRIMSON EYES.
YUAN...TAKE CARE OF YOUR BROTHERS AND SISTERS...
FOR WHAT KIND OF SECRET WOULD THE MIBU KILL ONE OF THEIR HIGHEST OFFICERS, ONE OF THE FOUR ELDERS? WHAT COULD POSSIBLY BE THE REASON?
WHAT?
AS SHE DIED, SHE TOLD ME THIS...

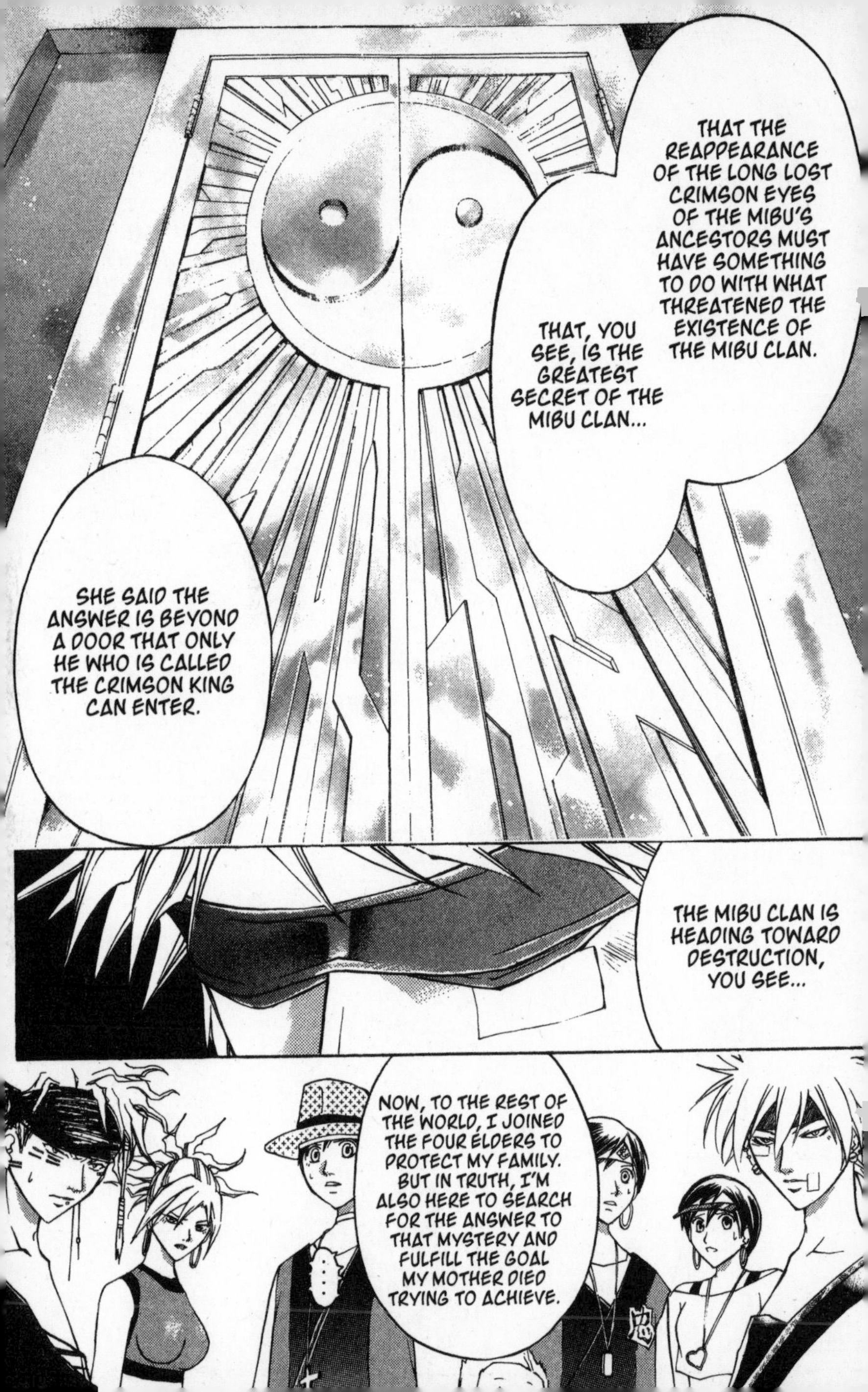
THAT THE REAPPEARANCE OF THE LONG LOST CRIMSON EYES OF THE MIBU'S ANCESTORS MUST HAVE SOMETHING TO DO WITH WHAT THREATENED THE EXISTENCE OF THE MIBU CLAN.
THAT, YOU SEE, IS THE GREATEST SECRET OF THE MIBU CLAN...
SHE SAID THE ANSWER IS BEYOND A DOOR THAT ONLY HE WHO IS CALLED THE CRIMSON KING CAN ENTER.
THE MIBU CLAN IS HEADING TOWARD DESTRUCTION, YOU SEE...
NOW, TO THE REST OF THE WORLD, I JOINED THE FOUR ELDERS TO PROTECT MY FAMILY. BUT IN TRUTH, I'M ALSO HERE TO SEARCH FOR THE ANSWER TO THAT MYSTERY AND FULFILL THE GOAL MY MOTHER DIED TRYING TO ACHIEVE.

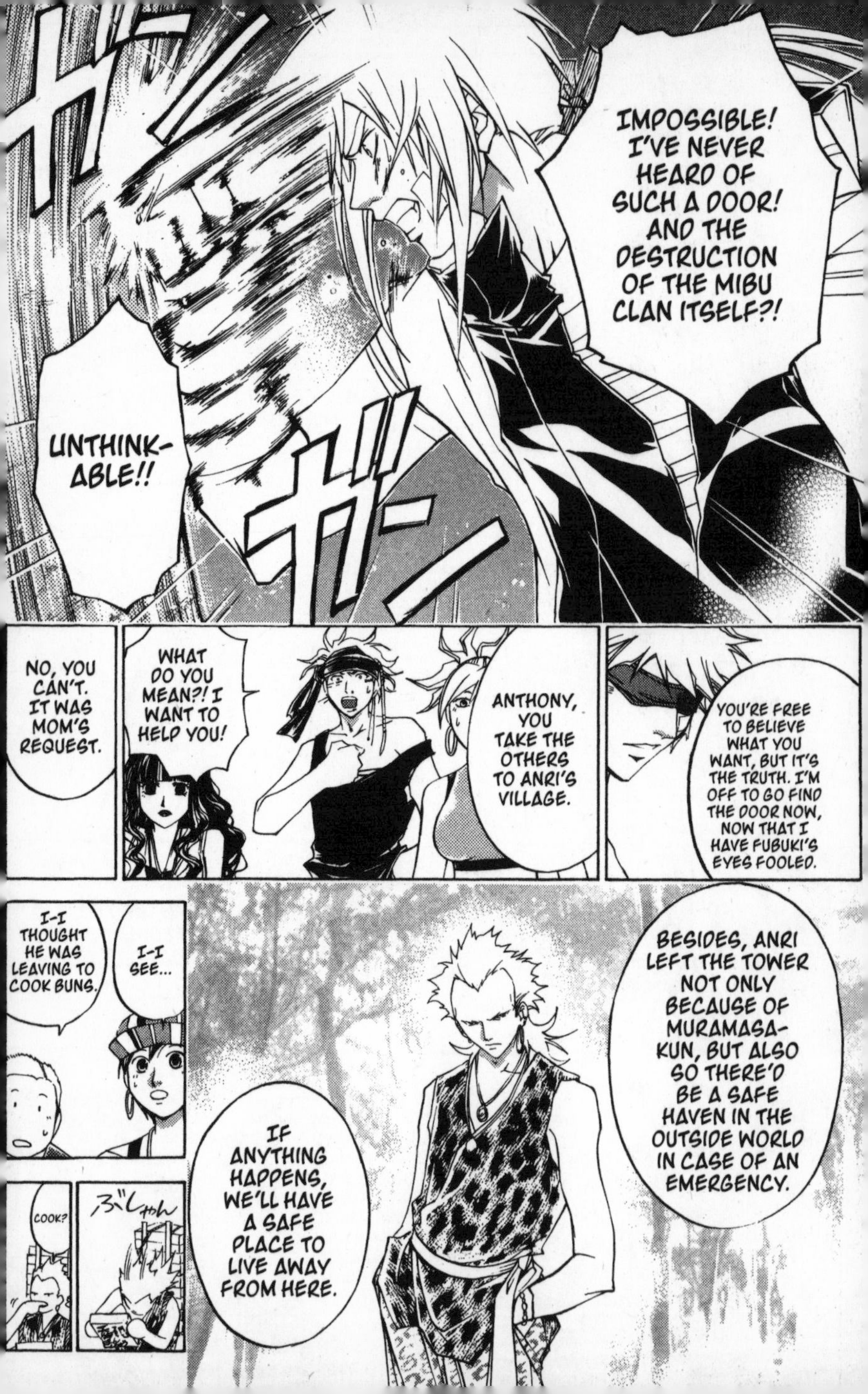
IMPOSSIBLE! I'VE NEVER HEARD OF SUCH A DOOR! AND THE DESTRUCTION OF THE MIBU CLAN ITSELF?!
UNTHINK-ABLE!!
YOU'RE FREE TO BELIEVE WHAT YOU WANT, BUT IT'S THE TRUTH. I'M OFF TO GO FIND THE DOOR NOW, NOW THAT I HAVE FUBUKI'S EYES FOOLED.
ANTHONY, YOU TAKE THE OTHERS TO ANRI'S VILLAGE.
WHAT DO YOU MEAN?! I WANT TO HELP YOU!
NO, YOU CAN'T. IT WAS MOM'S REQUEST.
BESIDES, ANRI LEFT THE TOWER NOT ONLY BECAUSE OF MURAMASA-KUN, BUT ALSO SO THERE'D BE A SAFE HAVEN IN THE OUTSIDE WORLD IN CASE OF AN EMERGENCY.
IF ANYTHING HAPPENS, WE'LL HAVE A SAFE PLACE TO LIVE AWAY FROM HERE.
I-I SEE...
I-I THOUGHT HE WAS LEAVING TO COOK BUNS.
ぶしゃぁ
COOK?

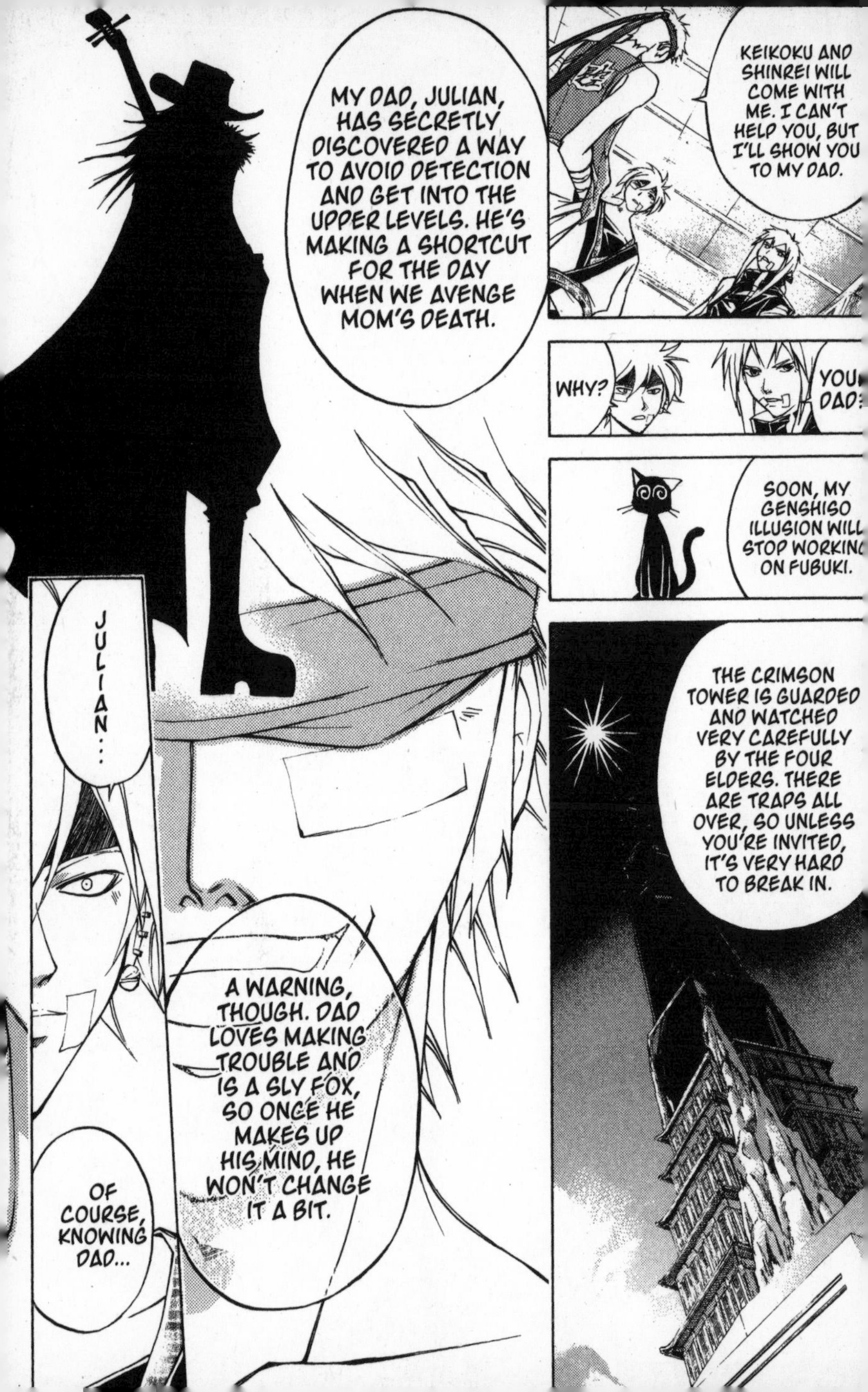
KEIKOKU AND SHINREI WILL COME WITH ME. I CAN'T HELP YOU, BUT I'LL SHOW YOU TO MY DAD.
YOU DAD?
WHY?
SOON, MY GENSHISO ILLUSION WILL STOP WORKIN ON FUBUKI.
THE CRIMSON TOWER IS GUARDED AND WATCHED VERY CAREFULLY BY THE FOUR ELDERS. THERE ARE TRAPS ALL OVER, SO UNLESS YOU'RE INVITED, IT'S VERY HARD TO BREAK IN.
MY DAD, JULIAN, HAS SECRETLY DISCOVERED A WAY TO AVOID DETECTION AND GET INTO THE UPPER LEVELS. HE'S MAKING A SHORTCUT FOR THE DAY WHEN WE AVENGE MOM'S DEATH.
JULIAN...
A WARNING, THOUGH. DAD LOVES MAKING TROUBLE AND IS A SLY FOX, SO ONCE HE MAKES UP HIS MIND, HE WON'T CHANGE IT A BIT.
OF COURSE, KNOWING DAD...

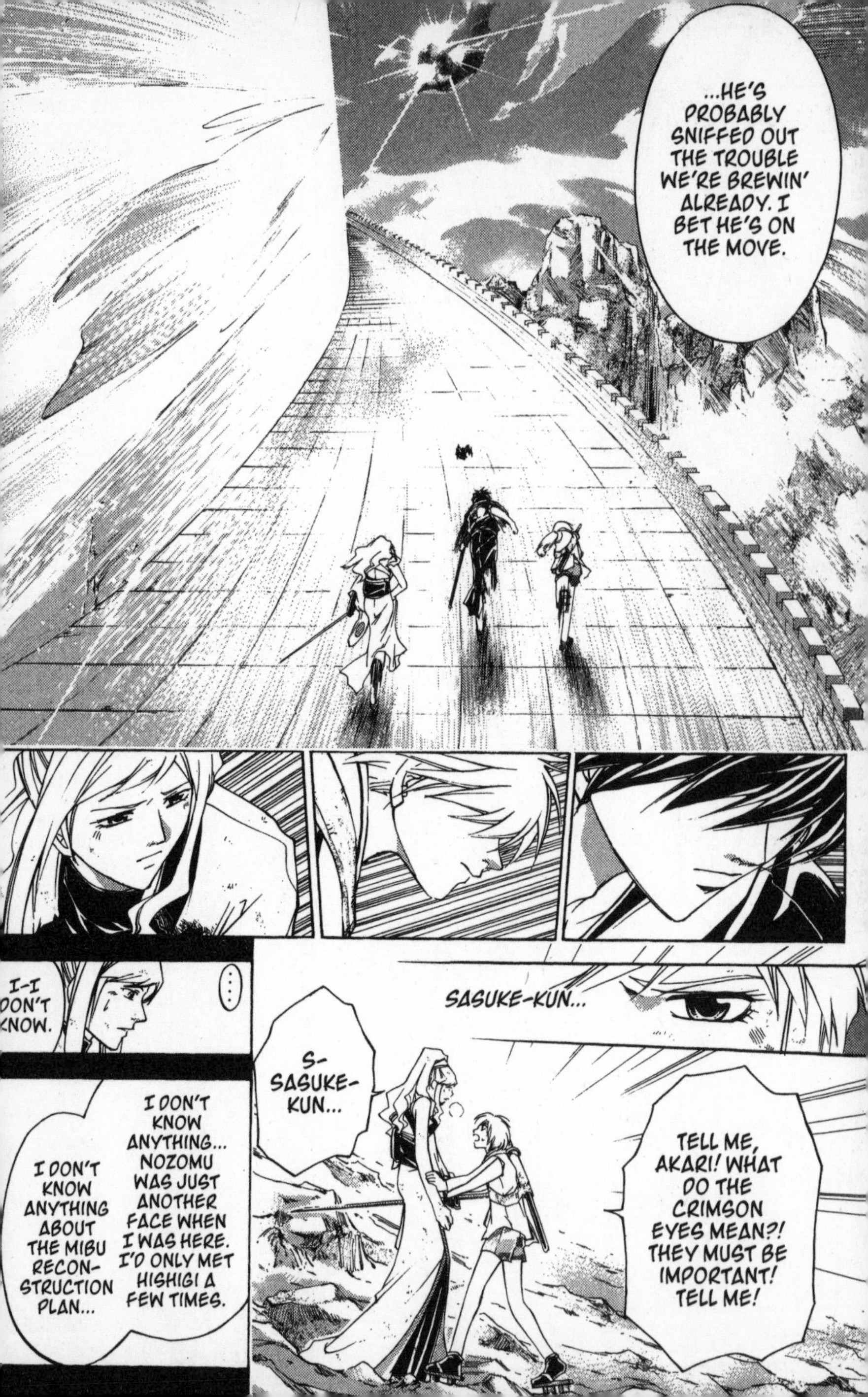
...HE'S PROBABLY SNIFFED OUT THE TROUBLE WE'RE BREWIN' ALREADY. I BET HE'S ON THE MOVE.
SASUKE-KUN...
TELL ME, AKARI! WHAT DO THE CRIMSON EYES MEAN?! THEY MUST BE IMPORTANT! TELL ME!
S-SASUKE-KUN...
...
I-I DON'T KNOW.
I DON'T KNOW ANYTHING... NOZOMU WAS JUST ANOTHER FACE WHEN I WAS HERE. I'D ONLY MET HISHIGI A FEW TIMES.
I DON'T KNOW ANYTHING ABOUT THE MIBU RECON-STRUCTION PLAN...

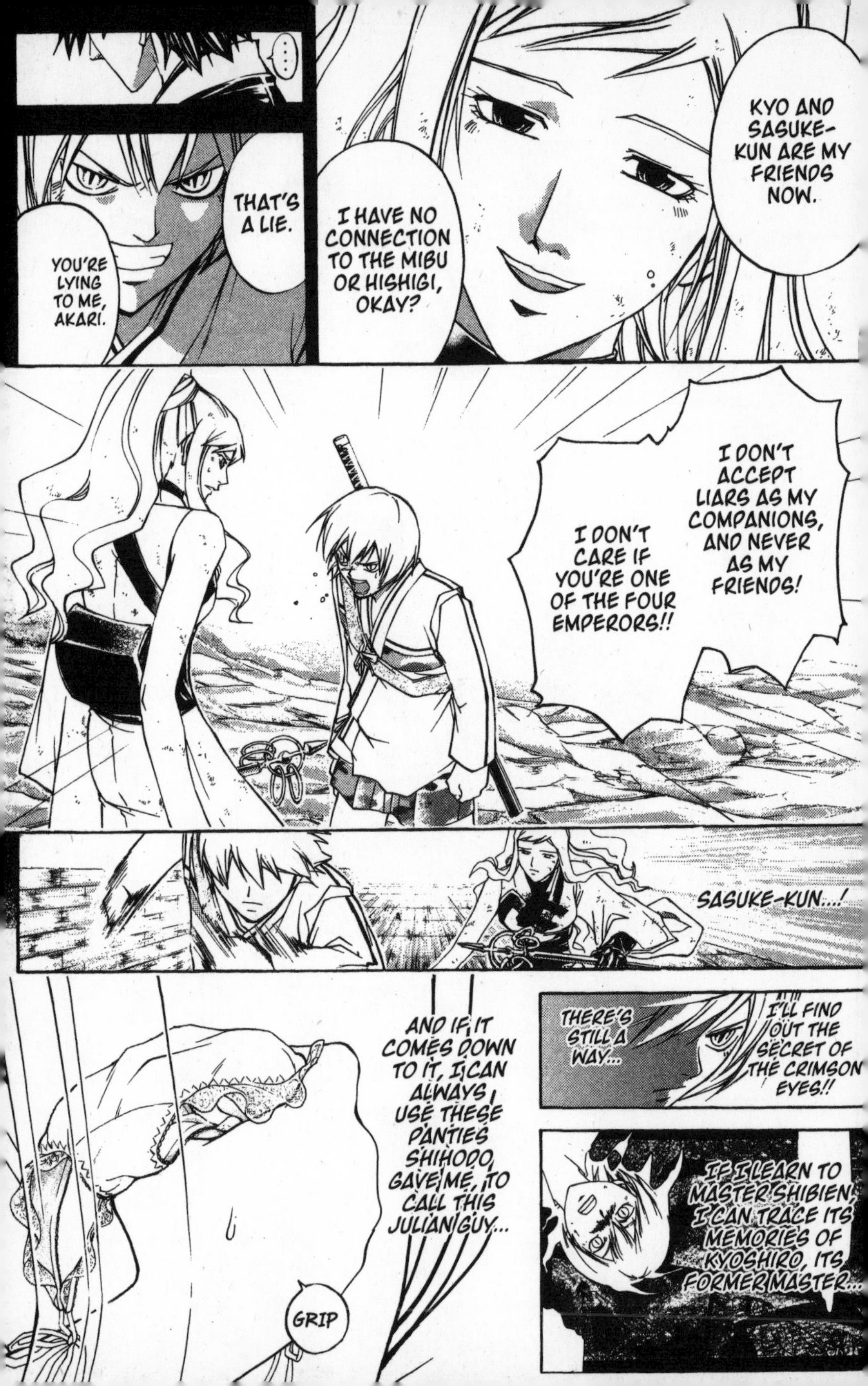
KYO AND SASUKE-KUN ARE MY FRIENDS NOW.
I HAVE NO CONNECTION TO THE MIBU OR HISHIGI, OKAY?
THAT'S A LIE.
YOU'RE LYING TO ME, AKARI.
...
I DON'T ACCEPT LIARS AS MY COMPANIONS, AND NEVER AS MY FRIENDS!
I DON'T CARE IF YOU'RE ONE OF THE FOUR EMPERORS!!
SASUKE-KUN...!
I'LL FIND OUT THE SECRET OF THE CRIMSON EYES!!
THERE'S STILL A WAY...
IF I LEARN TO MASTER SHIBIEN, I CAN TRACE ITS MEMORIES OF KYOSHIRO, ITS FORMER MASTER...
AND IF IT COMES DOWN TO IT, I CAN ALWAYS USE THESE PANTIES SHIHODO GAVE ME, TO CALL THIS JULIAN GUY...
GRIP

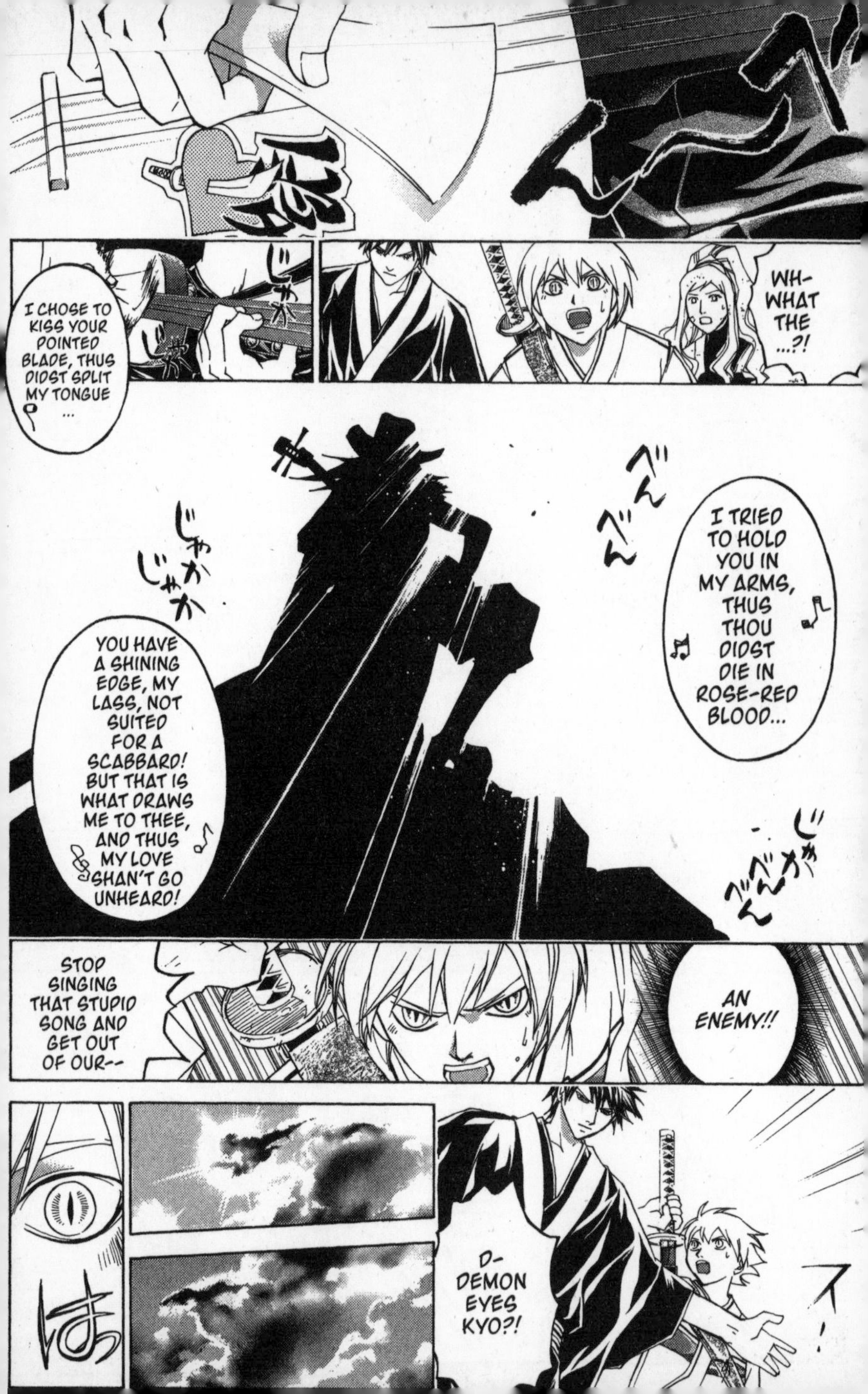
WH-WHAT THE ...?!
I CHOSE TO KISS YOUR POINTED BLADE, THUS DIDST SPLIT MY TONGUE ...
べんべん
I TRIED TO HOLD YOU IN MY ARMS, THUS THOU DIDST DIE IN ROSE-RED BLOOD...
じゃかじゃか
YOU HAVE A SHINING EDGE, MY LASS, NOT SUITED FOR A SCABBARD! BUT THAT IS WHAT DRAWS ME TO THEE, AND THUS MY LOVE SHAN'T GO UNHEARD!
AN ENEMY!!
STOP SINGING THAT STUPID SONG AND GET OUT OF OUR--
D-DEMON EYES KYO?!

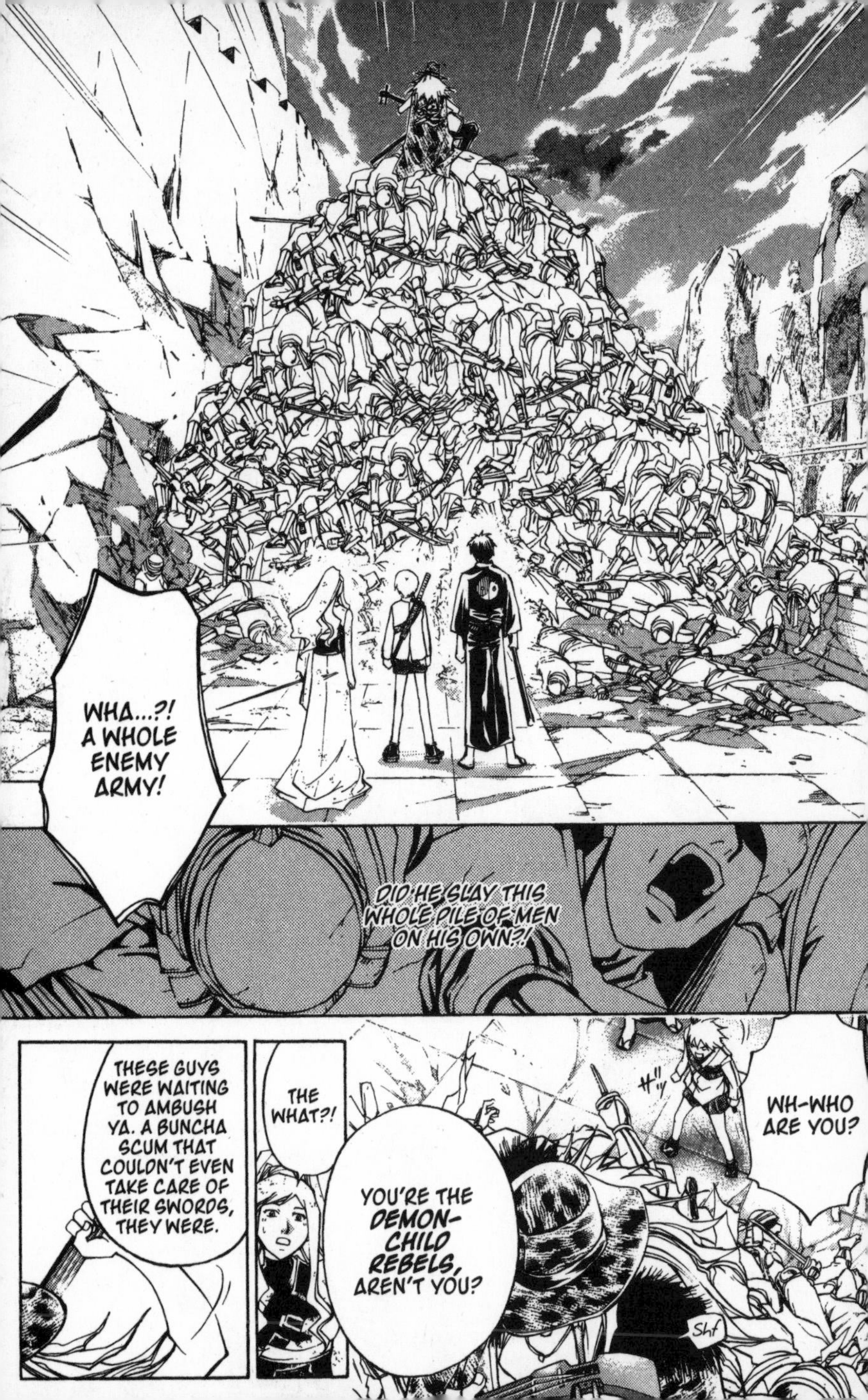
WHA...?! A WHOLE ENEMY ARMY!
DID HE SLAY THIS WHOLE PILE OF MEN ON HIS OWN?!
WH-WHO ARE YOU?
YOU'RE THE DEMON-CHILD REBELS, AREN'T YOU?
THE WHAT?!
THESE GUYS WERE WAITING TO AMBUSH YA. A BUNCHA SCUM THAT COULDN'T EVEN TAKE CARE OF THEIR SWORDS, THEY WERE.
Shf

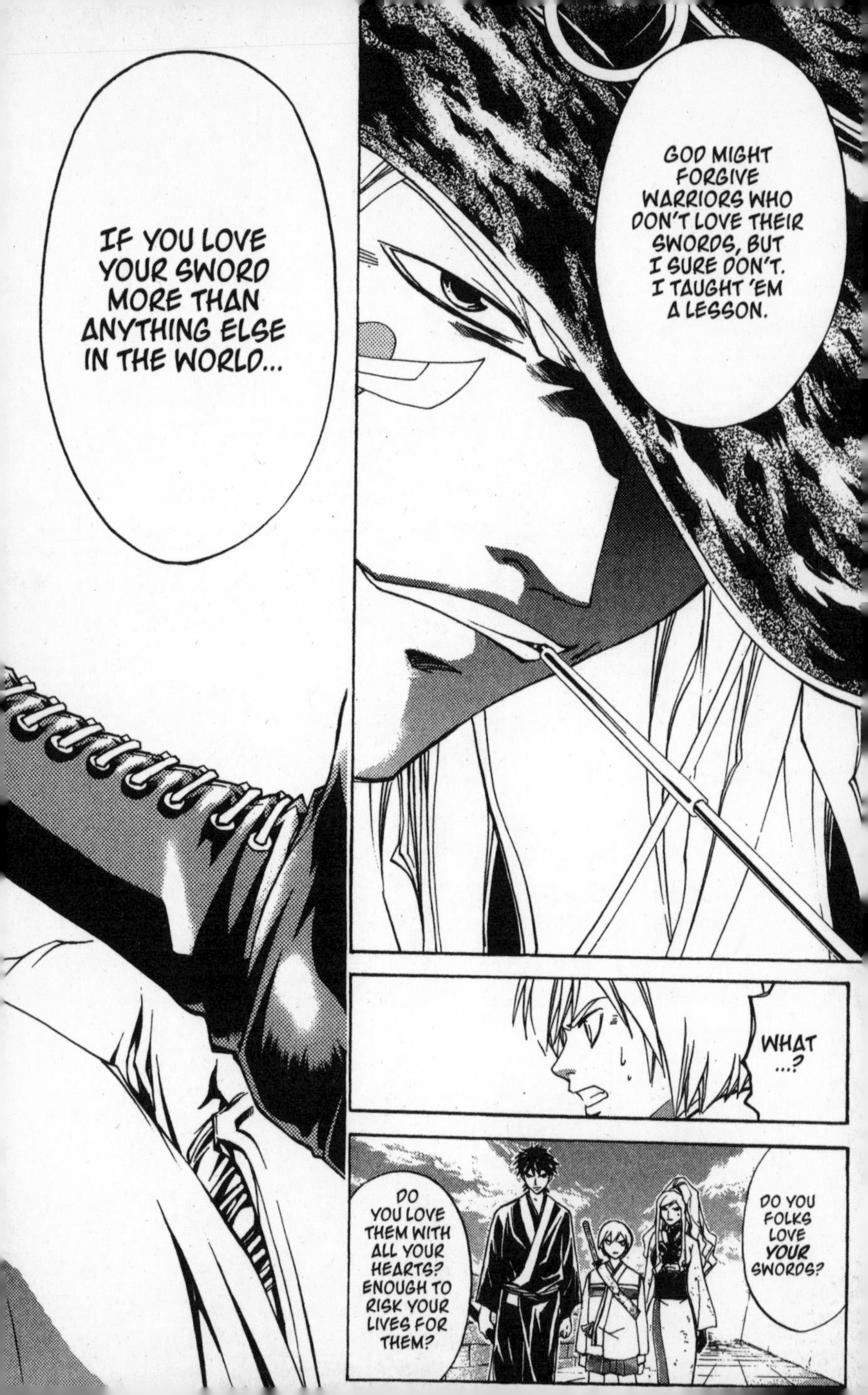
GOD MIGHT FORGIVE WARRIORS WHO DON'T LOVE THEIR SWORDS, BUT I SURE DON'T. I TAUGHT 'EM A LESSON.
WHAT ...?
DO YOU FOLKS LOVE YOUR SWORDS?
DO YOU LOVE THEM WITH ALL YOUR HEARTS? ENOUGH TO RISK YOUR LIVES FOR THEM?
IF YOU LOVE YOUR SWORD MORE THAN ANYTHING ELSE IN THE WORLD...

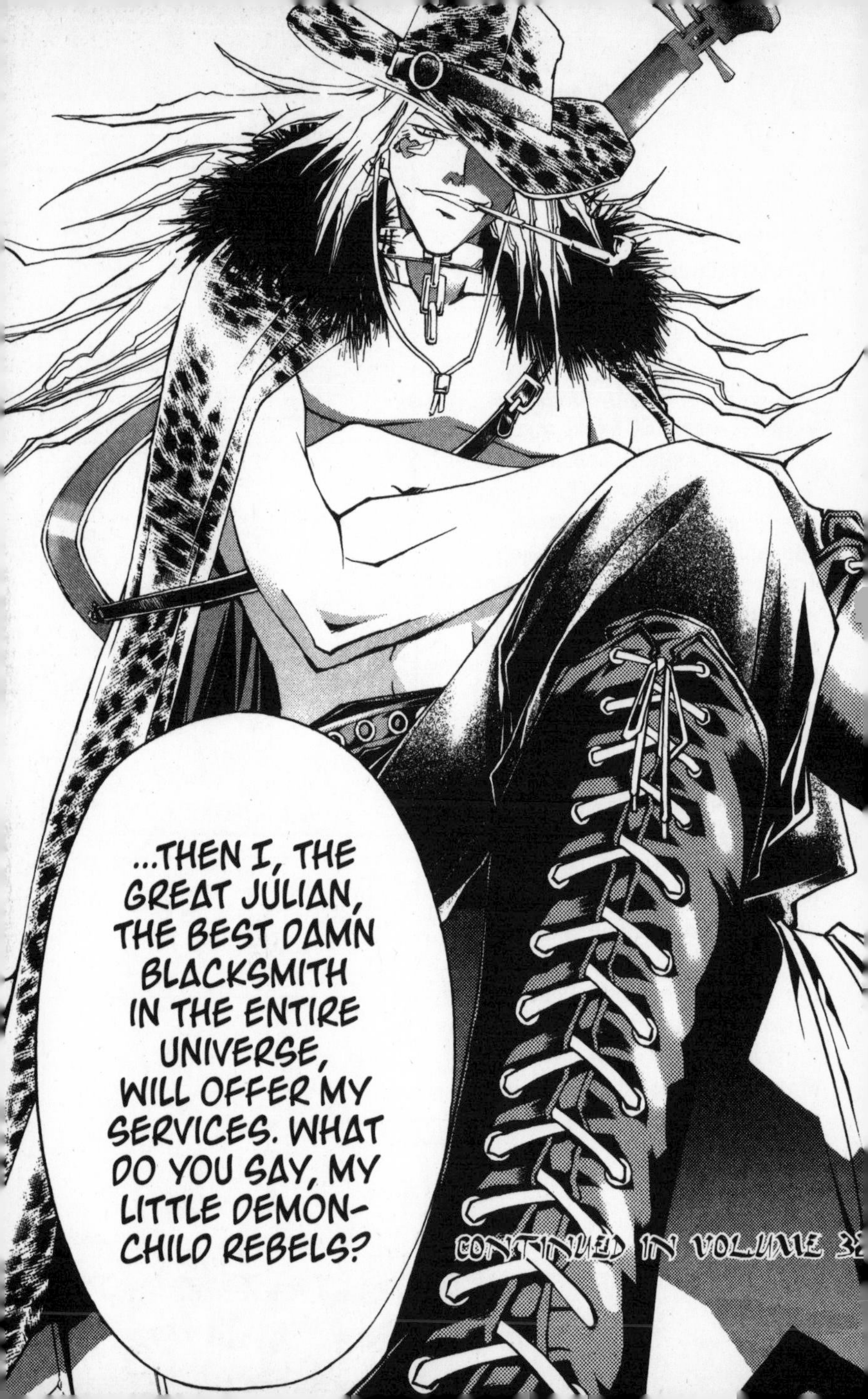
...THEN I, THE GREAT JULIAN, THE BEST DAMN BLACKSMITH IN THE ENTIRE UNIVERSE, WILL OFFER MY SERVICES. WHAT DO YOU SAY, MY LITTLE DEMON-CHILD REBELS?
CONTINUED IN VOLUME 3

Hey, folks! Kamijyo here. This here's Volume 31, which came out in regular and limited edition in Japan!

Just recently, *Weekly Magazine,* which is where SDK runs originally, started an "Author's Comment" section. So every week I'm sitting here thinking, "I know there's something funny I can talk about..." The problem is, I can never think of anything! I mean, I live a life of nonstop manga, every single day! It's awesome! But when I stop to think about it, there's not much else. On the other hand, whenever I look back on a particular week, there's always something that happened! Even if it's just a little funny thing. And I've been living through them each day without noticing! What a waste. So I've recently reaffirmed the need to appreciate my everyday life more. Makes me feel like a better person! Not that it's going to help me write better comments each week. Make sure to read them once in a while, and maybe you'll get a laugh.

GUESS THE FOOTPRINTS

HEY, CHECK OUT THE SNOW! I LOVE BREAKING THROUGH THE CRUST!
LOOK, YOU CAN SEE EVERY-ONE'S FOOT-PRINTS!
ざく
ざく
THAT'S GOTTA BE HOTARU-HAN'S.
AND HERE'S AKARI-HAN'S GETA SANDALS.
THIS LITTLE ONE'S GOTTA BE THAT BRAT SASUKE'S.
THIS ONE MUST BE KYO. HE'S TOTALLY DUCK-FOOTED.
HUH?!
WHAT'S THIS...?
BON-HAN'S, RIGHT?
'Cuz he's an animal!
UH...IS THAT RIGHT?
GROWL ...

DEEPER²

YUAN'S HOUSE

YOU FOLKS ARE ALL PART OF THE FAMILY NOW. FEEL FREE TO STICK AROUND ALL YOU WANT.
THANKS, ANNA!
JUST ONE THING...
COOKING
LAUNDRY
REFRIGERATION
CLEANING
...EVERYONE HAS TO HELP OUT!
WE GOTTA GO NOW. WE'RE TIRED.
WE LOVE VISITORS WHO CHIP IN!
NOBODY STAYS FOR FREE AT YUAN'S HOUSE...
YAY!

I've also done a bit of work for *Weekly Magazine's* sister publication, *Magazine Wonder.* Check it out if you're curious.

In the next volume a certain someone will be embarking on the greatest duel yet. Of course, I treat every duel like the greatest one yet, but this time that certain someone and I truly crossed a great barrier. I'm very proud of the result. I can't wait to share it! See you next volume!

Yuan's big family, from the house interior to the individual clothing design, was sheer hell on my assistance staff. Thanks, everyone!

*And thanks for all the letters! I'll do my best even without them, but I do my best **and** have fun with your support!*

DEEPER²

KAMIJYO REPORT

CD DRAMA PRODUCTION SECRETS
(SORRY, OUT ONLY IN JAPAN!)

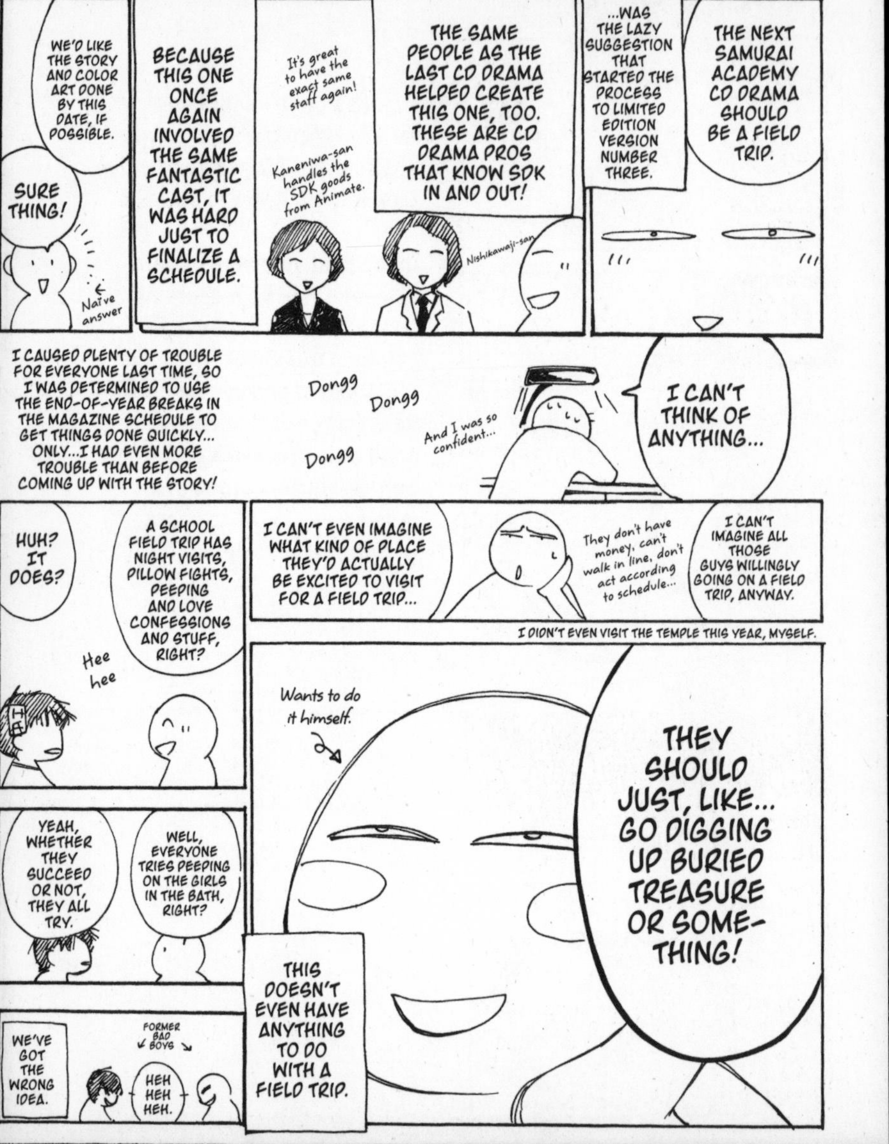
THE NEXT SAMURAI ACADEMY CD DRAMA SHOULD BE A FIELD TRIP.
...WAS THE LAZY SUGGESTION THAT STARTED THE PROCESS TO LIMITED EDITION VERSION NUMBER THREE.
THE SAME PEOPLE AS THE LAST CD DRAMA HELPED CREATE THIS ONE, TOO. THESE ARE CD DRAMA PROS THAT KNOW SDK IN AND OUT!
It's great to have the exact same staff again!
Kaneniwa-san handles the SDK goods from Animate.
Nishikawaji-san
BECAUSE THIS ONE ONCE AGAIN INVOLVED THE SAME FANTASTIC CAST, IT WAS HARD JUST TO FINALIZE A SCHEDULE.
WE'D LIKE THE STORY AND COLOR ART DONE BY THIS DATE, IF POSSIBLE.
SURE THING!
Naïve answer
I CAN'T THINK OF ANYTHING...
And I was so confident...
Dongg
Dongg
Dongg
I CAUSED PLENTY OF TROUBLE FOR EVERYONE LAST TIME, SO I WAS DETERMINED TO USE THE END-OF-YEAR BREAKS IN THE MAGAZINE SCHEDULE TO GET THINGS DONE QUICKLY... ONLY...I HAD EVEN MORE TROUBLE THAN BEFORE COMING UP WITH THE STORY!
I CAN'T IMAGINE ALL THOSE GUYS WILLINGLY GOING ON A FIELD TRIP, ANYWAY.
They don't have money, can't walk in line, don't act according to schedule...
I CAN'T EVEN IMAGINE WHAT KIND OF PLACE THEY'D ACTUALLY BE EXCITED TO VISIT FOR A FIELD TRIP...
I DIDN'T EVEN VISIT THE TEMPLE THIS YEAR, MYSELF.
A SCHOOL FIELD TRIP HAS NIGHT VISITS, PILLOW FIGHTS, PEEPING AND LOVE CONFESSIONS AND STUFF, RIGHT?
HUH? IT DOES?
Hee hee
Wants to do it himself.
THEY SHOULD JUST, LIKE... GO DIGGING UP BURIED TREASURE OR SOME-THING!
THIS DOESN'T EVEN HAVE ANYTHING TO DO WITH A FIELD TRIP.
WELL, EVERYONE TRIES PEEPING ON THE GIRLS IN THE BATH, RIGHT?
YEAH, WHETHER THEY SUCCEED OR NOT, THEY ALL TRY.
FORMER BAD BOYS
HEH HEH HEH.
WE'VE GOT THE WRONG IDEA.

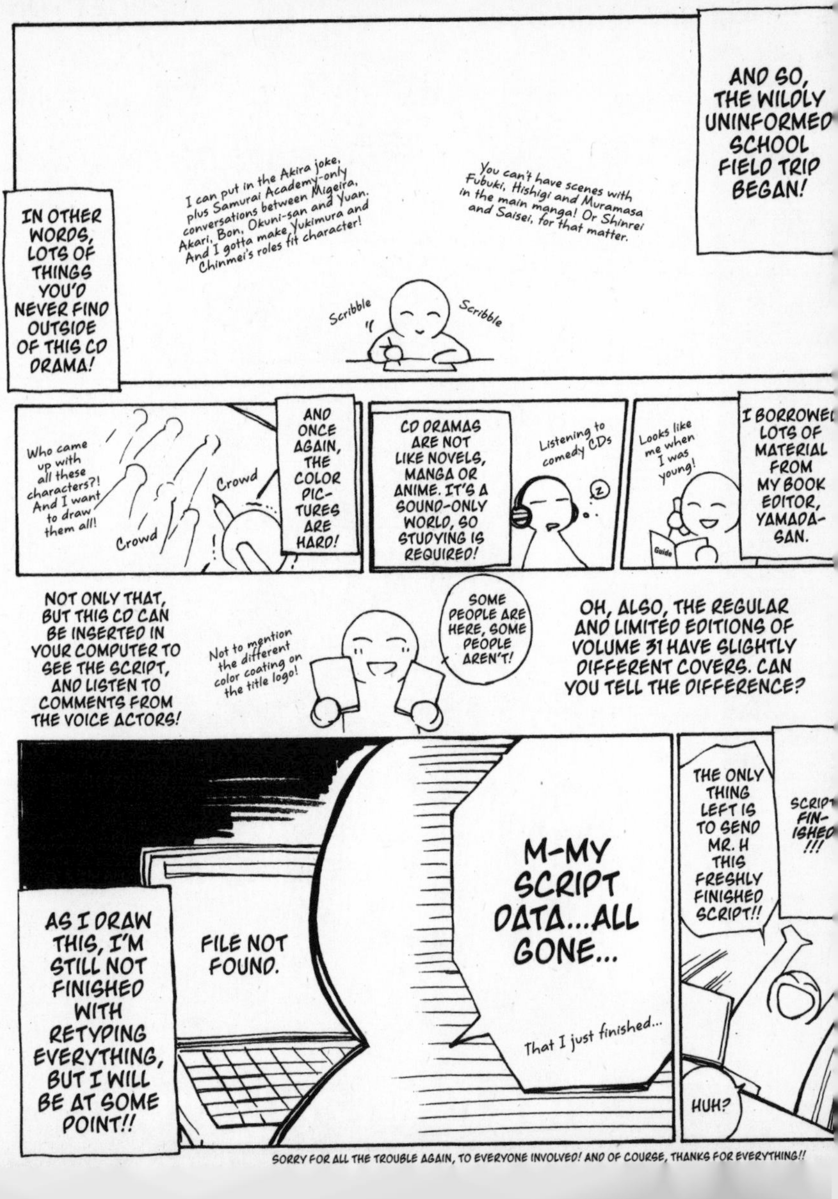
AND SO, THE WILDLY UNINFORMED SCHOOL FIELD TRIP BEGAN!
You can't have scenes with Fubuki, Hishigi and Muramasa in the main manga! Or Shinrei and Saisei, for that matter.
I can put in the Akira joke, plus Samurai Academy-only conversations between Migeira, Akari, Bon, Okuni-san and Yuan. And I gotta make Yukimura and Chinmei's roles fit character!
IN OTHER WORDS, LOTS OF THINGS YOU'D NEVER FIND OUTSIDE OF THIS CD DRAMA!
Scribble
Scribble
I BORROWE LOTS OF MATERIAL FROM MY BOOK EDITOR, YAMADA-SAN.
Looks like me when I was young!
Guide
CD DRAMAS ARE NOT LIKE NOVELS, MANGA OR ANIME. IT'S A SOUND-ONLY WORLD, SO STUDYING IS REQUIRED!
Listening to comedy CDs
Z
AND ONCE AGAIN, THE COLOR PICTURES ARE HARD!
Crowd
Who came up with all these characters?! And I want to draw them all!
Crowd
OH, ALSO, THE REGULAR AND LIMITED EDITIONS OF VOLUME 31 HAVE SLIGHTLY DIFFERENT COVERS. CAN YOU TELL THE DIFFERENCE?
SOME PEOPLE ARE HERE, SOME PEOPLE AREN'T!
Not to mention the different color coating on the title logo!
NOT ONLY THAT, BUT THIS CD CAN BE INSERTED IN YOUR COMPUTER TO SEE THE SCRIPT, AND LISTEN TO COMMENTS FROM THE VOICE ACTORS!
SCRIPT FIN-ISHED !!!
THE ONLY THING LEFT IS TO SEND MR. H THIS FRESHLY FINISHED SCRIPT!!
HUH?
M-MY SCRIPT DATA...ALL GONE...
That I just finished...
FILE NOT FOUND.
AS I DRAW THIS, I'M STILL NOT FINISHED WITH RETYPING EVERYTHING, BUT I WILL BE AT SOME POINT!!

SORRY FOR ALL THE TROUBLE AGAIN, TO EVERYONE INVOLVED! AND OF COURSE, THANKS FOR EVERYTHING!!

SAMURAI DEEPER KYO NEXT

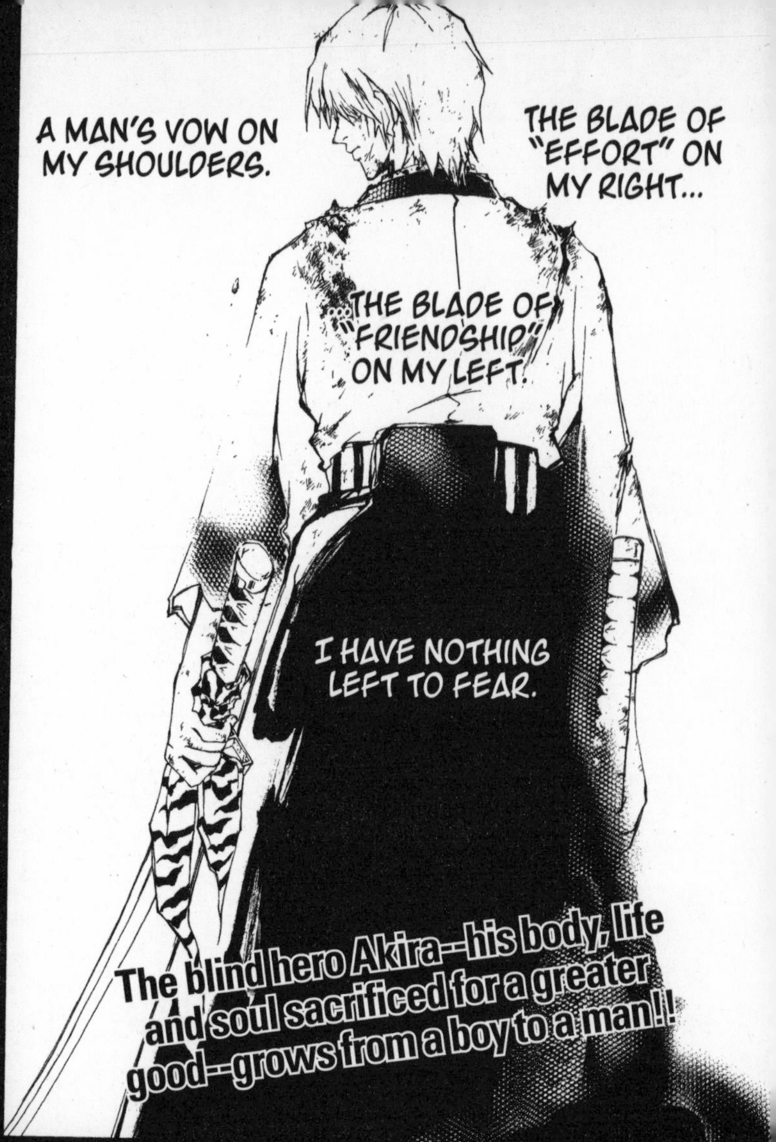

THE BLADE OF "EFFORT" ON MY RIGHT...
A MAN'S VOW ON MY SHOULDERS.
...THE BLADE OF "FRIENDSHIP" ON MY LEFT.
I HAVE NOTHING LEFT TO FEAR.
The blind hero Akira--his body, life and soul sacrificed for a greater good--grows from a boy to a man!!

Pure heart and purer soul in Volume 32!!

SAMURAI DEEPER KYO

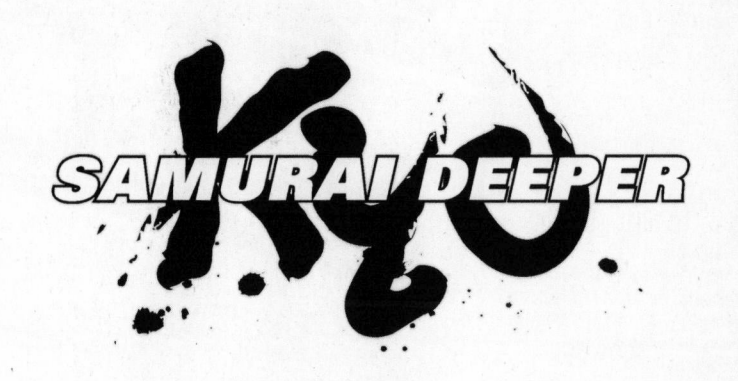

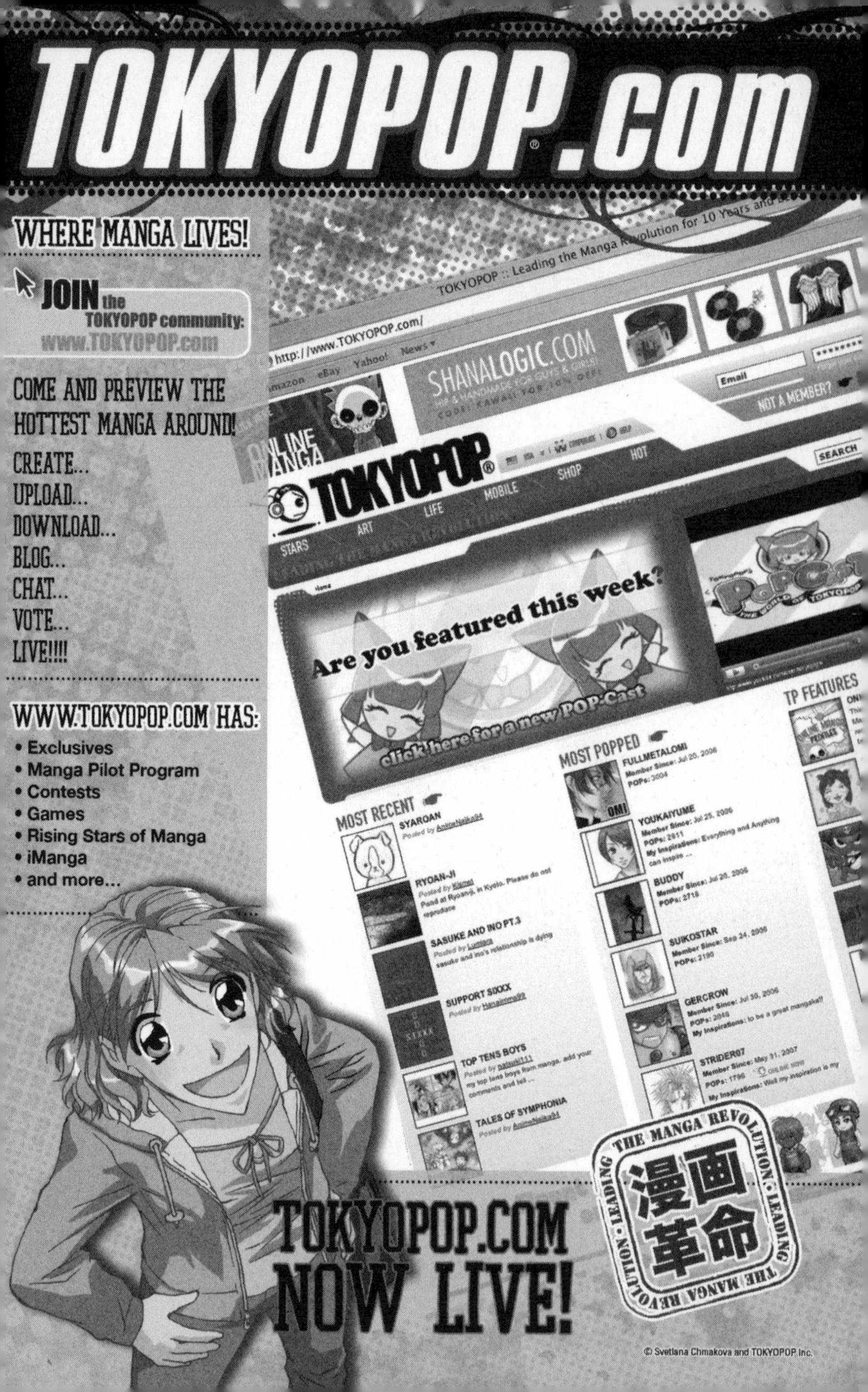
TOKYOPOP.com
WHERE MANGA LIVES!
JOIN the TOKYOPOP community: www.TOKYOPOP.com
COME AND PREVIEW THE HOTTEST MANGA AROUND!
CREATE...
UPLOAD...
DOWNLOAD...
BLOG...
CHAT...
VOTE...
LIVE!!!!
WWW.TOKYOPOP.COM HAS:
• Exclusives
• Manga Pilot Program
• Contests
• Games
• Rising Stars of Manga
• iManga
• and more...
Are you featured this week?
click here for a new POP-Cast
MOST RECENT
MOST POPPED
TP FEATURES
TOKYOPOP.COM NOW LIVE!
漫画革命
THE MANGA REVOLUTION • LEADING
© Svetlana Chmakova and TOKYOPOP Inc.

STOP!

This is the back of the book.
You wouldn't want to spoil a great ending!

This book is printed "manga-style," in the authentic Japanese right-to-left format. Since none of the artwork has been flipped or altered, readers get to experience the story just as the creator intended. You've been asking for it, so TOKYOPOP® delivered: authentic, hot-off-the-press, and far more fun!

DIRECTIONS

If this is your first time reading manga-style, here's a quick guide to help you understand how it works.

It's easy... just start in the top right panel and follow the numbers. Have fun, and look for more 100% authentic manga from TOKYOPOP®!